WORKING WITH DIAGRAMS

Studies in Social Analysis

Editors: Judith Bovensiepen, *University of Kent*
Martin Holbraad, *University College London*
Hans Steinmüller, *London School of Economics*

By forging creative and critical engagements with cultural, political, and social processes, anthropology explores the potential of social analysis to open new paths for thinking about human phenomena.

The focus of this series is on 'analysis', understood not as a synonym of 'theory', but as the fertile meeting ground of the empirical and the conceptual. It provides a platform for exploring anthropological approaches to social analysis in all of their variety, and in doing so seeks also to open new avenues of communication between anthropology and the humanities as well as other social sciences.

Recent volumes:

For a full volume listing, please see the series page on https://berghahnbooks.com/series/studies-in-social-analysis

WORKING WITH DIAGRAMS

Edited by

Lukas Engelmann, Caroline Humphrey,
and Christos Lynteris

berghahn
NEW YORK · OXFORD
www.berghahnbooks.com

Published in 2022 by

Berghahn Books

www.berghahnbooks.com

© 2022 Berghahn Books

Originally published as a special issue of *Social Analysis*, volume 63, issue 4.

Library of Congress Cataloging-in-Publication Data

A C.I.P. cataloging record is available from the Library of Congress
Library of Congress Cataloging in Publication Control Number: 2022019800

British Library Cataloguing in Publication Data

A catalogue record for this book is available from the British Library.

ISBN 978-1-80073-558-3 hardback
ISBN 978-1-80073-560-6 paperback
ISBN 978-1-80073-559-0 ebook

https://doi.org/10.3167/9781800735583

CONTENTS

ILLUSTRATIONS

INTRODUCTION
Diagrams beyond Mere Tools

Lukas Engelmann, Caroline Humphrey,
and Christos Lynteris

In a review of Bender and Marrinan's (2010) *The Culture of Diagram*, Martin Jay (2010–2011: 158) argues that there can be "no question that the role of the humble diagram in many different fields has been slowly earning recognition for some time." From studies of evolutionary tree diagrams (Catley and Novick 2008; Gontier 2011), the use of diagrams in semiotics (Stjernfelt 2000), and analyses of their impact on Euclidean geometry (Miller 2007; Norman 2006) to visualizing Foucault's abstract machines (Deleuze 1988; Elmer 2003) or exploring Deleuze's philosophy (Knoespel 2001; Teyssot 2012; Zdebik 2012), historians, philosophers, linguists, geographers, and science and technology studies (STS) scholars have over the past 20 years been dissecting and inter-rogating the diagrammatic heart of a number of sciences and disciplines. Of particular importance in these studies has been the examination of diagrams as epistemic images, which in the definition of Christoph Lüthy and Alexis Smets

Notes for this section begin on page 17.

(2009: 399) refer to "any image that was made with the intention of express-ing, demonstrating or illustrating a theory."[1] At the same time, the interest shown by cognitive science in the nature of diagrammatic representations since Larkin and Simon's (1987) classic paper on the subject has led to a prolifera-tion of studies of 'diagrammatic cognition'. In anthropology itself, new studies of the use of diagrams by both anthropologists (Bouquet 1996; Ingold 2007) and others (Bonelli 2015; Hallam 2008; Lynteris 2017) are markedly different from older reflections on the medium (e.g., Burr and Gerson 1965; Hage and Harary 1983) that took diagrams to simply be tools for visualizing data and data relations, but which could not in themselves add information. Moreover, as Matei Candea stresses in his contribution to this book, anthropologists have recently resumed their own use of diagrams "not simply as illustrations, but as key steps in argument."

These new studies across the discipline approach diagrams in a new onto-logical space, where, as Lorraine Daston (2014: 320) has argued, "the dis-tance between presentation and representation" is collapsed. Perhaps a famous literary parable summarizes this turn best. In Stefan Zweig's ([1941] 2013) acclaimed novella *A Chess Story*, Dr B tries to salvage his sanity from the tor-ture of "nothingness" to which he is subjected by the Gestapo by rehearsing in his head 150 historical chess matches whose diagrams were contained in a periodical he managed to steal from his torturers. When, years after his release, he comes across a real chess match on an ocean liner bound for Buenos Aires, he is both mesmerized and disoriented: "I stared at the board as if magnetized and saw my diagrams, my knight, rook, king, queen and pawns as real pieces cut from wood; to understand the situation in the match I first had to trans-form it back from my world of abstract notation into that of movable figures" (ibid.: 93). In his examination of the work of diagrams in architecture, Anthony Vidler (2000: 6) has argued that "operating between form and word, space and language, the diagram is both constitutive and projective; it is performative rather than representational." A good example of this might be found in a recent body of STS scholarship on the performativity of economics that has looked in particular at the influence of diagrams and charts, both digital and analogue, in the forecasting of trends and price indexes in economic reasoning (Callon 2006; MacKenzie 2009). In this field, "chartism" was coined by Alex Preda (2007: 41) to describe a specific form of expertise in which shapes and characteristic curves of diagrams, such as "breaking gaps, flat bottoms, sauce bottoms, falling flags," now populate the distinctive vocabulary of economists. In this case, the economists' work with diagrams has come to shape the iden-tity of their discipline as much as it has impacted the evaluation of economic risks and chances. Yet at the same time, as Yann Giraud (2014) has shown, the work of economic graphs, like Laffer curves, has become the object of critical examination and even parody by economists themselves (e.g., Gardner 1981), who point to the complex and indeed reflexive working of diagrams within professions and disciplines that employ them.

Our focus on 'working with diagrams' in this collection arises from the need to go beyond the semiotic, cognitive, epistemic, and symbolic reading of these visual devices that pervades the social sciences and the humanities. But why is the idea of 'work' so important when it comes to diagrams? Jay (2010–2011: 158) has argued that "the diagram has been more of a hybrid between ideas and perceptions," acting as what we may call, following historians of science Lorraine Daston and Peter Galison (1992), a 'working object'. Such objects "never duplicate a reality external to them, nor are entirely the result of pure imagination, but somehow fall productively between the two" (Jay 2010–2011: 158). So what is the work that this working object does? And why is it 'work' rather than just utility or efficacy? In other words, why is this collection about *working* with diagrams and not simply about using them?

The contributions to this book emphasize that diagrams inhabit a mediating space between representation and prescription, words and images, ideas and things, theory and practice, abstraction and reality. As many have pointed out before, diagrams find a strong place in key moments of scientific, technological, and intellectual innovation, leading to everyday uses in all spheres of social, political, economic, and cultural life. Conversely, employed across the disciplines as thinking tools, they hold the promise of transforming abstract ideas into graspable images and translating the unseen into intelligible and actionable form. This collection explores such transformations in relation to time (e.g., change or evolution that takes place when diagrams are copied repeatedly), scale (e.g., tiny anthropological samples used to model large theories), and cross-field transfers (e.g., diagrams originating in genetics used in anthropology, or from animation software used in architecture). But rather than attempting to define the deictic capacities of the diagrammatic across disciplines, the contributors to this volume draw together the work that diagrams do in the development of theories. They focus on the collaborative and cooperative work that scientists, architects, or anthropologists carry out with—and on—diagrams, while considering the question of how diagrams have been made to work.

First of all, such a focus on working with diagrams enables us to move beyond representational as well as cognitive approaches. Indeed, it requires us to understand diagrams less as images, and more as visual devices. Let us take the example of the most prolific diagram in Jewish mysticism: the Kabbalistic Tree of Life, which is generally seen as mapping "the topography of the Godhead, often imagined in terms of four gradually emerging worlds and ten luminous emanations," the Sefirot (Chajes 2016). The mapping in place in this diagram elucidates the "order and interconnections" of different emanations and the way in which this in turn forms the cosmos (ibid.). But the Tree of Life is not simply a description of the cosmos for philosophical contemplation—it is a working tool of Jewish mysticism. Yossi Chajes, the leading authority today on diagrammatic aspects of the Kabbalah, gives an illuminating example of this. In his essay for the British Library, "Kabbalistic Diagrams in the British Library's Margoliouth Catalogue," Chajes (2016) discusses the 1588 CE manuscript (Add MS 27091), which contains a number of intriguing diagrams. These are of course illustrations of the mystical text, but they are also more than just that. Take, for example, the following diagram (fig. 0.1) where in the center of

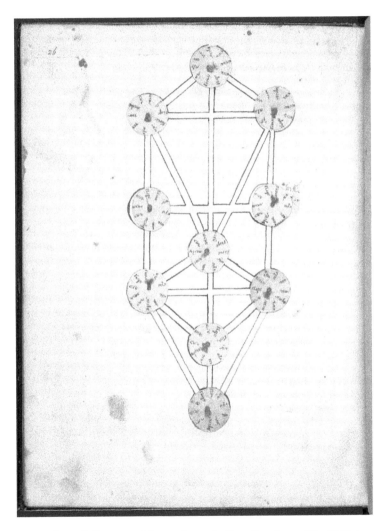

FIGURE 0.1: Arboreal diagram with rotating volvelles. Courtesy of the British Library (Add MS 27091, f. 26r). https://www.bl.uk/hebrew-manuscripts/articles/kabbalistic-diagrams-in-the-british-librarys-margoliouth-catalogue.

each Sefirah is visible a 'volvelle'. These medieval astronomical instruments of concentric rotating disks, Chajes argues, "illustrate the fractal ... concept of the *Sefirot.*" But this is not simply an illustration of a cosmological fact, namely, that "each *Sefirah* contains all ten of the *Sefirot.*" Rather, Chajes maintains, it has a key practical implication: "The idea of physically manipulating the discs gives tangible expression to the importance of practicing visual variations when contemplating the divine; the structure should be perceived as alive and bearing almost infinite potential" (ibid.).

For this collection, we take two important aspects from this arboreal mystical diagram. First, not all workings with diagrams find their purpose in methods of simplification, schematization, or standardization. On the contrary, the contributions to this book stress that diagrams might as well insist on the complexity of epidemic, anthropologic, or genetic configurations, that their production allows for pushing beyond the limits of theoretical frameworks, and that their mobilization is accompanied by translations and interferences, whereby clarity is lost rather than increased. Second, the scholarship on diagrams has predominantly focused on diagrams as products of a thought process, as the result of a research endeavor, or as the disseminated abstraction of a discovery. By contrast, our focus on the workings of diagrams enables us to also address the often ephemeral nature of diagrams within the processes of observation, analysis, research, and theorizing. Our contributions stress the co-production of epidemic theory between geographic sketches and understandings of disease: they extrapolate from spatial interior configuration to the diagrammatic conceptualization of the mind and demonstrate the sheer multiplicity of concepts in the repeated iteration of diagrammatic drawing. To this end, the chapters by Spankie and Steadman in this collection have integrated the performative nature of diagrams and diagrammatic reasoning into the development of their arguments. Both of them shift between a reading of diagrams and a diagrammatic visualization of readings.

In her contribution, Ro Spankie reads the diagram as an invitation to shift registers from theories about the mind to the design of the interior space of Freud's study and consulting room. With reference to Mary Douglas (1991), Spankie approaches Freud's interior as one that "exists in time and has aesthetic and cultural dimensions." It is one that folds the spatial coordinates of rooms, in which psychoanalytic work is carried out, into the interior of the mind, whose structures Freud aimed to work out. In her contribution, Spankie, herself an architect, works with diagrams to trace the processes of translation and extrapolation between physical and psychological spaces. She emphasizes that "as a technique, diagramming—working with diagrams—shifts the emphasis from physical form or appearance to latent structure." Following these implicit structural connections and associations, Spankie reconstructs the genealogy of Freud's psychoanalytical mind through a close reading of a range of diagrams, diagrammatic practices, and diagrammatic translations. This enables a different reading of Freud's work in which the significance of spatial metaphors becomes visible. Spankie suggests understanding Freud's descriptions of psychoanalysis "as a process of ordering one's thoughts in the same way as one might order one's things in a cluttered or disorderly interior." She re-engages with the kinds of visualizations that diagrams enable when she demonstrates the imprint of Freud's spatial arrangements on his diagrammatic representations of "dream structure." The chapter concludes by proposing the diagram as a means through which "invisible structures, rituals, and routines" are rendered visible as a contingent "visual analogy."

These cross-readings of diagrams in between spatial arrangements and theories of the mind circle around a theme that Philip Steadman, too, picks up in his epilogue to this collection: the relationship of ornament and order in and through diagrams. But Steadman asks how this relation is configured in diagrammatic processes of copying designs. He focuses on a technique of copying as applied by researchers investigating the capacities of visual memories. Rather than the expected deterioration of form and shapes toward chaos, the serial copying of drawings exposes "some tendencies toward schematization." From ornament to order, through repeated copying of drawings in experimental setups, it appears that a tendency toward diagrams can be observed. In experiments that Steadman carried out himself, pictures were "flattened out," objects were reduced to their boundaries, topological relationships were preserved, and only distances and angles changed. Without jumping to conclusions, Steadman argues that these results might indicate a diagrammatical way of thinking and a general diagrammatic tendency from ornament to order.

The mainstream of studies of diagrams places the work of diagrams in the realm of the schematization or simplification of complex processes in— or theories about—the world. Historians of science have long unpacked the use of diagrams as reductive representations of the cosmos (Kusukawa and Maclean 2006), as popularized schemes of complex physical models, or as accessible demonstrations of chemical processes (Eddy 2014). The field has usually looked at diagrams through the lens of the material culture of scientific practice and has largely been influenced by Bruno Latour's (1999) considerations of inscription. As a result, diagrams, including tables, graphs, chemical formulae, maps, and other abstract two-dimensional representations, have been addressed as a type of scientific iconography that has been mobilized by scientists to transform a scientific object into paper.

While much of the recent scholarship on the history of diagrams in science appears to follow Latour's proposition, more recent work on 'paper tools' has begun to emphasize a line of inquiry more comparable to the goals of this book. Beginning with the work of Ursula Klein (2003), paper tools and paper technologies were approached in the performative arrangements of laboratories or in the post-war teaching of physics as malleable, multiple forms that incite a myriad of uses and lay the groundwork for a complex, contingent 'diagrammatic reasoning', for example, in the educative and multivalent production of Feyman diagrams in theoretical physics (Kaiser 2005: 18). Contrary to Latour, David Kaiser shows how the educative work physicists have done with diagrams has served to draw theories apart, rather than bring things together (ibid.). The perspective cultivated in recent history of science and knowledge perceives diagrams not as reductive representations of a scientific object; instead, it focuses on the "fleeting, undetectable intermediates" (Nye and Weininger 2018: 5) that diagrams have produced, for example, in the history of chemistry, and on the productive, creative, and explorative elements of the formal and data-driven reasoning of diagrammatic practices, tools, and instruments.

A similar perspective has been developed in the recent historiography of paper technologies in clinical reasoning, identifying the forms, tables, graphs, and diagrams that organize pathological discourse, not only as instruments of standardization and formalization, but also as technologies that sustain and support narrative practices and enable a way of knowing on the basis of cases (Hess 2018; Hess and Mendelsohn 2010). This perspective then resembles scholarship on the significance and meaning of maps and spatial reasoning in and through diagrams. Here, historical scholarship has long pointed beyond the idea of maps as accurate representations of territory. The political and cultural dimensions of geographical maps have been emphasized (Harley 2001), and disease maps have been considered as a "method of assemblage within which ideas are constituted and then argued about" (Koch 2011: 13).

The contributions to this book all engage with the curious combination of simplification and multiplication that appears to structure most of existing scholarship on the topic so far. Following Nelson Goodman (1976), Laura Perini (2013: 274) explains that in comparison to other visual representations, diagrams are "relatively non-replete" insofar as in diagrams "relatively few visible features are used to convey content." And yet, if simplification may indeed be the case when it comes to some scientific diagrams, it cannot be said to be an inherent characteristic of diagrams as such. Indeed, to return to Chajes's work, diagrams may be employed explicitly so as to complicate a simplified image of the world. Hence the Trees of Life deriving from the sixteenth century Lurianic school of the Kabbalah (fig. 0.2) are "kaleidoscopically multiplied" in comparison to earlier diagrams, such as the one examined above. Based on a more "spatial-mechanical" cosmology of emanation, which saw "higher levels of divinity … transposed and expressed in the lower levels," Chajes (2016) argues, Isaac Luria's system made "diagrams more essential than ever to the aspiring kabbalist."

When examining 'working with diagrams', it is worth considering how different aspects of diagrams work, or how they can be deployed and transformed

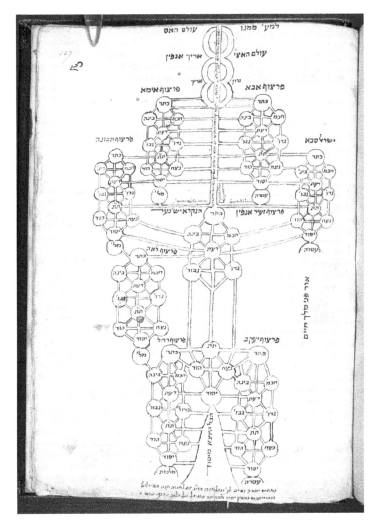

FIGURE 0.2: The denary tree, kaleidoscopically multiplied. Courtesy of the British Library (Add MS 27006, f. 227r). https://www.bl.uk/hebrew-manuscripts/articles /kabbalistic-diagrams-in-the-british-librarys-margoliouth-catalogue.

in ways that work. To what extent, for example, is the diagram's graphic form essential to its working or being workable? In some cases, like the Kabbalistic Trees of Life, form can be of the essence and cannot be substituted (as Sefirot are drawn as circles in order to represent their true spherical nature). In other cases, form can be both symbolic and conventional, but is not ontologically tied to the diagram. Take, for example, diagrams of zoonosis where animal to human infection is represented by arrows. This is, on the one hand, conventional in the sense that arrows generally convey causal relations in the sciences. But it is also symbolic insofar as pestilence has been represented by arrows in both narrative and visual sources, from the Iliad through to the Counter-Reformation (Lynteris 2017). And yet, if in the case of the Kabbalah a diagram that does not represent spheres would not work as a Tree of Life, in the case of epidemiology a diagram that does not employ arrows can still represent animal to human infection. If working with diagrams requires, at a minimum level, the ability of a human subject to transform and revise these diagrams to fit new situations, then that subject has to know the ontological value of the components of the diagram, or risk ending up with a diagram that no longer works.

This does not, however, imply that working with diagrams means one has to necessarily end up with them. In fact, sometimes the aim of diagrams is precisely to produce something non-diagrammatic. An example is the case of Marcel Baltazard, the renowned Pasteurian who, after establishing himself as a pioneer of the scientific investigation of plague in Morocco, founded his own regional Pasteur Institute in Tehran (Mainbourg 2007). There, in the 1950s, Baltazard directed far-reaching research in sylvatic plague, especially in Iran's Kurdish areas. Visually apt,[2] at some point he seemed keen to develop a popular means of communicating to the public how plague could be transmitted. What he produced was a beautiful single-page comic strip titled "Propagation of Plague in Iran's Kurdistan" (fig. 0.3), which predates today's movement of 'graphic medicine' (Czerwiec et al. 2015) by half a century.

The comic strip shows a gerbil dying of plague, with its fleas abandoning its cold cadaver so as to infest other rodents and eventually a turban-wearing bearded man, who appears to be scratching in evident irritation. The same man then develops first bubonic and later the contagious pneumonic form of plague, infecting his friend who in the last frame appears to be infecting another man by means of a transfer of human fleas. What lay behind this uniquely legible piece of public health communication was a far more messy and ungainly diagram (fig. 0.4). The protagonists of the comic strip are still there, but schemas, names, and the jumps of the fleas are rough drawings, with arrows between them. Although the details and even the context of the process are lacking, one thing is clear: here the work of the diagram is achieved by its transformation into a non-diagram—a comic strip used for public health campaigns.

At this point, it cannot be stressed enough that the work of diagrams is not limited to the work of their graphic elements, as these work only within specific non-graphic contexts. The most important—or at least immediate—of these is the surface on which diagrams are drawn. John Bender and Michael Marrinan (2010) have noted the importance of the white surface in some of the defining diagrams of modernity: the ones adorning the pages of Diderot's *Encyclopedia*. Discussing the copper plate on patisserie engraved by Robert Benard ("Pattisier, Tour à Pâte, Bassines, Mortier &c."), the two authors stress the lack of volume

FIGURE 0.3: Propagation de la peste au Kurdistan d'Iran. Archives Institut Pasteur – BLT.16 – Lieu: A4/131-132, C/Travaux scientifiques, 3_ Documentation; Propagation de la peste au Kurdistan d'Iran; maladie des rongeurs "mériones" dont l'homme est le révélateur. © Institut Pasteur/Archives Marcel Baltazard.

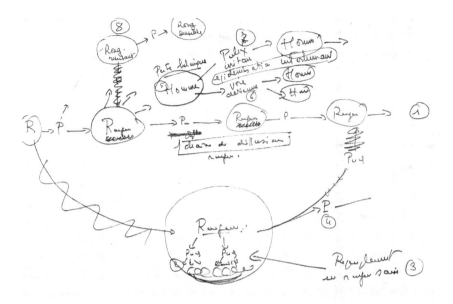

FIGURE 0.4: Cycle de propagation de la peste. Archives Institut Pasteur – BLT.16 – Lieu: A4/131-132, C/ Travaux scientifiques, 3_ Documentation; Cycle de propagation de la peste. © Institut Pasteur/Archives Marcel Baltazard.

in the figures of bowls, spoons, and so forth, which synthesize what we may call a meta-diagram of patisserie. The 'notation' of this diagram is in this case underlined by the lack of shadows on the white background of the figures. "This whiteness," Bender and Marrinan assert, "is an arena of potentiality that fosters connections without fixing them or foreclosing thought experiments" (ibid.: 23). It is a whiteness that, by "permeat[ing] the plates of the *Encyclopedia*," becomes "the field of Diderot's *rapport* that we call correlation. We take it [to] be a virtual space whose material presence—which joins together the disparate parts of the *Encyclopedia* plates—provides support for the composite play of imagery and cognition that is the motor-energy of diagram" (ibid.). Writing about epidemiological diagrams describing animal-to-human infection (zoonosis) in the twenty-first century, Lynteris (2017: 472) has noted the still pervasive operation of the blank background: "We need to consider the relation between geometric and iconographic components (lines and figures) of the diagram and its surface as a meaningful one; indeed, as a relation whose apparent invisibility is an important analytical component of its articulation." Lynteris follows Kenneth Knoespel (2001) in arguing that the work of the blank surface is that it allows the double operation of diagrams hinted at by their meaning in Greek: to both draw and erase (*diagrapho*). At one and the same time, in providing a surface for drawing the interrelation between significant components of zoonosis and for erasing the ecological and social context of the latter, the white/blank surface of epidemiological diagrams makes infection appear as an objective process, free from environmental or historical referents.

But the dialectic between the 'diagrammatic' and the 'diagraphic' (i.e., erasing) work of diagrams is not limited to their oft-used blank/white background. In her chapter in this volume, Nurit Bird-David examines kinship trees as "diagrammatic pilots of anthropological reasoning" (Lynteris 2017: 463), challenging us to consider how they "dis-work—in ethnographic accounts of other people's worlds." She asks: *"Do* these diagrammatic tools make fieldwork and its findings 'intelligible to others'—or, rather, to the contrary, in some cases do they obscure locals' lived-worlds and the fieldwork process?" The focus of Bird-David's chapter is on small-scale societies and hunter-gatherers of South India in particular. Stressing the importance of the scalar context, she begins by interrogating the impact of mapping in anthropological accounts of and relating with other peoples. Following Alfred Gell (1998) in stressing the non-indexicality of maps, Bird-David reflects on her own cartographic practices during fieldwork in the Nilgiri region, which culminated in the commissioning of a map of her field site. The map demarcates "a territory that the foragers are described as living *in,"* but it erases what in the forager's experience is far more crucial, that is, with whom they live—"not so much in space/system (environment, nature) but in a community of sentient beings with or alongside whom they live." Similarly, Bird-David argues, just as maps can show us the 'in' but obscure the 'with whom', the "kinship tree has its virtues" but also carries with it a work of erasure or obscuration.

Bird-David discusses how this is brought about by reflecting on W. H. R. Rivers's ([1910] 1968) much-adhered-to instructions for collecting kinship data and drawing kinship diagrams. Bird-David identifies three key problems. First is the fact that "Rivers's method is rooted in using personal names" as if these were concrete bases for genealogical sorting, whereas in her ethnographic experience they are impermanent and a "shaky basis for making pedigrees." "A second problem," Bird-David tells us, is that Rivers "was basing the method on father, mother, child, husband and wife relations." Demonstrating a nuclear-family-led bias of kinship, this ignored the fact that for societies like the Gorge foragers, siblingship is the primary relation. Third, Rivers's stress on "known status" (marriage, number of children) obscured the "performative basis of kinship relations," or what Bird-David aptly terms the "the minute work of 'relati*ng*' that constitutes relations" among foragers. The three problems with Rivers's genealogical instructions are both reflected in and complicated in actually drawn kinship diagrams. Explaining how following these instructions led her to robust but prejudiced diagrams, Bird-David begins by noting that "kinship diagrammatic tools embody a grammar of self and relations that obscures the foragers' sense of themselves and their community." While showing connections, kinship diagrams emphasize individuals as nodal points while reducing the actual object of their graphic work, the connecting lines, to "add-on relations" of usually dyadic nature. This, Bird-David stresses, draws out an ontology that has no bearing with the "foragers' primary sense of an intimate community into which one is born as a relative who is multiply connected to everyone else." The diagraphic work of diagrams in this case can thus be said to be the erasure of the Gorge foragers' "performative and strategic kinship experience" whereby "each person is at once relative(s) of multiple others."

In his contribution to this collection, Matei Candea reflects on the "distinctive power and limits of visual representation as an anthropological heuristic." Turning his attention to the meaning and work of 'graphic coherence', he asks: "When is a diagram coherent? And what is it supposed to be coherent with?" Assuming a 'practitioner's view' of the question of working with diagrams, Candea explores "where and to what effect diagrams accompany, prefigure, and exceed textual forms of anthropological argument." To do this, he compares diagrams with another neglected anthropological practice: the use of algebraic formulations. Both forms of non-textual description in anthropology have been criticized as problematic for lending a (pseudo)scientific authority to non-scientific statements, and for doing little more than repeating textual context. And yet, Candea argues, there is a key difference between the work of diagrams and that of algebraic formulations in anthropology. In contrast to mathematical notation, diagrams, as a visual form, are conceptually and indeed symbolically replete: "Circles imply closure and perfection; unbroken lines seem to suggest that objects have firm boundaries." As inherently polysemic visual forms positioned between 'visual excess' and 'visual coherence', diagrams, Candea tells us, require a textual reference or aid so that they may be read. Although this position runs against most current cognitive and epistemological studies of diagrams, it is important to consider here the 'work' that diagrams perform in the text-oriented context of anthropology. Could the dependence of diagrams on texts in anthropology account for their relative lack of success, both inside and outside the discipline? When read alongside other contributions to this collection, Candea's reflections on anthropological diagrams challenge us to consider the extent to which, in some cases, diagrams may indeed become so linked to texts that they surrender their diagrammatic properties and thus deliver a creative disturbance "at the intersection of conventions and inventions." Cutting across (but perhaps not challenging) the iconophobic bias of the discipline, anthropological diagrams-with-texts work toward new concepts on the basis of "a self-conscious play with conventional visual languages."

If Vidler (2000: 17) is right in that, in the digital age, "the diagram becomes less and less an icon and more and more a blueprint," we may ask here how this shift is already predicated in the work of what we may call 'transformational diagrams', such as epidemic maps or Conrad Waddington's 'epigenetic landscape'. Just like the model, the diagram suggests a change of medium, when it takes part in the scientific elaboration of a research object (Rheinberger 2015). And like the model, any diagram presupposes the transition from traces to data to then enable the tinkering with data configurations. In early epidemiology, as Engelmann argues in his contribution to this collection, the diagram's configurations produce and sustain the conceptual understanding of epidemics as configurations. The spatial diagram supported efforts of boundary work to bolster epidemiology's "notions of complexity, to preserve system-thinking" against the deductive principles of the laboratory. For Ljungberg (2016: 142), the spatial diagram is an instrument of hybridity that not only represents and abstracts networks of relationships, but also allows for the experimental discovery of new relationships and unknown elements. Engelmann thus demonstrates how spatial diagrams were used to open the frame for an exploration of the unusual, unexplained dimensions of an epidemic, contrary to the common misunderstanding of a diagram as a condensation of that which is known. To this end, Engelmann presents two maps produced to grasp the configuration of bubonic plague, the first during an outbreak of the disease in the Russian village of Vetlianka (1878) and the second during the 1899 outbreak in the Portuguese city of Porto. Engelmann compares the map produced in the former, as a diagram drawn ahead of the identification of plague's pathogen, with the one produced after this watershed moment in the history of the disease. He thus demonstrates the persistent commitment of epidemiology to conduct inductive surveys rather than deductive investigations. As Engelmann shows, this scientific ethos is sustained through diagrams. Here, where the radical epistemological indeterminacy of induction as a hallmark of epidemiological reasoning comes into focus, he argues that it is through the working of epidemiologists with diagrams that the modern understanding of the epidemic as an abstract object, as a conceptual entity, first emerged.

In her chapter for this collection, Caroline Humphrey returns to Daston and Galison's (1992) idea of the 'working object' in order to examine the defining image/object of epigenetics: Waddington's much-discussed 'epigenetic landscape' diagram. Humphrey poses a key question as regards scientific diagrams: to what extent can they be said to be "illustrations" of scientific theories, hypotheses, or observations? Defining illustration as "a representational visual depiction of something, an image that uses naturalistic artistic means to make that object or idea clear and vivid," she notes that what usually distinguishes diagrams from the former is that their work is not so much representational as explanatory or indeed "constitutive." However, when one examines what, following Isabelle Stengers (1987), we may call the 'nomadic' work of Waddington's epigenetic landscape diagram, the question about what makes this so adaptable and indeed inspirational across many different disciplines and fields arises. The answer, Humphrey claims, may be sought in the "illustrative character" of Waddington's diagram, which, by depicting a scene, requires "the viewer to imagine the completion of a process about to take place in it." This leads Humphrey to examine how the "visual and conceptual affordances of these diagrams can set off a process of imaginative 'work' in a new field." In going beyond both cognitive and epistemological discussions of diagrams, Humphrey's chapter seeks to elucidate the importance of the imagination (understood as a creative faculty in the strong, Castoriadean sense of the term) in the work of diagrams. Examining "the varied affordances of the diagram as a working object," Humphrey proposes that "diagrams can perhaps best be seen as a *means of transportation* of a set of ideas from one context to another." But both the transformational and transportational capacity of diagrams, Humphrey stresses, is not an unconditional trait of diagrams as such. Rather, it has to do with the way in which different diagrams embody relatedness or "the relations between parts." If for some diagrams, opting for openness, this remains both a constitutive and transformable faculty, for others relatedness is fixed or over-specified, resulting in a loss of their "imaginative potential"—these are "over-determined" diagrams that no longer entice the viewer to imagine, but instead instruct her or him "what to think."

This book thus introduces scholarship that addresses the ephemeral dimensions of scientists' interactions and collaborations with diagrams across different professions and disciplines. Moving beyond the perception of diagrams as mere inscriptions of objects and processes, we propose here an evaluation of diagrammatic reasoning as the work that is carried out with, on, and beyond diagrams. The reasoning curated in this collection can be considered diagrammatic as it is invested in the production, mobilization, repurposing, and annihilation of diagrams. *Working with Diagrams* brings together for the first time chapters concerned with practices and studies that highlight the significance of diagrammatic reasoning in and beyond the sciences, indifferent to any visibility or material trace of a diagram.

Acknowledgments

This book is the result of the conference "Diagrammatic: Beyond Description?" which was held in December 2016 at the Centre for Research in the Arts, Social Sciences and Humanities (CRASSH), University of Cambridge. We would like to thank Oliver Wright for his help in organizing the conference, our keynote speaker, Anthony Vidler, all our speakers and delegates for their discussion and feedback on the topic of working with diagrams, and CRASSH for its generous support of the event (funded by a CRASSH conference award). We would also like to thank Yossi Chajes for discussing with us his approach to diagrams. Research leading to this introduction was funded by a European

Research Council Starting Grant (under the European Union's Seventh Framework Programme/ERC grant agreement no. 336564) for the project "Visual Representations of the Third Plague Pandemic" (principal investigator, Christos Lynteris) and supported by the Challenge Investment Fund of the College of Arts, Humanities and Social Sciences of the University of Edinburgh (principal investigator, Lukas Engelmann).

Lukas Engelmann is a Senior Lecturer and Chancellor's Fellow in History and Sociology of Biomedicine at the University of Edinburgh. His work focuses on the history of epidemiological reasoning in the long twentieth century, and is funded by an ERC starting grant. Recent publications include *Mapping AIDS: Visual Histories of an Enduring Epidemic* (2018) and, co-authored with Christos Lynteris, *Sulphuric Utopias: A History of Maritime Fumigation* (2020).

Caroline Humphrey is a social anthropologist who has worked in the USSR/ Russia, Mongolia, Inner Mongolia, Nepal, and India. Until 2010 she was Sigrid Rausing Professor of Anthropology at the University of Cambridge, and she is currently a Research Director at the university's Mongolia and Inner Asia Studies Unit. Recent publications include *A Monastery in Time: The Making of Mongolian Buddhism* (2013), co-authored with Hurelbaatar Ujeed; *Frontier Encounters: Knowledge and Practice at the Russian, Chinese and Mongolian Border* (2012), co-edited with Franck Billé and Grégory Delaplace; and *Trust and Mistrust in the Economies of the China-Russia Borderlands* (2018).

Christos Lynteris is a Professor of Medical Anthropology at the University of St Andrews. A medical anthropologist investigating epistemological, bio-political, and aesthetic aspects of infectious disease epidemics, he is the principal investigator of the Wellcome-funded project, "The Global War Against the Rat and the Epistemic Emergence of Zoonosis." His recent publications include *Ethnographic Plague: Configuring Disease on the Chinese-Russian Frontier* (2016), *Human Extinction and the Pandemic Imaginary* (2019), and, co-authored with Lukas Engelmann, *Sulphuric Utopias: A History of Maritime Fumigation* (2020).

Notes

1. For a more recent approach, see Drucker (2014).
2. An avid photographer, Baltazard also produced a film on plague that is appreciated today as a unique visual document of Iranian architecture.

References

Bender, John, and Michael Marrinan. 2010. *The Culture of Diagram*. Stanford, CA: Stanford University Press.

Bonelli, Cristóbal. 2015. "To See That Which Cannot Be Seen: Ontological Differences and Public Health Policies in Southern Chile." *Journal of the Royal Anthropological Institute* (n.s.) 21 (4): 872–891.

Bouquet, Mary. 1996. "Family Trees and Their Affinities: The Visual Imperative of the Genealogical Diagram." *Journal of the Royal Anthropological Institute* 2 (1): 43–66.

Burr, Winthrop A., and Donald E. Gerson. 1965. "Venn Diagrams and Human Taxonomy." *American Anthropologist* 67 (2): 494–499. https://doi.org/10.1525/aa.1965.67.2.02a00260.

Callon, Michel. 2006. "What Does It Mean to Say That Economics Is Performative?" CSI Working Papers Series. Centre de Sociologie de l'Innovation (CSI), Mines ParisTech, August. halshs-00091596.

Catley, Kefyn M., and Laura R. Novick. 2008. "Seeing the Wood for the Trees: An Analysis of Evolutionary Diagrams in Biology Textbooks." *BioScience* 58 (10): 976–987.

Chajes, Yossi. 2016. "Kabbalistic Diagrams in the British Library's Margoliouth Catalogue." 29 February. https://www.bl.uk/hebrew-manuscripts/articles/kabbalistic-diagrams-in-the-british-librarys-margoliouth-catalogue.

Coopmans, Catelijne, Janet Vertesi, Michael Lynch, and Steve Woolgar, eds. 2014. *Representation in Scientific Practice Revisited*. Cambridge, MA: MIT Press.

Czerwiec, MK, Ian Williams, Susan Merrill Squier, Michael J. Green, Kimberly R. Myers, and Scott T. Smith. 2015. *Graphic Medicine Manifesto*. University Park: Pennsylvania State University Press.

Daston, Lorraine. 2014. "Beyond Representation." In Coopmans et al. 2014, 319–322.

Daston, Lorraine, and Peter Galison. 1992. "The Image of Objectivity." *Representations* 40: 81–128.

Deleuze, Gilles. 1988. *Foucault*. Trans. Seán Hand. Minneapolis: University of Minnesota Press.

Douglas, Mary. 1991. "The Idea of a Home: A Kind of Space." *Social Research* 58 (1): 287–307.

Drucker, Johanna. 2014. *Graphesis: Visual Forms of Knowledge Production*. Cambridge, MA: Harvard University Press.

Eddy, Matthew D. 2014. "How to See a Diagram: A Visual Anthropology of Chemical Affinity." *Osiris* 29 (1): 178–196.

Elmer, Greg. 2003. "A Diagram of Panoptic Surveillance." *New Media & Society* 5 (2): 231–247.

Gardner, Martin. 1981. "Mathematical Games: The Laffer Curve and Other Laughs in Current Economics." *Scientific American* 245 (6): 18–34.

Gell, Alfred. 1998. *Art and Agency: An Anthropological Theory*. Oxford: Clarendon Press.

Giraud, Yann. 2014. "Legitimizing Napkin Drawing: The Curious Dispersion of Laffer Curves, 1978–2008." In Coopmans et al. 2014, 269–290.

Gontier, Nathalie. 2011. "Depicting the Tree of Life: The Philosophical and Historical Roots of Evolutionary Tree Diagrams." *Evolution: Education and Outreach* 4 (3): 515–538.

Goodman, Nelson. 1976. *Languages of Art: An Approach to a Theory of Symbols*. Indianapolis, IN: Hackett Publishing.

Hage, Per, and Frank Harary. 1983. *Structural Models in Anthropology*. New York: Cambridge University Press.

Hallam, Elizabeth. 2008. *Anatomy Museum: Death and the Body Displayed*. London: Reaktion Books.

Harley, J. B. 2001. *The New Nature of Maps: Essays in the History of Cartography*. Ed. Paul Laxton. Baltimore: Johns Hopkins University Press.

Hess, Volker. 2018. "A Paper Machine of Clinical Research in the Early Twentieth Century." *Isis* 109 (3): 473–493.

Hess, Volker, and J. Andrew Mendelsohn. 2010. "Case and Series: Medical Knowledge and Paper Technology, 1600–1900." *History of Science* 48 (3–4): 287–314.

Ingold, Tim. 2007. *Lines: A Brief History*. London: Routledge.

Jay, Martin. 2010–2011. "*The Culture of Diagram* (Review)." *Nineteenth-Century French Studies* 39 (1–2): 157–159.

Kaiser, David. 2005. *Drawing Theories Apart: The Dispersion of Feynman Diagrams in Postwar Physics*. Chicago: University of Chicago Press.

Klein, Ursula. 2003. *Experiments, Models, Paper Tools: Cultures of Organic Chemistry in the Nineteenth Century*. Stanford, CA: Stanford University Press.

Knoespel, Kenneth J. 2001. "Diagrams as Piloting Devices in the Philosophy of Gilles Deleuze." *Theorie, Littérature, Enseignement* 19: 145–165.

Knoespel, Kenneth J. 2002. "Diagrammatic Transformation of Architectural Space." *Philosophica* 70: 11–36.

Koch, Tom. 2011. *Disease Maps: Epidemics on the Ground*. Chicago: University of Chicago Press.

Kusukawa, Sachiko, and Ian Maclean, eds. 2006. *Transmitting Knowledge: Words, Images, and Instruments in Early Modern Europe*. New York: Oxford University Press.

Larkin, Jill H., and Herbert A. Simon. 1987. "Why a Diagram Is (Sometimes) Worth Ten Thousand Words." *Cognitive Science* 11 (1): 65–100.

Latour, Bruno. 1999. *Pandora's Hope: Essays on the Reality of Science Studies*. Cambridge, MA: Harvard University Press.

Ljungberg, Christina. 2016. "The Diagrammatic Nature of Maps." In *Thinking with Diagrams: The Semiotic Basis of Human Cognition*, ed. Sybille Krämer and Christina Ljungberg, 139–159. Berlin: De Gruyter.

Lüthy, Christoph, and Alexis Smets. 2009. "Words, Lines, Diagrams, Images: Towards a History of Scientific Imagery." *Early Science and Medicine* 14 (1–3): 398–439.

Lynteris, Christos. 2017. "Zoonotic Diagrams: Mastering and Unsettling Human Animal Relations." *Journal of the Royal Anthropological Institute* 23 (3): 463–485.

MacKenzie, Donald. 2009. *Material Markets: How Economic Agents Are Constructed*. New York: Oxford University Press.

Mainbourg, Jean. 2007. *Balta, aventurier de la peste: Professeur Marcel Baltazard (1908–1971)* [Balta, plague adventurer: Professor Marcel Baltazard (1908–1971)]. Paris: L'Harmattan.

Miller, Nathaniel. 2007. *Euclid and His Twentieth Century Rivals: Diagrams in the Logic of Euclidean Geometry*. Stanford, CA: CSLI Publications.

Norman, Jesse. 2006. *After Euclid: Visual Reasoning and the Epistemology of Diagrams*. Stanford, CA: CSLI Publications.

Nye, Mary Jo, and Stephen J. Weininger. 2018. "Paper Tools from the 1780s to the 1960s: Nomenclature, Classification, and Representations." *Ambix* 65 (1): 1–8. https://doi.org/10.1080/00026980.2017.1419651.

Perini, Laura. 2013. "Diagrams in Biology." *Knowledge Engineering Review* 28 (3): 273–286.

Preda, Alex. 2007. "Where Do Analysts Come From? The Case of Financial Chartism." *Sociological Review* 55 (s2): 40–64.

Rheinberger, Hans-Jörg. 2015. "Preparations, Models, and Simulations." *History and Philosophy of the Life Sciences* 36 (3): 321–334. https://doi.org/10.1007/s40656-014-0049-3.

Rivers, W. H. R. (1910) 1968. "The Genealogical Method of Anthropological Enquiry." In *Kinship and Social Organisation*, ed. A. Forge, 97–113. London: Athlone Press.

Stengers, Isabelle. 1987. *D'une science à l'autre: Des concepts nomades* [From one science to another: Nomadic concepts]. Paris: Seuil.

Stjernfelt, Frederik. 2000. "Diagrams as Centerpiece of a Peircean Epistemology." *Transactions of the Charles S. Peirce Society* 36 (3): 357–384.

Teyssot, Georges. 2012. "The Diagram as Abstract Machine." *V!RUS* 7. http://www.nomads.usp.br/virus/virus07/?sec=3&item=1&lang=en.

Vidler, Anthony. 2000. "Diagrams of Diagrams: Architectural Abstraction and Modern Representation." *Representations* 72: 1–20.

Zdebik, Jakub. 2012. *Deleuze and the Diagram: Aesthetic Threads in Visual Organization*. London: Bloomsbury.

Zweig, Stefan. (1941) 2013. *A Chess Story*. Trans. Alexander Starritt. London: Pushkin Press.

Chapter 1

REVISITING SIGMUND FREUD'S DIAGRAMS OF THE MIND

Ro Spankie

> Home is represented, not by a house, but by a practice or set of practices.
> Everyone has his own. (Berger 1984: 64)

Sigmund Freud needs little introduction, being well known for having created a theory, a method of investigation, and a treatment for psychological disorders. What he is perhaps less well credited for is the construction of the interior arrangement that most psychoanalytic consulting rooms take today, which argu-ably features as an essential ingredient in the therapeutic process. This oversight is perhaps due to a curious historical break in Freud's consulting room and study as found today. Although it is possible to visit the study and consulting room at their original location in Berggasse 19, now the Freud Museum Vienna, the rooms are bare—because in 1938, after the Nazis annexed Austria, Freud (who was Jewish) and his immediate family were forced to leave Vienna and

Notes for this chapter begin on page 39.

make a new home in London. This exile late in Freud's life, at age 82, is why one finds the 'architecture' (the empty study and consulting room) in Vienna, while the 'interior arrangement' (consisting of the furniture and fittings) is in London.

I am an architect by training, and my research concerns the role of the drawing in the design process, in particular in relation to the creation of interior space. The word 'design' comes from the Italian word *disegno*, which means drawing but also the drawing out of an idea (Hill 2006: 33). Designers use the act of drawing as a means of visual thinking, while the finished drawing can be understood as the picturing of a spatial idea. Conventionally, interior design is seen as part of the discipline of architecture, constructed from physical form and represented using scaled orthographic techniques such as plan and section. If, however, one defines interiors as 'a practice or set of practices', one shifts the focus from physical form to function, which becomes more challenging in terms of drawing.

In my search for alternative methods of drawing out interior qualities, I came across a range of drawings by Sigmund Freud (see Gamwell and Solms 2006), which I divided loosely as carefully observed medical drawings of slides seen through a microscope and abstract diagrams in the form of freehand sketches used to think with and through the structure of the psyche, as well as graphics for publication. What is noticeable is that, at the point that Freud's investigations shifted from descriptive anatomy to brain function and the hypothetical structures of psychoanalysis, his drawings also shifted from the scaled and the observational to the abstract and the diagrammatic. Both the content of these later drawings and the way Freud seems to be using diagramming as a tool to think through an idea, as well as to visually explain that idea, suggested potential overlaps with how designers use drawings. I was intrigued to explore whether the shift from physical anatomy to the hypothetical structures of psychoanalysis could provide an analogous technique that might give insight into the relationship between the body/architecture and the mind/interior.

The chapter's approach is driven by two propositions. First, I suggest that interiors, regardless of their function, should be understood closer to Mary Douglas's definition of 'home' than the more traditional architectural notion of the inside of a house or building. In her article "The Idea of a Home: A Kind of Space," Douglas (1991: 287) defines home not as a physical place, but as "a pattern of regular doings," constructed and acted out by an embryonic community. While such a home is located in space, since it also exists in time, it is "not necessarily a fixed space," and "because it is for people who are living in that time and space, it has aesthetic and moral dimensions" (ibid.: 289). Thus, for Douglas a home is not made of bricks and mortar, but "is the realization of [a community's] ideas" (ibid.: 290) about a structured domesticity. Adapting this anthropological observation to architectural method, I would maintain that while an interior is framed by the architecture that contains it, it has a more fluid structure, being full of movable elements such as furniture and effects that the occupant arranges and rearranges according to his or her needs, tastes, and customs. An interior therefore exists in time and has aesthetic and cultural dimensions.

Second, I assume the motivations of the occupant, in this case Freud, to be different from those of an interior designer, suggesting that the desire to decorate, to furnish, and to arrange a space constitutes an expression of self, both conscious and unconscious, rather than solely a response to spatial or functional requirements. The act of arranging his or her space allows the occupant to establish his or her identity and create a personal interior architecture that challenges the traditional architectural understanding of interior design and the more professional concerns of form, function, and style. As the art critic Mario Praz ([1964] 2008: 21) put it: "This is the house in its deepest essence: a projection of the ego."

In this chapter I go a step further in demonstrating that Freud's approach to psychoanalysis shares a diagrammatic order with the interior in which he dwelled and practiced. Working with diagrams, the chapter exposes the intricate analogy between Freud's conceptual contributions and the spatial context in which they were developed. To this end, I will 'draw out' Freud's study and consulting room—two rooms that he furnished, arranged, and adapted to suit his practice over a period of 43 years—in order to shed light on the 'inner' (as opposed to bodily) qualities of the space.[1] The chapter's first section, "Reconstructing the Consulting Room and Study," offers a description of Freud's workspace as it can be found today, followed by a reconstruction of it during Freud's lifetime. The second section, "Diagramming Space," focuses on the interior qualities of the workspace, such as function, and suggests possible associations that the arrangement of furniture might have held for both Freud and his patients. The final section, "Diagramming the Mind," borrows the structure of a set of diagrams that Freud used to describe the dream process, so as to demonstrate the diagrammatical analogies in his description of the interior in terms of function, sequence, and effect. Throughout the chapter, drawing—more specifically, diagramming—is used as both a descriptive and an investigative technique.

Reconstructing the Consulting Room and Study

It is in the action of changing and creating it that the individual confers meaning on his environment. (Pawley 1968: 31)

What drew me to Freud's study and consulting room was the fact that the rituals and routines he created around the 'psychoanalytic setting'[2] are not specific to one location and, like Douglas's description of home, can be understood to exist both physically and in people's minds—in this case as a memory, a method, and a metaphor. Because of the curious transplanting of the interior from one architectural body to another, my first act was one of reconstruction, to imagine the furniture and effects back in the rooms in Vienna. Obviously conceptual, the task here was also speculative because what occurred in those rooms in Berggasse 19 essentially happened behind closed doors. Freud wrote virtually nothing about the arrangement of the rooms within which he worked and where he kept his famous collection of antiquities. Despite the lack of specific source material, however, there is a vast quantity of what could be described as chance references found in Freud's own writings, numerous biographies (M. Freud 1957; Gay 1989; Jones 1953, 1955, 1957; Sachs 1945), published letters (Boehlich 1990; Brabant et al. 1993; Masson 1985), and recollections from patients.[3] The most compelling visual evidence can be found in a set of black and white photographs of Freud's study and consulting room in Vienna, taken by a young photographer, Edmund Engelman (1998),[4] just before Freud left the city, as well as in the museum context of his final home at Maresfield Gardens, now the Freud Museum London.

Freud spent the greater part of his life in Vienna. From 1891 to 1938, he and his family lived on the second floor of Berggasse 19, an apartment block in Vienna's ninth district. In 1908 he moved his psychoanalytic practice into two rooms adjoining the family apartment, which he furnished as a study and consulting room. Although his practice had a separate front door, he effectively moved what was originally understood as a clinical practice out of the surgery and into a domestic setting. For the next 30 years, it was in these two rooms that he saw patients, wrote up his case histories and papers, and arranged his ever-growing collection of antique objects.

The first of the two rooms, the consulting room, contained the therapist's couch and Freud's armchair at its head (fig. 1.1a). Perhaps the most iconic element of the arrangement, the couch alone could be said to represent the practice of psychoanalysis. Given to him by a grateful patient in 1891, the couch, a piece of domestic furniture, referred back to the days when Freud was still a medical doctor and used techniques such as hypnosis in the treatment of nervous disorders. Even though the treatment shifted from the physical to the psychogenic, Freud continued to use the couch and established his own position at its head, out of the patient's view. This arrangement was intended to create an atmosphere conducive to free association,[5] the patient lying with feet warmed by the stove, in a perfusion of sensuous Oriental rugs and throw pillows, "draped in that flying carpet for unconscious voyaging" (Warner 1998: viii). Freud himself, a disembodied voice or a listening ear, made his presence apparent by the fumes of an aromatic cigar as the patient's unconscious mind was revealed through memories, dreams, and everyday events. That Freud considered this arrangement vital to his practice can be seen in a photograph[6] taken after he had had his armchair, the couch, and the rugs moved to his summer residence at Hohe Warte just outside Vienna,[7] so he could continue to treat patients during the summer months.

The adjoining room, connected by open double doors, was furnished as a study (fig. 1.1b). Referred to by Freud as his inner sanctum, this space contained a large wooden desk, his curiously shaped chair,[8] and his library. It was an inward-looking environment, with the desk placed adjacent to a large window, facing the double doors and the couch. One could describe the first room as housing the practice of psychoanalysis and the second as framing its theory, the two activities visually connected.

Freudian analysis requires analysts to give their complete attention during the analytic session; any notes are therefore written up from memory afterward. In Freud's case, on returning to his desk at the end of the day, he was literally reflecting back on his day's work, the visual connection aiding recall. Of course, Freud was not just writing up notes. What he heard at the head of the couch provided the raw material for the development of psychoanalysis as a whole. Over his lifetime he published 320 books, articles, and essays, the majority of which were drafted in longhand on this desk.

Today at 20 Maresfield Gardens, the desk is separated from the museum visitor by a rope. Curiously anonymous in comparison to the famous couch or the distinctively shaped chair, its surface is obscured by writing implements, smoking paraphernalia, and antique figurines that leave seemingly little space to write—and it is this arrangement that remains in the mind rather than the desk itself. One could argue, however, that if the couch represents the method of treatment, it is the desk that tells us about Freud's writing and the prodigious body of work that was written on its cluttered baize surface.[9]

However, the nature of this significance is harder to pin down than the arrangement of the consulting room. Since the desk lacks the usual paraphernalia one might expect, such as family photographs, a calendar, or a telephone, the temptation is to treat the 65 objects on it—in particular, the figurines—as a form of hieroglyph awaiting their Rosetta stone. But hieroglyphs, like any system of writing, require a collectively understood set of symbols, and the associations here are not so direct; for example, there is no figure of Oedipus on the desk, and few of the Egyptian figures that make up the majority of the figurines are mentioned in Freud's writing.

The word 'object' plays an important role in psychoanalysis. It is used to describe representations of significant figures within the psyche, as in 'mother object' or 'love object', and also when feelings for such figures are transferred onto actual objects, as in a 'transitional object'[10] or 'fetish object'.[11] Functioning both to provide pleasure and to ward off anxiety, such objects represent a complex emotional content to their owner, as well as any formal representation.

Research into the 65 objects on the desk reveals that they too hold multiple characteristics and associations, their stories relating both to the character they assume and to their role in Freud's life. An Osiris figure represents the complex myth of the Egyptian god of the underworld and was also a gift from a friend

FIGURE 1.1a: View of consulting room with couch and Freud's chair at the head. Photograph taken in 1938 by Edmund Engelman at Berggasse 19, Vienna. Courtesy of Freud Museum London.

FIGURE 1.1b: View of study from behind Freud's desk. Photograph taken in 1938 by Edmund Engelman at Berggasse 19, Vienna. Courtesy of Freud Museum London.

to celebrate the completion of Freud's *Totem and Taboo* in 1913. A centaur, a hybrid figure, both man and beast, recalls the strange composite figures created in dreams, as well as the trip to Innsbruck where it was purchased. We learn that Freud, responding to objects that appealed to all the senses, was in the habit of absentmindedly stroking the smooth marble surface of the Baboon of Thoth in the same way he stroked his pet dogs, and that he was unable to write without his favorite pen. For Freud, a lifelong smoker, the multiple ashtrays on the desk would have been infused with the immensely pleasurable association of the smell and taste of cigars (Spankie 2015: 30, 46, 48, 62, 92, 157).

Contemporary commentators also suggested the importance of the emotional content of the figures. An otolaryngologist and contemporary of Freud, Wilhelm Fliess speculated that the little figures that faced Freud as he wrote provided him with an audience that "offer[ed] rest, refuge, and encouragement" (Masson 1985: xvii), acting as markers or signposts to his thoughts. Or as the American poet and patient of Freud Hilda Doolittle (who published under the pseudonym H.D.) described: "The Professor said that his little statues and images helped stabilize the evanescent idea, or keep it from escaping altogether" (H.D. [1956] 2012: 175). Thus, the desk is not 'functional' in the way that a designer might use the term; rather, it created what the English psychoanalyst D. W. Winnicott (1967) referred to as a 'facilitating environment'. In other words, the arrangement of figures on the desk, plus certain writing implements and cigars, created a secure, creative space that allowed Freud both to think and to write.

It is here that, in order to understand the way in which the spatial arrangement of Freud's consulting room and study interacted with his conceptual work, I propose that the projections of occupants (in this case Freud) as well as their structured domesticity can be best observed, analyzed, and demonstrated through diagrammatic methods. I will thus proceed by working with diagrams, so as to draw out subjective qualities such as time, function, and association in relation to the human mind and interior space.

Diagramming Space

An architect's professional status is based on his or her knowledge of the discipline of architecture, demonstrated through an ability to create measured orthographic projections. These indicate not only what the building will look like but also how its interiors will be arranged (typically shown in plan view) as well as how it stands up, the structure, traditionally hidden or disguised behind the façade (is typically shown in section). The photographer Edmund Engelman (1907–2000) had trained as an engineer and drew a cutaway axonometric drawing of Berggasse 19 (fig. 1.2a) to show the location of Freud's study and consulting room in the apartment block.

Freud had originally trained as a medical doctor, and part of this training included producing closely observed drawings of slides seen through a microscope. Working in pen and ink, Freud drew in this way from 1876 to 1886 (see fig. 1.2b) and was a skilled draftsman. In a manner similar to an architect, a doctor's knowledge of a patient's condition is related to his or her understanding of the body's anatomy beneath the surface of the skin. Although both professions' expertise is based on the knowledge of things that are unseen (except through a microscope, on the operating table, or as the building is being constructed), they are essentially dealing with physical matter that—once revealed—can be seen. Freud's drawings are typical nineteenth-century scientific drawings based on a tradition of observation and analysis. I suggest that they can be compared to the orthographic drawings produced by architects because they are created in sectional cuts to reveal what is under the surface of the body tissue (rather than the building façade). Both methods of drawing are measured, to scale, and follow discipline-specific conventions.

Attempting to understand the interior created by Freud, I began my experiment with a measured drawing of Berggasse 19 during Freud's lifetime. To do this, I surveyed the study and consulting room at Berggasse 19 in Vienna's ninth district and the furniture arrangement at 20 Maresfield Gardens, London. Starting with Berggasse 19, I drew out the room plans and mentally placed the furniture back in position. I sat at an imaginary desk and looked at an imaginary couch. I sat in the corner of the consulting room facing the window and looked out to the courtyard, as Freud must have done, and then to my left through the double doors to where I had just imagined the desk. I then drew out my findings in two plans (figs. 3a, 3b) that compare the furniture arrangement in Vienna and London. I marked the visual connection between the desk chair and the couch with an arrow to suggest that the two activities stimulated each other, the desk representing theory and the armchair at the end of the couch, practice.

What can be seen is that the arrangement is similar: the relationships remain the same but not the exact position, as if all the elements were related to one another by elastic threads. Referring to contemporary discussions on 'topological thinking',[12] we see that Freud's interior architecture is capable of being compatible with a number of extensive qualities, such as distance, area, or volume, while retaining the same function. This is why it can be packed up and recreated. Like Engelman's axonometric drawing, my two plans locate important pieces of furniture and establish the visual connection between Freud's two main positions in the space. The drawings, however, fix the interior at a moment in time—1938—and say little about the rituals and routines that occurred within it or what the space represented to Freud or his patients.

The word 'diagram' comes from the Greek διαγραμμα, defined by the *Oxford English Dictionary* (OED) as "that which is marked out by lines." In contrast to orthographic drawings, diagrams should be understood graphically

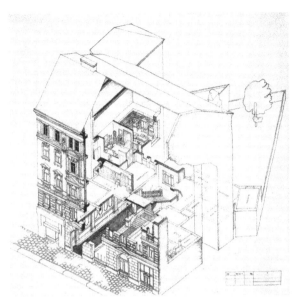

FIGURE 1.2a: Axonometric showing the street façade of Berggasse 19 cut back to reveal the two rooms used by Freud as his consulting room and study. Drawn by Edmund Engelman in 1938. Courtesy of Freud Museum London.

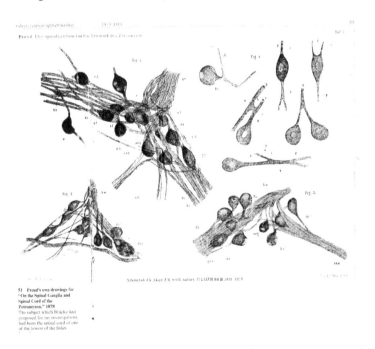

FIGURE 1.2b: On the spinal ganglia and spinal cord of Petromyzon. Drawn by Freud in 1878. Courtesy of Freud Museum London.

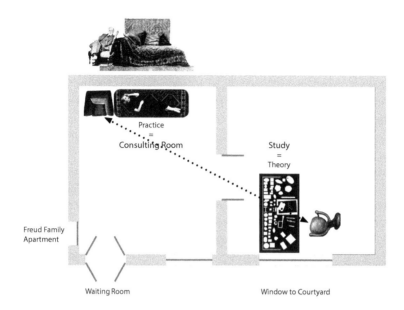

FIGURE 1.3a: Diagrammatic room plan of Berggasse 19, Vienna, showing the consulting room with the patient lying on the couch, the analyst sitting at the head out of sight and the study with the desk facing the couch that is viewed through a screen of objects. Drawn by author.

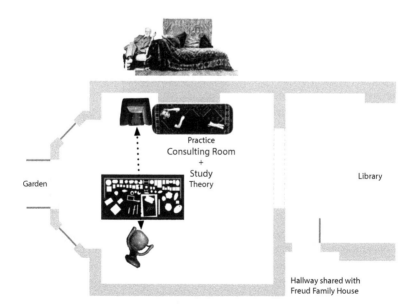

FIGURE 1.3b: The same arrangement at 20 Maresfield Gardens London. Drawn by author.

as representations rather than projections. Diagrams rely on lines, symbols, images, and text to communicate; their purpose is to draw out or connect ideas rather than depict what something looks like. The crucial point is that, as a technique, diagramming—working with diagrams—shifts the emphasis from physical form or appearance to latent structure, offering a tool to 'draw out' or reveal unseen qualities, such as the relationship between elements and their psychological function.

The distinction made between projection and representation is important. The dictionary tells us that the word 'projection' comes from the Latin prōiectiōn-, with prōiectiō meaning the "action of projecting or throwing forward" (OED). In drawing, this translates as "a representation of a figure on a surface according to a particular system of correspondence between its points and the points of the surface" (OED). The projection, therefore, regardless if drawn out in lines of sight, light, or pencil lead, implies a correspondence between the original object and its projection. For architects, this correspondence is made through scale and measure. A representation, on the other hand, is "something which stands for or denotes another symbolically; an image, a symbol, a sign" (OED), the correspondence to the 'other' being through association or analogy rather than points in space. It is this ability of diagrams to depict associative, analogous qualities that makes them so potent in drawing out the interior.

The ability of diagrams to edit out superfluous information and clarify complexity means that architects use them as both an analytical and a generative tool. However, for the most part, such techniques apply discipline-specific conventions. As my interest shifted from the architectural to the interior qualities described earlier, I saw the potential of studying Freud's diagrams to draw out his workspace with particular reference to his diagrams of the mind.

I began with the sketches. Throughout his life, Freud corresponded widely with letters to family, friends, and colleagues, which he would illustrate with sketch diagrams—most intriguingly for me, including some spatial layouts. As part of his medical studies, Freud (aged 20 at the time) spent four weeks at the University of Vienna's biological station in Trieste. His task was to study the anatomy of eels, using the scientific model of observation, analysis, and reflection to search for evidence of the male eel's testicle as a way to identify its sex. Despite dissecting 400 specimens, he had no success. However, in writing to his friend Eduard Silberstein in 1876, he included sketches not only of an eel, but also of his workroom, his worktable surface (carefully recording the position of his microscope and other equipment), and one of his chairs, with his body's position indicated by arrows (see sketches in Boehlich 1990: 143–147).

What is interesting about these sketches is the consideration Freud gave to the arrangement of his workspace, which suggests a close relationship in his mind between the spatial layout and his working method and the importance of details, such as the position of the window and his own body's position in the chair. Freud, explaining to Silberstein two years earlier, wrote: "I am one of those human beings who can be found most of the day between two pieces of furniture, one formed vertically, the armchair, and one extending horizontally, the table, and from these, as social historians are agreed, sprang all civilization" (Boehlich 1990: 48–49).

Another example is a sketch plan included in an 1883 letter to his then fiancée Martha Bernays describing his accommodations at the Vienna General Hospital—the first of three letters sent to Martha that day (see sketch in Grubrich-Simitis et al. 2013: 308). The plan is just an outline, but what is intriguing are Freud's annotations explaining how he has divided the space into two sides: one for studying (writing, reading, thinking), which he terms his *animalische* side, and one for living, which he calls *vegetativer* (sleeping, washing, dressing) (ibid.: 308). Rather than just locating the functional requirements of student life against the spatial layout, Freud associated them with psychic concepts. By describing the animal functions as "higher," he also suggested an ordering of the two, with the discomfort of the vegetative part disturbing the concentration of the animal part. Again, the plan locates important pieces of furniture and describes pictures on the wall, while the window is annotated with the words "air and light," and the door, the "outer world."[13]

I was unable to find any such descriptions of the study and consulting room, so in reference to these sketches and the layout of the study and consulting room in both Vienna and London I redrew Freud's workspace as a diagram focusing on the arrangement of activities and their associations rather than the architecture (fig. 1.4). His most important activities were the acts of consulting—'practice' (observation and analysis)—and of studying—'theory' (reflection). I suggest that in Freud's mind the study and consulting room represented his *animalische* side and the family apartment, the *vegetativer*. Meanwhile, I also noticed the window—Freud was right-handed and always positioned the desk with the window to the left—and the entrance from the waiting room and exit via a side door.

Curiously, my diagram reveals that Freud's spatial arrangement at the end of his life is not dissimilar to his workspace at age 20 in Trieste. This suggests that he repeated certain rituals and routines or 'patterns of doing' throughout his life, adapting them to different circumstances. There is, however, one significant difference: Freud's method of observation changed from looking to listening. By 1896, Freud had swapped the microscope for the couch, moving himself out of the patient's view (and them out of his). This arrangement remains accepted psychoanalytic practice today and is considered an essential component of the therapeutic process. This was a hugely significant development, as noted by psychoanalyst Ilse Grubrich-Simitis (1997: 24): "There can be no doubt that the radical revolutionization of clinical perception was fully accomplished only when 'hearing' too came to be incorporated into the

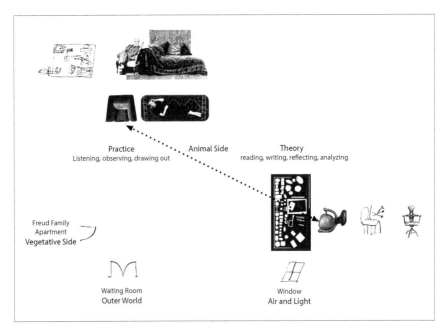

FIGURE 1.4: Diagram of study and consulting room showing activities and associations. Drawn by author.

perceptual process." This is because listening requires that, unlike the eels of Trieste, the subject being studied is alive.

I was mindful that this interior space was one with two users—Freud and the patient (also referred to as 'analysand' or sometimes 'student')—and I directed my attention to the experience of the patient or 'living subject'. Freud discouraged his patients from taking notes, "fearing such conscious activities would interfere with the deeper, spontaneous processes of the mind" (Warner 2012: 412). Despite this, one patient, H.D., did keep notes from the period of analysis she underwent with Freud between 1933 and 1934, which she published later in a 1956 volume titled *Tribute to Freud*. A skilled poet and founding member of the Imagist movement, H.D. structured her text like an analytic session, allowing it to wander from Freud's study and consulting room to her childhood, to the myths and characters embodied in the ancient figurines, to wartime London, and back to her childhood, offering a beautiful and visual description of the consulting room and the experience of free association. Describing her own analysis, H.D. ([1956] 1971: 20–21) wrote:

> My imagination wandered at will; my dreams were revealing, and many of them drew on classical or Biblical symbolism. Thoughts were things, to be collected, collated, analyzed, shelved, or resolved. Fragmentary ideas,

apparently unrelated, were often found to be part of a special layer or stratum of thought and memory, therefore to belong together; these were sometimes skillfully pieced together like the exquisite Greek tear-jars and iridescent glass bowls and vases that gleamed in the dusk from the shelves of the cabinet that faced me where I stretched, propped up on the couch in the room in Berggasse 19, Wien IX.

What is interesting in this passage is that H.D., like Freud, connects the space and the mind, describing psychoanalysis as a process of ordering one's thoughts in the same way as one might order one's things in a cluttered or disorderly interior. H.D. unwittingly alludes to something that architectural historian Antoine Picon (2013: 37) describes as the paradoxical status of ornament and ordering: "The Latin word for ornament, *ornamentum*, shares, for instance, a common etymological origin with the verb *ordino*, meaning to organise, to order, as if an ornament, any well-conceived ornament, expressed the underlying order of things." Thus, while the study and consulting room look on the surface like a typical fin-de-siècle Viennese interior, underneath, as the description of the desk implied, the furniture and effects acted as markers or signposts, to both Freud and his patient's thoughts.

The psychoanalytic process asks patients not to focus on the present, but to allow their mind to wander back to childhood as well as to consider the future. In a remarkable passage, H.D. ([1956] 1971: 29–30) maps this idea of time onto the consulting room:

> Length, breadth, thickness, the shape, the scent, the feel of things. The actuality of the present, its bearing on the past, their bearing on the future. Past, present, future, these three—but there is another time-element, popularly called the fourth-dimensional. The room has four sides. There are four seasons to a year. This fourth dimension, though it appears variously disguised and under different subtitles, described and elaborately tabulated in the Professor's volumes ... is yet very simple. It is as simple and inevitable in the building of time-sequence as the fourth wall to a room. If we alter our course around this very room where I have been talking with the Professor, and start with the wall to my left, against which the couch is placed, and go counter-clockwise, we may number the Professor's wall with the exit door 2, the wall with the entrance door ... 3, and the wall opposite the couch 4. This wall actually is largely unwalled, as the space there is left vacant by the wide-open double doors.

H.D.'s description adds another layer—that of time—to my original diagram (see fig. 1.4). In spatializing the past, present, and future, the couch is the analytic instrument dealing with the past, while the Freud family apartment and the exit door to everyday life are the present. The double doors to the waiting room represent the outside world and the future, and, finally, the space left vacant, containing the study and desk, are the fourth dimensional (fig. 1.5). I understand H.D.'s term 'fourth dimensional' as the imagination or the creative and unconscious power of such psychic spaces. Adding these annotations next to the graphic symbols of the important furniture elements, the diagram is no longer a spatial layout but a representation of H.D.'s 'psychoanalytic setting'.

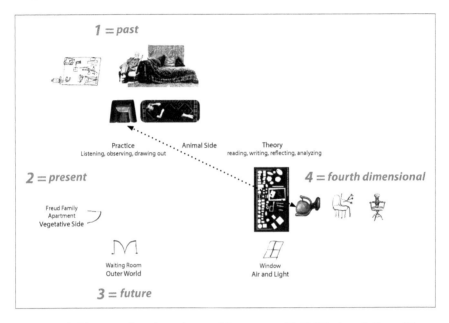

1 = past

Practice
Listening, observing, drawing out

Animal Side

Theory
reading, writing, reflecting, analyzing

2 = present

4 = fourth dimensional

Freud Family
Apartment
Vegetative Side

Waiting Room
Outer World

Window
Air and Light

3 = future

FIGURE 1.5: Diagram of study and consulting room with H.D.'s description of time added. Drawn by author.

Diagramming the Mind

> When I myself had begun to publish papers, I had been obliged to make my own drawings to illustrate them. (Freud 1900; SE vol. 4: 172)

In his own spatial diagrams as described above, Freud mapped psychic concepts onto actual space. As his clinical work shifted from neuropathology to neuropsychology and then to metapsychology, he increasingly found himself attempting to apply psychic concepts to the anatomy of the brain. In a set of sketch diagrams intended to illustrate an unpublished essay, "Introduction to Neuropathology," from about 1886, Freud drew looping lines to connect various nodes intended to show how the body (arms, face, hands) are represented in areas of the brain. At the time these drawings appeared, many neurologists presumed the body was somehow mirrored in the brain, perhaps altered in form but recognizable, intact. Yet in these sketches and others like it, Freud speculated that the brain worked differently. As he put it in his 1891 monograph entitled *On Aphasia*, the brain's fibers and cells "contain the body periphery in the same way as a poem contains the alphabet, in a complete rearrangement" (quoted in Gamwell and Solms 2006: 91). Later research supported Freud's novel idea that "the body periphery is not *projected* onto the cortex in a simple and direct fashion ... but rather it is *represented* there" (ibid.).

The concept that the mind represents the body not concretely but functionally, abstractly, and symbolically was a breakthrough for Freud. Some observers have suggested that it was the moment when the 'mind' entered his scientific work (Gamwell and Solms 2006: 91; Strachey 1970: 14). Of course, mental functions, unlike body tissue and structure, are dynamic and exist over time, and they involve processes that cannot be seen and cannot easily be drawn. Unsurprisingly, this was the point at which Freud gave up observational drawings and began to use diagrams.

As Freud developed the theory of psychoanalysis, he used diagramming to think through psychological structures that are not only invisible but also hypothetical. In these sketches of the ego and the id (fig. 1.6), one can see him trying to work out the best way to describe the structure of the psyche for the "New

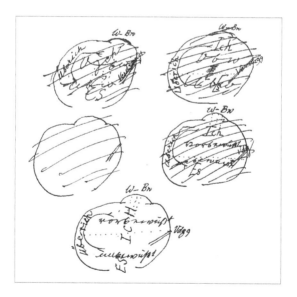

FIGURE 1.6: Diagrams from the fair copy of the "Neue Folge der Vorlesungen zur Einführung in die Psychoanalyse [New Introductory Lectures on Psychoanalysis]." Where W-Bw = Pcpt.-Cs.; Uberich = Superego, Es = Id, Ich = Ego vorbewusst = Preconscious, unbeusst = Unconscious, Vdg or Verdrangt = Repressed. (Grubrich-Simitis 1997: 156, Plate 9.1). By permission of The Marsh Agency Ltd. on behalf of Sigmund Freud Copyrights.

Introductory Lectures on Psycho-analysis" (Freud 1933; SE vol. 22). If the earlier drawings were about observation and analysis, one could suggest that these later diagrams are 'design drawings' because Freud is 'drawing out' an idea and speculating on what it might be.[14] Similar to a *mappa mundi*, the concern is not spatial accuracy, but rather the desire to explain one idea in relation to another. As Lynn Gamwell points out: "Einstein once said that when he thought about science, he thought visually, he thought in pictures, and this appears to be the case with Freud" (cited in Carey 2006).

The Dream Diagrams

Perhaps Freud's most intriguing diagrams were published in what he considered his most important work. "The Interpretation of Dreams" was written between 1895 and 1897, although it was not published until 1900. Chapter 7, "The Psychology of the Dream Processes," contains three abstract 'figures' that at first glance could be mistaken for Egyptian hieroglyphs. Freud tells his reader that they are diagrams (or figures) to help explain the dream process—a function of the mind that cannot be seen and has no physical locality, due to being dynamic and existing over time.

Freud offers his reader an analogy to aid interpretation: "I shall carefully avoid the temptation to determine psychical locality in any anatomical fashion. I shall remain upon psychological ground, and I propose simply to follow the suggestion that we should picture the instrument which carries out our mental functions as resembling a compound microscope or a photographic apparatus, or something of the kind" (1900; SE vol. 5: 536). The microscope returns, this time as an analogy, to make the invisible visible. Freud explains that just as the lenses in an instrument "are located one behind the other," so in certain psychical processes functions "go through a definite temporal sequence in their arousal" (ibid.).

So how does the diagram work? Reading from left to right, using line, symbol, and text, figure 1.7a illustrates how one's perception (Pcpt) is activated by experiences or stimuli (either internal or external) indicated by the upward arrow. These are stored in the mind as a memory or memory trace (Mnem). The memory trace is not just the content of the perception itself but the associations and sensations that come with it, as well as links to other memories. Over a lifetime, these build up, represented by the dots, and for the most part are forgotten, ending up in the unconscious (Ucs). The unconscious also stores our 'wishes' and 'fears', the oldest and most powerful of which derive from memory traces laid down in childhood when we are most impressionable. Responses to new stimuli or experiences may be motivated by these unconscious wishes and fears, now brought into the conscious mind by the Preconscious (Pcs) that controls motor activity (M) indicated by the downward arrow on the right.

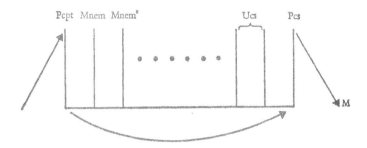

FIGURE 1.7a: Diagram from "The Interpretation of Dreams" where Pcpt = perception, Mnem = memory, Ucs = unconscious, Pcs = Preconscious, M = motor activity. By permission of The Marsh Agency Ltd. on behalf of Sigmund Freud Copyrights.

Freud tells his reader that it is the time sequence of this psychic process, as indicated by the arrows, that is important rather than the spatial order, and that in dreams the process described is reversed. Dreams, beginning as wishes (or fears) in the unconscious, work their way back through the memory traces before they surface as dream-images in the sleeping perceptual system. This 'regressive' process effectively returns an idea back into the sensory image from which it was originally derived. As Freud emphasizes: "In regression the fabric of dream-thoughts is resolved into its raw material" (1990; SE vol. 5: 543). He continues:

> Analogies of this kind are only intended to assist us in our attempt to make the complications of mental functioning intelligible by dissecting function and assigning its different constituents to different component parts of the apparatus ... We are justified, in my view, in giving free reign to our speculations so long as we retain the coolness of our judgement and do not mistake the scaffolding for the building ... strictly speaking, there is no need for the hypothesis that the psychical systems are actually arranged in a spatial order. It would be sufficient if a fixed order was established by the fact that in a given psychic process the excitation passes through the systems in a particular temporal sequence. (Ibid.: 536–537)

One could substitute the word 'diagrams' for 'analogies', and the quote would still make perfect sense.

My own earlier diagrams had mapped psychic structures onto the space of the study and consulting room, but now Freud's dream diagrams suggested the possibility of mapping the interior space onto the dream structure. So I borrowed Freud's dream diagrams as a 'scaffold' to explain how his interior arrangement functioned, adding images of the furniture and figurines described earlier over the black dots to symbolize the associations and sensations embodied in the objects around him. In figure 1.7b, the dotted arrow pointing to the right indicates that

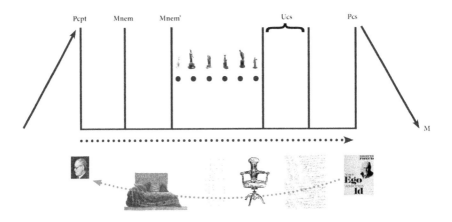

FIGURE 1.7b: Third dream diagram reworked to describe the effect of Freud's study and consulting room on his working method. Drawn by author.

the case histories Freud heard at the end of the couch informed his writing, while the curved dotted arrow going in the opposite direction indicates that theories developed in his writing would direct his interest in particular aspects of case histories, suggesting a process of simultaneity. A representation rather than a projection, my diagram refers to temporal sequence rather than spatial arrangement, separating out function instead of form. The ideas embodied in and associated with the couch, the desk, and the antique figurines functioned as visual references. The building blocks of Freud's imagination, they were endlessly rearranged in his subconscious "in the same way as a poem contains the alphabet," as Freud had put it in *On Aphasia*. Repeating this pattern of regular doings—day in, day out—gave Freud a scaffold against which to build his theories.

Conclusion

In "The Interpretation of Dreams," Freud writes that "the most striking psychological characteristic of the process of dreaming: a thought, and as a rule a thought of something that is wished, is objectified in the dream, represented as a scene, or, as it seems to us, is experienced" (1900; SE vol. 5: 534). However, citing G. T. Fechner, Freud speculates "that the theatre where our dreams are enacted is a different one from the scene of action where our ideas are generated in waking life" (ibid.: 536). Interior space can be described as a series of scenes or backdrops against which we live out our lives. Like the architecture that contains them, it is possible to describe the physical layout of an interior in orthographic projections. But there is another space, created by the occupant over time—a personal interior architecture that resists such techniques by being highly subjective and emotive. Using Sigmund Freud's study and consulting room as an example, this chapter has argued that diagramming offers a more rewarding technique to describe such interiors. In stripping back the architecture of a given space to reveal its invisible structures, rituals, and routines, diagramming allows for visual analogy and speculation. But most importantly, it provides tools to work with as well as think with.

Acknowledgments

The author gratefully acknowledges the following: Philip Steadman for advice given during the development of this chapter, the opportunity to present a draft version at the conference "Diagrammatic: Beyond Inscription?" and the feedback given at that point, and the peer reviewers, in response to whose comments this chapter has been greatly improved. The author also wishes to acknowledge financial support received from the University of Westminster for image funding.

Ro Spankie is a designer, teacher, and researcher. She is a Principal Lecturer and Assistant Head of the School of Architecture + Cities at the University of Westminster, London. She is Co-Editor of the journal *Interiors: Design/Architecture/Culture*. Her PhD in Architectural Design, awarded by University College London, focused on the role of drawing as an investigative tool in relation to three case study interiors, one of which was the study and consulting room of Sigmund Freud. Her publications include "Within the Cimeras: Spaces of Imagination" in *The Production Sites of Architecture* (2019), edited by Sophia Psarra, and *An Anecdotal Guide to Sigmund Freud's Desk* (2015).

Notes

1. Freud had lived in apartment number 5 on the second floor of Berggasse 19 from 1891 to 1938, a period of 47 years. From 1896 to 1908, he practiced from a three-room apartment (consisting of a waiting room, consulting room, and study) on the floor below. In 1908, he was able to move his practice up into the adjoining apartment (number 6) on the same landing as the family home. This arrangement continued until the Freuds left Vienna in 1938.
2. The 'psychoanalytic setting' is the 'pattern of regular doings' (to borrow Douglas's term) set between the analyst and the patient, such as rules about time and money, the use of the couch, and so forth (see Freud 1912; SE vol. 12: 111–112). Please note that references to *The Standard Edition of the Complete*

Psychological Works of Sigmund Freud (SE), edited by James Strachey (1953–1974), are abbreviated throughout as presented here.

3. One of Freud's more famous patients was Sergei Pankejeff, to whom Freud (1918; SE vol. 17) gave the pseudonym 'Wolf-Man'. Pankejeff later wrote about the experience, describing the space as follows: "I can remember, as though I saw them today, his two adjoining studies, with the door open between them and with their windows opening on a little courtyard. There was always a feeling of sacred peace and quiet here. The rooms themselves must have been a surprise to any patient, for they in no way reminded one of a doctor's office but rather an archeologist's study … A few potted plants added life to the rooms, and the warm carpet and curtains gave them a homelike note. Everything here contributed to one's feeling of leaving the haste of modern life behind, of being sheltered from one's daily cares" (cited in Gardiner 1972: 139).

4. The apartment was photographed by Engelman in May 1938 just before it was packed up for shipping. These photographs were not published until 1998.

5. Free association, a psychoanalytic technique, encourages patients to put into words whatever thoughts or fantasies spontaneously occur in their minds, "without selection or censorship," and in this way to stop giving any conscious direction to their thoughts (Freud 1912; SE vol. 12: 112).

6. This arrangement can be seen in a photograph of Freud sitting at the end of the couch at Hohe Warte. The image, IN26 "Sigmund Freud, 1933," can be viewed at https://www.freud.org.uk/photo-library/freud-portraits/.

7. In the summer, the Freud family would rent a house on the outskirts of Vienna to escape the heat of the city. During these periods, Freud would continue to write and, in order not to disrupt their analysis, would continue to see some of his patients. Remarkably, in order to facilitate this, every year the couch and other pieces of furniture, as well as a substantial part of the collection of antiquities, would travel with the family to the summer residence.

8. The desk chair was made in 1930 by the architect Felix Augenfeld as a gift from his daughter Mathilde. Augenfeld wrote: "She explained SF had the habit of reading in a very uncomfortable body position. He was leaning in this chair, in some sort of diagonal position, one of his legs slung over the arm of the chair, the book held high and his head unsupported. The rather bizarre form of chair I designed is to be explained as an attempt to maintain this habitual posture and make it more comfortable" (Warner 1998: 57).

9. Again, the ability to be relocated offers a clue. It is recorded that each summer the desk and many of the objects on it were transported to the various family summer residences. When the Freud's possessions arrived in London in 1938, it was a matter of pride that the objects on the desk were arranged in the same order in which they had appeared in Vienna. This act of recreation indicates that the arrangement was in some way significant to Freud.

10. An example of a transitional object might be a teddy bear (see Winnicott 1967).

11. An example of a fetish object might be a woman's stocking (Freud 1927; SE vol. 18: 152–157).

12. Here the term 'topological thinking' refers its use in Manuel DeLanda's (2002) article "Deleuze and the Use of the Genetic Algorithm in Architecture."
13. Translations from this collection are my own. Later in life, Freud struggled with the reception of his work by the outer world, and it is possible even in these early days that he saw his room as a sanctuary from external criticism.
14. Examples of diagrams used to think through an idea include Darwin's 'tree of life' diagram, Lévi-Strauss's diagram of the 'raw' and the 'cooked', Lacan's L-scheme, Waddington's epigenetic landscape, and Crick's pencil sketch of the DNA double helix.

References

Berger, John. 1984. *And Our Faces, My Heart, Brief as Photos*. New York: Pantheon Books.

Boehlich, Walter, ed. 1990. *The Letters of Sigmund Freud to Eduard Silberstein, 1871–1881*. Trans. Arnold J. Pomerans. Cambridge, MA: Belknap Press.

Brabant, Eva, Ernst Falzeder, and Patrizia Giampieri-Deutsch, eds. 1993. *The Correspondence of Sigmund Freud and Sándor Ferenczi. Vol. 1: 1908–1914*. Trans. Peter T. Hoffer. Cambridge, MA: Belknap Press.

Carey, Benedict. 2006. "Analyze These." *New York Times*, 25 April. https://www.nytimes.com/2006/04/25/health/psychology/analyze-these.html.

DeLanda, Manuel. 2002. "Deleuze and the Use of the Genetic Algorithm in Architecture." In *Designing for a Digital World*, ed. Neil Leach, 117–120. Chichester: Wiley-Academy.

Douglas, Mary. 1991. "The Idea of a Home: A Kind of Space." *Social Research* 58 (1): 287–307.

Engelman, Edmund. 1998. *Sigmund Freud, Vienna IX, Berggasse 19*. Photographs and epilogue, Edmund Engelman; introduction and legends, Inge Scholz-Strasser. Vienna: Verlag Christian Brandstätter.

Freud, Martin. 1957. *Glory Reflected: Sigmund Freud—Man and Father by His Eldest Son*. London: Angus and Robertson.

Freud, Sigmund. 1900. "The Interpretation of Dreams." Reprinted in Strachey 1953–1974, vols. 4, 5.

Freud, Sigmund. 1912. "Recommendations to Physicians Practising Psycho-analysis." Reprinted in Strachey 1953–1974, vol. 12: 109–120.

Freud, Sigmund. 1918. "From the History of an Infantile Neurosis." Reprinted in Strachey 1953–1974, vol. 17: 7–123.

Freud, Sigmund. 1927. "Fetishism." Reprinted in Strachey 1953–1974, vol. 18: 152–157.

Freud, Sigmund. 1933. "New Introductory Lectures on Psycho-analysis." Reprinted in Strachey 1953–1974, vol. 22.

Gamwell, Lynn, and Mark Solms. 2006. *From Neurology to Psychoanalysis: Sigmund Freud's Neurological Drawings and Diagrams of the Mind*. Binghamton: Binghamton University Art Museum, State University of New York.

Gardiner, Muriel, ed. 1972. *The Wolf-Man and Sigmund Freud*. London: Hogarth Press and the Institute of Psycho-Analysis.

Gay, Peter. 1989. *Freud: A Life for Our Time*. New York: Anchor Books.

Grubrich-Simitis, Ilse. 1997. *Early Freud and Late Freud: Reading Anew "Studies on Hysteria" and "Moses and Monotheism."* Trans. Philip Slotkin. London: Routledge.

Grubrich-Simitis, Ilse, Albrecht Hirschmüller, and Gerhard Fichtner, eds. 2013. *Sigmund Freud und Martha Bernays. Die Brautbriefer Band 2: Unser "Roman in Fortsetzungen"* [The Letters during Their Engagement, vol. 2: Our "Novel in Installments"]. Frankfurt am Main: S. Fischer.

H.D. (pseud. Hilda Doolittle). (1956) 1971. *Tribute to Freud*. Oxford: Carcanet Press.

H.D. (pseud. Hilda Doolittle). (1956) 2012. *Tribute to Freud*. 2nd ed. New York: New Directions.

Hill, Jonathan. 2006. *Immaterial Architecture*. London: Routledge.

Jones, Ernest. 1953. *The Life and Work of Sigmund Freud*. Vol. 1: *The Young Freud 1856–1900*. London: Hogarth Press.

Jones, Ernest. 1955. *The Life and Work of Sigmund Freud*. Vol. 2: *Years of Maturity 1901–1919*. London: Hogarth Press.

Jones, Ernest. 1957. *The Life and Work of Sigmund Freud*. Vol. 3: *The Last Phase 1919–1939*. London: Hogarth Press.

Masson, Jeffrey, ed. 1985. *The Complete Letters of Sigmund Freud to Wilhelm Fliess 1887–1904*. Cambridge, MA: Belknap Press.

Pawley, Martin. (1968) 2007. "The Time House or Argument for an Existential Dwelling." In *The Strange Death of Architectural Criticism*, ed. David Jenkins, 24–34. London: Black Dog Publishing. Picon, Antoine. 2013. *Ornament: The Politics of Architecture and Subjectivity*. West Sussex: John Wiley & Sons.

Praz, Mario. (1964) 2008. *An Illustrated History of Interior Decoration: From Pompeii to Art Nouveau*. Trans. William Weaver. London: Thames & Hudson.

Sachs, Hanns. 1945. *Freud: Master and Friend*. London: Imago.

Spankie, Ro. 2015. *An Anecdotal Guide to Sigmund Freud's Desk*. London: Freud Museum London.

Strachey, James, ed. 1953–1974. *The Standard Edition of the Complete Psychological Works of Sigmund Freud*. London: Hogarth Press and the Institute of Psychoanalysis.

Strachey, James. 1970. "Sigmund Freud: A Sketch of His Life and Ideas." In *Two Short Accounts of Psycho-Analysis*, Sigmund Freud, 11–24. Middlesex: Penguin Books.

Warner, Marina. 1998. *20 Maresfield Gardens: A Guide to the Freud Museum*. London: Serpent's Tail.

Warner, Marina. 2012. *Stranger Magic: Charmed States and the Arabian Nights*. London: Vintage.

Winnicott, D. W. 1967. *Playing and Reality*. London: Tavistock Publications.

Chapter 2

DIS/WORKING WITH DIAGRAMS
How Genealogies and Maps Obscure Nanoscale Worlds
(a Hunter-Gatherer Case)

Nurit Bird-David

In this chapter I examine the ordinary use of diagrams in anthropology, with a special focus on locational maps and kinship diagrams.[1] These visuals are standards in the ethnographic genre. Monographs that do not include them are hard to find. I examine these signatures of the ethnographic text that have contributed to a nascent anthropological discussion of diagrams among philosophers of science, historians, and cognitive psychologists (Lynteris 2017). Anthropologists have been looking at eighteenth-century chemical diagrams (Eddy 2014), public health 'protocolscapes' (Bonelli 2015), diagrams used by anatomy students (Hallam 2016), and zoonotic cycles diagrams for the study of animal-human infection in the life sciences (Lynteris 2017). Here, I turn to anthropology's own staple visuals—locational maps and kinship diagrams—which I approach from a participant-observer stance, drawing on my own use of them in my ethnographic work. I explore whether using these "diagrammatic pilots of anthropological

Notes for this chapter begin on page 60.

reasoning" (ibid.: 463) has a distortive effect on the anthropological project of understanding other peoples' worlds, in both the cultural and ontological senses.

Using kinship diagrams in anthropology goes back to the discipline's early days. It is not an over-exaggeration to say that the 'genealogical method', introduced by W. H. R. Rivers ([1910] 1968) into the study of exotic peoples, marked the twin birth of anthropology as a science and of ethnography as its unique comparative basis for developing modern theories. Maps seem to have had an unmarked entry into anthropology's visual canon, as part of the general modern visual regime. Ethnographers need no reminder that they have to show on a map where their study subject lives, while kinship diagrams are something that they are prompted to provide. Producing genealogical charts is described as the ethnographer's "minimum obligation" to help make fieldwork "intelligible" to others (Barnes 1967: 121). Every ethnographer, "whether kinship specialist or not," wrote Barnard and Good (1984: 1), "is expected to come home from the field with a description of 'the kinship system.'" The ordinary deployment of both visual signatures of ethnography has continued uninterrupted today, remarkably surviving the 1960s cultural critique of the 'old' and then re-emergence of the 'new' kinship studies, and the 2000s debates on alternative epistemologies and ontologies. The resilience of these diagrammatic tools, if nothing else, warrants reflecting on how they affect anthropological understandings of other people's lives. Following the little attention previously given to these standard visuals as cultural objects,[2] this chapter asks whether they work—or, rather, dis/work—in ethnographic accounts of other people's worlds. Do these diagrammatic tools make fieldwork and its findings 'intelligible' to others—or, rather, in some cases do they obscure locals' lived worlds and the fieldwork process?

I pursue these questions with a special focus on cases involving communities so minuscule that for good reason we may brand them 'nano-societies' (Bird-David 2017b). The smallest of those once branded 'small-scale societies', they are subsumed today within economic, regional, and political categories (e.g., hunter-gatherers, Amazonian societies, indigenous peoples). Surveying such intimate communities is logistically challenging, in some cases politically charged, and often conceptually murky. However, their order of size is undeniably and startlingly small, with estimates of local communities numbering as few as several dozen relatives, and entire populations ranging from a few hundred to a few thousand (Bodley 1996: 12; Smith and Wishnie 2000: 493). Their plural identity categories and modes of societal imagination contribute to their group size in functioning as downscaling projects of a sort (Bird-David 2017a, 2017b). Joining a 'scalar turn' in the social sciences, anthropologists have begun addressing issues of agential scaling and scalability, for the most part focusing on the large-scale end of the scalar continuum and on multi-scalar issues within it.[3] Here, I adapt this perspective to the small-scale end of the scalar spectrum. I take scale to involve population size inseparably from societal imagination and cultural projects, with the attendant phenomenological and cultural/onto-logical concomitants. I use the prefix 'nano-' (justifiable for populations of few, compared with hundreds of millions) as a rhetorical reminder of the radically small-scale case of scalar diversity, and as a trigger to inquire into the plural and culturally distinct phenomena at this end.

I draw on my study of a forest people living in South India. Without going here into the complexity of this anthropological comparative category, they can be described as 'hunting and gathering people', or, for short, 'foragers'. Hunter-gatherers are among the smallest groups of indigenous societies. In the 1960s, the so-called magic number range for local group size was 25 to 50 men, women, and children, while the average size was calculated at 28.4 persons (Kelly 1995; Lee and Devore 1968). The scalar context of forager (and other miniscule) societies has persistently been ignored in the study of their worlds and, moreover, in comparative anthropology that draws on it. In recent work (Bird-David 2017a, 2017b, 2018a, 2018b, 2019), I have tried to redress this neglect and show that scalar context is crucial to understanding these worlds. With the benefit of current theoretical sensitivities, and with the hindsight gained from following the changes these foragers have undergone since I first encountered them, I have scale-sensitively rewritten what I call a 'late ethnography', focusing on my baseline 1970s fieldwork, a decade before development and government organizations would start working in the area, and two decades before they would reach these particular forest people. Novices worrying about their career prospects understandably shy away from relating their problems with meeting the 'minimum obligation' of providing maps and kinship diagrams, but I could do so in writing this ethnography. In interludes interspersed between its substantive chapters, I examined how the genre's conventions hindered describing the 1970s foragers' world. This chapter draws on and develops two of those interludes. I start with a brief, scale-sensitive introduction of the fieldwork context relevant to this chapter, and then discuss one by one some problems I had with maps and kinship diagrams, in both the fieldwork and the post-fieldwork (or textwork) phases.

Nayaka, Foragers Who Call Themselves "Us, Relatives"

During 1978–1979, I shared a hut with a forager family. Our hut was one of six that constituted a forager hamlet, which was large by local standards. The other hamlets in my study group comprised two to three huts. The distance between those hamlets could be traversed by a two- to six-hour walk through the forest. The dwellers constantly journeyed between those hamlets, their visits lasting a few days or up to a few months at a time, and sometimes even longer. Our local group maintained weaker ties with relatives living in two more distant hamlets, about a day's walk away. Links with those 'satellite' hamlets often involved searching for and marrying spouses, and, in time, the growing traffic of visits could and did change the contours of the local community. Everyone who lived within visiting range referred to and addressed each other mostly by kinship relation terms and referred to the collective as *nama sonta*, best translated (per their usage) as "us, relatives." This plural category limits the collective to those constantly engaging with each other, in stark scalar and ontological contrast to the scalable ethnonymic category that others use for them—Kattunayaka, that is, the forest Nayaka (Bird-David 2017a). State recognition of the latter for purposes of positive discrimination entitlements has led to a rapid increase of identity claimers (already over 50,000), many of whom are urban dwellers. Below, I focus strictly on the foragers who 'we designate' themselves as "us, relatives," even when for clarity I sometime use the proper name and noun Nayaka.

The main five hamlets of my study group are scattered on both sides of a gorge going down a valley that narrows as it descends to the Kerala plains. These hamlets constitute the multi-focal core of what the local foragers called *nama sime* (our home area), referring to the unbounded area that expands outward from this core, and that I, for want of a proper name, call the Gorge. The actual spatial reach of the foragers within it was reflected in their circumstances and personalities. However, a general idea can be given by focusing on a man I call Kungan, my adoptive father. He sometimes walked up to Pandalur, the little market village on the country road crossing through the region, which was a two-hour steep climb from his hamlet. Once, taking a local bus, he visited Gudalur, the capital of the taluk (administrative district), which is 20 kilometers from Pandalur. He never visited Ooty, capital of the Nilgiris district, which is 50 kilometers beyond Gudalur. Pandalur lay within his everyday vivid imagination, and Gudalur figured occasionally at the horizons of his concerns. But Ooty did not exist at all for him at that time. He led a rich life with his relatives within the walking horizons of their hamlets, which should not be mistaken for isolation. From time to time, outsiders (forest traders, surveyors, smugglers) passed through the Gorge, and some (plantation laborers, field managers, timber workers, ethnographers) even settled there, temporarily or permanently. Where those people had come from did not concern the foragers as much as learning how to live with or alongside them in their *sime* (home place). Those with whom they closely engaged were considered by them in certain contexts to be *nama sonta* (us, relatives).

The Ethnographer's Map

Maps have received anthropological attention in discussions of the spatial knowledge involved in wayfinding and navigation compared with that embodied in maps. Explored in this context has been the general nature of this special artifact, especially how what the map shows relates to the world shown. Gell (1998) argued that, unlike other visual images, the map is 'non-indexical' in that it encodes beliefs or propositions about the location of places that are true (or taken to be true) independently of where one is currently positioned in the world. Ingold (2000) noted that the common metaphorical use of the term 'map' when discussing cultures, cognition, communication, and much more affects its understanding as a cartographic object. Using 'map' for an overarching framework into which we can fit specific data of observation makes "*actual* maps" appear as "schematic representations of the real world, which do not index any position but upon which it should be possible to plot the position of everything in relation to everything else" (ibid.: 224). Following such arguments, I ask how the standard inclusion of maps in the ethnographic text affects the anthropological project of revealing other people's worlds.

Typically, a map of the country being discussed is provided in ethnographies, with an arrow pointing to the location where the studied group lives (see fig. 2.1). In ethnographies of nano-societies, there is usually also a map of the particular region with the country reduced to an inset (see fig. 2.2), and in some work there is also a large-scale map of the particular locality being studied (see fig. 2.3). The task of producing such maps may seem trivial in these days of Google Maps and Google Earth. Detailed maps and aerial photography can be easily retrieved from the Internet, even for fieldwork in out-of-the-way places such as the Gorge, and with the touch of a finger one can digitally move between them and up and down scales to achieve a desired balance of area covered and detail. However, throughout much of the life span of anthropology, these turn-of-the-twenty-first-century means were not yet available, and maps had to be constructed even for tiny communities at the margins of Third World countries. How ethnographers have procured those maps has been rarely related, nor has its connection to the ethnographic project. I next describe and reflect on my experience as a way to examine what the genre's cartographic standards 'do' to the subject being studied.

I traveled from Cambridge to my field site by car, a Citroën 2CV, one of the last vehicles to caravan the overland route from Europe to Australia before troubles broke out in Iran and Afghanistan. Large-scale maps of Europe, Asia, and India were readily available in bookshops, showing the main routes and the countries those routes crossed through. These maps were redundant to my ethnographic project once we crossed the border into India. While it is "possible to plot the position of everything in relation to everything else" (Ingold 2000: 224), anthropologists exercise a specific choice. The ethnographic standard is to locate the fieldwork site on a map of the country in which one works, not to show where the former is in relation to where the ethnographer comes from.

The separate map of India that I had purchased in England guided us through the 3,000 kilometers or so across India to the Nilgiri region, and it was also the

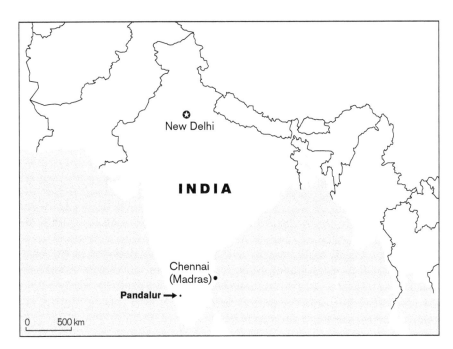

FIGURE 2.1: Field site location in India. Originally published by University of California Press.

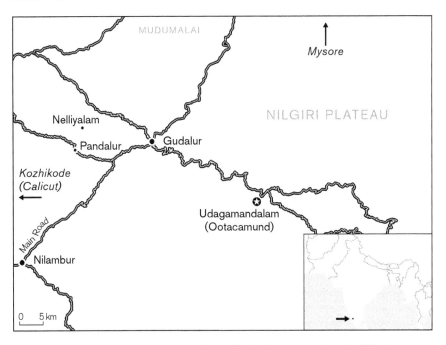

FIGURE 2.2: The Nilgiris region. Originally published by University of California Press.

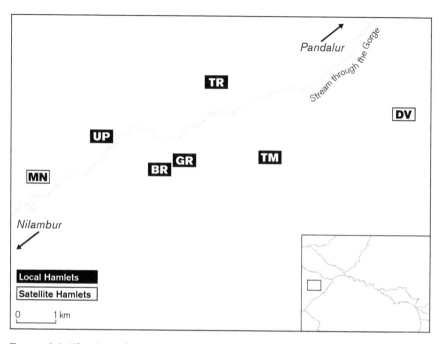

FIGURE 2.3: The Gorge hamlets and satellite hamlets, based on Mohandes's sketch. Originally published by University of California Press.

basis of producing figure 2.1. No doubt, this map affords instant recognition of where the ethnographic subject lives. However, recognition is dependent on readers' spatial imaginations and at the cost of colossal distortion when it comes to nanoscale worlds. A centimeter on this map represents 44 kilometers, marking a distance greater than any that Kungan normally traveled to visit relatives or would even care to contemplate. The little roadside marketplace of Pandalur, which he sometimes visited, is enlarged to absurdum on this map.

Figure 2.1 also seriously distorts the foragers' ontological sense of their world by locating their home place, or *sime*, in an imagined nationalistic space. Country maps such as this evolved within colonial and state regimes. Anderson ([1983] 2006) argued that the map-as-logo turned into a powerful emblem of the nation, a part of nationalism itself. Together with surveys and museums, such maps foreground national ideas of territory, peoplehood, and identity (ibid.). Among other things, a country is based on the idea of a national territory (always vast compared with the local home place, especially in India with its 3,287 million square kilometers), the idea of its nationals populating this territory (always a large number of people, and especially India with its population of 1,324 billion), and lastly the idea of solidarity based on sameness of nationality, however dispersed its citizens are and irrespective of whether they know or possibly can know each other. Locating the foragers' home place on this map carries these national ideas into their world and subverts their alternative plural categories, which, as I have argued elsewhere (Bird-David 2017a), are rooted not in sameness among dispersed strangers but in intimacy among relatives of infinite diversity.

Acknowledging spatial disconnects, ethnographers of miniscule communities/societies are expected to provide a map of the region, with the country reduced to an inset. Such maps were hard to acquire in South India in the late 1970s (and still are, decades later). I traveled to Madras, and managed to buy from a government office copies of a map of the Nilgiris district (scaled 1:126,720) and one of the Gudalur taluk (scaled 1:63,360). The title of the first one, which provided the basis of figure 2.2, leaves no doubt about its origin and purpose. The *Nilgiri District Map for the Use of Touring Officers* was a reproduction of a map produced in colonial times. Its main purpose, as the title indicates, was to orient colonial administrators who were new to the region during their tour of duty there. A typical instance of this genre, figure 2.2 shows what matters to touring people: the main settlements and the routes connecting them. At the same time, its scale allows for realistically showing the horizons of the foragers' spatial reach, the horizons of their concerns and imagination, and the horizons of their scaling projects. But only the far horizons—Pandalur and Gudalur. Had I realistically marked their hamlets on this regional map, the foragers' lived world would appear as closely spaced dots, and the forest between and surrounding them—their world, their *sime*—would be indiscernible. Meanwhile, the miniature map of India in the inset keeps the state in mind as the frame of reference, with its nation-scale ontology of territory, peoplehood, and identity.

Continuing my search for maps, I chanced to find in a small municipal archive in Ooty a rare series of land-use maps—nine large sheets (scaled 1:7,920, undated) showing state-recognized boundaries between forest and plantation estates in the Nilgiri-Wynaad area. One of those sheets covered the area of the plantation next to which I worked. However, besides marking its borders and the jeep-drivable 'white road' going toward it, the bulk of the map was empty, a large expanse of unmarked heavy paper that had yellowed over the years.

Maps provide overviews of a territory that those who intimately walk through do not have or need. The foragers I lived with did not have or need a map of their intimate home place on paper or as a mental template. Neither did I during my fieldwork as I moved with them, eventually growing intimately familiar with their *sime* myself. Toward the end of my fieldwork, to meet future academic expectations, I employed Mohandes, a surveyor from a little township near Gudalur. He walked the steep, narrow footpath through the forest down to Kungan's hamlet, and, with me and Kungan at his side, paced off the dimensions of the huts and the distances between them and so roughly estimated the locations of and the distances to the other hamlets. Back in his hometown, in his shabby one-room office, Mohandes drew sketches of the five hamlets and a rough map showing their locations in the forest, translating the distances he had paced off into metric data that he recorded in a conventional modern representation of the area. Mohandes's sketches were the cartographic basis of figure 2.3.

The spatial reach of this huge-scale map accords with that of the foragers' familiar world. Yet it, too, skews their spatial register, not to mention the banal detail that, by rebuilding their huts every so many months, their hamlets 'crawl' across the landscape, changing position in relation to one another. On this map, in common with the previously discussed maps, we demarcate a territory that the foragers are described as living 'in': in India, in the Nilgiris, in the Gorge, in the forest, in a hamlet. The seemingly innocent preposition 'in' is a tricky Trojan horse that sneaks into their world a sense of space and society, and of nature too, as abstract containers in which individuals live. As I show elsewhere (Bird-David 1999), foragers' cultural energies as animists are invested not so much in *where* they live as in those *with whom* they live. They are not so much in space/system (environment/nature), but in a community of sentient beings with or alongside whom they live.

All the maps I had amassed remained stored away during my fieldwork. It was only when I was back at the PhD students' room in Cambridge's Department of Social Anthropology that I hung them on the wall facing my desk, as did my fellow students. The walls of our shared room were covered with maps of different parts of the world, orienting us—or, rather, I argue, *disorienting* us—by obscuring issues of scale/scaling and scalability, by prioritizing the viewpoint of foreign tourers over locals, and by immersing us in the social imagination and ontology of nations.

Coevals' Kinship Diagrams

While maps are intended to introduce the fieldwork site, kinship diagrams are integral to the ethnographic analysis. A kinship tree has its virtues, certainly for some fields of scholarship and for helping readers follow complicated ethnographic analyses. For the latter purpose, ethnographers often use segments—small kinship diagrams—that showcase connections between the protagonists in an ethnographic event to aid understanding its analysis. Their usefulness acknowledged, I want to dwell here on problems of working cross-culturally and cross–scalarly with these diagrammatic forms, especially in ethnographies of people who do not use such diagrams themselves. Despite their role in the ethnographic text, kinship diagrams have received only a little attention, mostly in broad work on anthropology's visual methods (e.g., Banks 2001:

24–28; Grimshaw 2001: 35–43; Ingold 2007: 104–119). Bouquet (1996) asked why genealogical trees were used by Rivers to visualize kinship, and she traced the roots to the prevalence of tree imagery for secular, religious, and scientific purposes in eighteenth- and nineteenth-century Europe (cf. Ingold 2007). This being the case, we could expect problems with producing such diagrams in working with forager (and other nanoscale) societies, but ethnographers rarely discuss them. Cashing in on what 'late ethnography' affords, I do so by following the process from fieldwork through to the post-fieldwork stage. Again, I start with my ethnographic experience, turning to the ethnographer's work of producing these diagrams before examining the distortive effects of their use in the ethnography of intimate worlds.

Rivers ([1910] 1968) provided careful and detailed instructions for producing kinship pedigrees and genealogies. A half-century later, in the authoritative volume *The Craft of Social Anthropology*, Barnes (1967: 106) wrote that these instructions "scarcely can be improved." Rivers ([1910] 1968: 97) advised to use only a few terms denoting kinship: father, mother, child, husband, and wife. The inquiry was to proceed in separate sessions with informants, a particular informant each time. The informant was to be asked first for the names of his/her father and mother (the 'real' ones, not anyone for whom he/she might use such terms); second, for the names of his/her parents' children in order of age; and, third, for the names of those children's respective spouses and offspring. The informant then was asked to go through the same three-stage process for his/her parents' parents, and so up the generational ladder "till the genealogical knowledge of his family possessed by [the] informant was completely exhausted" (ibid.: 98). The pedigrees so produced were then to be connected in the 'upside-down tree' form that Bouquet (1996) discussed. Rivers ([1910] 1968: 99) paid great attention to stylistic details, for example, the names of males were to be written in capital letters and those of females in ordinary type, the name of the husband should be written to the left of that of his wife, and so forth. Reading these instructions, the task seems straightforward and easy. What could possibly obstruct asking for basic and simple information, such as personal names, marriage details, and parental connections? It turns out that much could.

Setting about the job of mapping kinship relations early in my fieldwork, I tried to follow River's instructions, but the foragers were reluctant to play their part in his script. Their patience was exhausted well before my inquiries were completed. Often muttering that they were going to "collect firewood" (a common excuse for disengaging from nagging relatives), they stood up and left. Some of their answers, at any rate, were perplexing. For example, when I asked about relatives of the third ascending generation, at times I was told, "I did not live with them, so I do not know them" (or words to that effect). When I inquired about their own children, only those co-residing in the same hamlet would be mentioned. With regard to marriages, couples could be described by some informants as married and by others as not, with the same people sometimes changing their view from day to day. When I asked whether a particular couple was married, sometimes I was told, "People say that they are married. I have not seen."

Due to the inabillity of obtaining reliable information, I stopped conducting those sessions and let time do my job. There is much kinship talk, and talk through kinship, in a small community of relatives. Year-long fieldwork within an intimate community produces a large volume of fragmentary kinship information, if one vigilantly records what turns up in the ordinary run of everyday life, in spontaneous conversations, and during special events. My field notes filled up with such information, and additionally I found a good partner to my obsessing about the foragers' kinship connections in Mathew, the bookkeeper of the small marginal plantation on which some of those foragers had worked off and on for nearly two decades (Bird 1983). Mathew had arrived at this out-of-the-way plantation in the early 1950s, taking leave once a year to visit his family in Kerala. We spent long evenings trying to link our jigsaw pieces of knowledge and draw kinship diagrams. He brought temporal depth to the task and a cultural readiness to give diagrammatic form to his implicit knowledge.

Yet, ultimately and tellingly, I completed producing those kinship diagrams in the students' room at Cambridge, 8,000 kilometers from the Gorge. My technique was allegorical as much as it was pragmatic. Using copies of my fieldwork diaries and a pair of scissors, I literally extracted kinship-relevant bits from all my field notes, spread those bits of paper on my desk, sorted and resorted, cross-checked, reshuffled, and moved them around. Then, one by one, I collated them into small kinship diagrams, as in figure 2.4, which eventually became the complex-looking result presented in figure 2.5 (a professional reproduction of my original). This kinship tree connects 147 people, practically every individual I knew personally or was told about.

With hindsight and without precluding other causes, I examine in the first subsection below what could have caused the early fieldwork problems, and, in the second, the distortive attendants of succeeding in producing the kinship diagrams. In both cases, special attention has been paid to problems involving scalar and ontological slippages.

Problems with the Method

Rivers's method is rooted in using personal names, which are popularly presumed to be universal, a view shared by some scholars (e.g., Alford 1988). Yet, as mentioned, these Nayaka foragers usually referred to and addressed each other by kinship terms, a common phenomenon among hunter-gatherer (and other tiny) indigenous communities. Personal names were bestowed on these populations by non-kin outsiders who required individuals' identification for

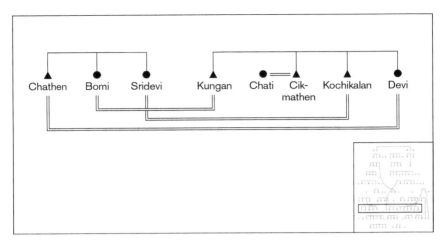

FIGURE 2.4: Kinship ties among Gorge hamlet's core members. Originally published by University of California Press.

their own needs.[4] The foragers used those names, if at all, changing between the names available for each person. My experiences included, for example, asking a man for the name of his brother-in-law. The former paused and asked the latter, "*Bhava[n]* [brother-in-law], what are you called here these days?" Then he turned to me and said that his *bhava(n)* is called now Mathen in the plantation. On another occasion, when I asked a man for the name of his young daughter, he turned to his wife and asked her for the name, apologizing to me that "we do not remember names." In working with a nanoscale forager community of relatives, personal names were a shaky basis for making pedigrees.

A second problem was basing the method on father, mother, child, husband, and wife relations. This instruction reflects Rivers's scientific thoughtfulness, yet also the modern idea of the nuclear family with husband-wife and parents-children as its cardinal relations, and siblingship only a second-order relation between co-children. As is commonplace among hunter-gatherer and other nanoscale communities (see, e.g., Marshall 1979; Mason 1997; Myers 1986; Nuckolls 1993), siblingship was a primary relation for the Gorge foragers. Siblings, their spouses, and their children often co-resided, constituting the hamlet's residential core and, in those tiny hamlets, often the majority (Bird-David 2017b: chap. 3). Had I started my early fieldwork sessions asking about sibling relations, I wonder whether those sessions would have been more productive.

Lastly, Rivers's styled inquiry is driven by known status rather than processual performance, a perspective in which marriage status and the number of children are decisive factitive matters. But students of hunter-gatherers have long observed the strong performative basis of kinship relations that, in these societies, largely inheres in perpetual sharing and demand-sharing conditional

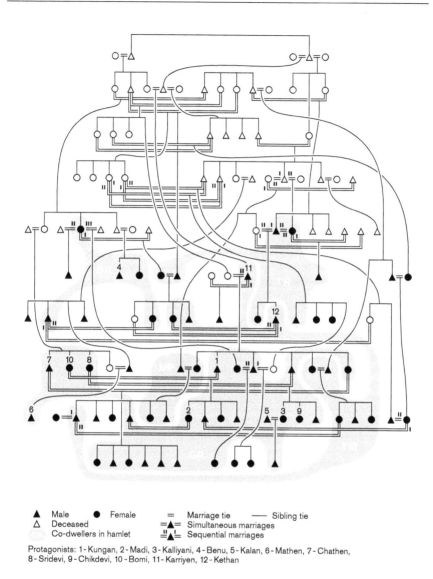

Male △ Female   = Marriage tie   —— Sibling tie
△ Deceased   =▲= Simultaneous marriages
Co-dwellers in hamlet   ⸗▲⸗ Sequential marriages

Protagonists: 1- Kungan, 2- Madi, 3- Kalliyani, 4- Benu, 5- Kalan, 6- Mathen, 7- Chathen, 8- Sridevi, 9- Chikdevi, 10- Bomi, 11- Karriyen, 12- Kethan

FIGURE 2.5: Kinship tree of relatives in the Gorge. Originally published by University of California Press.

on co-presence achieved by visiting and communal life.[5] Relations depend on such performances, and the foragers observed the minute work of 'relat*ing*' that constitutes relations, over and above the status inferred from such work over time. This cultural disposition had perhaps attuned my interlocutors to the children with them at the time and to the indeterminate state of a fluctuating conjugal cohabitation, when I formally asked them to list their children and describe certain marital statuses.

Problems with Kinship Diagrams

Rivers ([1910] 1968: 107) extolled the genealogical method for providing "more definite and exact knowledge than is possible to a man who has lived for many years among the people," unintentionally pointing out the method's weakness as a tool for understanding locals' praxis and understandings. To the best of my knowledge, the diagrams I pieced together based on cumulating data in my fieldwork diaries provide a good-enough representation of descent and affinity paths linking Gorge foragers. All the same, and partly for this reason, they prejudice understanding the forager nanoscale world. Below I point to several ways in which they do so, starting with the small kinship diagram genre, which showcases the links between the protagonists in an ethnographic tale.

The kinship diagrammatic tools embody a grammar of self and relations that obscure the foragers' sense of themselves and their community. Paradoxically, a kinship diagram shows how people are connected, but in doing so it posits discreet individuals (the nodes) and the links between them (the lines) as add-on relations. Moreover, it shows how each two persons are connected through one dyadic tie or a chain of ties. This ontology of singular persons and two-based relations is far removed from the foragers' primary sense of an intimate community into which one is born as a relative who is multiply connected to everyone else, with these links constituting his/her identity (Bird-David 2017b). The foragers' sense of themselves is embodied in calling themselves "us, relatives." In fact, in everyday life in such an intimate community, one can hardly focus on a single individual or on a single relation and ignore all the pluripresent others: doing so would be considered ill-mannered behavior. Kinship here is about 'plurality of being', stepping up from Sahlins's (2013) concept of kinship as 'mutuality of being'. Each person is at once a relative of multiple others. The kinship diagrammatic tools obscure this critical experience that underscores the foragers' scalar identity categories and social imaginations.

The small kinship diagram is the ordinary genre. The rarer large kinship tree reveals what the former conceals. The small diagram highlights a set of relations that the ethnographer considers pertinent to the analysis at hand. The large tree shows how those individuals are cut apart from the field of kinship relations that connect the majority of the community and, in a small world, are inseparable from and affect those on whom the diagram focuses. For an example, figure 2.4 shows the sibling and affinal ties between core members of the Gorge hamlet in which I lived to illustrate my argument about the key place of siblingship in the hamlet. On its own, this segment could have been read as an instance of sibling exchange marriages of the kind canonized by Lévi-Strauss ([1949] 1969). However, the smallness of the community shown by the kinship tree indicates that scarcity of spouses must play a role as well. In relating to me how they came to marry their spouses, the protagonists themselves emphasized that they visited their married sibling, met the sibling's spouse's sibling, and married him or her—sometimes against their initial desire—for dearth of other options at the time. The genealogical tree reveals a highly inbred community, not to be confused with isolation or endogamy. Foragers married close kin or sometimes outsiders from neighboring ethnic groups because scarcity of spouses is chronic in a minuscule group.[6] A small diagram seriously distorts an understanding of the ethnographic tale in a nanoscale world: the relevant cast here is the entire community, in their presence or absence.

The genealogical tree, while showing the foragers' field of intricate connections, precludes an expression of their performative and strategic kinship experiences. Its iconographic form goes back to modern European traditions (Bouquet 1996), and so does its purpose. In those large-scale modern contexts, as often as not it would show the common long-dead ancestors of descendants who are dispersed and live among non-kin. Strathern (1992a: 84) observed that, in such contexts, "one's kin are part of a wider population, but not a part that is in any way equal to it." Exported to forager (and other nanoscale) communities of kin, inattentively to scalar slippages, this diagrammatic tool is a Trojan horse. One of its paradoxical outcomes is showing connections between neighbors in a tiny hamlet, who often are close kin, through long-dead ancestors. Thus, for example, to trace the kinship link between 'ego' and his second-cousin neighbor, "one would proceed upward on the tree from ego to ego's parent, then farther upward to ego's parent's parent, then laterally to ego's parent's parent's sibling, then downwards to ego's parent's parent's sibling's child, and finally, down to ego's parent's parent's sibling's child's child, the cousin with whom ego lives. Certainly a convoluted calculus to describe two people who essentially share lives" (Bird-David 2017b: 92). The kinship tree in this case ends up distancing close relatives, instead of showing the closeness of distant ones.

Furthermore, just as cartographic maps do, a kinship tree provides an overview of a territory that those who intimately walk through do not have or need. The Gorge foragers did not turn to a diagrammatic representation, concrete artifact, or mental map for the facts of their kinship connections. They learned those 'on the move', in actually engaging with one another. Using kinship terms as a means of appellation helps them to do so. Children learned kinship-relation terms along with their situated, plural, and perspectival nature. One learned to respond with the appropriate term to the term one was addressed by, for example, 'uncle-nephew'. One learned to align with terms used among surrounding kin. For instance, if Kungan regarded me his 'daughter', and I him as my 'father', then his 'brother' could regard me as his 'niece', and I him as my 'uncle'; his 'daughter' could regard me as her 'older sister', and I her as my 'younger sister', and so forth. The foragers exploited the options available to them within their highly inbred community, the scope of which the genealogical tree does show. They strategically navigated their way through the field of kinship relations. For example, one chose the closest kinship option when asking for a food share, and a distant option to hold off claims on what one had (cf. Widlok 2017).

Lastly, the nature of the performative basis of foragers' kinship relations is obscured by the kinship tree, and equally by its absence, in a roundabout and paradoxical way. In the growing general tide of interest in performative kinship, much attention has been given to 'post-natal' relations that are constituted through the culturally appropriate action in each case, for example, commensality, co-residence, shared memories, shared suffering, and so forth (Sahlins 2013). This orientation has filtered into analyses of foragers' kinship relations, ignoring cross-scalar slippages. Generally, in the scale-blind tradition of cultural analysis in anthropology, the forager society is taken to be the assemblage of its individual members. Their kinship relations are a separate subject, if discussed at all, and through various discursive practices they are left out of analyses of other cultural institutions, for example, even sharing (Bird-David 2019). In turn, the emphasis on sharing as constitutive of kinship relations obscures the fact that in this nanoscale context most relations *are* based on birth and marriage links to start with. For the most, post-natal relations are not alternative and additional to birth relations; rather, here, performance has the capacity to censor given natal/affinal relations. If these relations are not continuously performed, they fade from culturally guided conscious attention. "He used to be my relative," is how one of Barbara Bodenhorn's (2006) informants eloquently described an actual kin with whom he was no longer in touch, a sentiment extending to even close blood relatives. Thus, the kinship tree I have constructed gives a good-enough representation of affinal and descent relations, but not of all of them, only those censored by performance.

Conclusions

Attentive to cross-scalar as much as cross-cultural issues, this chapter has examined the distortive effect of our disciplinary diagrammatic practices on understanding the worlds of foragers. I approached their community as an example of a broader class that I find useful to shorthand as 'nanoscale societies' in order to foreground their long-neglected scalar framework, encompassing group size and, inseparably, modes of societal imaginations and plural identities. As part of the modern, ubiquitous application of diagrammatic visuals across the sciences, maps and kinship diagrams have become a part of the DNA of ethnographies. The little attention paid to them as objects of anthropological analysis has not previously led to examining their effects on knowledge production in anthropology itself. By deliberately describing in banal detail my fieldwork and post-fieldwork experience of producing these conventional visuals, I hope to have shown that these long-lasting signatures of the ethnographic text, which ethnographers are expected to provide as their professional obligation, in fact obscure the nanoscale worlds that they are supposed to help make intelligible to readers.

Within the space limitations, I have focused here on how these standard diagrammatic pillars of ethnographic analysis present the ethnographic analysis within a framework that is unfavorable to understanding the foragers' world of humans. It is vital to continue examining how these diagrammatic practices constitute ontological shifts that immensely complicate, if not outright preclude, understanding the foragers' animistic world. How do maps that locate foragers *in* space, let alone in an imagined nationalistic space, obscure understanding that their cultural energies are invested not so much in *where* they live as in those *with whom* they live, non-humans as well as humans? How do kinship diagrams frame *a priori* only humans as kin and complicate understanding how other-than-humans can be kin, too? How does tracing connections between coevals through long-dead ancestors complicate understanding that foragers culturally recalled their past predecessors not as specific individuals but as an amalgamate, "our *big* parents," humans and non-humans who continued to participate in their world? How do maps and kinship diagrams transform local intimate worlds of vivid 'beings-with', transpersonal worlds of beings 'with-us', trans-species communities of relatives, into space and time that individual beings live *in*?

Foragers' and other nanoscale worlds were and have remained anthropology's mainstay in developing its unique comparative theory and perspective. We have to continue addressing what these diagrammatic pillars of ethnographic analysis show, what they conceal, and what they distort, mindful of the effects of their cross-scalar travel. We have to critically observe each time we use them whether they are analytical gifts or Trojan horses.

Nurit Bird-David received her PhD in Social Anthropology from the University of Cambridge and is a Professor of Cultural Anthropology at the University of Haifa. She is the author of *Us, Relatives: Scaling and Plural Life in a Forager World* (2017), and dozens of her articles have appeared in leading journals. Her research interests include hunter-gatherers' environmental perceptions and ontologies, shifting scales of practice and imagination, alternative notions of nation and community, neo-liberal notions of personhood, home, and security, and the new algorithmic-based 'sharing economy'.

Notes

1. On kinship diagrams, see Banks (2001: 24–28), Bouquet (1996), Grimshaw (2001: 35–43), and Ingold (2007: 104–119). On maps, see Gell (1998), Ingold (2000: 219–242), and Turnbull (1991). For reviews, cf. Partridge (2014) and Wilson (2018).
2. See, among others, Latour (2005), Strathern (1991, 1992a, 1992b, 1995), Tsing (2012), and Xiang (2013) for discussions on these issues.
3. On naming practices during colonial administration, see Alia (2007), Bruck and Bodenhorn (2006), and Widlok (2000).
4. For further discussion on the performative basis of kinship relations, see, for example, Bird-David (1994, 2017b), Bodenhorn (2000), Myers (1986), Nuttall (2000), Peterson (1993), and Widlok (2013, 2017).
5. For a detailed analysis of the role played by the scarcity of spouses in nanoscale worlds, see Bird-David (2017b: chap. 3).
6. For other, similar cases, see also Bodenhorn (2000), Nuttall (2000), and Widlok (2013, 2017).

References

Alford, Richard D. 1988. *Naming and Identity: A Cross-Cultural Study of Personal Naming Practices*. New Haven, CT: HRAF Press.

Alia, Valerie. 2007. *Names and Nunavut: Culture and Identity in Arctic Canada*. New York: Berghahn Books.

Anderson, Benedict. (1983) 2006. *Imagined Communities: Reflections on the Origin and Spread of Nationalism*. New York: Verso.

Banks, Marcus. 2001. *Visual Methods in Social Research*. London: Sage.

Barnard, Alan, and Anthony Good. 1984. *Research Practices in the Study of Kinship*. London: Academic Press.

Barnes, John A. 1967. "Genealogies." In *The Craft of Social Anthropology*, ed. A. L. Epstein, 101–128. London: Transaction Publishers.

Bird, Nurit. 1983. "Wage-Gathering: Socio-Economic Change and the Case of the Naiken of South India." In *Rural South Asia: Linkages, Change and Development*, ed. Peter Robb, 57–89. London: Curzon Press.

Bird-David, Nurit. 1994. "Sociality and Immediacy: Or, Past and Present Conversations on Bands." *Man* (n.s.) 29 (3): 583–603.

Bird-David, Nurit. 1999. "'Animism' Revisited: Personhood, Environment, and Relational Epistemology." *Current Anthropology* 40 (S1): S67–S91.

Bird-David, Nurit. 2017a. "Before Nation: Scale-Blind Anthropology and Foragers' Worlds of Relatives." *Current Anthropology* 58 (2): 209–226.

Bird-David, Nurit. 2017b. *Us, Relatives: Scaling and Plural Life in a Forager World*. Oakland: University of California Press.

Bird-David, Nurit. 2018a. "Persons or Relatives? Animistic Scales of Practice and Imagination." In *Rethinking Relations and Animism: Personhood and Materiality*, ed. Miguel Astor-Aguilera and Graham Harvey, 25–34. London: Routledge.

Bird-David, Nurit. 2018b. "Size Matters! The Scalability of Modern Hunter-Gatherer Animism." *Quaternary International* 464: 305–314.

Bird-David, Nurit. 2019. "Where Have All the Kin Gone? On Hunter-Gatherers' Sharing, Kinship and Scale." In *Towards a Broader View of Hunter-Gatherer Sharing*, ed. Noa Lavi and David E. Friesem, 15–24. Cambridge: MacDonald Institute for Archaeological Research, University of Cambridge.

Bodenhorn, Barbara. 2000. "'He Used to Be My Relative': Exploring the Bases of Relatedness among Iñupiat of Northern Alaska." In *Cultures of Relatedness: New Approaches to the Study of Kinship*, ed. Janet Carsten, 128–148. Cambridge: Cambridge University Press.

Bodley, John H. 1996. *Anthropology and Contemporary Human Problems*. 3rd ed. Mountain View, CA: Mayfield Publishing.

Bonelli, Cristóbal. 2015. "To See That Which Cannot Be Seen: Ontological Differences and Public Health Policies in Southern Chile." *Journal of the Royal Anthropological Institute* (n.s.) 21 (4): 872–891.

Bouquet, Mary. 1996. "Family Trees and Their Affinities: The Visual Imperative of the Genealogical Diagram." *Journal of the Royal Anthropological Institute* 2 (1): 43–66.

Bruck, Gabriele vom, and Barbara Bodenhorn, eds. 2006. *The Anthropology of Names and Naming*. Cambridge: Cambridge University Press.

Eddy, Matthew D. 2014. "How to See a Diagram: A Visual Anthropology of Chemical Affinity." *Osiris* 29 (1): 178–196.

Gell, Alfred. 1998. *Art and Agency: An Anthropological Theory*. Oxford: Clarendon.

Grimshaw, Anna. 2001. *The Ethnographer's Eye: Ways of Seeing in Anthropology*. Cambridge: Cambridge University Press.

Hallam, Elizabeth. 2016. *Anatomy Museum: Death and the Body Displayed*. London: Reaktion Books.

Ingold, Tim. 2000. *The Perception of the Environment: Essays on Livelihood, Dwelling and Skill*. London: Routledge.

Ingold, Tim. 2007. *Lines: A Brief History*. London: Routledge.

Kelly, Robert L. 1995. *The Foraging Spectrum: Diversity in Hunter-Gatherer Lifeways*. Washington, DC: Smithsonian Institution Press.

Latour, Bruno. 2005. *Reassembling the Social: An Introduction to Actor-Network-Theory*. Oxford: Oxford University Press.

Lee, Richard B., and Irven DeVore, eds. 1968. *Man the Hunter*. New Brunswick, NJ: Transaction Publishers.

Lévi-Strauss, Claude. (1949) 1969. *The Elementary Structures of Kinship*. Ed. Rodney Needham; trans. James H. Bell, John R. von Sturmer, and Rodney Needham. Boston: Beacon Press.

Lynteris, Christos. 2017. "Zoonotic Diagrams: Mastering and Unsettling Human-Animal Relations." *Journal of the Royal Anthropological Institute* 23 (3): 463–485.

Marshall, Mac, ed. 1979. *Siblingship in Oceania: Studies in the Meaning of Kin Relations*. Ann Arbor: University of Michigan Press.

Mason, Alan. 1997. "The Sibling Principle in Oronao' Residence." *Ethnology* 36 (4): 351–366.

Myers, Fred R. 1986. *Pintupi Country, Pintupi Self: Sentiment, Place, and Politics among Western Desert Aborigines.* Washington, DC: Smithsonian Institution Press.

Nuckolls, Charles W., ed. 1993. *Siblings in South Asia: Brothers and Sisters in Cultural Context.* New York: Guilford Press.

Nuttall, Mark. 2000. "Choosing Kin: Sharing and Subsistence in a Greenlandic Hunting Community." In *Dividends of Kinship: Meanings and Uses of Social Relatedness*, ed. Peter P. Schweitzer, 33–60. London: Routledge.

Partridge, Tristan. 2014. "Diagrams in Anthropology: Lines and Interactions." Life Off the Grid. https://anthropologyoffthegrid.wordpress.com/ethnograms/diagrams-in-anthropology.

Peterson, Nicolas. 1993. "Demand Sharing: Reciprocity and the Pressure for Generosity among Foragers." *American Anthropologist* (n.s.) 95 (4): 860–874.

Rivers, W. H. R. (1910) 1968. "The Genealogical Method of Anthropological Enquiry." In *Kinship and Social Organization*, A. Forge, ed, 97–113. London: Athlone Press.

Sahlins, Marshall. 2013. *What Kinship Is—And Is Not.* Chicago: University of Chicago Press.

Smith, Eric A., and Mark Wishnie. 2000. "Conservation and Subsistence in Small-Scale Societies." *Annual Review of Anthropology* 29: 493–524.

Strathern, Marilyn. 1991. *Partial Connections.* Savage, MD: Rowman & Littlefield.

Strathern, Marilyn. 1992a. *After Nature: English Kinship in the Late Twentieth Century.* Cambridge: Cambridge University Press.

Strathern, Marilyn. 1992b. "Parts and Wholes: Refiguring Relationships in a Post-Plural World." In *Conceptualizing Society*, ed. Adam Kuper, 75–104. London: Routledge.

Strathern, Marilyn. 1995. *The Relation: Issues in Complexity and Scale.* Cambridge: Prickly Pear Press.

Tsing, Anna L. 2012. "On Nonscalability: The Living World Is Not Amenable to Precision-Nested Scales." *Common Knowledge* 18 (3): 505–524.

Turnbull, David. 1991. *Mapping the World in the Mind: An Investigation of the Unwritten Knowledge of the Micronesian Navigators.* Victoria: Deakin University Press.

Widlok, Thomas. 2000. "Names That Escape the State: Hai//om Naming Practices versus Domination and Isolation." In *Hunters and Gatherers in the Modern World*, ed. Peter P. Schweitzer, Megan Biesele, and Robert K. Hitchcock, 361–379. New York: Berghahn Books.

Widlok, Thomas. 2013. "Sharing: Allowing Others to Take What Is Valued." *HAU: Journal of Ethnographic Theory* 3 (2): 11–31.

Widlok, Thomas. 2017. *Anthropology and the Economy of Sharing: Critical Topics in Contemporary Anthropology.* London: Routledge.

Wilson, Ara. 2018. "Visual Kinship." *History of Anthropology Newsletter* 42, 24 July. http://histanthro.org/clio/visual-kinship/.

Xiang, Biao. 2013. "Multi-scalar Ethnography: An Approach for Critical Engagement with Migration and Social Change." *Ethnography* 14 (3): 282–299.

Chapter 3

ON VISUAL COHERENCE AND VISUAL EXCESS
Writing, Diagrams, and Anthropological Form

Matei Candea

Unlike some of the other chapters in this book, this one is written primarily from a practitioner's point of view. Parts of it might even be labeled 'confessions of a budding diagrammatist'. But there is a broader aim here: the chapter explores anthropological diagramming as an entry point into questions about form and formalism in anthropological knowledge production. I will examine some of the critiques against and uneasiness with the use of diagrams in anthropology and examine the recurrent (counter-)claim that diagrams and other kinds of formal representation—including anthropology's very brief love affair with algebra—are useful because they clarify, reduce, and act as a productive limit on the proliferation of verbal arguments. Although this claim is persuasive in some respects, it is also partial. I argue below that diagrams and other formalisms can also suggest new possibilities and vistas, to which the accompanying text in turn acts as a productive limit. In sum, this chapter makes an argument for the value of formalism in anthropological knowledge production, while seeking to expand our understanding of how formalism might be valuable.

Alongside analyses of some historical uses of anthropological diagrams, the chapter draws on a reflexive examination of trials and errors in my own recent attempt to use diagrams to build an argument about anthropological comparison (Candea 2018). The topic of that book is in principle incidental—any diagrammatic argument would have served as an example, the main point being merely to unpick stages and moments in the process of articulating pictures to words and vice versa. However, I will argue in the conclusion below that these two themes (diagrams and comparison) are not randomly connected. This chapter's core argument is that diagrams are productive because they strain against the text they accompany. This is also in essence the book's argument about the way anthropological comparisons keep the discipline together, that is, precisely through its internal tensions—an argument developed partly through diagrams, as I will outline below. On both scales, this is a story about a particular epistemic device: formalism as a means for fostering internal multiplicity.

Back to the Drawing Board?

Diagrams are back. Once a mainstay of anthropological exposition, diagrams fell out of favor in the 1980s and 1990s in part as a result of the 'literary turn'. Writing in the late 1990s, Alfred Gell (1999: 31) described it as "a moment of verbalism, in which the graphic impulse is checked on ideological grounds, because graphics are associated with science, high-tech and particularly, engineering [which] is from the standpoint of the cultural studies mindset, Disciplinary Enemy No 1." Now, however, diagrams seem to be making a comeback in some quarters. Gell's own 'Strathernogram' was an early trailblazer. Bruno Latour's profuse use of diagrams in various works (see, e.g., Latour 1993, 2004) has become a key device also for the exposition of his ideas by others. No university lecture on actor-network theory is complete without one or another of Latour's diagrams being presented to an initially puzzled audience. Eduardo Viveiros de Castro (2001), Martin Holbraad, and Morten Axel Pedersen (Holbraad 2012; Holbraad and Pedersen 2009) have used diagrams not simply as illustrations, but as key steps in arguments. The purely 'trendy' aspect of anthropology's spat with diagrams might thus seem to be at an end. Right now it is the literary turn that is fashionably being shunned, so it is perhaps not surprising that ideological strictures against the 'graphic impulse' have loosened.

And yet there is continuing unease with diagrams in some quarters. These are not are not viewed in a matter-of-course way as they were in the mid-twentieth century. Those who cede regularly to the graphic impulse tend to attract amused comments and asides from colleagues and simply brush off rebuttals such as "diagrams just don't do anything for me." Few are the contemporary anthropological diagrammatists who do not perform the art with a measure of flamboyant self-consciousness and/or a pinch of tongue-in-cheek.

At least two widely stated and fundamentally solid objections to the use of diagrams in contemporary anthropology are not just about intellectual trends. The first is the thought that diagrams often add little to the text they accompany. Since they typically require explanation, why not simply provide the explanation? As Barnes (1962: 406) once wrote of the brief love affair with algebraic formulae in anthropology, "plain English is easier to understand and cheaper to print." A stronger version of this critique focuses not simply on the claim that diagrams add nothing, but points furthermore to what diagrams take away. Ingold (2000: 140) has criticized kinship diagrams' "decontextualizing linearity." As Partridge (2014) reports in a wide-ranging review of anthropological diagramming, a number of critics feel that diagrammatic representation "threatens to conceptualise social relations as static social facts rather than as 'dynamic phenomena,' offering a particularly empty conception of social life." In sum, diagrams, through their very form, are sometimes felt to leech away context, time, dynamism, and life itself.

The second objection is most clearly stated in an observation that Gell (1999: 31) attributed to Marilyn Strathern, according to which "diagrams can give a spurious logic to texts which are, in fact, discursively incoherent." This charge echoes another widespread discomfort about diagrams, which centers on the claim that they lend a spurious authority to the text. Historians of the discipline have noted that early anthropological uses of diagrams such as Rivers's genealogical charts were self-conscious attempts to establish anthropology as a positivist scientific enterprise on a par with other sciences (Bouquet 1996), and those desires persist in some quarters. More recent diagrammatists might be suspected instead of trying to appear to be not as boring as biologists, but rather as highfalutin as philosophers.

Yet as Partridge (2014) notes, there are many kinds of anthropological diagrams, and they have been used to many ends and purposes. Not all seek positivist reduction—some, on the contrary, try to expand the interpretive reach of the text they accompany. And the precise kind of authority they seek or achieve depends very much on context. One might say, with Partridge, that "questions around how diagrams are used in anthropology are as numerous as the forms they adopt" (ibid.). I will, however, try to say something a bit more specific than that.

But first let me be clear about what this chapter will not be attempting. A proper historical exploration of diagramming in anthropology would need to take into account the many institutional, political, and interdisciplinary contexts in which various kinds of diagramming emerged and spread. It would need to consider diagrams as 'paper tools' (Foks 2019) through which the discipline produced various forms of institutional and political effects, both internally and externally. I will not be trying to do anything on that scale here. Rather, this chapter provides a complementary angle by zooming in, rather myopically, on a seemingly technical question: how do diagrams and text interact within particular anthropological arguments? What exactly do they add or remove? And how might we think about the question of diagrams' coherence, raised above? In response to the charge that diagrams lend a spurious coherence to texts, Gell (1999) sets out his own goal as that of producing both graphic coherence and textual coherence simultaneously. Yet while we have some sense of what textual coherence looks like, it is not entirely clear what 'graphic coherence' means. When is a diagram coherent? And what is it supposed to be coherent with? Itself? How would it not be? The text it accompanies perhaps? But then we are back to the first objection: if a diagram merely recapitulates the text, then why provide the diagram?

I am going to explore these questions in two different ways. As noted above, the first is a kind of auto-ethnography of my recent conversion to diagrams. It reflects on the process of building a book-length argument through, with, and alongside what Gell (1999) terms a 'visual channel'. The following sections consider this case alongside others from the anthropological record, to examine some broader questions concerning the distinctive power and limits of visual representation as an anthropological heuristic. Here the chapter rejoins the key themes explored by other contributors to this book, who show, as the editors put it, that "diagrams inhabit a mediating space between representation and prescription, words and images, ideas and things, theory and practice, abstraction and reality." But my key concern will be to decompose this mediation in order to identify more precisely where and to what effect diagrams accompany, prefigure, and exceed textual forms of anthropological argument. I will focus in particular on the question of how far diagrams borrow from more or less elaborate conventional visual codes, situating this in comparison to anthropology's short-lived mid-twentieth-century romance with algebraic formulations. These seemingly technical questions of 'code' will lead to some broader conclusions about the interplay of invention and convention and the dynamics of graphic coherence within single anthropological arguments and broader disciplinary discussions.

Thinking through Diagrams

I had for long been doodling out ideas, but had never before actually published a diagram of my own. Yet my book *Comparison in Anthropology* (Candea 2018) carries no fewer than 17 diagrams, suggesting something of the convert's zeal.

This section describes the way some of these diagrams were devised, and their interrelation with the developing argument of the text. Recounting one's own writing/drawing process in this way might seem a rather self-indulgent thing to do. But crucially, this is not presented as a mastered or particularly elegant process—because it was not. The point of the description, rather, is to pinpoint precisely the contingencies, mistakes, and rethinking that accompany the interweaving of thoughts, words, and pictures in one specific case. Such a decomposition of the writing/drawing process—which only the author can give and which we can only surmise in the case of published works—provides good material for exploring the two questions raised above, namely, that of visual excess (when do diagrams do more than replicate the text?) and that of visual coherence (when do diagrams lend a spurious coherence to an otherwise incoherent discussion?). We shall see that these questions await us at every step of the way.

It all began with figure 3.1 below, which I first doodled for my own purposes to help me think through the interplay of analogies and contrasts in anthropological comparison. The book at that point was half-written, and various individual arguments were lying there, resisting my attempts to assemble them into a coherent whole. Those concerning the interplay of difference and similarity in anthropological comparison went as follows. First, it has been a recurrent feature of anthropological musings on comparison to draw a stark distinction between comparisons that aim at establishing similarities—often in order to build generalizations—and comparisons that aim at establishing or making difference. These alternatives form a fundamental conceptual but also political and ethical fork in the road for many contemporary anthropologists.

Second, a persistent strand of writing on comparison, from at least John Stuart Mill (1856) onward, has focused on the way in which analogies and contrasts are procedurally interwoven in the building of specific comparisons. Comparisons that point to a key similarity between things otherwise different

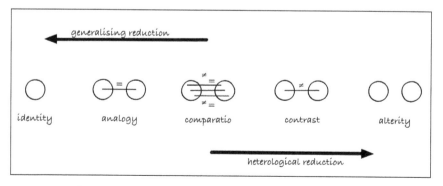

FIGURE 3.1: Identity and alterity. Drawn by author. Originally published by Cambridge University Press.

and comparisons that point to differences between things otherwise similar are two classic permutations. But there are many others. Third, and relatedly, there is a fundamental sense in which analogy and contrast are mutually entailed in *any* anthropological comparison. Minimally, even a clear and sustained analogy starts from the point that it operates between two different objects; conversely, any contrast, however stark, involves some preliminary or implicit form of commensuration. Finally, most sustained ethnographic comparisons are more that single contrasts or analogies; rather, they deploy a thick skein of interwoven similarities and contrasts. As an avatar of this thick interweaving of analogies and contrasts, I had struck upon the classic rhetorical figure of *comparatio* (Goyet 2014)—the systematic and slow drawing out of analogies and contrasts between two things, whose most well-known contemporary descendant is the compare and contrast essay.

Figure 3.1 originated as an attempt to visually represent these various arguments alongside one another, to see how they might fit together. Without giving this initial decision much thought, I figured the objects of comparison as circles and the relations made between them as lines, marking some of these relations as analogies by adding $=$ and some as contrasts by adding $\neq$. This basic visual convention then led to figuring the various terms of the argument above (alterity, identity, *comparatio*, analogy, contrast) as in figure 3.1—although not, at first, in any particular order.

Placing these individual figures alongside each other made me see the sense in which they came with an implicit order in terms of the 'thickness' of relations. At the extremes, both identity and radical alterity marked a non-comparative horizon—there can be no comparison between a thing and itself,[1] just as there can be no comparison by definition between two entities that are completely and utterly different from one another. These horizons are 'ends' of comparison, both in the sense that anthropological comparisons usually point toward one or the other, and in the sense that they are the point at which comparison ends, finishes, is extinguished. The thickest comparative interweaving of analogies and contrasts seemed to sit naturally at the midpoint between these two radical horizons. Single analogies and contrasts marked the intermediaries.

In its final form, the diagram represented two arguments that the practice of drawing it had helped me to hone. First, while the aims to which anthropologists put comparison are themselves incommensurable, their actual practices form a disciplinary common ground. Second, there is an inverse relation between the thickness of a comparison and its closeness to its aim, that is, to the 'point' it is intended to make. These two arguments are essentially captured in the overall shape of figure 3.1, with its thick middle of comparative practice weaving together incommensurable thin ends, along which one can travel in both directions to make a point.

These two arguments now formed the bedrock of the book. However, the process of writing it involved the transposition of this basic argumentative and visual form in a number of additional directions. The first such expansion derived in part from a dissatisfaction with my own visual convention of representing objects as closed circles and comparative relations as lines between them. Those circles seemed rather too closed. Are the objects of anthropological comparison really that discrete? Surely a key point of contention among anthropologists concerns the very nature of what we are comparing. Are we comparing things, units, entities in the world, or are we comparing relations, configurations, flows?

The visual/textual argument developed around figure 3.1 encouraged me to cast it again as a tension between 'ends' or 'purposes'. The rather otiose metaphysical debate between those who see relations everywhere and those who see entities everywhere becomes more tractable and more interesting when it is figured as a parting of ways between two opposed projects. Is the purpose of comparison that of reducing a confused initial glimpse of flows, states, and relations to a stable vision of identifiable objects, elements, and states? Or is it, on the contrary, to unravel an all-too-easy belief in states and objects into their constituent flows, processes, and relations? This alternative is as stark as that between alterity and identity as aims of comparison. And yet again, in practice, actual anthropological comparisons invoke both objects and relations, both states and flows, both events and processes. The shape of these observations now seemed familiar. They invited a transposition of figure 3.1 into a new figure 3.2, in which some initial circles—the unproblematized 'things' of figure 3.1—became evanescent and 'melted' into flows and intensities, themselves now figured as arrows. What remained stable was the overall visual form of a thick middle of comparative practice (in which attention was paid to flows, intensities, objects, and transitional states) that thinned out toward two different and incommensurable

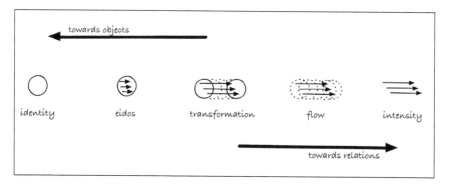

FIGURE 3.2: Identity and intensity. Drawn by author. Originally published by Cambridge University Press.

'ends': on the one hand, pure identity and its clearly delineated objects and, on the other, pure intensity and a world of flows and perpetual transformation.

Crucially, though, I was not ready to let go of figure 3.1. Figure 3.2 mapped out not an improvement of figure 3.1, but rather a second, parallel problematic. Yet somehow parallelism was not quite what was at stake. How might one represent these two as aspects of the same comparative practice? Putting it like this suddenly made available a new visual possibility that I had not initially envisaged. Figure 3.1 and figure 3.2 had one term in common—identity. What if one mapped these two figures as two dimensions of a plane, with identity as their common origin, as in figure 3.3? At first blush, the move made sense: after all, tensions between similarity and difference and between relations and entities could be applied simultaneously to any single anthropological comparison. The two figures were not describing parallel lines, but rather perpendicular axes of the same problematic (cf. Corsín Jiménez 2011).

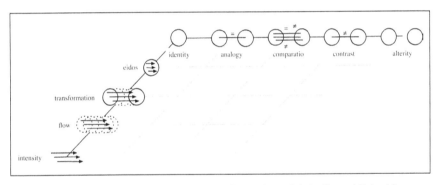

FIGURE 3.3: A plane of comparison. Drawn by author. Originally published by Cambridge University Press.

Here, however, more than at any earlier point in the process, the diagram drove the conceptual argument. If, with figure 3.2, I found myself trying to work out a coherent visual representation of a set of conceptual arguments, now I suddenly had to scramble to draw out the conceptual implications of an enticing visual possibility. What would it mean to imagine comparisons on a plane? Did such an image actually make sense when put into words, and what would be its implications? Was it coherent to combine 'identity as sameness' and 'identity as objecthood' (self-sameness)? Did the new implication of a 'coordinate system', with difference, identity, and intensity as variables, help or hinder an understanding of how comparison actually operates in anthropology? Each of the previous diagrams had highlighted an intricate midpoint of thick comparison—could one imagine a midpoint of these midpoints? Without going into further detail at this point, a reader of *Comparison in Anthropology* will readily see that some of these questions are addressed explicitly in the resulting text, others implicitly, and others not at all. The diagram exceeds the text in a number of directions.

This developing diagrammatic convention begged another fundamental question, however. All of these figures focused on the objects and relations of comparison, but where might the observer be located? Reconsidering those diagrams in light of that conceptual question, they suddenly seemed to carry an blindness to what is probably the most fundamental problematic of most anthropological discussions of comparisons, namely, that of the relationship between observer and observed. This observation about the limits of the diagrams rejoined a distinction I have drawn elsewhere (Candea 2016) between 'lateral' comparisons, which focus on the lining up of cases ('this and that'), and 'frontal' comparisons, in which the observer's own context is one of the terms of the comparison (canonically in anthropology, a comparison between 'us and them'). All of the diagrams above were essentially about lateral comparison. Introducing the problematic of the observer required another addition to the visual language, as in figure 3.4.

The multiple permutations of the relationship between observer and observed—the forms and valences of frontal comparison—in turn suggested the necessity of a third axis, turning the two-dimensional plane of comparison in figure 3.4 into a three-dimensional space, as in figure 3.5. Without tracing this third axis in any detail, the broader point is that, again, the addition of this third dimension thickened and expanded my initial argument.

In a nutshell, the final core argument of *Comparison in Anthropology* is that anthropologists use comparison in pursuit of divergent if not incommensurable

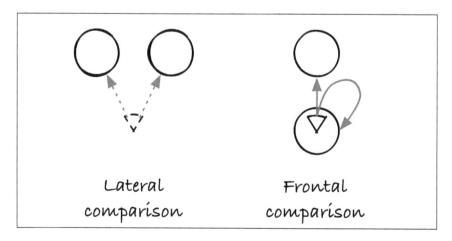

FIGURE 3.4: Lateral/frontal comparisons. Drawn by author. Originally published by Cambridge University Press.

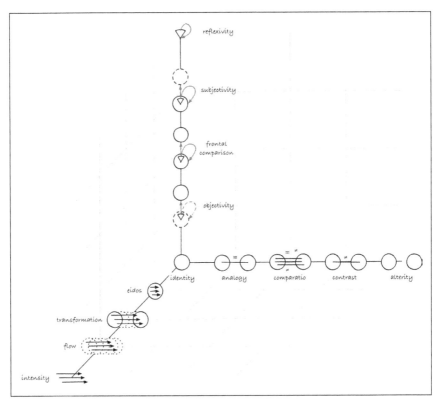

FIGURE 3.5: A three-dimensional space of comparison. Drawn by author. Originally published by Cambridge University Press.

ends: to generalize from particulars or to challenge generalizations; to unpick purported entities into flows and processes or to identify shared ideals or concrete forms behind disparate processes; to provide accounts of the world as it is or to challenge their own analytical or cultural presuppositions. However, these different ends are all pursued through techniques of comparison that are built out of the same basic building blocks: analogies and contrasts, relations and intensities, objectivities and subjectivities. Combined and recombined, these form intricate heuristic arrangements adequate to the variety of purposes outlined above. While some anthropologists have held up the 'thickness' of comparison as an epistemic ideal, the vision of a three-dimensional space also provides a shorthand for imaging what maximal comparative thickness might consist of. A comparison that attends to difference *and* similarity, relations *and* processes, the world *and* the observer's own situated perspective would sit somewhere in the middle of the space mapped out in figure 3.5.

This section has illustrated the back-and-forth motion between diagrammatic and textual representation in one anthropological argument. This account raises two sets of questions that pertain to our initial problematics of visual excess and visual coherence. The first set of questions asks about the 'translation' (a problematic metaphor in many ways) of words into pictures and pictures into words. When do diagrams betray the words they sit alongside, and the converse? And if the goal is perfect correspondence between image and text, where does the added value of diagrams lie in relation to the words they accompany? The second set of questions focus on coherence, not between individual diagrams and the text, but across a series of diagrams themselves. What are the value and effects of visual conventions (and visual inventions) in anthropological diagrams, whether these conventions obtain within a single work, as in this example, or in a broader disciplinary conversation? How do visual conventions intersect with visual inventions? The remaining sections explore these questions in relation to other instances of anthropological diagramming.

On Graphic Excess: Logical Relations and Unwanted Implications

Those who see value in diagrams have a paradoxical response to claims that diagrams are useless and add nothing to the text because they require textual explanation. The value of diagrams lies, proponents retort, not in saying *more* than the text but in saying *less*. From Peirce onward, as the editors remind us in their introduction, diagrams have been praised as "a skeleton-like sketch of its object … constructed from rational relations" (Stjernfelt 2000: 363). In this view, what diagrams add inheres precisely in what they cut away: verbose description and its thick unintended implications and echoes. By leaving a mere skeleton, diagrams make conceptual relations, patterns, and structures visible.

In this respect, diagrams can be interestingly juxtaposed to another form of graphic convention that some anthropologists briefly experimented with in the mid-twentieth century, and which is definitely *not* making a comeback. This was the thought that one might profitably seek to express generalizations about social relations in terms of an algebraic language. In his book *The Theory of Social Structure*, Siegfried Nadel (1956), a key proponent of this idea, sought to devise and propound such a notational language, combining the conventions of mathematics and formal logic. To take only two early and very simple examples, the thought that a social role (ρ) is made up of a series or sum (Σ) of attributes might be noted as

$$\rho = \Sigma \ a, b, c \ldots n$$

If one wishes to note that a role includes one pivotal attribute (p) and that some of its attributes are optional, this could be written as

$$\rho = \Sigma \ p, a, b \ldots l/m/n$$

The complexity of these formulae escalates throughout the book, such that the reader will later find the illuminating thought that

> if E : A [≳ (crb)] is such that
> ErA E (ca) A
> ∴ ErA → A [≳ (crb)]

In fairness, it must be said that Nadel was characteristically cautious about the power and limits of his proposed system of notation. It aim was primarily "to help in demonstrating certain complicated situations more simply and accurately than can be done by verbose descriptions" (ibid.: 6). He did occasionally suggest that the notation might enable a kind of calculus, making visible some entailments that would not have been discovered if the situation had merely been stated in conventional language (ibid.: 56–57). Fundamentally, though, the aim of the formulae was to induce a certain kind of rigor to the discussion: "They certainly produce, in those who use them, a new attitude, a new way of looking at the material to be handled: which is probably the decisive step" (ibid.: 7).

Nadel's notation, perhaps unsurprisingly, did not catch on. On the rare occasions when it is remembered, it is with more than a smattering of derision (e.g., Ingold 2008: 72–73). This was already a contemporary response. In a scathing review of the book, Edmund Leach (1976) described Nadel's attempt to devise a logical notation as 'disastrous', adding that "none of these symbolic statements has any meaning until Nadel has himself explained them in his accompanying text and none of them leads to conclusions which are not much more readily propounded in simple English. The only positive effect of this excursion into 'mathematics' is to deter the reader from trying to understand the argument" (ibid.: 133).

And yet, somewhat paradoxically, in his Malinowski lecture given the following year, Leach himself would propound the virtues of algebraic notation in terms rather similar to those of Nadel. In a now famous critique of the structural-functionalist study of kinship, Leach (1966: 10) began by noting the way some standard anthropological kinship terminology betrays ethnographic realities: "If the Trobrianders say—as they do say both in word and deed—that the relation between a father and his son is much the same as the relation between male cross-cousins and as the relation between brothers-in-law, but absolutely different from the relation between a mother and her child, then we must accept the fact that this is so. And in that case we delude ourselves and everyone else if we call such a relationship *filiation*." Leach then demonstrated, using a pair of diagrams to which I return below, that a much clearer sense of the ethnographic situation could be garnered by decomposing 'filiation' into two variables: filiation with the father (q) and filiation with the mother (p).

The various comparative questions relating to filiation (including the then current debates around patrilineal, matrilineal, and complementary descent systems) could then be stated in terms of various ratios Z, where $Z = p/q$.

Leach (1966: 17) anticipated critics making much the same observation that he himself had thrown at Nadel the previous year:

> In a way this is all very elementary. Those of you who teach social anthropology may protest that, leaving out the algebra, this is the sort of thing we talk about to first year students in their first term. And I agree; but *because* you leave out the algebra, you have to talk about descent and filiation and extra-clan kinship and sociological paternity and so on and your pupils get more and more bewildered at every step. In contrast what I am saying is so easy that even professors ought to be able to understand! It is not algebra that is confusing but the lack of it. After all, you professionals have long been familiar with both the Trobriand and the Kachin ethnographic facts, but I suspect that you have *not* until this moment perceived that they represent two examples of the same pattern—you have been unable to perceive this because you were trapped by the conventional categories of structural classification. Now that I have pointed out the mathematical pattern the similarity is obvious ... But let me repeat. I am not telling you to become mathematicians. All I am asking is: don't start off your argument with a lot of value loaded concepts which prejudge the whole issue.
>
> The merit of putting a statement into an algebraic form is that one letter of the alphabet is as good or as bad as any other. Put the same statement into concept language, with words like paternity and filiation stuck in the middle of it, and God help you!

In sum, Leach's defense of algebraic notation overlaps substantially with Nadel's.[2] Algebraic notation makes description simple and accurate by avoiding unintended verbal implications, and it induces a new way of seeing. And, again not unpredictably, what Leach himself described as a "pseudo-mathematics" (ibid.: 8) was greeted with the same skepticism with which he had greeted Nadel's. As Barnes (1962: 406) observed, "a characteristic of pseudo-mathematics is that each symbolic pseudo-statement has to be translated into words as we go along."

— • —

This brief excursion through the mostly forgotten episode of algebraic anthropology provides a comparative perspective on our discussion of diagrams. We find algebra and diagrams being criticized for the same reasons—that they merely repeat the textual content, and that they can lend an air of scientific rigor to observations that are themselves not necessarily rigorous. We find their proponents praising them precisely for the same reasons—that they produce a

skeletal representation which cuts away unintended or irrelevant verbal implications, and that they thus make visible logical relations in otherwise familiar
material. Both diagrams and logical notation are a way of seeing otherwise.

The previous discussion suggests one important difference, however. Algebraic notation was praised for cleaning up unwanted implications, since one
letter of the alphabet was as good as any other. In this particular respect, the
mid-twentieth-century vision of algebra as a means of anthropological communication shares some of the long-standing rhetorical force of scientific appeals
to quantification—namely, the thought that, as Leibniz put it, "most disputes
arise from the lack of clarity in things, that is, from the failure to reduce them
to numbers" (quoted in Daston 1995: 9). As historians of science have noted,
this particular vision of quantification implied a moral economy of commu-
nicability and unification, one that was "sociable but intolerant of deviation"
(ibid.; cf. Porter 1992). Nadel's and Leach's praise for algebra's purported
virtue of cutting away terminological imprecision evokes similar visions of
disciplinary unification.

The same cannot automatically be assumed of diagrams. Certainly, diagrams
do cut away some implications, but they also add others. Even the simplest
visual forms are rich with conceptual implications, many of them entirely ancil-
lary to the logical relations that the author initially wished to convey: circles
imply closure and perfection; unbroken lines seem to suggest that objects have
firm boundaries; arrows figure a kind of linear progression, although they might
only be intended to suggest entailment, or the reverse; relative size can always
seem to imply importance even if it was only meant to ensure readability.

The notion of a diagram that can stand on its own and be read without textual explanation—the sort of ideal implied by critics who complain that a diagram adds nothing if it has to be explained by the text—is thus fundamentally
misguided. Diagrams are inherently polysemic. They fundamentally require
exposition and 'control' by a textual explanation that pinpoints which features
the reader ought to attend to, and which are incidental or even misleading. In
this respect, diagrams are no different, of course, from the text itself. Just as
ideas like 'filiation' or 'paternity' carry unwanted implications or obfuscatory
possibilities, so do circles, arrows, and dotted lines. The same sort of work of
definition and control has to go into the framing of both.

So what, then, is the added value of diagrams? It lies precisely in the fact
that the entailments and implications—the conceptual 'drift' and 'bleed', one
might say—of words and figures is not the same. Language lies with all the force
of etymological echoes, tautology, poetic fudges, and non-linear expositions of
various kinds that paper over incoherences and gaps in argument. Diagrams
have a way to cut through all of these obfuscations, to keep the text honest. But
images also lie, through a different kind of polysemy and through the constant
ambiguity between what is being figured and what is merely a convenient way

to draw something. Is the distance between these two forms, their respective size, or the thickness of the line meant to be relevant, or is it merely the clearest way to arrange a picture on the page? The text that accompanies diagrams keeps them honest in turn by pointing to what matters and what does not.

Language lies and so do figures (cf. Partridge 2014)—but they lie at cross-purposes. As a result, they can productively act as a control for each other. The initial Peircean idea of diagrams as a skeletal assemblage of rational relations is only half of the picture. Yes, diagrams can do this productive work of cutting away the drift and bleed of language, but only if their own drift and bleed have first been cut away by some explanatory text. Diagrams are 'clean' because the accompanying words clean them. They are, to parody Bourdieu (1977: 72), "structured structures which are predisposed to function as structuring structures." They are 'predisposed' because of the inherent tension between the way in which words and images leak meanings. Keeping a verbal channel and a visual channel open alongside each other acts as a form of two-way control.

However, this talk of rigor and control is all very stern. There is a more positive point to be made, for as we saw in my initial example, it is also in the ways that text and images exceed each other, escape each other's control, that they can act together as a productive engine for driving an argument forward. As we saw in the previous section, new ideas can stem precisely from the ways in which a figure cannot adequately render a conceptual point—or, conversely, from the ways in which drawing something out suggests unintended entailments that exceed the arguments previous spelled out in words. Perhaps Nadel's thought that notation might lead to calculus was not entirely misplaced. At the very least, rendering a verbal argument into images will often suggest hypothetical further entailments, which would then need to be worked out. The ongoing struggle of fitting and refitting images and words to each other is a path to both control and creativity.

On Graphic Coherence: Between Convention and Invention

While in the previous section we have been mainly dealing with the question of excess (what does a diagram add to the text?), this discussion has taken us into a consideration of coherence. We ended up, in effect, with the observation that the constant—and often difficult—striving for coherence between texts and diagrams can confer a certain kind of rigor to arguments that combine them. The fact that such coherence is never perfect lends a certain spark to the process and opens up new possibilities.

But the brief excursus through algebraic anthropology suggests another, complementary set of observations. For what distinguishes algebraic notation from the dominant way in which diagrams are used by anthropologists today is its conventional nature. Algebraic notation is a code—its terms are defined once and for all, and they are kept stable through multiple permutations and iterations in the same text or, ideally (if the notation catches on) in multiple texts.

By contrast, anthropological diagrams, as they are being used today, are mainly what one might call 'single-use' diagrams: each is a specific, stand-alone visual device for representing a particular conceptual point, relationship, or argument. There is no assumption that the elements of any given diagram will be carried forward to any other diagram in the same text. Each diagram is a monad, a contingent, single-purpose figuration. Any visual coherence is entirely a local matter of the relationship between this particular image and the immediately adjacent text, raising the sorts of questions we have explored above.

Between the extremes of logical notation and single-use diagrams, however, lies the use of diagrams as described in the first section of this chapter. Here the text is accompanied by a series of diagrams that share a set of visual elements. Once a symbol has been established, it remains stable in subsequent diagrams: the diagrams share a visual convention. It thus becomes possible to ask, not only whether diagrams are coherent with the text that is immediately adjacent, but also whether they are coherent with the other diagrams in the series. Another classic instance of this is Gell's (1999: 29–75) essay "Strathernograms," with which I began this chapter, which sets out to give a diagrammatic representation of Gell's reading of Marilyn Strathern's (1988) arguments in *The Gender of the Gift*.

While Gell himself does not state this, I suspect that in introducing the notion of graphic coherence, what he is primarily evoking is precisely this effect of seriality. What "Strathernograms" turns on is not merely coherence between the text and the 'graphic channel', but also coherence within the graphic channel itself, ensured by the use of a consistent graphic convention. Gell (1999: 36–37) defines his own convention explicitly: 'terms' are figured by boxes, 'relations' by circles or ovals, and 'appearances' by lozenges (see fig. 3.6). While Gell does not tell us this, he is in fact drawing on an existing diagrammatic convention—the 'entity-relationship' model developed by computer scientist Peter Chen (1989). In order to illustrate Strathern's argument, Gell uses the entity-relationship convention in 19 diagrams of increasing complexity (some of them matching that of Nadel's formulae), interspersed with other diagrams and line drawings.

Once again, I am interested in the form rather than the substance of the argument here. The distinction between single-use diagrams and serial diagrams is worth attending to, for it raises the broader question of the 'conventional' in anthropological uses of diagrams. Unlike single-use diagrams, serial diagrams that deploy a shared visual convention, as in Gell's case, introduce a different, additional requirement of coherence. Such diagrams need to be coherent with the text they accompany, of course, but they also need to be coherent among

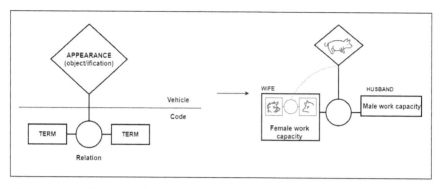

FIGURE 3.6: Gell's convention. Drawn after the original in Gell (1999). Originally published by Cambridge University Press.

themselves. This second requirement makes it harder to cheat, to give a mere 'air of logic'. It ties graphic coherence to a broader standard.

This is even clearer in cases where graphic conventions are shared, not simply within one text, but within a broader conversation. The classic graphic convention in anthropology was of course that of kinship diagrams, which involved three kinds of formal relationships—alliance (=), filiation (|), sibling-ship (-)—between two distinct and mutually exclusive genders (circles and triangles). Each of these relations and entities was taken to form a complete set. We are in fact only one step short of a logical notation. Graphic coherence here is scaffolded by a stock set of visual terms. Through this convention, kinship diagrams spoke to each other, not only within a single text, as in Gell's case, but across different texts. It would be very easy to point out, within this convention, what it might mean for a kinship diagram to be 'incoherent', although we shall see in a moment that incoherence in the sense of a bending of convention need not be a bad thing. Conversely, it would be rather difficult to mask textual incoherence through such conventional, formalized visual representation—one would more likely make such incoherence evident.

Unpacking the notion of graphic coherence has thus led us to a contrast between what one might think of as convention and invention in anthropological uses of diagrams (cf. Wagner 1981, another great diagrammatist). Single-use diagrams are self-conscious inventions: each proposes a new, bespoke visual form to map, express, or indeed constitute a particular conceptual configuration. At the opposite end of the scale, just short of the move out of diagrams and into logical notation, classic kinship diagrams are thoroughly conventional, providing a stock visual vocabulary that frames new permutations.

Stated like this, however, the difference is unhelpfully stark. On the one hand, even single-use diagrams tend to draw on a set of conventional geometrical figures (lines, circles, etc.), and we saw in the previous sections how these simple geometrical forms carry much conventional baggage. Conversely, the power of 'conventional' visual languages often lies precisely in the novel inventions they enable. Minimally, every new kinship diagram, insofar as it is not a direct reproduction of a previous one, is an inventive reconfiguration of conventional elements—meaning, in this sense, that is always premised on invention (Holbraad and Pedersen 2017; Wagner 1981). Less trivially, some of the best diagrams in the history of anthropology have relied on a self-conscious play with conventional visual languages. In sum, the contrast between diagrammatic invention and convention speaks to the way—picked up by other contributors to this book—in which description and prescription are interwoven in diagrams. Formal, conventional, diagrammatic languages are prescriptive. Working with and against the grain of such prescriptions can be an intensely inventive act.

As to the former point (convention as prescription), kinship diagrams are a perfect and classic example. The kinship diagram convention derives its power and durability in part from its ability to remain coherent across texts hailing from radically different conceptual perspectives. The classic debates over the 'real' or merely 'conceptual' existence of social structure (Dumont [1971] 2006; Evans-Pritchard 1950; Leach 1966; Lévi-Strauss 1958; Nadel 1957; Radcliffe-Brown 1940) nicely pinpoint this issue. While structuralists and functionalists differed profoundly as to their ontological commitments concerning the nature of the social, and more specifically of kinship relations, they could unproblematically share their kinship diagrams. Everyone shared in essence the thought that one might visually represent men and women, alliance, filiation, and siblingship, even though what each of these figures indexed in ontological terms (statistical patterns, formal rules, roles, individuals, etc.) was thoroughly up for grabs. The graphic coherence of a conventional diagrammatic language stemmed from and underpinned a conceptual coherence—the outline of a shared disciplinary conversation, however contentious.

And yet, while the convention of kinship diagrams was broad enough to accommodate radical differences of opinion, it nevertheless required some questions to remain unasked. As Bouquet (1996: 44) notes, quoting Jameson via Clifford, "visualizing kinship in the genealogical diagram reflects 'the limits of a specific ideological consciousness, [marking] the conceptual points beyond which that consciousness cannot go, and between which it is condemned to oscillate.'" As soon as 'kinship' itself came to be seen as a specifically Euro-American cultural figuration (Carsten 2000; Schneider 1984), the vision of two mutually exclusive and jointly exhaustive genders and of three fundamental relationships lost some of its shine. The very idea of cross-culturally stable forms of personhood and relation has fallen away, and with it the meaningfulness of *any* standard visual language in which to represent such things. The conceptual features of a given 'culture of relatedness' (Carsten 2000) might be the object of a particular diagrammatic representation, but the idea of drawing all of these different diagrams from the same stock visual terminology seems to serve no purpose. For what, after all, would such stock visual terminology itself index? It is a truism to say that anthropologists today would find it hard to agree on any given list of fundamental relationships. Kinship diagrams persist, of course, but they have been robbed of their fundamental theoretical 'footing'. The forms they pick out as their building blocks now seem arbitrary and problematically—rather than productively—partial. Their graphic coherence is the ghost of a conventional vision of social life that anthropologists no longer share.

Any visual convention, in other words, is restrictive and comes with blind spots. Even single-use diagrams suffer from this limitation, since, as we noted above, they draw on a stock of geometrical figures (circles, lines, arrows, squares, and the like), each of which carries its own unintended conceptual echoes, however slight. No diagram is a complete invention.

Conversely however, it is often precisely this conventional undertow that enables invention. Consider, for example, Leach's (1966: 11–12) use of diagrams in *Rethinking Anthropology*. In order to illustrate his iconoclastic critique of functionalist kinship theory, and specifically of the concept of 'filiation', Leach amends standard kinship diagrams in various ways. First, he grafts a whole range of extraneous relations and factors onto a standard kinship diagram. The point is explicitly to provide a visual summary of Malinowski's arguments about Trobriand kinship, witchcraft, and exchange, showing the complex interrelation of different elements of cultural behavior. Crucially, however, this is not merely an addition. Rather, what is normally a single vertical line denoting filiation, stemming from the = denoting marriage (fig. 3.7a), is here decomposed into two lines: a descent line stemming directly from the mother to the son, and a diagonal line marked "'resemblance' (influence)," which does not quite join the father and the son (fig. 3.7a). In sum, this diagram breaks the convention of kinship notations by multiplying filiation and setting it out—visually—as simply one among a multiplicity of relationships of various kinds. From a strictly canonical perspective, as a kinship diagram, it might be seen as tending toward incoherence, yet it is perfectly coherent in relation to the text it accompanies. The diagram visualizes a complex theoretical point, namely, that descent as commonly figured by anthropologists is only one among many forms of relationship, and a decomposable form at that. The diagram that follows (fig. 3.7b) recomposes this multiplicity of relations into a focused illustration of Leach's alternative, 'algebraic' mode of generalization. Once we have decomposed descent, it is possible to imagine formalizing two components—one coming from the mother and another from the father. This provides a stepping-stone to Leach's algebraic generalizations. Leach's inventive reconfiguration of generalizations about descent relies on a direct and knowing play with an existing visual convention.[3]

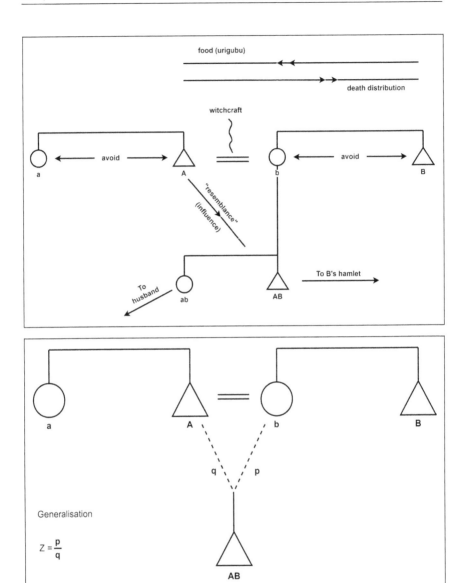

FIGURE 3.7a,b: Leach's inventions. Drawn after the originals in Leach (1966). Originally published by Cambridge University Press.

Any diagrammatic convention can become a device for invention. To return to an example mentioned above, Gell 'invents' with Chen's entity-relationship model in a number of ways. For instance, by placing rectangles or lozenges inside other rectangles or lozenges—a possibility that makes little sense in the terms in which this visual convention was first outlined—Gell illustrates the fractal character of Strathern's Melanesian aesthetic. Conversely, any diagrammatic convention also constrains. Thus, by comparison with kinship diagrammatic conventions, Gell's entity-relationship model might seem to be almost infinitely capacious, since it merely indexes 'relationships' and 'terms'. Could one imagine a less constraining figuration? And yet, even here, the limits of convention bite back. Thus, recognizing the conventional aspect of Gell's diagrams casts interesting light on a fundamental point of contention surrounding his representation of Strathern's argument about relations. As Gell (1999: 35) puts it:

> What is a 'relation'? Strathern does not tell us this, but, on her behalf, I assert that a relation is a connection between two terms ... I think that one can justifiably criticize Strathern for not doing enough to elucidate the concept of relationship, as I have just done, and in particular for saying so much about relationships without introducing the logically essential concept of terms, i.e., what relationships relate. She took all this for granted. In what follows, relationships are necessarily between terms, and terms are treated as constituted out of the relationships in which they participate.

Gell's rendering of Strathern's arguments is thus structured by the reintroduction of a binary contrast between terms and relations. And yet, Strathern (2014) herself has argued that one key affordance of the notion of 'relation' is precisely the ability to invoke relations without specifying their terms. My aim is not to enter into that dispute, but simply to note that the relations/terms binary speaks directly to the visual possibilities and restrictions of an entity-relationship model (as the name of that model suggests). It would be fascinating to know which came first as Gell was writing that piece—his choice of the entity-relationship visual model, or his recognition of an absence of 'terms' in Strathern. Without such insight into Gell's process, one can only say that the diagrammatic conventions and the theoretical possibilities and limitations of his argument (about Strathern's argument) are in some general sense mutually constitutive. Thus, even this seemingly infinitely capacious visual convention is restrictive and comes with blind spots.

In sum, the point of this section is that the existence of a conventional visual language gives visual invention something productive to strain against. The dynamic is similar to the broader one described in earlier sections, whereby diagrams both complement and strain against the text they accompany.

Conclusion

Despite signs of a renaissance in diagramming after the literary turn, many anthropologists remain skeptical of diagrams, while those who use them have rarely sought to mount a defense of the practice in principle. In the absence of such a defense, it is easy to accuse diagram-wielding anthropologists of obfuscation or scientistic posturing—and of course the charge may in some cases fit. But there is more to diagrams than bluster, rhetoric, and style. I have sought in this chapter to lay out some of the positive arguments for working with diagrams in anthropology.

Thinking about diagrams from the 'inside', as it were, provides a new perspective on the two critiques we started from—the critique that diagrams are reductive, and the critique that they lend a spurious consistency and authority. Like all of such critiques, these need to be substantiated in particular cases. Critiques that identify particular omissions are valuable, but they are hardly a reason to abandon diagramming altogether. While they are admittedly flawed tools, diagrams do have value—in some ways, their value lies precisely in their limitations.

This value, I have argued, lies not primarily in diagrams' inherently logical nature, or in a propensity to always clarify words. Diagrams can also be tricky, polysemic, and confusing—they can have a spurious coherence. But then, words are tricky too. The value of adding what Gell terms a 'visual channel' to anthropological texts stems, I would argue, from the different ways in which the trickiness of words and of graphics is configured at the intersection of conventions and inventions. The strain of seeking to maintain coherence both within and between these two channels simultaneously helps to make arguments more robust. The creative flashes produced when this coherence is disturbed provide an unparalleled engine of conceptual invention.

This defense is very much in the same spirit as Rumsey's (2004) defense of tropes in anthropological writing. It has become commonplace to undercut the authority of anthropological texts by pointing at the way in which they deploy literary tropes and devices (Clifford and Marcus 1986). Yet this critique seems to imply a crypto-positivism of its own, as if tropes stood in the way of representational truth or accuracy. As Rumsey notes, the formal devices deployed to macro-structure ethnographic monographs—whether this be on the classic holistic part-whole model (Thornton 1988), or in the genre of intentionally fragmentary collections held together by a thematic trope, as Rumsey notes of Anna Tsing's (1993) *In The Realm of the Diamond Queen*—are not only inescapable, but can be extremely productive. The use of such macro-tropes and structural devices, Rumsey (2004: 288) concludes, "has contributed in an essential way to anthropological understanding, in at least some cases running ahead of related developments in theory rather than merely changing in response to them." To be aware of such tropes and structural devices is to be in a position to use them in novel ways and devise new ones to suit new purposes.

Rumsey's discussion reminds us that ethnographic texts themselves already work in some diagrammatic-like ways (Rupert Stasch, pers. comm.). They deploy form and structural devices in order to scale down and provide 'sketches' of an object elsewhere. This is the converse of saying, as I have at various points, that diagrams perform in some ways rather like a language (e.g., that they 'lie'). And yet recognizing these echoes between how texts work and how diagrams work does not reduce the core point I am making here, which is that texts and diagrams operate on fundamentally different principles, and the tensions introduced by trying to assemble them as two simultaneous channels in the same argument can have distinctive effects. The effect is similar to that which would be achieved, for instance, if one were trying to simultaneously run an argument in two languages—as indeed many ethnographies in effect do, moving back and forth between indigenous terms and necessarily imperfect translations or equivocations (cf. Viveiros de Castro 2004).

In other words, I am pointing to a broader formal device—that of fostering internal multiplicity. As I said at the outset, this argument about diagrams is not unrelated to my argument about anthropological comparison. The relationship is analogical. The particular formal device I have described here within one text—the way in which a visual channel and a textual channel can work to both curtail and extend each other—is a scaled-down version of a broader dynamic in the discipline of anthropology. As Andrew Abbott (2001) has suggested of academic disciplines more broadly, anthropology as a practice, as a discipline, exists in the tension of its internal differences. Anthropology is subdivided into groups pursuing incommensurable ends and visions, as I have suggested above in relation to comparison. Some of us use comparison to generalize, others seek to highlight difference, some see the self-critique of Western concepts as their main goal, while others envisage anthropology as a device for the pursuit of social justice. We are also subdivided into groups constituted around the knowledge of and passionate engagement with particular areas and themes, different theoretical schools, national traditions, and political imaginaries. These differences are not stable or essential; they shift and churn in relation to one another. Yet this does not mean anthropology is just an empty signifier. Rather, the discipline lives through the actual institutional spaces in which these differences are forged, sustained, and exhibited—in seminars, in departments, in conferences, in peer-reviewed journals, in book reviews, in edited volumes, and the like. In such settings, these myriad projects, purposes, and expert visions rub up against each other, simultaneously curtailing each other's flights of fancy and extending them (Candea 2018).

Nor do anthropologists speak just to one another. Our arguments are buffeted not only by the requirements and challenges of differently situated anthropologists, but also by academics from other disciplines, and beyond that by different people, including those with whom anthropologists work, and beyond that still by a world of non-human entities of various kinds that may also raise objections to our accounts. Like the internal resistances of anthropology, these external resistances put our accounts to the test, and in the process strengthen them. We find here, writ large, the same dynamic I have tried to elucidate at the intersection of visual and verbal channels inside an anthropological text—that particular model of rigor and invention points to a broader epistemic form in anthropology writ large.

Acknowledgments

The writing of this chapter was supported by the European Research Council (ERC) under the European Union's Horizon 2020 Research and Innovation program (grant agreement 683033).

Matei Candea is a Professor in Social Anthropology at the University of Cambridge. He is the author of *Corsican Fragments* (2010) and *Comparison in Anthropology: The Impossible Method* (2018), and the editor of *The Social after Gabriel Tarde* (2010) and *Schools and Styles of Anthropological Theory* (2018). He has worked on alterity and belonging in Corsica and on human-animal relations in biological science. He is currently the Principal Investigator of an ERC-funded research project comparing the ethics, epistemics, and heuristics of freedom of speech in Europe.

Notes

1. Although that possibility is explored by the introduction of intensity, as discussed below.
2. This overlap exists even though Leach (1966: 8) attempted—less than conclusively—to distinguish himself by suggesting that Nadel sought to apply a mathematical procedure to his arguments, whereas one ought to use only a mathematical notation.
3. More recently, Knut Rio (2005, 2007) has operated similarly intriguing distortions of the kinship diagram convention.

References

Abbott, Andrew. 2001. *Chaos of Disciplines*. Chicago: University of Chicago Press.
Barnes, J. A. 1962. "Rethinking and Rejoining: Leach, Fortes and Filiation." *Journal of the Polynesian Society* 71 (4): 403–410.
Bouquet, Mary. 1996. "Family Trees and Their Affinities: The Visual Imperative of the Genealogical Diagram." *Journal of the Royal Anthropological Institute* 2 (1): 43–66.

Bourdieu, Pierre. 1977. *Outline of a Theory of Practice*. Trans. Richard Nice. Cambridge: Cambridge University Press.

Candea, Matei. 2016. "De deux modalités de la comparaison en anthropologie sociale" [On two modalities of comparison in social anthropology]. *L'Homme* 218: 183–218.

Candea, Matei. 2018. *Comparison in Anthropology: The Impossible Method*. Cambridge: Cambridge University Press.

Carsten, Janet. 2000. "Introduction: Cultures of Relatedness." In *Cultures of Relatedness: New Approaches to the Study of Kinship*, ed. Janet Carsten, 1–36. Cambridge: Cambridge University Press.

Chen, Peter Pin-Shan. 1989. "The Entity-Relationship Model: Towards a Unified View of Data." In *Readings in Artificial Intelligence and Databases*, ed. John Mylopoulos and Michael L. Brodie, 98–111. San Francisco: Morgan Kaufmann.

Clifford, James, and George Marcus, eds. 1986. *Writing Culture: The Poetics and Politics of Ethnography*. Berkeley: University of California Press.

Corsín Jiménez, Alberto. 2011. "Daribi Kinship at Perpendicular Angles: A Trompe l'Oeil Anthropology." *HAU: Journal of Ethnographic Theory* 1 (1): 141–157.

Daston, Lorraine. 1995. "The Moral Economy of Science." *Osiris* 10: 2–24.

Dumont, Louis. (1971) 2006. *An Introduction to Two Theories of Social Anthropology: Descent Groups and Marriage Alliance*. Ed. and trans. Robert Parkin. New York: Berghahn Books.

Evans-Pritchard, E. E. 1950. "Social Anthropology: Past and Present: The Marett Lecture, 1950." *Man* 50: 118–124.

Foks, Freddy. 2019. "Constructing the Field in Colonial Africa: Power, Persona and Paper Tools." Paper presented at the Senior Seminar, 25 January, Department of Social Anthropology, University of Cambridge.

Gell, Alfred. 1999. *The Art of Anthropology: Essays and Diagrams*. Ed. Eric Hirsch. Oxford: Berg.

Goyet, Francis. 2014. "Comparison." In *Dictionary of Untranslatables: A Philosophical Lexicon*, ed. Barbara Cassin, Emily Apter, Jacques Lezra, and Michael Wood; trans. Steven Rendall, Christian Hubert, Jeffrey Mehlman, Nathanael Stein, and Michael Syrotinski, 159–164. Princeton, NJ: Princeton University Press.

Holbraad, Martin. 2012. *Truth in Motion: The Recursive Anthropology of Cuban Divination*. Chicago: University of Chicago Press.

Holbraad, Martin, and Morten Axel Pedersen. 2009. "Planet M: The Intense Abstraction of Marilyn Strathern." *Anthropological Theory* 9 (4): 371–394.

Holbraad, Martin, and Morten Axel Pedersen. 2017. *The Ontological Turn: An Anthropological Exposition*. Cambridge: Cambridge University Press.

Ingold, Tim. 2008. "Anthropology Is Not Ethnography." *Proceedings of the British Academy* 154: 69–92.

Ingold, Tim. 2000. *The Perception of the Environment: Essays on Livelihood, Dwelling and Skill*. London ; New York: Routledge.

Latour, Bruno. 1993. *We Have Never Been Modern*. Trans. Catherine Porter. London: Harvester Wheatsheaf.

Latour, Bruno. 2004. "Why Has Critique Run Out of Steam? From Matters of Fact to Matters of Concern." *Critical Inquiry* 30: 225–248.

Leach, Edmund. 1966. *Rethinking Anthropology*. London: Athlone Press.

Leach, Edmund. 1976. "Social Anthropology: A Natural Science of Society?" *Proceedings of the British Academy* 62: 157–180.

Lévi-Strauss, Claude. 1958. *Anthropologie Structurale* [Structural anthropology]. Paris: Plon.

Mill, John Stuart. 1856. *A System of Logic, Ratiocinative and Inductive, Being a Connected View of the Principles of Evidence, and the Methods of Scientific Investigation*. Vol. 2. London: John W. Parker and Son.

Nadel, Siegfried F. 1957. *The Theory of Social Structure*. London: Cohen & West.

Partridge, Tristan. 2014. "Diagrams in Anthropology: Lines and Interactions." Life Off the Grid. https://anthropologyoffthegrid.wordpress.com/ethnograms/diagrams-in-anthropology/.

Porter, Theodore M. 1992. "Quantification and the Accounting Ideal in Science." *Social Studies of Science* 22 (4): 633–651.

Radcliffe-Brown, A. R. 1940. "On Social Structure." *Journal of the Royal Anthropological Institute of Great Britain and Ireland* 70 (1): 1–12.

Rio, Knut M. 2005. "Discussions around a Sand-Drawing: Creations of Agency and Society in Melanesia." *Journal of the Royal Anthropological Institute* 11 (3): 401–423.

Rio, Knut M. 2007. *The Power of Perspective: Social Ontology and Agency on Ambrym Island, Vanuatu*. New York: Berghahn Books.

Rumsey, Alan. 2004. "Ethnographic Macro-Tropes and Anthropological Theory." *Anthropological Theory* 4 (3): 267–298.

Schneider, David M. 1984. *A Critique of the Study of Kinship*. Ann Arbor: University of Michigan Press.

Stjernfelt, Frederik. 2000. "Diagrams as Centerpiece of a Peircean Epistemology." *Transactions of the Charles S. Peirce Society* 36 (3): 357–384.

Strathern, Marilyn. 1988. *The Gender of the Gift: Problems with Women and Problems with Society in Melanesia*. Berkeley: University of California Press.

Strathern, Marilyn. 2014. "Reading Relations Backwards." *Journal of the Royal Anthropological Institute* 20 (1): 3–19.

Thornton, R. J. 1988. "The Rhetoric of Ethnographic Holism." *Cultural Anthropology* 3 (3): 285–303.

Tsing, Anna Lowenhaupt. 1993. *In the Realm of the Diamond Queen: Marginality in an Out-of-the-Way Place*. Princeton, NJ: Princeton University Press.

Viveiros de Castro, Eduardo. 2001. "GUT Feelings about Amazonia: Potential Affinity and the Construction of Sociality." In *Beyond the Visible and the Material: The Amerindianization of Society in the Work of Peter Rivière*, ed. Laura M. Rival and Neil Whitehead, 19–43. New York: Oxford University Press.

Viveiros de Castro, Eduardo. 2004. "Perspectival Anthropology and the Method of Controlled Equivocation." *Tipití* 2 (1): 3–22.

Wagner, Roy. 1981. *The Invention of Culture*. Rev. ed. Chicago: University of Chicago Press.

Chapter 4

CONFIGURATIONS OF PLAGUE
Spatial Diagrams in Early Epidemiology

Lukas Engelmann

Spatial diagrams have long been essential instruments in visualizing epidemics. They configure epidemics on maps and enhance the recognition of epidemic processes spanning time and space, at the same time integrating an indefinite series of ecological, environmental, biological, social, and cultural aspects. They draw together the structures, concepts, systems, theories, and ideas that are brought into significant relation through an epidemic. When they attach the topography of a series of disease cases to the geographical coordinates of a place, they shape the dynamic nature of an outbreak over time and serve the purpose of situating epidemics on the ground. In this chapter I will argue that epidemiology's spatial diagrams come closest to 'representing' the epidemic itself. In the history of epidemiology as science, the epidemic has always been

Notes for this chapter begin on page 107.

a rather peculiar object. Neither a natural object like bacteriology's pathogens, nor a social entity like demography's populations, the epidemic maintains a tension between observed event and conceptual framework—a tension best preserved and presented in the spatial diagram.

The term 'spatial diagram', as used throughout this chapter, is not coincidently borrowed from architecture and landscape design (Vidler 2000). The principal purpose of such diagrams is to provide the location and integration of a conceptual entity, a design, or a structure within a given landscape or environment. To this end, spatial diagrams offer a clear iconographic distinction between the visualization of the given context, often found in a common map, and the representation of an envisioned structure as an abstract or diagrammatic entity. The spatial visualization of an epidemic involves a comparable combination of a map of a given environmental context with references to the spatial and temporal pattern of a series of cases of a disease. Within the terms of epidemiological reasoning, the spatial diagram is perhaps best understood to be a hybrid between maps and functional diagrams. While both maps and topological diagrams of, for example, the hierarchy of cases have been widely employed in epidemiology and public health, it is the spatial diagram that captures most reliably and consistently the abstract entity of an epidemic (Koch 2011).

In recent social science literature, maps and diagrams of epidemic events have received a range of attention. Many perceive the epidemic map and diagram as instruments of social control—visualizations of power structures, blueprints of containment strategies—or as strategic investments in the normalization of societies and pathological behavior (Monmonier 2010). Maps and diagrams of epidemics can be seen as simulations of possible worlds, as models for worlds of social relations, or as "animated social theories" (Opitz 2017: 394) structured by contagious and infectious phenomena. For Carlo Caduff (2015), maps and diagrams can be addressed as cybernetic ways of knowing the epidemic, where reductionism and incompleteness express immediacy and urgency, without aiming for comprehensive accounts and stabilized sets of information. On the other hand, Christos Lynteris (2017: 464) argues that the zoonotic diagram in particular "embodies and reproduces fundamental principles of interspecies relations" that inform bio-political human-animal relationships.

These authors have analyzed epidemic diagrams to grasp the effects enabled by and the technologies of power incorporated into these graphic devices and visual modes of reasoning. Here, I focus on a different question. Stepping back from an analysis of the political implications and power dynamics of epidemic diagrams and maps, I ask instead about the relationship between what we consider to be an epidemic and how this precarious object of knowledge is captured and demarcated in visual representations. This inquiry is methodologically located in a history of science to unpack the hardened traditions of visualizing epidemics that have structured epidemiological representations up to the present day. Here, I take two exemplary historical cases of spatial diagrams of the same disease during a crucial period when disciplinary boundaries were set in epidemiology. Both cases convey a clear picture of an epidemiological diagrammatic of configuration that maintained epistemological distance from questions of origin or causation.

The historian of medicine Charles Rosenberg has offered a now famous answer to the question, what is an epidemic? Prompted by the developing AIDS crisis, Rosenberg (1992) proposes that we grasp epidemics as events, rather than as trends. He suggests a 'dramatic' framing for understanding the spatial and temporal development of an outbreak as a series of choreographic events. Moreover, Rosenberg identifies two conceptual frameworks through which people have explained epidemics and made sense of the epidemic event in the past. The first, 'configuration', emphasized a systems view, in which epidemics were explained as "a unique configuration of circumstances" of categorical equal significance (ibid.: 295). Communal and social health were seen as a balanced and integrated relationship between humankind and environmental constituents, in which epidemics appeared not only as the consequence, but also as the origin of disturbance, crisis, and catastrophe. Rosenberg's second framework, 'contamination', focused on a different view, one that prioritized particular and identifiable causes for an epidemic event. Whereas configuration implies holistic concepts, the contamination perspective suggests a disordering element, a *causa vera*, and implies a reductionist and monocausal way of thinking. As Rosenberg emphasizes, both of these themes have existed since antiquity in epidemiological reasoning, but it is particularly in the late nineteenth century, with the emergence of bacteriological science, that we see a proliferation of these themes in polemical dichotomies. Already seeded with conflicts between contagionists and anti-contagionists throughout the nineteenth century, the theme of configuration became overwhelmingly identified with the sanitary beginnings of epidemiology. The bacteriological laboratory, on the other hand, introduced bacteria as a superior principle of contamination. But contrary to the stock narrative of the bacteriological revolution, the principle of contamination never achieved autarchy in the explanation of epidemics, and the laboratory was kept at a critical distance from the epistemology of epidemiology.

As Olga Amsterdamska (2005) has argued, epidemiology long struggled to constitute itself as a discipline; indeed, many of the doctors and health officers who were involved in the observation, analysis, and classification of epidemic events would hardly call themselves epidemiologists far into the twentieth century. But throughout the late nineteenth and early twentieth centuries, during this period of disciplinary demarcation and boundary work, epidemiology continued to preserve its commitment to systems, to ideas of equilibrium and balance. Epidemiologists carried out boundary work to safeguard their own inductive modes of reasoning against the reductionist simplifications of the equation that found if one microbe leads to one disease, a number of them would lead to an epidemic. Instead, the turn of the nineteenth century was characterized by a distinctive proliferation of theories and concepts that integrated bacteriology seamlessly into other modes of epidemiological reasoning, including history, sociology, demography, and early versions of ecology. Amsterdamska (2004: 486) contends that "epidemiologists reacted to the advent of the germ theory of disease neither with hostility and rejection nor with the belief that the new theory implied a subordination of their own findings to those of the bacteriological laboratory." Andrew Mendelsohn (1998: 306) argues in a similar direction when, citing Flexner, he channels epidemiologists' persistence in defining their field "in terms wider than the microbic incitants." The traditional basis of epidemiology—history, environment, statistics—never disappeared in the face of bacteriological science, but rather became a 'counter-trend'. Contrary to a popular picture, epidemiology did not require bacteriological expertise about pathogens, nor did bacteriology or germ theory offer a missing piece to epidemiological puzzles. In point of fact, epidemiology had already developed a distinctive and robust set of practices, methods, and ways of reasoning to observe, articulate, and analyze the configuration of epidemic events.

In this chapter I argue that spatial diagrams have long been substantial tools for the boundary work undertaken by epidemiologists to safeguard notions of complexity, to preserve system thinking, and—most importantly—to study epidemic phenomena without adhering to the identification of contaminations suggested by bacteriological investigations. In other words, the spatial diagram has furthered the tradition of inductive reasoning committed to open-ended observation and association, which was akin to epidemiology and stood in strong contrast to the deductive methods of the laboratory (Bauer 2013; Parascandola 1998). The history of spatial diagrams in epidemiology has the capacity to challenge common misunderstandings that still exist today when epidemiological maps and spatial diagrams are read and interpreted as proof of causality and origin.

According to Christina Ljungberg (2016: 142), maps as well as spatial diagrams share the capacity to "structure domains into networks of relationships" to achieve "both likeness and hybridity. That hybridity is what makes the map an efficient tool not only for exploring unknown territories but also for discovering new relationships that no verbal description could reveal." Since John B. Harley's (1989) critical commentary on cartography, we have clearly moved beyond a perception of maps as reproductions of an objective image of the epidemic's reality. But Harley also reminds us that we still need to consider the map's epistemological and cultural investment in the production of objects of research that affect values and politics around the issues drawn up in geographic visualizations (ibid.: 4). In his reading of the disease map, Koch

(2011) picks up on this perspective and pushes it a step further. For him, the disease map is inherently an instrument from the epidemiologist's workbench, implicated in ongoing research questions, rather than an instrument of representation or demonstration. Disease maps belong to a sophisticated "method of assemblage within which ideas are constituted and then argued about specific experiences" (ibid.: 13).

The spatial diagram of an epidemic is therefore a conjunction of analytic presentation and experimental presentation in visual exposition. With reference to Hans-Jörg Rheinberger's (1999) 'experimental systems', Koch (2011) suggests that we first see the disease map as an assemblage of known aspects, secured facts, and well-established understandings—of environment, climate, hygienic status, population-density, cultural customs, and built structures, as well as characteristics of a disease, virulence of a bacteria, and any other factor deemed relevant—which then goes on to emphasize those aspects that are unknown, unusual, and seek further exploration and explanation.

The history of plague is uniquely qualified to demonstrate the capacity of spatial diagrams as a way to emphasize the configuration of an epidemic event over principles of contamination. The beginning of the Third Pandemic coincided with the bacteriological identification of its agent, later known as *Yersinia pestis*, but plague and its medieval heritage had long been a favorite object of epidemiologists (Echenberg 2007; Lynteris 2016). The recurrence of plague in the late nineteenth century, when bacteriological science enjoyed outstanding popularity, indeed offered a pathway in which the epidemic seemed to have become an object of the laboratory—an infectious disease seen almost exclusively through the lens of contamination (see Cunningham 1992). But, as I argue here, despite the microbe's stabilized ontology, epidemiologists continued to invest in and strengthen their approaches to studying outbreaks as complex configurations while maintaining their professional indifference to arguments of contamination, causality, and origin.

The two cases discussed here inhabit distinct positions in the historical arch of the third plague pandemic (1894–1952). The first diagram was produced a few years ahead of the pandemic, covering a small outbreak in the Russian village of Vetlianka in 1878. The second was produced in 1899 in the Portuguese city of Porto as the pandemic reached European shores. The spatial diagrams produced for both outbreaks allow us to unearth a series of unique epidemiological perspectives on the disease, which emphasized a view of plague as a superimposition of historical narratives, environmental descriptions, and disease topographies—a view that stressed uncertainty and resisted the premature attribution of causality and responsibility.

The examples furthermore enhance a historical sense of an epidemiological practice that was not yet subsumed under biostatistics and mathematical proofing but consisted in the assemblage and open-ended superimposition of a variety of fields of knowledge. In 1878, we see diagrammatical reasoning about plague in Vetlianka before bacteriological explanations were readily available. The arrival of plague on Europe's shores in 1899 demonstrates how epidemiology's diagrammatic reasoning persisted despite the availability of monocausal frameworks. Both cases serve to excavate a forgotten practice of epidemiological reasoning: that epidemiologists working with and on diagrams assumed a capacity of radical epistemological indeterminacy. Almost any perspective, viewpoint, theory, and concept could be considered and arranged into the networks of relationships, the models of configuration, and the diagrams of epidemics that they were observing and drawing together.

Plague in 1878 Vetlianka: A House and Family Epidemic

A map of the 1878 plague outbreak in the Russian fishing village of Vetlianka on the banks of the Volga provides us with a remarkable diagram (see below). The iconic references appear opaque, and the diagram's conceptual propositions require as much explanation as do the circumstances of its production. The aesthetic qualities of the picture mimic the isolated and outstanding position of the outbreak in Vetlianka at the time. It was the first severe epidemic of plague on the European continent in the nineteenth century, which had considerable geopolitical consequences for the hygienic reputation of the Russian Empire and attracted attention from newspapers across the English-, French- and German-speaking worlds (Heilbronner 1962). Plague was considered at the time to be contained in the Far East, India, and North Africa and was believed to be unlikely to ever appear again in modern, hygienic Europe. With Vetlianka bearing evidence to the contrary, the members of an international commission all wrote reports, drew maps, and plotted graphs and diagrams to understand the precise conditions under which the epidemic had defied the advancements of European sanitation. Crucially, they wanted to know whether if it could progress further West.

On the Volga, the outbreak was understood to be the result of a series of smaller cases spanning the second half of the nineteenth century in the wider region of Astrakhan. Isolated cases tended to be attributed by local physicians to soldiers returning from China. The outbreak in the small and isolated fishing village of Vetlianka, 200 miles north of Astrakhan, probably began in mid-October 1878, but it took until December for its arrival to be publically announced. Russian authorities immediately sent doctors to investigate the circumstances of the surprising outbreak. But as news traveled, and out of growing concern for the hygienic reputation of the Russian Empire, an international commission from 11 European countries was invited to investigate the occurrence (Pirogovskaya 2014: 139). The commission arrived in Astrakhan in December

1878, only to discover that most Russian physicians had already succumbed to plague, although the outbreak itself seemed to have slowed down.

Historically, the outbreak occurred at a pivotal moment. With early bacteriology beginning to find footing in the German and French centers of medicine, and with ongoing controversies regarding concepts of disease transmission that involved contagious and sanitary conditions, Vetlianka offered an opportunity for the systematic observation of plague *in situ*, and for the precise definition of its epidemiological characteristics. But this should not be mistaken for an interest in the bacteriological identification of plague's microbe, as the commission's members were doctors and health officers who cared little for bacteriology. Instead, they sought to define the precise configuration of the local conditions in the fishing village that had turned individual cases—which had occurred before—into clusters, heaps, and series. Their interest was to capture the climatic and hygienic conditions of the local environment, as well as the susceptibility of the population, their living conditions, and in particular the 'pestilential' *watagas*—the large salt brine vats where the villagers cured fish (Lynteris 2016: 47). While the principle of a contagion was acknowledged by the commission's delegates, at the time of the Vetlianka outbreak it played only a minor conceptual role. A microbe that might have transmitted plague and the principle of contagion itself remained under-theorized in the proceedings of the commission's members, as these notions were widely ignored in early Russian epidemiology (Hutchinson 1985; Mikhel 2018).

Russian and Western European newspapers hurried to attribute the outbreak of Vetlianka to the catastrophic hygienic circumstances in the Astrakhan region. Russian physicians blamed social deprivation, growing poverty, and the unhygienic local fishing industry for having introduced conditions ripe for plague, which had led to the outbreak (Pirogovskaya 2014). One newspaper quoted a river boat captain who described Vetlianka as a "malodorous place," where passengers would cover their noses when passing by. Some papers went so far as to suggest that plague was not an import at all, but that the living conditions of the poor in Vetlianka had bred plague into existence (ibid.: 150).

The reports published by Russian, German, French, and English members of the commission painted a different picture. All of the reports follow a characteristic structure of systematic epidemiological observations in the late nineteenth century (see, e.g., Hirsch and Sommerbrodt 1880; Lawrence-Hamilton 1875; Zuber 1880). Extensive historical narratives of the ancient and more recent origin of plague were significant, as were the climatic conditions of the Volga valley. The professional occupation of the plague victims—most were fishermen—was considered with the same rigor as the relationship of settlements to their surrounding landscape, commonly referred to as "environs" (Radcliffe 1881: 3). What occasionally reads as pedantic and detailed accounts of seemingly disconnected elements and random aspects of an unusually widely framed historical and geographical context constitutes the driving principles of epidemiological reasoning at the time, whereby the history, the environment, and the population were all considered (Mendelsohn 1998).

Perhaps surprisingly, the commission members seemed rather unconcerned about an opposition between contagion and individual constitution, or between sanitary states and miasmatic influences. Rather, their writing and drawings suggest a pragmatic approach and an explicit interest in the configuration of the networks of relationships that the epidemic had made visible. The German epidemiologist August Hirsch took the isolated occurrence of the outbreak, which had caused no more than a few individual cases in neighboring villages, to be indicative of Vetlianka presenting a rare opportunity to study those circumstances that allow plague to thrive. The "detailed investigation of the local circumstances were essential," Hirsch argued, "as this plague appears to be an isolated epidemic, which mirrored in its appearance the properties [*eigenthuemlich*] of the local conditions" (Hirsch and Sommerbrodt 1880: 5; my translation). Hirsch then went on to discuss in detail the origin of this outbreak, which he assumed to be found in the Russo-Turkish wars. He assumed that returning Cossack soldiers, who comprised almost half of the population in the region, might have brought the disease with them. But he also considered the topography of the landscape, the humid climate, and the geology of the region before he engaged with the hygienic circumstances and their connection to the cultural habits of the Cossacks. Finally, Hirsch provided an overview of the history of other epidemics, such as malaria, in the same region before turning to the outbreak itself. He remarked that the plague in Vetlianka followed a unique pattern: cases seemed to have been confined strictly to families and their homes. Indeed, for both the first and second wave of the outbreak, almost all cases could be shown to have occurred along kinship lines. This pattern, he argued, suggested that the common belief that hygienic circumstances drove the epidemic was in need of urgent revision.

The English report, penned by J. Netten Radcliffe (1881), opened an equally wide framework. It considered the historical, geographical, and climatic influences before turning to the structure of the local population to capture the 'social conditions' of plague victims. After lengthy considerations of the geography, accompanied by maps, Radcliffe also gave much detail over to descriptions of the impoverished fishing village—the makeshift wooden structures of the dwellings, the poor sanitary state of the streets, and the leaking cemetery. He then relied on statements written by Russian doctors who had witnessed the outbreak in December to discuss the different waves and phases with which the plague had presented itself. He, like Hirsch, focused on the remarkable fact that almost the entirety of cases had been confined to families and seemed to have spread among close relatives: "The outbreak, indeed, consisted of a series of *houses* and *family epidemics*" (ibid.: 15; emphasis in original). Not only direct relatives were affected by these 'family epidemics', but also "persons brought into most familiar communication with the family" (ibid.). As an example, Radcliffe points to the four Russian doctors who had been sent to investigate the epidemic. All but one of them succumbed to plague, as had the entirety of the village's staff of feldshers (health care providers) after they visited infected houses.

G. N. Minkh, a professor of pathological anatomy at the University of Kiev, did not join the international commission, but instead went to Vetlianka on his own initiative, eager to report on the precise shape of the plague outbreak. A protagonist of experimental medicine influenced by Rudolf Virchow, he spent four months in the region to conduct research on the outbreak. Minkh's (1898) report, published after his death in 1896, was written with two principal goals in mind. First, he conducted a survey of the historical geography of plague to demonstrate that the spread of the disease out of the region was highly unlikely. Accompanying the report was a series of maps of the region that visualized the geopolitical significance and historical trajectory of cases along the Caspian Sea. Second, Minkh agreed in principle with the prominent members of the commission who found that the local conditions of Vetlianka were of special interest as they seemed to have allowed an epidemic to take hold that otherwise would not have settled in Europe. Understanding and mapping the conditions under which plague flourished there—and nowhere else—would thus allow for a generalized epidemiological picture of plague to be produced.

As he turned to the outbreak itself, Minkh focused on the two distinct periods of the epidemic. The first seemed to have developed slowly, was marked by classic signs of bubonic plague, and had only a moderate mortality rate. The second period was characterized by many pneumonic cases, a greatly increased mortality rate, and a far quicker death in most cases. Not only did both periods follow family lines, as pointed out by other commission members, but the second period also began in the particularly wealthy family of Osip Belov. For Minkh, this was reason enough to abandon any investigation into the hygienic state of dwelling or the hygienic living conditions of plague victims. Instead, he developed a different research question that followed the kinship structure of the epidemic.

Yet the concept of a 'family epidemic', as put forward by Radcliffe, did not make for a sufficient explanation of the observable pattern in Vetlianka. Minkh questioned whether the epidemic indeed followed a genealogy, and why some members of the same family who also had been in touch with sick family members were not affected. Furthermore, if the epidemic was to be understood in terms of proximity and contagion alone, why were dwellings next to infected houses often spared? His diagram of the topography of the outbreak of plague in Vetlianka followed these two questions (fig. 4.1). Minkh used a geographic map of the village, which showed the river in the north and the structure of dwellings throughout the town. To provide a representation of the social space, he

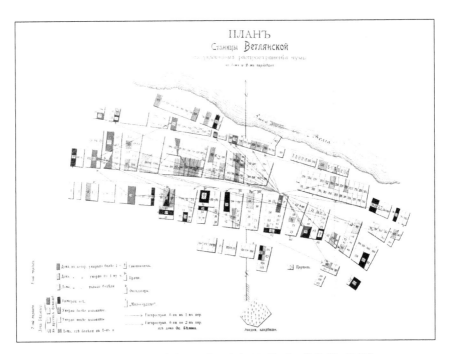

FIGURE 4.1: Spatial diagram of the outbreak in Vetlianka (Minkh 1898).

indicated the position of churches, the doctor's and feldshers' homes, and the cemetery. Minkh then developed a unique system of icons, arrows, and visual statistics to visualize the temporal and spatial characteristics of the epidemic. All remaining iconographic references were dedicated to the visualization of the spatial structure of morbidity and mortality, and the assumed spread of plague.

In Minkh's diagram, houses marked as red, orange, or yellow were those affected by the first, mild outbreak. Red houses were those in which more than one person had died; orange houses indicated that at least one case had been fatal. Yellow were all the remaining dwellings in which people with plague had recovered. Red arrows indicated the direction of transmission of the first period of the disease. Minkh identified the transmission from house #10 to house #58 as the origin of the second period, which was visualized with blue arrows. The structure of the second wave is split into two principal clusters. Three shades of blue indicate all houses belonging to the Belov family, with the darkest blue pointing to the total extinction of households, while the second and third shade signify a larger or a smaller mortality. Three shades of gray were then used to indicate the houses of other families not directly related to the Belovs, with a similar codification of fatalities.

Minkh argued that the diagram visualized a more complicated pattern than just an epidemic of family houses or of bloodlines. Rather, he could show that the two periods of the epidemic appeared in different spatial configurations. The first seemed to have largely been contained in the east of the village, with only isolated cases breaking out in other areas. The second, more violent period had also begun within a family, the Belovs, but had caused cases and pockets of outbreaks throughout the village. Most importantly, this map shows that this outbreak was neither structured solely by family bloodlines, nor did it follow a clear pattern of spatial distribution. Through his complex visualization, Minkh was able to show that the characteristics of plague in Vetlianka needed to be seen as both a plague of 'family epidemics' and as a disease of contagious nature, distributed beyond the families on the basis of contact and connections that were not explicable in terms of dwelling conditions, environmental aspects, or human-animal vectors.

In Vetlianka, the spatial diagram delivered a portrait of the epidemic's configuration in which two common perceptions of plague were drawn together to let a different network of relations emerge. Minkh's visualization presented plague as an epidemic of the village population that appeared to strike in two highly selective ways. Both were traceable through family lines as well as through proximity. His spatial diagram brought together concepts of lineage with questions about space and the immediate urban environment. His epidemic configuration thus resisted both a simple hygienic argument, such as those carried by many newspapers at the time, and arguments promoted by the British report, which considered this to be an epidemic of families and houses. Rather, Minkh's diagram insisted on the complexity of the spatial and temporal coordinates of the outbreak. Instead of attributing a cause, it integrated and sustained uncertainty in its accurate representation of the configuration of the plague epidemic, which in turn appeared as a system of interlocking factors and multiple influences.

Plague in 1899 Porto: Standardizing the Pattern of the Plague

The arrival of plague in the south of Europe three decades later offers a good case for comparison. At first sight, much of the epidemiological analysis undertaken in Porto resembles the endeavors of the commission in Vetlianka. An international commission was sent to the Portuguese city to investigate the circumstances under which the epidemic had managed to establish a focus in a European port. And similarly to Vetlianka, interpretations of causality were overwhelmingly focused on urban sanitary conditions. Different from Minkh's sophisticated visualization of an epidemic topography, the maps of plague in Porto illuminate another way that epidemiologists worked with spatial diagrams. Instead of inventing an innovative configuration of the epidemic, the Pasteurian Albert Calmette utilized the spatial diagram to combine different registers of observation in order to visualize and standardize what he considered to be a characteristic and universal picture of a plague outbreak.

The epidemic of Porto happened in a historical and geographical context that was very different from Vetlianka. The geopolitical landscape of Europe had undergone drastic changes, and this epidemic, which was believed to have originated in 1894 in Hong Kong, had in the meantime become a global pandemic. In the same year, the Japanese bacteriologist Shibasaburo Kitasato and the Pasteurian Alexandre Yersin had identified the bacterial agent responsible for plague. Yet until the end of the nineteenth century, most European and American public health authorities were convinced that plague bacteria could not survive in the sanitary environment of European and American cities. Following the Porto outbreak in July 1899, a chain of plague outbreaks took place in San Francisco, Sydney, and Buenos Aires in the same year, provoking conceptual reconsideration of what had been considered favorable conditions for plague to thrive.

The first case in Porto appeared when a Galician stevedore died after unloading a shipment of unknown origin at the local port. In a matter of days, many of his roommates, some of whom had sat in vigil for their friend, also died, and so did five women who worked and lived in neighboring houses (Echenberg 2007: 107). Ricardo Jorge, the local chief medical officer, was informed in July of the cluster of unusual cases, and after weeks of laboratory testing, he confirmed the presence of the plague bacillus in the corpses. Two months later, after Jorge's diagnosis had been confirmed, Camara Pestana of the Lisbon Royal Institute of Bacteriology declared a plague emergency. The outbreak further increased over the following months and gradually declined as winter set in. The final tally reported 322 cases of plague with 115 fatalities.[1]

Within a matter of weeks, the outbreak attracted doctors from Spain, Germany, England, Sweden, Norway, Italy, the United States, and Russia, with instructions to conduct epidemiological analysis. Most arrived just before a sanitary cordon was erected around the entire city on 24 August, lasting until 22 December (Almeida 2013: 893). While almost all the foreign doctors agreed that the quarantine was relatively useless and probably caused more harm to the local population than the plague itself, their focus was directed to an entirely different aspect of the epidemic. The French delegation, composed of Drs. Albert Calmette and Alexandre Salimbeni, arrived from Paris with an antiplague serum that promised effective immunization against the disease.[2] But Jorge (1899), among others, remained skeptical about the safety of the new serum and claimed that the success of its application to curb the epidemic was dubious. Instead, he proposed to remove the poorest populations from a particular form of habitation that had come to characterize the deprived part of the city around the port (ibid.: 12).

The *ilhas* or 'islands' were backyards on long and narrow plots in which only the front was occupied by traditional middle-class buildings. The remainder of the plot, accessibly only through a narrow underpass from the street, was crowded with small dwellings and shacks. Heavily overpopulated, these patches housed over 45,000 people in 1899, almost a third of the city's population. According to Jorge (1899), the *ilhas* had turned the city into a graveyard. Plague, an "exotic pestilence," had implanted itself in a "contagious, immoral, and miserable neighborhood" (ibid.: 16; my translation). To Jorge, the conclusion was therefore clear: "It is an epidemic of houses" (ibid.). Only rigorous sanitary measures and the forcible removal of citizens from these deplorable circumstances would contain the epidemic. But the drastic interventions, including compulsory bathing for whole streets, were greeted with strong opposition from the population. The investigating doctors were attacked with stones, and cavalry forces had to intervene to control a city that had suffered economic hardship as a result of the strict quarantine (Cohn 2018: 357). Jorge's program of combined social and hygienic improvement did not succeed. He handed in his resignation in September 1899 and left the city to advance his career in Lisbon.

The Pasteurians, arriving in Porto in August 1899, rejected the simple identification of plague with unhygienic conditions of overly cramped housing. Rather, Calmette and Salimbeni were investigating the outbreak as a test case for a specific French approach to bacteriology and epidemiology at the turn of the century. They were interested in the particular configuration of the epidemic as a relationship between bacteria, the environment, and the host, but they considered each of the systems that included the pathogen to be a variable factor. Driven by the theory that undergirded the Pasteurians' production of an immunization serum, they looked at the epidemic mainly through the conceptual framework of 'virulence' (Mendelsohn 2002). The bacterium was not considered a fixed entity but one whose capacity of infection fluctuated in correspondence to external factors, thus explaining the waxing and waning of outbreaks (Amsterdamska 2004). Accordingly, it was important not only to investigate the living conditions of people infected with the bacterium, but also to establish a picture of how the conditions of a European population in its specific environment affected its capacity to ignite an epidemic. "It was necessary," Calmette (1900: 108) wrote, "to determine with exactitude if the microbe was identical with that studied by Yersin in India, and if, following the inception of the virus in the European race, its characteristics had not changed."

Indeed, the bacteria in Porto was observed to be extremely virulent, and Calmette and Salimbeni witnessed a considerable number of pneumonic cases, which prompted further investigation into the modes of transmission in the city. But their greatest interest was to find out the extent to which the serum they had brought would have a beneficial effect and a measurable impact on mortality. The serum was used exclusively in the plague hospital, both as an immunization for staff and as a treatment for patients at an early stage of the disease. To prove the efficacy of the serum, they had to establish a detailed register of all treated cases in the hospital and compare it with all untreated cases in Porto. Many of these cases were never brought to the attention of doctors as families tended to hide patients, and those cases could thus be used as a control group. Here, Calmette and Salimbeni could demonstrate the reduced mortality among patients treated with their serum and also that houses and *ilhas* were not to blame for an increased occurrence of plague. Once they had assembled all the cases, with their individual characteristics, and had arranged them on a map (fig. 4.2), the conclusion had to be drawn that European populations were just as vulnerable to plague as Indian or Chinese people.

The paperwork that went into the production of this spatial diagram consisted of comprehensive reconstructions of individual cases before they were arranged on the map. In Calmette's research papers, we find a stack of individual case reports, each containing a detailed description of the clinical history of the patient, dates of the onset of the plague infection, descriptions of the symptoms, dates of mortality, and dates of convalescence for those who survived. Most importantly, Calmette (1900) noted when the serum was prescribed and its effects on the patients. The dates and fever curves were plotted onto graphs for each case. These representations of the cases, both descriptions and graphs,

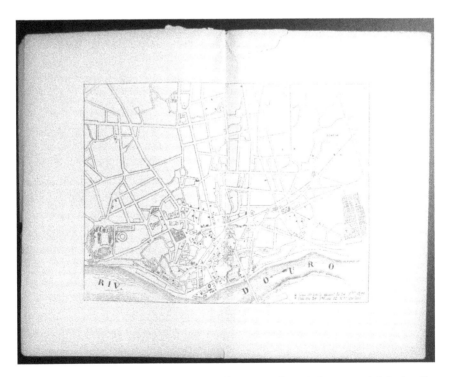

FIGURE 4.2: Dot map of the plague outbreak in Porto from Calmette and Salimbeni's report (Calmette 1900).

were then tied together through the map, where each case appears to be represented through a dot. The sketch of a spatial pattern of the epidemic had thus been transformed into the dot map printed in Calmette's report (see fig. 4.3).

At the time of the Pasteurians' report, the aesthetically inconspicuous spatial diagram was used in the visualization of many outbreaks of plague, as well as other diseases. Commonly referred to as dot maps—originating from the first and most famous one drawn by John Snow to show cholera in 1854 London—the form is built around the incidence of cases (Koch and Denike 2010; Snow 1855). With each dot representing a case, the nominative map produces a visual account of cases, placing them on the map to infer spatial and sometimes temporal patterns.

In the case of Calmette's map, nothing out of the ordinary can be observed. Similar to the diagram of Vetlianka, the outbreak is separated into two periods,

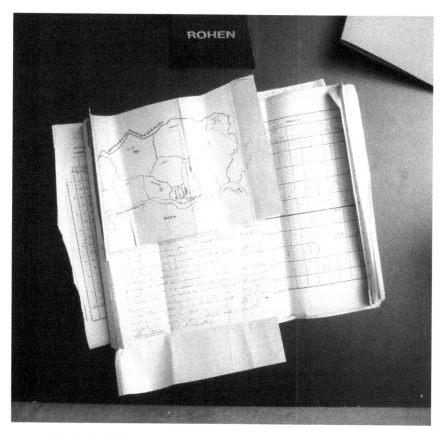

FIGURE 4.3: Archival photograph of the notes and graphs of Calmette's paperwork, stacked together with a map of Porto, in which the position of cases has been marked. Courtesy of Institut Pasteur, DR.OM 2, case files.

one dedicated to cases observed until 24 July 1899, and the other for all cases seen until 12 October of the same year. Calmette could clearly demonstrate that while the dense occurrence of cases in houses and *ilhas* close to the port might have originally suggested a configuration of plague as a disease of impoverished housing conditions, the second period's distribution across the city—and indeed across social divisions—rendered such framings fully inadequate. Instead, the message of this spatial diagram and its diagrammatic contribution to the discussions around Porto was simply to state that plague seemed to follow the exact same pattern in Europe as it did in comparable outbreaks—and maps of outbreaks—in India (Evans 2019).

The spatial diagram allowed Calmette to corroborate the characteristic distribution of plague known from previous outbreaks in non-white populations and to infer that the first modern occurrence of the disease in a white, European population seemed indeed to have no effect on the virulence of the bacteria. Instead, the spatial diagram supported the account of a non-specific spatial distribution of plague in European urban environments. This conclusion enabled Calmette to conveniently attribute the comparable harmlessness of the Porto outbreak not to the assumed superiority of the European race, nor to modern hygienic standards, but rather to the success of the serum therapy and thus to the triumphant intervention of the Pasteurians. The implied configuration of plague was one in which neither houses nor families or individuals were brought into a causal relation, but one in which the focus shifted onto other factors that could explain the spatial and temporal distribution of the disease. Almost in passing, Calmette and Salimbeni's report concluded that the role of rats, mice, and fleas deserved further investigation, as traces of these animals appeared to have a persistent presence around cases.[3]

What the Pasteurians established was a network of relations between the European hosts, the environment of a European port city, and the pathogen. The simple dot map presents here a configuration of three interlocking systems—the host, the environment, the pathogen—each considered to be a variable with the capacity to act on the other systems. Plague's visualization did not infer causality and origin; rather, it sought to establish the patterns and dynamics characteristic of the configuration that the epidemic implied. In Porto, Calmette and Salimbeni used the spatial diagram not to trace the pathogen or to identify its transmission pathways, but to visualize an expectable and repeatable pattern of plague that had been observed globally. Their spatial diagram definitely did not take on the position of an explanation of the epidemic: it failed to provide further information as to how the specific conditions of Porto or the *ilhas* might have influenced the spread of the disease. Instead, the diagram appears to have been an instrument of exploration and observation, through which the characteristic spatial pattern of plague was identified as configuration and thus effectively universalized.

Conclusion

Epidemics have always resisted definition, but since the mid-nineteenth century, doctors and public health officers have aimed to define the epidemic with the instruments and tools of modern scientific inquiry. The observation of epidemics like plague was often guided by the apparent phenomenon that the aggregate occurrence of a disease in a population seemed to be structured by laws and patterns that were different from an individual case of the same disease. However, these laws and patterns were notoriously elusive entities, and throughout the nineteenth century epidemiology struggled to earn the badge of a medical science by trying—and failing—to arrive at satisfying accounts of the networks, structures, patterns, and rhythms of epidemics. Nonetheless, the challenge of identifying repeatable, characteristic, and recognizable patterns was the principal aim of early epidemiologists' scholarly work. And spatial diagrams, I have argued here, not only supported these inductive epidemiological investigations. They also helped to establish the epidemic as an object of configuration, as a network of systems, and as an abstract entity—a series or pattern—that appeared within an environment, a population, or a combination of both.

In both cases of plague, the spatial diagrams were developed not to support theories of causality or to argue about attributable origins of the disease, but to advance a thinking of epidemics beyond monocausal and deductive explanations. Neither the always suspicious sanitary conditions nor the overwhelming attraction of bacteriological agency was privileged in the accounts of Minkh and of Calmette and Salimbeni. Both the Ukrainian doctor and the Pasteurians rejected simplified and popular explanations, choosing to propose, with their spatial diagrams, an alternative way of seeing that pointed beyond dated sanitary anxiety and resisted the allurement of the modern laboratory. Their work on the outbreaks in Vetlianka and in Porto insisted instead on the value of epidemics as unique configurations of a set of circumstances. Their tradition of epidemiological reasoning was committed to the exposure of the relations, the systems, and the networks between humans, animals, the material environment, climatic seasonality, historical conditions, and pathogens.

Diagrams enabled an epidemiological practice grounded in technologies of observation and conceptual combination, bringing topographies of a disease to bear on environmental and social characteristics of places. Through diagrams, epidemiologists were able to combine spatial and temporal dimensions, include hygienic considerations, develop aspects of population density and susceptibility, integrate notions of variable virulence, and express a notion of the epidemic as a configuration. In spatial diagrams, epidemiologists could render the epidemic as a conceptual entity, as an object of research that had accrued value for epidemiologists without needing to be an instrument that clarified causality or served as a blueprint for strategies of containment.

The intent of this chapter has been to reinvigorate a sense of the historical contingency of epidemiological reasoning and to showcase epidemiology's spatial diagram as an instrument of inductive reasoning with a broad range of disciplinary and theoretical capacity. In the spatial diagram we find traces of the radical epistemological indeterminacy that characterizes many of the endeavors of making an epidemiological science. I leave it to following research to trace the residues of this tradition in the epidemiological visualizations of today's global health and digital medicine. But epidemics like plague continue to resist being known as well-defined objects of inquiry, and their occurrence still poses serious challenges to the discipline that aims to master their observation, analysis, and representation (Kosoy and Kosoy 2017). This chapter has not attempted to deliver another, more comprehensive definition of epidemics, nor has it sought to remove the conceptual precariousness of epidemiology's object of research. Rather, I have argued that, in the case studies examined here, the status of the epidemic as a scientific object with blurred boundaries and contested ontologies required the representational capacities of the spatial diagram. The diagrams of Minkh and Calmette and Salimbeni framed and suspended the concept of an epidemic in an open-ended way that perhaps had no other purpose than to grasp the multi-layered, unusual, and inconclusive formation of the epidemic.

Acknowledgments

This chapter was initially developed for the 2016 conference "Diagrammatic: Beyond Inscription?" at CRASSH, and has profited substantially from the discussions at the meeting, as well as from collaborating with Caroline Humphrey and Christos Lynteris. The research leading to these results has received funding from the European Research Council under the European Union's Seventh Framework Programme (FP7/2007-2013)/ERC grant agreement number 336564.

Lukas Engelmann is a Senior Lecturer and Chancellor's Fellow in History and Sociology of Biomedicine at the University of Edinburgh. His work focuses on the history of epidemiological reasoning in the long twentieth century, and is funded by an ERC starting grant. Recent publications include *Mapping AIDS: Visual Histories of an Enduring Epidemic* (2018) and, co-authored with Christos Lynteris, *Sulphuric Utopias: A History of Maritime Fumigation* (2020).

Notes

1. These figures are probably not accurate case numbers as the city's mortality report sees a 20 percent increase for 1899 in Porto, suggesting at least another few hundred cases (Almeida 2013).
2. As with other vaccines developed at the Institut Pasteur, the serum was made by culturing attenuated bacteria in horses. The serum had only limited efficiency, and its capacity to immunize was and remained highly contested.
3. At that time, the animal vector of plague was still subject to speculation, but many were intrigued by the pivotal role of animal vectors in the distribution of the disease, adding yet another layer to the complex configuration of plague.

References

Almeida, Maria Antónia de. 2013. "Epidemics in the News: Health and Hygiene in the Press in Periods of Crisis." *Public Understanding of Science* 22 (7): 886–902.

Amsterdamska, Olga. 2004. "Achieving Disbelief: Thought Styles, Microbial Variation, and American and British Epidemiology, 1900–1940." *Studies in History and Philosophy of Science Part C: Studies in History and Philosophy of Biological and Biomedical Sciences* 35 (3): 483–507.

Amsterdamska, Olga. 2005. "Demarcating Epidemiology." *Science, Technology & Human Values* 30 (1): 17–51.

Bauer, Susanne. 2013. "Modeling Population Health: Reflections on the Performativity of Epidemiological Techniques in the Age of Genomics." *Medical Anthropology Quarterly* 27 (4): 510–530.

Caduff, Carlo. 2015. *The Pandemic Perhaps: Dramatic Events in a Public Culture of Danger.* Oakland: University of California Press.

Calmette, Albert. 1900. "The Plague at Oporto." *North American Review* 171 (524): 104–111.

Cohn, Samuel K., Jr. 2018. *Epidemics: Hate and Compassion from the Plague of Athens to AIDS.* New York: Oxford University Press.

Cunningham, Andrew. 1992. "Transforming Plague: The Laboratory and the Identity of Infectious Disease." In *The Laboratory Revolution in Medicine*, ed. Andrew Cunningham and Perry Williams, 209–244. Cambridge: Cambridge University Press.

Echenberg, Myron J. 2007. *Plague Ports: The Global Urban Impact of Bubonic Plague,1894–1901.* New York: New York University Press.

Evans, Nicholas H. A. 2019. "The Disease Map and the City: Desire and Imitation in the Bombay Plague, 1896–1914." In *Plague and the City*, ed. Lukas Engelmann, John Henderson, and Christos Lynteris, 116–138. New York: Routledge.

Harley, J. B. 1989. "Deconstructing the Map." *Cartographica* 26 (2): 1–20.

Heilbronner, Hans. 1962. "The Russian Plague of 1878–79." *Slavic Review* 21 (1): 89–112.

Hirsch, August, and M. Sommerbrodt. 1880. *Mittheilungen über die Pest-Epidemie im Winter 1878–1879, im russischen Gouvernement Astrachan* [Reports on the plague epidemic in the winter of 1878–1879 in the Russian district of Astrakhan]. Berlin: C. Heymann.

Hutchinson, John F. 1985. "Tsarist Russia and the Bacteriological Revolution." *Journal of the History of Medicine and Allied Sciences* 40 (4): 420–439.

Jorge, Ricardo. 1899. *La peste bubonique de Porto, 1899: Sa découverte, premiers travaux* [The bubonic plague in Porto, 1899: Its discovery, first measures]. Porto: Teixeira.

Koch, Tom. 2011. *Disease Maps: Epidemics on the Ground*. Chicago: University of Chicago Press.

Koch, Tom, and Ken Denike. 2010. "Essential, Illustrative, or … Just Propaganda? Rethinking John Snow's Broad Street Map." *Cartographica* 45 (1): 19–31.

Kosoy, Michael, and Roman Kosoy. 2017. "Complexity and Biosemiotics in Evolutionary Ecology of Zoonotic Infectious Agents." *Evolutionary Applications* 11 (4): 394–403.

Lawrence-Hamilton, J. 1875. "The Report of the Imperial German Medical Commission on the Plague Which Prevailed in the Province of Astrakhan during the Winter of 1878 and 1879." *Transactions of the Epidemiological Society of London* 4: 376–390.

Ljungberg, Christina. 2016. "The Diagrammatic Nature of Maps." In *Thinking with Diagrams: The Semiotic Basis of Human Cognition*, ed. Sybille Krämer and Christina Ljungberg, 139–159. Berlin: De Gruyter.

Lynteris, Christos. 2016. *Ethnographic Plague: Configuring Disease on the Chinese-Russian Frontier*. Basingstoke: Palgrave Macmillan.

Lynteris, Christos. 2017. "Zoonotic Diagrams: Mastering and Unsettling Human-Animal Relations." *Journal of the Royal Anthropological Institute* 23 (3): 463–485.

Mendelsohn, J. Andrew. 1998. "From Eradication to Equilibrium. How Epidemics Became Complex after World War I." In *Greater Than the Parts: Holism in Biomedicine, 1920–1950*, ed. Christopher Lawrence and George Weisz, 303–331. New York: Oxford University Press.

Mendelsohn, J. Andrew. 2002. "'Like All That Lives': Biology, Medicine and Bacteria in the Age of Pasteur and Koch." *History and Philosophy of the Life Sciences* 24 (1): 3–36.

Mikhel, Dmitry. 2018. "Чума и Эпидемиологическая Революция в России: 1897–1914" [Plague and epidemiological revolution in Russia, 1897–1914]. SSRN Scholarly Paper, 30 March. https://papers.ssrn.com/sol3/papers.cfm?abstract_id=3153128.

Minkh, G. N. 1898. *Chuma v Rossii (Vetlyanskaya Épidemiya 1878–1879gg.)* [Plague in Russia (epidemic of Vetlianska 1878–1879)]. Kiev.

Monmonier, Mark. 2010. "Maps as Graphic Propaganda for Public Health." In *Imagining Illness: Public Health and Visual Culture*, ed. David Serlin, 108–125. Minneapolis: University of Minnesota Press.

Opitz, Sven. 2017. "Simulating the World: The Digital Enactment of Pandemics as a Mode of Global Self-Observation." *European Journal of Social Theory* 20 (3): 392–416.

Parascandola, Mark. 1998. "Epidemiology: Second-Rate Science?" *Public Health Reports* 113 (4): 312–320.

Pirogovskaya, Maria. 2014. "The Plague at Vetlyanka, 1878–1879: The Discourses and Practices of Hygiene and the History of Emotions." *Forum for Anthropology and Culture* 10: 133–164.

Radcliffe, J. Netten. 1881. "Memorandum on the Progress of the Levantine Plague." In *Ninth Annual Report of the Local Government Board 1879–80*, Supplement, 1–89. London: Spottiswoode.

Rheinberger, Hans-Jörg. 1999. "Experimental Systems: Historiality, Narration, and Deconstruction." In *The Science Studies Reader*, ed. Mario Biagioli, 417–429. New York: Routledge.

Rosenberg, Charles E. 1992. *Explaining Epidemics and Other Studies in the History of Medicine*. Cambridge: Cambridge University Press.

Snow, John. 1855. *On the Mode of Communication of Cholera*. 2nd ed. London: John Churchill.

Vidler, Anthony. 2000. "Diagrams of Diagrams: Architectural Abstraction and Modern Representation." *Representations* 72: 1–20.

Zuber, Hubert-Jules César. 1880. "Rapport sur une missione médicale en Russie: La peste du gouvernement d'Astrakhan" [Report on a medical mission in Russia: The plague in the district of Astrakhan]. In *Recueil des travaux du Comité Consultatif d'Hygiène Publique de France et des actes officiels de l'Administration Sanitaire* [Collection of the works of the French Public Hygiene Advisory Committee and Official Acts of the Health Administration] 9, 87–167. Paris: A. Lahure.

Chapter 5

A NOMADIC DIAGRAM
Waddington's Epigenetic Landscape and Anthropology

Caroline Humphrey

It had been argued, against the representational visual regime of a naively empiricist notion of science, that the diagram should be seen as a hybrid between ideas and perceptions, acting as a 'working object'. Such objects do not "duplicate a reality external to them, nor are [they] entirely the result of pure imagination, but somehow fall productively between the two" (Daston and Galison, referenced in Jay 2010–2011: 158). This idea applies well to the biologist Conrad Hal Waddington's epigenetic landscape (EL) diagrams from the 1950s, which depict the process of cell development. Waddington's path-breaking conceptual legacy has been tied closely to what has been called his 'pictorial methodology'. Both of these have been controversial, but lately they have had a wide and renewed impact throughout the life sciences and certain branches of sociology and anthropology. Indeed, they have migrated even further, being taken up in the emergent fields of graphic medicine, landscape architecture, and

Notes for this chapter begin on page 127.

bioArt (Squier 2017; Terranova 2017), the sustainability of technological inno-
vations (Baedke 2013: 763), and a move from topology to the nature of catastrophic form in ecosystemic change (Petryna and Mitchell 2017). This chapter
will trace a particular path relevant to sociology and anthropology amid this
welter of applications. It will focus on the graphic character of the EL diagrams,
explaining first how the diagrammatic form produced scientific working objects
for Waddington himself, then briefly discussing some of the social and disciplinary pressures that led to his temporary abandonment of this kind of diagram,
and finally addressing their reprise in anthropology both as working tools and
as inspirational schema in recent years.

Waddington expressed his ideas about genetics in prose in scientific articles
and books, but it seems to have been specifically the EL diagrams and the 'epigenetic landscape' metaphor that traveled so well, migrating far beyond their
initial fields to completely different academic domains, including the social
sciences. Attempts have recently been made to account for the 'allure' and compelling quality of Waddington's diagrams (Allen 2015), but they have neither
specified which of the many kinds of diagrams he employed had such magne-
tism, nor identified who was attracted to them. This chapter will suggest that
many of the diagrams scattered through Waddington's works were not alluring
at all—that they were irritatingly difficult to decipher or were useful only to certain groups of scientists. Instead, what needs to be explained is the fertility and
reusable quality of two 'iconic' EL diagrams in particular. Unlike Waddington's
prose explanations, which were subtle, complex, and of course changed over
his career, these diagrams were iconic in the sense that they seemed to represent
something important beyond the image and yet something that was 'done' by
it—not by words but by graphic means. I will suggest that their relative simplicity, and for that reason their enigmatic quality, has been agentive in their
capacity for mobility. Attempting to account for this, I will later discuss Isabelle
Stengers's (1987) notion of 'nomadic concepts' (ideas that move between scientific disciplines). However, I will shift attention from the ideas themselves to
what it is about the form in which they are expressed (in this case, diagrams)
that makes them apt for mobility and reinvigoration in new environments.

Looking at Waddington's use of visual materials, one can picture a spectrum
ranging between the illustration and the diagram. By illustration I refer to a
representational visual depiction of something, an image that uses naturalistic
artistic means to make that object or idea clear and vivid. A diagram, on the
other hand, is intended to explain rather than represent; it is a graphic mode
that uses radical simplification to show the workings of something and/or the
relations between parts. The diagram indeed may be constitutive. In architecture, for example, it has been suggested that "the diagram has become 'the
matter of architecture' itself, as opposed to its representation" (Somol, cited in
Vidler 2000: 5). In the field of embryology, this may also be true of the role of

the EL diagrams in Waddington's innovative theory of cell development. Yet it will be argued here that one reason why these diagrams have been inspirational in other, even non-biological fields is that, while condensing a complex idea into a simple explanatory image, they also retain a certain illustrative character. They seem to depict a 'scene', and they require the viewer to imagine the completion of a process about to take place in it. The visual and conceptual affordances of these diagrams can set off a process of imaginative 'work' in a new field. By imagination I refer here to a creative response to the suggestion that the EL diagrams make out of a series of possible definite but as-yet-to-be-determined metamorphoses of entities in time. This will be shown by contrasting the open-ended character of epigenetic landscape diagrams with more schematic or prescriptive diagrams, which serve rather to foreclose options.

Arriving at the Epigenetic Landscape Diagrams

There is no need for a complicated idea to be represented diagrammatically. Mattei Candea observes (this book) that scientists, including anthropologists, have often opted for other forms of representation, such as mathematical formulae. We could also mention alternatives such as tables, pie charts, hand sketches, series of images that depict sequential changes, cartoons, or pictorial illustrations. The advantage of a diagram is that it demonstrates multiple relations in the simplest possible way, using graphic conventions that the viewer is expected to understand. The method, of course, can be disadvantageous too. The diagram is always a construct of "semiotic flattening" on a formatted surface (Krämer and Ljungberg 2016: 1): it may be too simple for a given problem, and its conventions may be misinterpreted or misleading in a given context. Nevertheless, when a really new idea is afoot, the diagram is a very efficacious way of getting it across to the uninitiated, especially in the visually oriented Euro-American culture. It is also a cognitively intense way for the author to work on and hone the concept itself.

This 'working toward the idea' was the problem of representation that faced Waddington. Born in 1905, he trained as a geologist and explored the philosophy of evolutionary change before moving into developmental biology at the beginning of the 1930s. At the time, there was a scientific and institutional gap between genetics and embryology—that is, between the study of the inheritance and expression of genes and that of the development of a pluripotent embryo into cells with specific functions in the adult body, the phenotype. Waddington was in search of ideas to found a developmental biology that would reconcile them. What was startling and controversial about his new theory was that it was synthetic: it suggested that the emerging specificity of cells is determined not just by their own initial genetic make-up as a set of factors that play themselves out, but also by the potentialities arising from their organizing arrangement and interactions during their development, as seen in position effects, translocations, inversions, and so forth. This process could "give rise to new types of tissue and organ not present originally" (Waddington 1935: 154–155; see also Nicoglou 2018: 7–9). In effect, this was to set the scene for his later argument about the importance of environmental effects experienced over time during cell development. Waddington was to coin the word 'epigenetic' (i.e., beyond genetic) to express this set of ideas.

In the 1930s, and again after the interruption of the war, Waddington was dissatisfied with what he saw as unrealistic 'atomist' models of gene selection and trait evolution. He felt that the neo-Darwinians of the time had wrongly neglected the phenomenon of extensive and highly complex gene interactions that mitigate the effect of dominant individual genes. He therefore argued that the modeling of the development of cells, eggs, and embryos should be probabilistic or stochastic, rather than deterministic. But this was long before gene sequencing, and it was impossible to render such a dynamic process mathematically. This impracticability is one reason why Waddington's ideas were ignored or bypassed by most conventional geneticists of the time. He went ahead, however, convinced that in this situation visual representations as a complex whole could be useful, not as records of experiments, but as intuitive maps of the way things might be, which would suggest avenues for research. Waddington (1940: 11) thought of 'landscape' as a metaphor, a new virtual domain for envisioning "the whole complex system of actions and interactions which constitute differentiation." The differentiation he was after was the channeling of the development of cells/eggs/embryos into varied, highly specific forms over time.

However, it took some time for him to arrive at a diagram of such a process. In fact, the frontispiece to Waddington's (1940) book *Organisers and Genes* was an illustration, a moody quasi-naturalistic painting by his friend the artist John Piper, which depicted a river flowing between the craggy banks of one main and several side channels (fig. 5.1). Far from diagrammatic schematization, this image includes lowering clouds, a distant sea, and what look like bramble bushes in a terrain reminiscent of the Yorkshire fells. The idea, though, was to represent, by means of the tumbling river, a temporal process in a visual form. Waddington wanted to convey his thought that cell development, like the flowing river, is a classical philosophical paradox: the cell changes and grows over time under diverse influences, and yet it remains the same entity. It seems to be this paradox that is represented in the impossibility depicted by Piper, for his river appears to flow in two directions: both 'upward' into the sea and 'downward' toward the viewer.[1] His image looks like an illustration and not at all like a diagram, yet it forces the viewer to try to work out what is going on.

The disciplinary conventions of biological science in mid-twentieth-century Britain were not able to accept anything like Piper's confusing painting, which

FIGURE 5.1: The epigenetic landscape. Illustration by John Piper (frontispiece to Waddington 1940).

in any case did not clearly indicate Waddington's idea. A diagram was called for. Waddington had already tried to represent developmental mutations and reactions by branching-track diagrams, which looked not unlike railway tracks[2] or kinship genealogies (Allen 2015; Gilbert 1991). But the problem with this was that the two dimensions and over-linear, over-definite final points could not express what Waddington knew was a multi-dimensional process, one that occurred in time with probabilistic outcomes. Next, he tried a phase-space diagram of development from egg to adult, which at least included the time dimension (fig. 5.2). But the bare box did not indicate the encompassing environment in which the cell develops, and even with this reduction the image was complicated to read and understand.

It was not until 17 years after the Piper painting that the 'classic' epigenetic landscape (EL1) took shape in Waddington's (1957) *The Strategy of the Genes*, this time in diagrammatic form (fig. 5.3). The caption for the EL1 figure reads: "The path followed by the ball as it rolls down toward the spectator corresponds

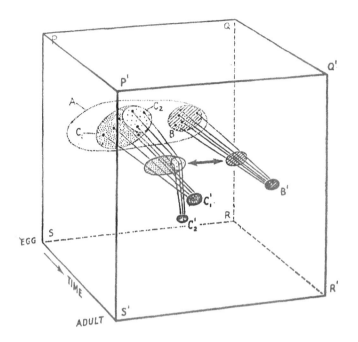

FIGURE 5.2: Phase-space box diagram (Waddington 1957: 28).

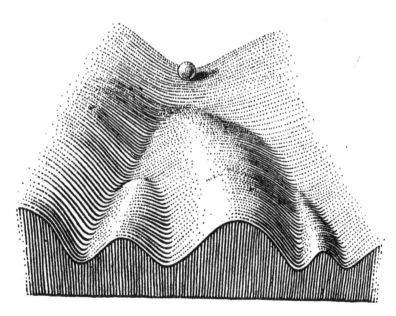

FIGURE 5.3: Epigenetic landscape EL1 (Waddington 1957: 29).

to the developmental history of a particular part of the egg. There is first an alternative, toward the right or the left. Along the former path, a second alternative is offered; along the path to the left, the main channel continues leftwards, but there is an alternative path which, however, can only be reached over a threshold" (ibid.: 29). Here, the undulating surface is tilted to indicate time, so that points representing later states are lower than those representing earlier ones. If something such as a ball (denoting a cell or an egg) were placed on the surface, it would run down toward some end state along the bottom edge. Yet this classic EL image does not indicate the possible differentiations at the final point.

In an earlier paper, when working on drosophila, Waddington had written "wing," "upper leg," "lower leg," "antennae", and so on at the end of each 'valley' in the landscape, indicating the final development of each type of tissue or organ (see Waddington et al. 1954). However, the greater specificity via labeling of this early image paradoxically made the diagram more difficult to interpret, since it was not clear if the balls at the top represented eggs or cells, or whether they ended up as differentiated cells or different types of cells. In addition, it was difficult to understand what process of development could lead from a single cell to 'typical' organs, since organs are composed of several different kinds of cells. This earlier version of the EL has remained unnoticed and unquoted (Nicoglou 2018: 14).

Abandoning labeling inside the diagram, Waddington was after a more general idea. One advantage of his easy-to-read classic image is that the visualization of development along channels can represent several processes at once—the influence on the cell of its surroundings, the robustness of its own genetic programming, and its own effects on its environment. The end states are differentiated; yet with alteration (tilting) in the landscape, the ball may roll slightly up one 'hillside' but itself compensate for this disturbance by falling back into the same 'valley' it would have normally run down. The invention of this image certainly helped Waddington to convey—and probably also to crystallize conceptually for himself—the new theoretical concepts he was proposing: 'canalization' (the ability to sustain a developmental direction despite environmental disruptions), 'homeorhesis' (the process by which the developing organism stabilizes its different cell lineages while it is still constructing itself),[3] and 'temporal and spatial scaling' (the perceptual/conceptual properties that enable the model to be applicable to both cellular differentiation and organismal development). Along with canalization and homeorhesis, Waddington, coined a further new term, 'chreode',[4] for the dedicated developmental pathways. What is significant for this chapter is that although these ideas have been influential, most of the words Waddington invented have not. The scientific neologisms fell into the waste bin of discarded attempts at biological theorizing, but the visual condensation of the ideas in the diagram has borne fruit in diverse fields, as I will indicate later.

But what are the constituents and workings of this 'landscape' in which the entity develops? Waddington (1957: 35) explains that its surface contours are dependent on an underlying network of interactions that is vastly more complicated. The EL2 diagram is Waddington's attempt to visualize this idea (fig. 5.4).[5] We (the viewers) are situated in the opposite position from the perspective of the first diagram. Here we are under the top 'initial' rim of the landscape, which floats above our heads and slopes down toward the 'end state' in the distance. The pegs represent genes and the guy-ropes represent the interacting chemical forces of these genes in the environment of the cell (or, at a different scale, of the fertilized egg). In this way, the surface of the landscape is shown to be not like fixed rock but more like a membrane, an undulating and topologically shifting surrounding, affected by the chemical tendencies of a myriad of interacting genes.

What was particularly unwelcome to standard genetics was not just the idea that how a gene expresses itself will not depend on that gene alone but on multiple networks and feedback processes. Equally unwelcome was Waddington's more radical decoupling of variations in the end result (the phenotype) from genetic variations, since he held that external environmental effects along the way, such as heat or chemical additions, also shape the landscape epigenetically. To take a simple example, the differences between a worker bee

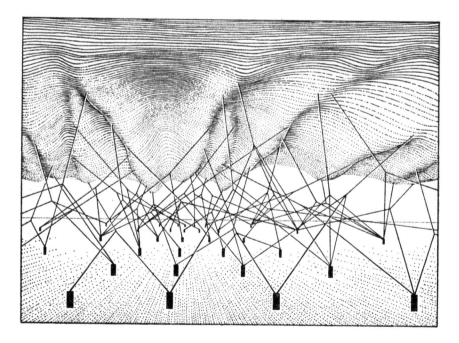

FIGURE 5.4: The underside of the epigenetic landscape EL2 (Waddington 1957: 36).

and a queen bee are epigenetic, not genetic, because whether a larva becomes a worker or a queen depends on the way that it is fed during development (Jablonka and Lamb 2002: 86). Plasticity—the ability of a single genotype to generate variant forms of morphology, physiology, or behavior—was therefore a key idea. Plasticity can be limited and predictable, such as seasonal changes in color, but it can also involve unpredictable, novel adaptive responses, such as when animals learn new behavior (Tavory et al. 2012). Waddington conducted a series of experiments showing that environmental shocks during development could result in inheritable genetic changes. As a result of this work on 'genetic assimilation', he increasingly came to see the 'thing' in his landscape (the cell, the fertilized egg, the embryo) as agentive, not inert.

Note that both of the EL diagrams retain a certain illustrative quality. They use the graphic technique of hatching, familiar from centuries of engraving in Western art, to depict distance, roundness, and shadows, and thus also to depict the crucial 'threshold' at which a cell might swerve from one path into another. The images also seem to convey the idea of 'horizons' and therefore to suggest a hilly 'landscape' that reaches toward them. Matthew Allen (2015: 132) argues that the stylized hatching technique was employed by Waddington to communicate not artistic license but rather the scientist's precise experimental control. However, this seems far-fetched if one considers the conventional diagrams in biological publications at the time. As I will now explain, for the scientific community Waddington's EL diagrams were deemed *not diagrammatic enough*.

Temporary Retreat from EL Diagrams

The rise of molecular biology from the 1960s onward, with its single gene focus, seemed to have put an end to Waddington's ideas. In attempting to unite embryology and genetics, Waddington was in fact trying to bridge a divide between two disciplines that had utterly different conceptual premises. The geneticists of the 1930s and the molecular geneticists of the 1960s to 1990s prized a reductionist account of biology. Scientific credibility in these fields was tied to the possibility of minimalizing the entities considered and formalizing their relations—a prospect that was likely if an organism could be explained in terms of its genes alone. Embryologists, on the other hand, were holistic thinkers. Commenting on this, Donna Haraway (1976) argued that the organism in its totality is as essential to an explanation of its elements as its elements are to an explanation of the organism. And Waddington was concerned even more broadly, not just with this end state totality, but with the evolution of developmental mechanisms and the plasticity of the phenotype in different environmental conditions. Such seemingly extraneous, irresolvable plurality was too much for most mainstream scientists. Waddington's diagrams were derided as 'metaphorical' and inexact. As the historian of science Scott Gilbert (1991: 151) puts it: "Even today, formal model building is not the forte of developmental biology. Moreover, given that the channels and spheres had no physical reality, what was an embryologist supposed to do with them? Very little. They cannot be purified, transplanted, cloned, or localized with a monoclonal antibody."

Through Jacob and Monod's (1961) analysis of the *lac* operon,[6] the first genetic regulatory mechanism was discovered and understood clearly. After this, mainstream molecular biology abandoned holistic epigenetic ideas. Indeed, Waddington himself was important in promoting the new direction as he helped introduce the operon model into developmental biology: "Here were chemicals that determined which path a cell was to take. With lactose in its environment, the bacterium produced one set of enzymes; without lactose, they synthesized another set" (Gilbert 1991: 151). As Susan Squier (2017: 38) observes, Waddington's temporary withdrawal from holism and complexity coincided with his semi-retreat from Whitehead's philosophy as a key inspiration and his immersion in orthodox experimental science. Later, Waddington (1969: 81) was to explain the socio-institutional circumstances that led his shift in focus—the bullying, Alpha-male professors and the high prestige of conventional science—when he wrote: "Since I am an unaggressive character, and was living in an aggressively anti-metaphysical period, I chose not to expound publicly these philosophical views." Squier (2017: 38) concludes that by opting for a more conventional approach and excluding affect and context from his scientific work, Waddington was backing away from the implications of his own concept (of epigenetics), narrowing and closing down its potential applications. Certainly, *lac* operon diagrams seem designed not to allow for imaginative expansion. They consist of straight lines labeled DNA with color patches representing inhibitor and activator genes and proteins, and they are festooned with arrows, standard shapes, and texts detailing the precise process going on.

However, in the late 1960s to 1970s, Waddington returned to an enhanced version of his EL framework, taking into account the more explicit advances made by the operon model. To do this, he reinterpreted the EL in terms of an 'attractor' surface backed up by topological approaches from mathematics.[7] This version, he argued, should be able to mathematize and quantify complex phenomena in development without succumbing to reductionism (Baedke 2013: 759). Even so, in his book *Tools for Thought*, Waddington (1977: 112) illustrated this idea with a defiantly swirly and non-arithmetical sketch made by his friend the artist Yolanda Sonnabend.

From the 1990s onward, the meaning of the term 'epigenetics' took on new contours in the context of molecular biology and the mapping of the human genome (Speybroeck 2002). However, the euphoria of the idea that the genome would explain everything soon collapsed. After it became clear that simple genetic programming could not account for particular outcomes, that there was no one gene X for effect Y, it was gradually recognized that epigenetics would be an expanding subdiscipline of biology. Today, the field of 'genetics' deals with the transmission and processing of information in DNA, while 'epigenetics' (although its definition is disputed) is generally held to deal with the effects of the integration of DNA information with non-genetic sources and the question of whether such changes are hereditable. Epigenetics in this sense, which is mostly laboratory-based and focused on hereditability, has wide practical applications, ranging from epigenetic changes responsible for cancers to epidemiology, cloning, agriculture, and plant science (Jablonka and Lamb 2002). The focus of this contemporary epigenetics is so different from Waddington's idea that there have been calls to abandon the word. But there are many other terms in biology (e.g., Johanssen's 'gene', Bateson's 'genetics', the concept of the 'organism') that have remained key concepts despite changes of meaning (ibid.: 88; Wolfe 2014). The meanings of such terms not only transform within a disciplinary network, but are subject to constant reification, transfer, and translation as they move across disciplines and non-scientific domains. As of today, the word 'epigenetics' is a catch-all term covering many different approaches.

Repurposed Landscape Diagrams in the Natural Sciences

In the 1960s and 1970s, Waddington's landscape imagery was taken up outside biology by the mathematician René Thom in his work on catastrophe theory. The two men were in close contact, and Thom used the image of mountains, watersheds, and river valleys to help him create a topological theory that could then develop a mathematical language to demonstrate the 'thresholds' that might signal abrupt change, for example, potential catastrophe (Baedke 2013). Adriana Petryna and Paul Mitchell (2017) have described how Thom's theory, despite a period of criticism, has recently returned in a revised form that is highly relevant to today's 'abrupt change science' and to the analysis of unforeseen ecosystemic behaviors.

Long after Waddington's death in 1975, the now separate discipline of developmental biology revived not so much his specific theories or terminology as the interactive approach suggested by his EL diagrams. Stem cell biology showed that cells could be reprogrammed and thus de- and transdifferentiated. Waddington's diagrams did not distinguish between pathways of differentiation and reprogramming, but his EL1 image was apt for later biologists to adapt in order to depict the new 'phenomenon-to-be-explained' (see fig. 8 in Baedke 2013: 764). It was the 'valleys' (canalization) of the EL1 diagram that now enabled the conceptualization of a new variety of developmental pathways, including, for example, reverse, transverse, repositioned, and stochastic tracks, which took on new explanatory functions. In an article entitled "Quantifying Waddington's Epigenetic Landscape," Shi et al. (2018) took on the task of estimating the differentiation potential of single cells based on experiments with mouse and human cells. They used a redrawn version of EL1 to illustrate how mathematical models that integrated single-cell RNA-sequence data with complex signaling processes involving protein interaction networks could produce robust, quantifiable potency estimates. In developmental psychology, it was the graphic technique of hatching to produce a 'landscape' of curves and hollows that was deployed to represent dynamic change over time. Each hatching line forming the surface of the landscape could represent a particular stage-change and indicate a number of incremental cognitive and behavioral developmental possibilities. One such EL1-like image (see fig. 7 in Baedke 2013: 763) has initiated its own pictorial tradition and has been used extensively in fields such as locomotor development and language development. Computer graphics have been used in an extraordinarily diverse number of fields to produce EL modifications, adding colors, graded surfaces, and three-dimensional perspectives. The continued generation of new EL diagrams shows that the original EL images, which demanded that the viewer visualize what was *not* depicted (what was going to happen to that ball?), were almost 'magical' spurs to creative imagination for diverse scientists. An example of such projective visualization is a recent diagram to explain genetic variation that almost playfully depicts what would happen to the surface in EL2 if pairs of scissors lurked among the guy-ropes: it would balloon here and sag there, when one or another of the guy-ropes is snipped (Paaby and Rockman 2014: 250; for further references, see Baedke 2013).

The EL Diagram as a 'Nomadic Concept'

The idea of 'nomadic concepts' has undergone serious change since Isabelle Stengers first introduced it in 1987. She used the term to denote the trajectory of general concepts like 'complexity' or 'correlation' as they moved from hard into soft sciences or vice versa, and she was concerned with the question of whether they kept the same meaning. But since then, post-colonial and feminist theory has redefined the idea of 'the nomad' by attending to the encroachment and violence committed by—as well as experienced by—nomads. Stengers's nomadic concept has been rephrased more prosaically as 'shorthand theory', referring to an idea that is underdetermined but at the same time carries certain information as it moves into a new setting and can be a valuable tool for innovation (Surman et al. 2014: 128). The later literature suggests that cross-disciplinary transfers usually work through 'hard' or intrusive metaphors or analogies, such as the machine metaphor when used to conceptualize living systems. It was pointed out that machine thinking has been pervasive in developmental biology and evolution, for example, in the understanding of natural selection as an engineer or watchmaker. Another example that has been accused of 'epistemic violence' is the invasion of the legal metaphor of 'inheritance' into biology (ibid.). In another direction, as it were, Haraway (1991) showed that some concepts and areas of modern biology, for instance, the clone, the cyborg, or nanotechnology, were influenced by ideas that arose first in science fiction.

So how has 'epigenetic landscape' fared as a nomad when it appears in the domains of sociology and anthropology? Far from being a hard or conquering idea, it has crept rather modestly into only certain fields. To see why this is so, we need to distinguish the Waddingtonian EL from the most common notion of 'epigenetics' found in contemporary social sciences. The latter, as mentioned earlier, is understood as the study of inheritable environmental chemical modifications to DNA and their impact, and it has become a sizable anthropological subfield. Such studies investigate environmental pressures, such as malnutrition, migration, psychologically damaging events, and so forth, and ask whether these produce 'epigenetic marks' that are carried down through generations.[8] Waddington's epigenetic landscape is more or less absent from such studies.

In contrast, there are some studies of social change/stasis over time in which it is indeed Waddington's EL1 diagram that is the inspiration. The diagram in this case acts to mediate between a problem in embryology and a quite different set of social data by visualizing certain shared background assumptions. These include assuming an undifferentiated starting point, the potential to develop along multiple trajectories, and termination at different end states in a dynamical system operating over time. An example of such work is Tavory et al. (2014), which describes how the EL1 diagram is heuristically useful in conceptualizing the causal processes and outcomes of persistent urban poverty. The authors do not deal with genes as such, but rather base their analysis on the dynamics of self-sustaining feedback interactions among multiple resources, schemas, and activities that lead to the channeling of a social pattern over time. Then they look at temporal departures from this tendency to persistence. They argue that this approach is necessitated by the fact that ongoing urban poverty over generations is a highly complex phenomenon with multiple structural causes, but it is also influenced by interaction with people in other socio-economic positions and by institutional interventions. Since some people escape from poverty, it cannot be understood deterministically. Yet there is a tendency for relatively stable cross-generational outcomes: most poor people's descendants remain poor. This, they argue, can be conceptualized via the EL1 as a dynamically stable path of canalization that people tend to 'flow' into if they are born poor. Figure 5.5 shows two alternative social paths leading to an end 'attractor state', A or B, with the width of the arrow indicating the probability of following a given path. Individuals may develop

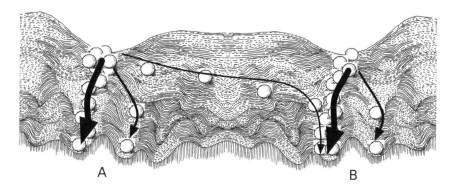

FIGURE 5.5: A social developmental landscape (Tavory et al. 2014: fig 14.2).

along different trajectories, usually ending up reproducing something like the end attractor state. Movement between attractors is also possible.

Tavory et al.'s (2014) explanation of their 'social landscape' introduces several differences from Waddington's initial idea: first, it works at a group and not an individual developmental level; second, the underlying peg and guy-ropes are *constitutive* of the landscape, not external causal inputs; and, third, the constitutive resources that interact are not made up of the same 'fabric' but belong to different domains (genetic, epigenetic, ecological, institutional, symbolic, linguistic, etc.). The advantage to sociology of this rejigged idea is that it offers a way of conceptualizing a 'landscape' of constraints and possibilities (composed by the diverse, interactive fabrics) that offers opportunities as time passes, and that also, when some 'decision' has been made, tends to push the most diverse actors, from drug dealers to formal economy minimum wage earners, back into stable channels of disadvantage.

Tavory et al. (2012, 2014) compare their approach with several other social science explanations for the stability of social forms, such as cultural influence models, meme analysis, and evolutionary and ecological theories. They focus in particular on Sperber's work on the evolution of cultural representations, which proposes that cognitive biases and cultural products are the 'attractors' that pull actors back into the channels. But they argue that their approach is more capable of dealing with the heterogeneous make-up of the landscape and the complexity of the trajectories of individuals within the group, and that it is better at asking questions about how different practical activities create trajectories that end up in the same hollows (attractor states). Essentially, in this case the EL diagrams work to suggest that there are analogies between developmental and socio-cultural processes that are helpful in understanding problems of order and the dynamic persistence of certain group patterns over time—an approach that has been used to inspire several ethnographic studies.[9] The crucial ideas here are feedback mechanisms, co-regulation, and self-sustaining interactions within the networks that sustain social landscapes, all ideas derived in inspiration from the EL1 and EL2 diagrams (Tavory et al. 2014: 313).

Note that in the hands of these authors, the landscape diagram itself is still a working object: it is 'peopled' by the multiplication of the balls nestling in 'valleys' (fig. 5.5), thus retaining an illustrative quality to the image. However, the wider imaginative potential given by grace of the simplicity of the original diagram has been lost. Now, with a thicket of lines, dots, balls, and arrows, the viewer is instructed what to think. Waddington's EL1 was a diagram of potentiality in the strong sense of the term. Once it had migrated into this branch of sociology, the diagram became overdetermined. It does express the authors' argument, but through over-inscription, its potential for further migration has evaporated.

Another trend in anthropology takes up a broad encompassment of both 'epigenetics' as it is now usually understood in the social sciences and the Waddingtonian 'landscape' approach, melding them together. The main aim has been to achieve analytical/programmatic/ethical accounts that address the question of how anthropology should proceed in the age of the Anthropocene. There are many important ideas here, which I can do no more than sketch. They take up the idea of the mutual interaction of biological development, the environment, and the social suggested by Waddington's later concept of epigenetics and invent new terms to express this. They suggest, for example, that 'nature' and 'nurture' are indistinguishable, that human variation occurs in 'situated biologies', and that the unit of analysis should be 'embedded bodies' or 'biosocial beings'—or even 'biosocial becomings' (Ingold and Palsson 2013)—that take part in 'naturecultures'.[10] The notion of 'landscape' in some of this work is expanded to align with Canguilhem's idea of the 'milieu', which is explicitly opposed to biological reductionism, being, as Lock and Palsson (2016: 157) characterize it, "a restless nature/nurture comingling of global proportions, one that never holds still in large part because of our ceaseless tinkering." These authors argue that while the 'miniaturization' of the idea of the environment found in mainstream epigenetics may work to pinpoint some effect inside an individual body, it results in an unfortunate tendency to neglect the larger impact of historical trauma, social inequality, and other political and economic variables that can contribute to epigenetic effects (ibid.: 98).

Finally, it is important to note that the field for thought proposed by the combination of EL1 and EL2—of processes of change over time taking place within a shifting 'landscape' made up of complex interactions—also enabled new approaches to be taken in evolutionary thinking in anthropology. Waddington's (1959) own application of his concept to human developmental potentialities and his thoughts about how these related to evolution (including cultural evolution) have been among several factors influencing the emergence of 'relational' evolutionary approaches in anthropology. A survey by Emily Schultz (2009) describes how these ideas have been attractive to anthropologists like Tim Ingold (1986, 2007), who were dissatisfied with the current 'neo-Darwinian' hegemony and seeking more holistic frameworks.

Conclusion

I would like to conclude by returning to the varied affordances of the diagram as a working object. Discussing the twentieth-century architectural maxim 'form follows function', Philip Steadman (1979: 198) observes that however many functions the designer brings to the table, he nevertheless "must bring some *specific* proposed form, some design hypothesis, into conjunction with its context before he may embark on any testing and evaluation," or draw the plans for any actual building. This observation leads to the question, what kind of thought process produces this initial design as an outcome?

Matthew Allen suggests (2015: 135), I think rightly, that Waddington's shifting descriptions of the epigenetic landscape should be seen as part of a conversation spanning decades between himself and his colleagues (or the institution of science more generally). Thinking about the invention of EL1 and EL2 in this light, it is interesting to recall that experimentation with various ways of visually grasping embryonic development went back and forth among the members of the Theoretical Biology Club in the 1930s. Joseph Needham, for example, invented a way of depicting Waddington's 1932 experiments on cell increase during bird embryo development by crafting a mountain-like model out of plaster, with the wider base of the mountain representing the great number of cells (Baedke 2013: 758). From this to John Piper's craggy painting was but a step visually, but the channeled movement of the river flow in the latter attempted to represent what was a conceptual breakthrough for Waddington. As I have argued, these initial visualizations involved the depth and extraneous complexity characteristic of illustration. Yet something resembling Steadman's '*specific* proposed form' was already present in the Piper painting. In the decision to shift away from this to the diagram, we see the importance of representational choices.

Waddington's two best-known EL diagrams are deliberately simple and condensed, yet at the same time open-ended. In this they differ from his later, more complicated diagrams of the same processes. Allen has likened the effect of the latter to Alfred Gell's (1998: 83) notion of "mind-traps," which we experience as "pleasurable frustration" when attempting to decipher, for example, the pattern of "an intricate oriental carpet." Trying to match up the features of an analogical diagram to concrete biological phenomena, Allen (2015: 138) suggests, is a similarly frustrating, pleasurable, and productive mental exercise.

But whatever Waddington may have intended to suggest, the EL diagrams are condensers of theory, not biological facts, and what they 'do' is open questions. Originally viewed as a 'dissident' step in biological theory (Schultz 2009: 227–228), they were often reproduced as a kind of historic icon in textbooks. However, as this chapter has shown, the questions they raised continued to be interesting, with the result that the diagrams were endlessly worked upon, tweaked, reprogrammed, and adapted to cope with different scientific problems. I have suggested that because EL diagrams retained certain illustrative graphic techniques and perspectives, they offered affordances, not only for non-verbal understanding, but also for visually imagined inventiveness. They therefore had advantages compared to the overspecific aridity of the *lac* operon diagram and to modes of verbal description.

When these diagrams nomadized out of biology into different fields, such as anthropology and sociology, another process was set in motion. No longer adaptable blueprints, the diagrams can perhaps best be seen as a 'means of transportation' of a set of ideas from one context to another—nomads on horses, as it were. Asked to deal with utterly different materials and processes, these transporters retain traces of their old forms and meanings while becoming subject to the tension brought about by new kinds of evaluation. Charles Wolfe (2014) has aptly written on the 'organism' as one such go-between concept. The organism as an idea was invoked as 'natural' by some thinkers to justify their metaphysics; however, laden with its academic history, it was presented by others as over and against the natural world (ibid.: 151).

A similar distinction applies to the recent fate of Waddington's epigenetic landscape. In Tavory et al.'s and similar studies, the epigenetic landscape is a metaphor for talking about the way a social situation is actually (i.e., 'naturally') molded. But in the hands of anthropologists like Lock and Palsson, the epigenetic landscape becomes something different, more like an ancient foundational charter that is scientifically completely out of date, but precious for the values it seems to represent when used to convey the openness and variability of life processes. Even so, the ghostly presence of the two diagrammatic images seems to linger in these anthropological accounts, the one pointing to the process of developmental change of any entity and the other to the complexity of its environmental influences.

Acknowledgments

I am very grateful to Tim Ingold, Eva Jablonka, Gisli Palsson, Charissa Terranova, and Jonathan Weitzman for generous access to their writings, and to the reviewers of this chapter for their helpful advice.

Caroline Humphrey is a social anthropologist who has worked in the USSR/Russia, Mongolia, Inner Mongolia, Nepal, and India. Until 2010 she was Sigrid Rausing Professor of Anthropology at the University of Cambridge, and she is currently a Research Director at the university's Mongolia and Inner Asia Studies Unit. Recent publications include *On The Edge: Life Along the Russia-China Border* (2021), co-authored with Franck Billé; *Trust and Mistrust in the Economies of the China-Russia Borderlands* (2018); and *Frontier Encounters: Knowledge and Practice at the Russian, Chinese and Mongolian Border* (2012), co-edited with Franck Billé and Grégory Delaplace.

Notes

1. For further illuminating discussion, see Susan Squier (2017: 22–26).
2. In an early book, Waddington (1935: 97) had used a photograph of Whitemoor Marshalling Yard of the L.N.E.R. railway to suggest an analogy between the biological switches in developmental pathways and wagons running downhill and sorted out by a system of points into different sidings.
3. Homeorhesis is contrasted with homeostasis, the process through which adult organisms are able to stay alive by maintaining their internal systems in a relatively stable state. See further discussion in Squier (2017: 131–132).
4. Coined by combining the Greek roots for 'necessary' and 'path'.
5. Waddington (1957: 35) writes that this image is not to be interpreted in any literal way, but it may bring home a point more vividly than a verbal description to those who tend to think in terms of visual images.
6. A unit of genetic material required for the transport of and metabolism of lactose in many enteric bacteria.
7. See Baedke's (2013: 761) discussion of the influence on Waddington of the 'ravines' notion of the Russian mathematical topologists Gel'fand and Tsetlin.
8. For more on this topic, see the survey in Thayer and Non (2015).
9. These studies are too numerous to cite here in full, but one example is Tavory et al.'s (2014) investigation into the continued reproduction over generations of Orthodox Jewish life in Los Angeles, even though this was a highly specific way of life that the modern city was supposed to erode and extinguish.

10. As Palsson (2004: 19–20) expresses it: "While the perspectives of the 'biosocial' and 'naturecultures' are far from mainstream in biology and the social sciences, and definitely less so in biology, they do respond to a growing pressure on current epistemic thought, seeking to address some of the critical aspects of the modern world: growing evidence of epigenetic signatures, the social histories of conflated microbiomes, shifting metagenomes, blurred supra-organisms, anthropogenic impact on the planet, the refashioning of 'life itself' through synthetic biology, bioengineering for medical purposes, and prosthetic cyborgs fusing bodies and artificial technologies."

References

Allen, Matthew. 2015. "Compelled by the Diagram: Thinking through C. H. Waddington's Epigenetic Landscape." *Contemporaneity* 4: 119–142.

Baedke, Jan. 2013. "The Epigenetic Landscape in the Course of Time: Conrad Hal Waddington's Methodological Impact on the Life Sciences." *Studies in History and Philosophy of Science Part C: Studies in History and Philosophy of Biological and Biomedical Sciences* 44 (4): 756–773.

Gell, Alfred. 1998. *Art and Agency: An Anthropological Theory*. Oxford: Clarendon Press.

Gilbert, Scott F. 1991. "Epigenetic Landscaping: Waddington's Use of Cell Fate Bifurcation Diagrams." *Biology & Philosophy* 6 (2): 135–154.

Haraway, Donna. 1976. *Crystals, Fabrics, and Fields: Metaphors That Shape Embryos*. New Haven, CT: Yale University Press.

Haraway, Donna. 1991. *Simians, Cyborgs and Women: The Reinvention of Nature*. New York and London: Routledge.

Ingold, Tim. 1986. *Evolution and Social Life*. Cambridge: Cambridge University Press.

Ingold, Tim. 2007. "The Trouble with 'Evolutionary Biology.'" *Anthropology Today* 23 (2): 13–17.

Ingold, Tim, and Gisli Palsson. 2013. *Biosocial Becomings: Integrating Social and Biological Anthropology*. Cambridge: Cambridge University Press.

Jablonka, Eva, and Marion Lamb. 2002. "The Changing Concept of Epigenetics." *Annals of the New York Academy of Sciences* 981 (1): 82–96.

Jacob, François, and Jacques Monod. 1961. "Genetic Regulatory Mechanisms in the Synthesis of Proteins." *Journal of Molecular Biology* 3 (3): 318–356.

Jay, Martin. 2010–2011. "The Culture of Diagram (Review)." *Nineteenth-Century French Studies* 39 (1–2): 157–159.

Krämer, Sybille, and Christina Ljungberg. 2016. "Thinking and Diagrams—An Introduction." In *Thinking with Diagrams: The Semiotic Basis of Human Cognition*, ed. Sybille Krämer and Christina Ljungberg, 1–20. The Hague: De Gruyter Mouton.

Lock, Margaret, and Gisli Palsson. 2016. *Can Science Resolve the Nature/Nurture Debate?* Cambridge: Polity Press.

Nicoglou, Antonine. 2018. "Waddington's Epigenetics or the Pictorial Meetings of Development and Genetics." *History and Philosophy of the Life Sciences* 40: 1–25. https://doi.org/10.1007/s40656-018-0228-8.

Paaby, Annalise B., and Matthew V. Rockman. 2014. "Cryptic Genetic Variation: Evolution's Hidden Substrate." *Nature Reviews Genetics* 15: 247–258.

Palsson, Gisli. 2004. "Epigenetic Routes through Epistemic Landscapes." Unpublished manuscript.

Petryna, Adriana, and Paul W. Mitchell. 2017. "On the Nature of Catastrophic Forms." *BioSocieties* 12 (3): 343–366.

Schultz, Emily. 2009. "Resolving the Anti-Antievolutionism Dilemma: A Brief for Relational Evolutionary Thinking in Anthropology." *American Anthropologist* 111 (2): 224–237.

Shi, Jifan, Andrew E. Teschendorff, Weiyan Chen, Luonan Chen, and Tiejun Li. 2018. "Quantifying Waddington's Epigenetic Landscape: A Comparison of Single-Cell Potency Measures." *Briefings in Bioinformatics*. Open access article published by Oxford University Press. https://doi.org/10.1093/bib/bby093.

Speybroeck, Linda Van. 2002. "From Epigenesis to Epigenetics: The Case of C. H. Waddington." *Annals of the New York Academy of Sciences* 981: 61–81.

Squier, Susan M. 2017. *Epigenetic Landscapes: Drawings as Metaphor*. Durham, NC: Duke University Press.

Steadman, Philip. 1979. *The Evolution of Designs: Biological Analogy in Architecture and the Applied Arts*. Cambridge: Cambridge University Press.

Stengers, Isabelle, ed. 1987. *D'une science à l'autre: Des concepts nomades* [From one science to another: Nomadic concepts]. Paris: Seuil.

Surman, Jan, Katalin Straner, and Peter Haslinger. 2014. "Nomadic Concepts in the History of Biology." *Studies in History and Philosophy of Science Part C: Studies in History and Philosophy of Biological and Biomedical Sciences* 48: 127–129.

Tavory, Iddo, Eva Jablonka, and Simona Ginsburg. 2012. "Culture and Epigenesis: A Waddingtonian View." In *The Oxford Handbook of Culture and Psychology*, ed. Jaan Valsiner, 662–676. New York: Oxford University Press.

Tavory, Iddo, Simona Ginsburg, and Eva Jablonka. 2014. "The Reproduction of the Social: A Developmental System Theory Approach." In *Developing Scaffolds in Evolution, Culture and Cognition*, ed. Linnda R. Caporael, James R. Griesemer, and William C. Wimsatt, 307–326. Cambridge, MA: MIT Press.

Terranova, Charissa N. 2017. "The Epigenetic Landscape of Art and Science, *c.* 1950." In *The Routledge Companion to Biology in Art and Architecture*, ed. Charissa N. Terranova and Meredith Tromble, 263–284. New York: Routledge.

Thayer, Zaneta M., and Amy L. Non. 2015. "Anthropology Meets Epigenetics: Current and Future Directions." *American Anthropologist* 117 (4): 722–735.

Vidler, Anthony. 2000. "Diagrams of Diagrams: Architectural Abstraction and Modern Representation." *Representations* 72: 1–20.

Waddington, C. H. 1935. *How Animals Develop*. London: George Allen & Unwin.

Waddington, C. H. 1940. *Organisers and Genes*. Cambridge: Cambridge University Press.

Waddington, C. H. 1957. *The Strategy of the Genes: A Discussion of Some Aspects of Theoretical Biology.* London: George Allen & Unwin.

Waddington, C. H. 1959. "Evolutionary Systems—Animal and Human." *Nature* 183: 1634–1638.

Waddington, C. H. 1969. *Behind Appearance: A Study of the Relations between Painting and the Natural Sciences in This Century.* Edinburgh: Edinburgh University Press.

Waddington, C. H. 1977. *Tools for Thought.* London: Paladin.

Waddington, C. H., B. Woolf, and M. M. Perry. 1954. "Environmental Selection by Drosophilia Mutants." *Evolution* 8 (2): 89–96.

Wolfe, Charles T. 2014. "The Organism as Ontological Go-Between: Hybridity, Boundaries and Degrees of Reality in Its Conceptual History." *Studies in History and Philosophy of Science Part C: Studies in History and Philosophy of Biological and Biomedical Sciences* 48: 151–161.

EPILOGUE
Abstraction and Schematization in the Repeated Copying
of Designs

Philip Steadman

It took a very short time, following the publication of *On the Origin of Species* in 1859, for Darwin's theoretical framework to be applied to material culture. One of the first in this field was the founder of scientific archaeology, General Augustus Lane Fox Pitt-Rivers. Pitt-Rivers (1906) was interested in the evolution of useful tools, especially—since he was a military man—in weapons. But he also studied the evolution of decorative patterns in pre-industrial societies and in folk art. As his colleague Henry Balfour (1906: v) said: "Through noticing the unfailing regularity of this process of gradual *evolution* in the case of firearms, [Pitt-Rivers] was led to believe that the same principles must probably govern the development of the other arts, appliances, and ideas of mankind."

Pitt-Rivers and Balfour imagined that traditional patterns of ornament might change over time through being repeatedly copied. This copying would be the equivalent of genetic inheritance in organic evolution. The copies would not, however, be completely accurate. Craft workers would tend to introduce small alterations, either deliberately or by accident. These changes would be equivalent to the variations in organic form that provide the raw material for natural selection. And so the designs would undergo gradual processes of 'artificial evolution'. With decoration, unlike useful tools, it was more difficult to see what the criteria might be for their 'artificial selection'. Perhaps these would be aesthetic criteria (Steadman 1979). Other criteria are suggested in what follows.

Figure E.1 shows an example from a paper by John Evans (1875) titled "On the Coinage of the Ancient Britons and Natural Selection." The series is numbered in chronological order. At the start is a classical coin with on one side a portrait of Philip of Macedon, and on the reverse a chariot with a driver and horses. This design was copied repeatedly by local British craftsmen. See how the laurel wreath on Philip's head is transformed into an ear of corn, and his ear and eye become crescent moons.

Pitt-Rivers and friends made some practical experiments, copying drawings repeatedly, to try to simulate and understand these processes. One of the founders of the Anthropology Department at Cambridge University, Alfred Haddon (1895), wrote about these experiments in a book titled *Evolution in Art*. As Haddon explains: "He [Pitt-Rivers] gave a certain drawing to some one (A) to copy; his rendering was sent on to another person (B) to copy, this copy was handed on to a third individual (C), and so on, each copyist having only the preceding person's performance before him" (ibid.: 311).

Inspired by the General's example, Balfour (1893: 26, 29), who became the first curator of the Pitt-Rivers Museum, carried out some similar experiments. Two of these are shown in figure E.2. The first series starts with a drawing of the head and shoulders of Patroclus. The final version, after 11 copies, is not too different from the starting point, the main change being that the warrior's pectoral muscles have turned into a cloak. The second of Balfour's series has more interesting results. The starting image shows a snail on a twig. This persists for a time, until the body becomes separated from the shell and turns into a fish shape. At a late stage, the whole image is turned upside down—since there was no indication of the original orientation—and the series ends with a kind of bird/fish wearing checked trousers. The snail's shell survives as a kind of large wart on the bird's chest. One might on first thought imagine that in this process of repeated copying, designs would deteriorate, detail would be lost, and all would eventually dwindle away to nothing. On the contrary, as figure E.2 demonstrates, designs come to take on lives of their own.

In the 1930s, the psychologist Sir Frederic Bartlett used similar copying techniques in his studies of memory. Bartlett was one of the founders of cognitive psychology and also worked at Cambridge. He knew Haddon's book *Evolution in Art* and must have seen Balfour's drawings. Bartlett (1932) published the results of his work in his very influential book *Remembering*. His experiments

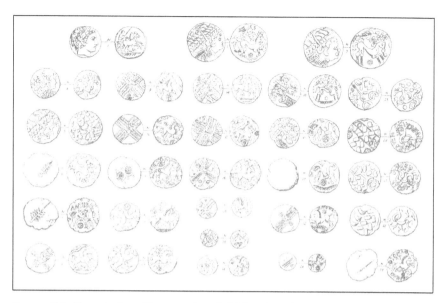

FIGURE E.1: Repeated motifs on ancient British coins, showing on the two sides the head of Philip of Macedon and a horse-drawn chariot (Evans 1875).

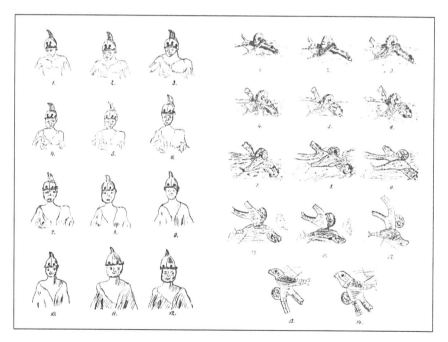

FIGURE E.2: Experiments made by Henry Balfour and friends in which drawings were copied successively by different individuals, each working from the immediately preceding copy, without reference to the original (Balfour 1893: 26, 29).

differed in a significant way, however, from those of the evolutionary anthropologists. Since Bartlett was interested in memory, he asked a subject to look at a drawing for a short time and then took it away. The subject had to make his or her copy from memory. This copy was shown briefly to a second subject, who had to remember it and reproduce it in turn, and so on.

Figure E.3 illustrates one of the resulting series. The starting point is a schematic ancient Egyptian drawing of an owl, which turns rather quickly into a cat. This is presumably because the curve of the owl's wing suggests a tail. The wing sinks lower and assumes the correct position for the tail. After the tenth copy, the design stabilizes as a classic back view of a black cat. The owl's beak is reinterpreted as a ribbon around the cat's neck. Bartlett says that the same thing happened when the procedure was initiated a second time from the same starting image. Figure E.4 is the most famous of Bartlett's series, which has been reproduced in psychological textbooks ever since. It starts with a highly stylized human face, something like an African tribal mask, labeled in French "Portrait d'homme." After nine rememberings and redrawings it becomes a conventionalized smiling face—although mysteriously the caption "Portrait d'homme" has changed into "L'homme Egyptien."

Bartlett (1932) drew a number of conclusions from these and other similar copying experiments. Most important, he saw a tendency to transform "in the direction of the familiar" (ibid.: 178)—in the direction of "accepted conventional representations" (ibid.: 185). The African mask becomes a standard icon for 'face'; the owl becomes a nursery image of a domestic cat. Bartlett carried out other experiments, getting subjects to remember and reproduce written stories. He built on all these results to develop his theory of mental schematization.

In essence, Bartlett's idea is that previous knowledge affects the processing of visual interpretation. A person tends to adapt what he or she sees to some appropriate pre-existing mental schema. The schema focuses the viewer's attention onto selected features of the image in preference to others. To quote a recent paper by the psychologists Claus-Christian Carbon and Sabine Albrecht (2012: 2258–2259) on Bartlett's work: "In the course of repeated reproduction, a face-like but somehow ambiguous visual stimulus will increasingly be changed towards a simple and prototypical face." Bartlett also recognized that giving the original drawing a caption like "Portrait d'homme" helped provide a strong steer to the subsequent direction of change.

All this seems reasonable and plausible. However, more recent work has failed to replicate Bartlett's results. Carbon and Albrecht (2012: 2269, fig. 5) used Bartlett's original Egyptian mask to try to recreate his best-known experiment. The top row in figure E.5 shows the typical result from a whole series of trials. Despite being labeled "Portrait des Menschen," the process—at least after five copyings—fails to produce a standard iconic face. The same happens in a second series with another mask, shown below. In both cases, the result

Original Drawing

' Cf. pp. 58, 93.   ² See pp. 21-2.

FIGURE E.3: Experiment on remembering by Frederic Bartlett in which a drawing was shown to one person for a short time, taken away, and the person asked to make a copy from memory. This copy was then shown to a second person who copied it from memory; and so on (Bartlett 1932: 180).

is a kind of Humpty Dumpty figure, recognizably a creature, but hardly conventionalized. Carbon and Albrecht say that surprisingly little work has been done by psychologists since the 1930s to follow up on Bartlett, and that his experiments, despite their suggestiveness and influence, were "hardly more than controlled anecdotes" (citing Roediger and Thompson, ibid.).

I will return to research in psychology. Meanwhile, mention should be made of a game—called "Dessin successif" (successive drawing), or sometimes "Jeu de dessin communiqué" (the game of copied drawings)—which was played in Paris in the late 1930s by a group of Surrealist artists and writers. This was the invention of Robert Rius, Benjamin Peret, Remedios Varo, and André Breton (the "Pope of Surrealism"), and followed exactly the format of Bartlett's experiments (Galerie 1900/2000 1999). The starting drawing was shown to someone for three seconds and was then taken away; that person copied it from memory, gave it to another, and so on. It is possible that the Surrealists had seen Bartlett's book, which had recently been published.

Figure E.6 reproduces one of the series from the game. Some of those playing were of course highly accomplished artists. The player who made the fifth copy

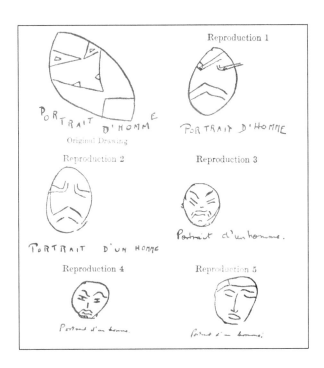

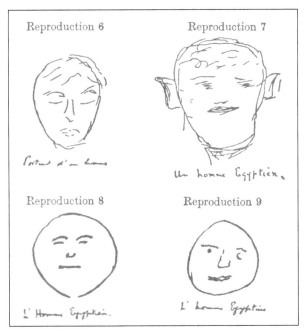

Figure E.4a,b: A second similar experiment conducted by Bartlett (1932: 178–179).

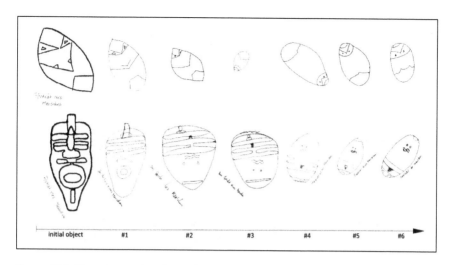

FIGURE E.5: Experiments by Claus-Christian Carbon and Sabine Albrecht attempting to reproduce Bartlett's results. The series at the top uses the same starting drawing as one of Bartlett's experiments (cf. figs. 4a, 4b). The series below takes a different tribal mask as the point of departure (Carbon and Albrecht 2012: 2269).

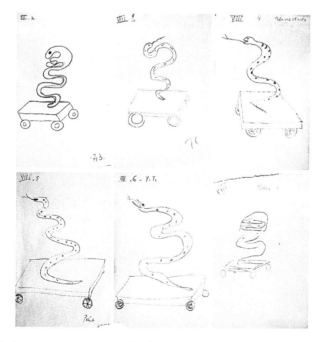

FIGURE E.6: "Jeu de dessin communiqué." Successive copyings made from memory, as in Bartlett's experiments, by the Surrealists Robert Rius, Benjamin Peret, Remedios Varo, and André Breton. Courtesy of Galerie 1900/2000, Paris.

obviously had an excellent visual memory. What is interesting here is how, from a rather schematic starting image, the drawings become quite naturalistic, and then revert again to something very sketchy. Of course, these games were not meant as scientific experiments. They were deliberately intended to stimulate invention and draw strangeness from the players' shared unconscious. But the Surrealists nevertheless imagined that the copying process in itself would play a large part in generating that strangeness.

What is the bearing of all these examples of copying on the subject of diagrams? My proposal is that we can see in these copying processes some tendencies toward schematization, but in a rather different sense from Bartlett's schemata. My suggestion, specifically, is that we can see processes that turn drawings of different kinds, by stages, into something more like diagrams. By studying these processes, we might, in turn, possibly throw light on how diagrams can serve to present information in clear and easily assimilated forms.

In the 1970s, I conducted some copying experiments of my own, inspired by Pitt-Rivers's example, with a group of students from the Cambridge University School of Architecture. I will use these drawings as extra material with which to support my argument. We can detect several systematic trends, I believe, in these sequences.

- There is a tendency for pictures to become 'flattened out', for perspective effects to be removed, in particular, the removal of effects of perspective occlusion in which parts of objects are hidden behind other objects.
- There is a tendency for objects to become represented by their boundaries, without shading or modeling. In these distortions of the geometry of objects, topological relationships of connectivity, touching, and containment are preserved.
- Parallel lines that are close together are moved farther apart, and narrow angles become wider.

Let us take these effects in order. First is the removal of perspective and the flattening of solid forms. Figure E.7 shows two coins from John Evans's (1875) paper: the Roman original, and a later British copy (cf. fig. E.1). The copy is numbered 21, presumably on the basis of its date. But I do not think it would

FIGURE E.7: Details from figure E.1 to show motifs on the two sides of two British coins, one presumably copied (perhaps at many removes) from the other (Evans 1875).

be possible to say how many times the original has been copied here. Look at the chariot and horses on the reverse sides of the coins. The original has two horses, one largely concealed behind the other. The chariot is drawn in perspective, with a wheel that appears as an ellipse. In the copy, there is a single horse, whose parts are flattened and separated out. The chariot is represented just by a wheel that has come loose and is seen frontally as a true circle. Otherwise, all traces of perspective have disappeared.

Figure E.8a is one of the drawings copied by the Cambridge students. The students did not know what was represented—presumably the root or bulb of some kind of plant—so they had no preconceptions. Figure E.8b shows what happened after seven copyings. The suggestions of three-dimensionality in the original have largely disappeared. Most of the perspective occlusion, where one feature masks another, has been removed. The main structure has become much more clearly a flat ring, with attachments. The basic topology is nevertheless preserved. The number of knobs or 'limbs' remains roughly the same.

The same initial drawing was started off again. Figure E.8c shows the result after seven copyings this second time around. Now the central outline of the ring has shrunk into a messy knot at the bottom. But the transformation of the outer ring is much the same as before. We see here my second tendency, for objects to become represented by their outlines.

This is an effect shown very clearly by one of the Surrealists' games of "Jeu de dessin communiqué" shown in figure E.9. Robert Rius's original (top left) is quite mysterious: could it perhaps be some sort of device for collecting electricity in the inverted pyramid? But André Breton's interpretation in the fourth

FIGURES E.8a,b,c: Results of experiments in the repeated copying of designs, inspired by Pitt-Rivers's example, made by Cambridge students of architecture. E.8a is the starting drawing; E.8b shows the result after seven copyings; E.8c shows the result of a second experiment with the same starting drawing, again after seven copyings.

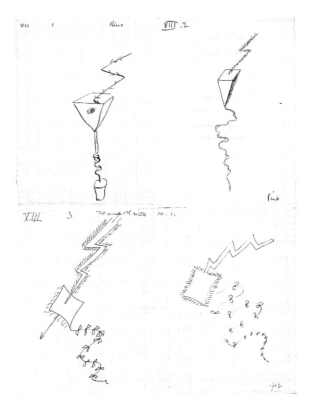

Figure E.9: A second sequence from the Surrealists' "Jeu de dessin communiqué." Courtesy of Galerie 1900/2000, Paris.

drawing (lower right) is much more obvious: lightning is striking a tasseled kite with a long tail. Maybe Breton had in mind Benjamin Franklin's efforts to draw lightning to the ground with a kite.

In Breton's version, the perspective of the pyramid is lost, and all three items—lightning, kite, and tail with bows—are laid out flat and defined by their outlines. Ironically, this sequence seems to have gone in exactly the opposite direction from what the Surrealists wanted: a rather opaque starting image has turned into a couple of conventional icons for the lightning and the kite. Bartlett's schemata are in action here.

My final trend is for parallel lines that are close together to move apart, and for narrow angles to get wider. This phenomenon is illustrated in figure E.10 by a very peculiar series of an American type of coffee pot, drawn by the Cambridge students. The part in the center holds the coffee grounds. See what happens to the spout. At every step, the angle of the spout drops lower and lower, until by the end any water poured into the pot would flow straight out again. Note that none of the copyists could have known that the spout was moving

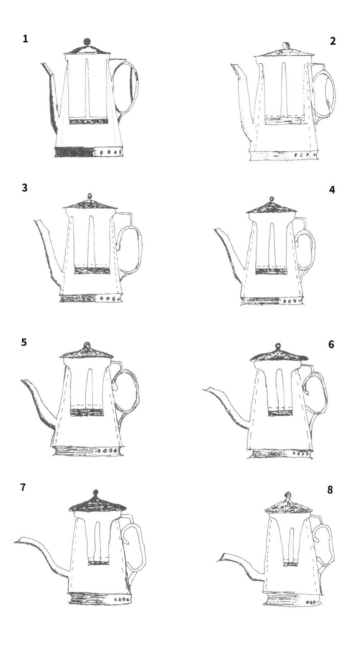

FIGURE E.10: Repeated copyings of a drawing of an American coffee pot by the Cambridge students. Notice the movements of the spout and of the container for the coffee grounds in the middle of the pot.

always in this downward direction. Each person has seen only the immediately preceding version.

The narrow angle at which the spout is set initially is made progressively wider. There seems to be some kind of graphical force of gravity acting on the copying. See what happens at the same time to the container for the coffee grounds inside the pot. Vertical lines that are close together at the start become separated, so that by the end their spacing is much more equal.

We can follow similar effects in another sequence, which starts from an original, figure E.11a, that is already highly diagrammatic: an electrical valve and associated circuitry. This drawing was also set off on the copying process more than once. Figures E.11b and E.11c are copies reached at the eighth stage in two experiments starting from the same original. In both cases, the structure at the center of the valve has shrunk, like the central part of the coffee pot. The vertical wires with coils have moved over to the right and become separated from each other. And the wires to the battery at the bottom of the picture have also become more widely spaced. Notice how in both cases the key letters have remained unchanged, except in a few cases where copyists have overlooked them and they have been lost. These are of course schemata of the most stable kind: every copyist knows how to reproduce letter forms.

A final example, figure E.12, shows a cartoon dog and child. After 16 copyings, this drawing has hardly changed at all. Arguably, this is because it has all the characteristics of a diagram to start off with: flattened forms, simple outlines, clearly distinguished parts whose topological relationships are preserved. Only the internal structures have been transformed: the dog's teeth and the child's arm and hand.

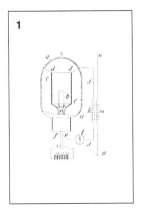 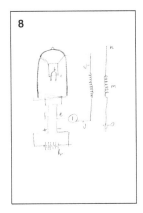 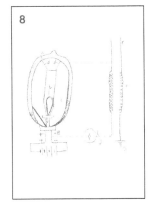

Figures E.11a,b,c: Results of repeated copyings by the Cambridge students: E.11a is the starting drawing; E.11b shows the result after seven copyings; E.11c shows the result of a second experiment with the same starting drawing, again after seven copyings.

FIGURE E.12: Result after the copying of a cartoon 17 times by the Cambridge students.

I have suggested that we see here a series of tendencies in these processes of copying, leading toward results that are more 'diagrammatic'. There have been trends of flattening, removal of perspective, the separation of closely spaced lines, the widening of narrow angles, all while preserving the underlying topology. What might explain these trends? I hesitate to put forward cognitive explanations. But could it be that there are certain characteristics of the ways in which we *see* designs, and in the ways that we *represent* them mentally and in memory, that lead us when making copies to transform what we pick out and draw, and to change them in those directions? Do we somehow *think* diagrammatically, that is to say? Do our 'mental diagrams' somehow steer what we pick out to copy, or how we change what we see?

In his extremely influential book *Vision*, the psychologist David Marr (1982) makes some speculative proposals about how the processes of interpretation of visual images in the brain might end up as 'three-dimensional' representations of shapes, which can then be recognized and classified. Marr concentrates on models of different species of animal. The models are based on 'shape primitives' in the form of generalized cones or cylinders, whose central axes are joined into different configurations, something like stick figures. What is important is not the outline or silhouette, but the connectivity of the relationships between torso, limbs, and head, and the relative lengths and diameters of these primitives. Incidental effects of light and shadow are ignored. Figure E.13 shows a set of examples, of varying degrees of specificity, going from top to bottom of the figure. The models, one might say, are three-dimensional diagrams. Similar principles could be applied in two dimensions, for example, in the mental modeling of human faces and their features.

Marr discusses how a retinal image of a creature seen obliquely might be recognized by the configuration of the axes of its component primitives. The

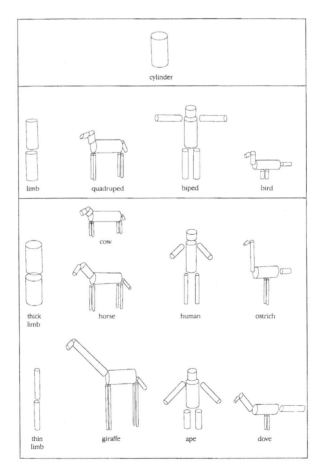

Figure E.13: Mental shape descriptions of animals constructed from cylindrical primitives. The descriptions lower on the page are more specific (Marr 1982: 319, figs. 5–10).

model could be rotated mentally to obtain a 'canonical' view as in figure E.13. Ambiguities introduced by specific perspective views can thus be avoided. Marr (1982: 314) points to the major difficulties created for vision by perspective occlusion, taking the case of horses: "For example, although the torso-based coordinate system for the overall shape of the horse is easily obtained from a side view, it is difficult to obtain when the horse faces the viewer." (A frontal view of a horse does, on the other hand, give an excellent view of its face.)

This is all extremely speculative. But if we can accept Marr's general ideas, then these could have a bearing on the processes I have diagnosed in the copying experiments. If copyists are referring what they see to something like Marr's models, then this might possibly account for the tendencies toward canonical views, flattening, and the removal of occlusion. This is what seems to be happening, for example, to the two horses on the British coins. The occluded horse is removed, the remaining beast is flattened into a canonical side view, and the body is clearly analyzed into its legs, torso, neck, and head. Yet we still easily read it as a horse.

I will leave these large questions unresolved and end with some modern examples of the production of diagrams proper. Arguably, we can see in these examples some of the features found in the results of the copying. The starting point for the copyings I have illustrated were almost all naturalistic images, or somewhat abstracted naturalistic images of real objects. In this context, we are excluding from consideration all kinds of diagrams that represent purely abstract or mathematical relationships such as flow charts, bar charts, or graphs. We are focusing rather on *pictograms*.

Figure E.14 shows Harry Beck's 1933 map of the London Underground, one of the world's most famous and frequently copied diagrams. Beck's map is contrasted with an older underground railway map of 1921. It might be objected that Beck's design is an abstract network diagram, but it is abstracted from an aerial view of the real (partly underground) geography of London. Beck preserves the topology, of course—that is the point. But to make this more readily comprehensible, Beck straightens and separates out those lines that are close together and spaces them more equally. There are no narrow angles in his map, and all the lines are placed horizontally, vertically, or at 45 degrees.

Beck drew his inspiration, as is well known, from electrical circuit diagrams. Figure E.15 shows three diagrams of Wheatstone bridges from 1884, 1890, and 1898 (Gregory 1970: 156–158). This is the period in which the graphical representation of circuits was being worked out, formalized, and standardized. At the top (a), the representation is naturalistic to a degree, with pictorial images of the wires and the bulb whose resistance is being measured. The interesting comparison for us is between the middle and bottom diagrams (b and c). The board on which the terminals are fixed in (b) is seen obliquely in perspective, complete with shading and shadows. The wires wander here and there. The

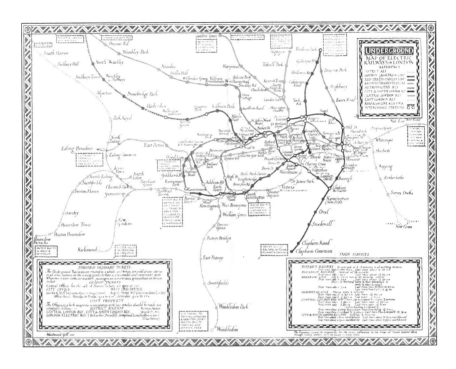

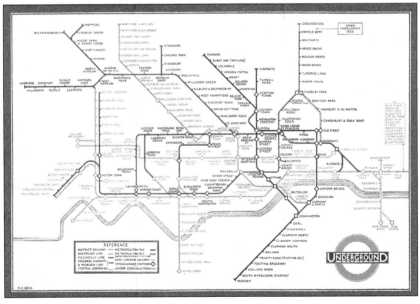

FIGURE E.14a,b: London Underground railway map of 1921 (top) compared with Harry Beck's map of 1933 (below).

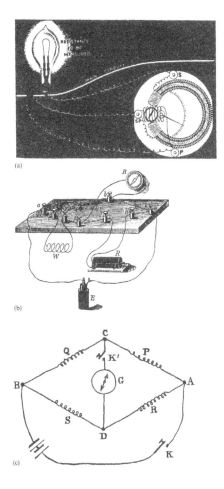

FIGURE E.15a,b,c: Nineteenth-century drawings of Wheatstone bridges (Gregory 1970: 156–158).

separate battery E and variable resistance R are also in perspective and cast their own shadows, although the galvanometer B is in plan view.

In the lower diagram (c), all irrelevant information—the board, the shadows—has been removed. The components are reduced to conventional symbols, and the wires have been sorted out, straightened, widely separated (like the wires in figs. 11a, 11b, 11c), and placed at oblique angles like Beck's tube lines. The essential topology has been maintained and clarified. The realistic picture of (a) is well on its way to becoming a modern circuit diagram at (c).

These properties are shared by many of the modern pictograms that are seen everywhere in signage, instructional manuals, and packaging. There is rarely any perspective occlusion. Human figures, animals, and inanimate objects are shown in canonical front or side views. Many consist of simple flattened outlines without shading, filled with uniform color.

These pictograms, the circuit diagram, and Harry Beck's map are not of course the results of mindless copying; they are the outcome of careful thought and deliberate design. But they clarify and organize in some of the ways, I would suggest, that diagrams are produced through the repeated copying of designs.

Philip Steadman is Emeritus Professor of Urban and Built Form Studies at University College London and a Senior Research Fellow at the UCL Energy Institute. He trained as an architect and has taught at Cambridge University and the Open University. His main research interests are the geometries of buildings and cities and their relationship to energy use. He has published several books on geometry in architecture and computer-aided design. In 2017 he published a book of essays, *Why Are Most Buildings Rectangular?* He also works in art history and published *Vermeer's Camera: Uncovering the Truth Behind the Masterpieces* (2001). His most recent book is titled *Renaissance Fun: The Machines Behind the Scenes* (2021).

References

Balfour, Henry. 1893. *The Evolution of Decorative Art*. London: Rivington, Percival.
Balfour, Henry. 1906. "Introduction." In Pitt-Rivers 1906, v–xx.
Bartlett, Frederic C. 1932. *Remembering: A Study in Experimental and Social Psychology*. Cambridge: Cambridge University Press.
Carbon, Claus-Christian, and Sabine Albrecht. 2012. "Bartlett's Schema Theory: The Unreplicated 'Portrait d'homme' Series from 1932." *Quarterly Journal of Experimental Psychology* 65 (11): 2258–2270.
Evans, John. 1875. "On the Coinage of the Ancient Britons and Natural Selection." *Proceedings of the Royal Institution* 7: 476–487.
Galerie 1900/2000. 1999. *Jeu de dessin communiqué* [The copied drawings game]. Paris: Galerie 1900/2000.
Gregory, R. L. 1970. *The Intelligent Eye*. London: Weidenfeld & Nicolson.
Haddon, Alfred C. 1895. *Evolution in Art, as Illustrated by the Life-Histories of Designs*. London: Walter Scott.
Marr, David. 1982. *Vision*. San Francisco: W. H. Freeman.
Pitt-Rivers, Lt-Gen A. Lane-Fox. 1906. *The Evolution of Culture and Other Essays*. Ed. J. L. Myres. Oxford: Clarendon Press.
Steadman, Philip. 1979. *The Evolution of Designs: Biological Analogy in Architecture and the Applied Arts*. Cambridge: Cambridge University Press.

AFTERWORD
The Work of Diagrams

Lukas Engelmann, Caroline Humphrey,
and Christos Lynteris

Philip Steadman's epilogue suggests that the copying of drawings (and its study) by anthropologists, psychologists, architectural students, and Surrealists is revealing not only of processes of diagrammatization but also of the fact that there is something 'diagrammatic' about the way in which designs are represented mentally, which affects how they are seen and altered when they are reproduced. The work of diagrams, not only as visual objects but also as mental processes, is shown by the chapters in this book to play a central role in fields as diverse as psychoanalysis, anthropology, epidemiology, and biology. More often than not, the synergy between these fields is facilitated, and sometimes catalyzed, by shared diagrammatic practices. As the studies examined in the epilogue demonstrate, diagrams form a privileged *visual* field of interdisciplinary dialogue and exchange. But importantly, they also facilitate a way of information processing—what the editors of this book call 'diagrammatic reasoning'—through which data are processed, presented, and reconfigured in clear and easily assimilated forms.

All of the contributions to this book have emphasized a similar process concerning the respective body of knowledge at stake in each field and discipline. However, the authors have also highlighted the very diverse trade-offs (or disadvantages) of formalizations of knowledge, which in all cases include a process of redrawing, reshaping, reconceptualizing, and redesigning. Bird-David shows how the diagram seems to offer a line of clarification and increased intelligibility, but in fact, in the context of anthropology, obscures the family relations of "other people's worlds." Maps, as Engelmann argues, replace simplistic concepts of causality in favor of forwarding a clear sense of epidemics as configurations, while Humphrey has demonstrated that the clear form of diagrams lends itself to an instructive, constitutive, and highly mobile quality, as in the case of Waddington's epigenetic diagram. A persuasive take on the capacity to translate and simplify complex theories of the mind has been demonstrated by Spankie, as she shifts the register on Freud, redrawing his concepts as designs of the interior. Finally, Candea has reflected on the drawing process in his own anthropological work, exposing the alluring quality of "graphic coherence" when rethinking theories. In summary, all of these contributions have covered (some explicitly, some more implicitly) processes of graphical production and visual formalization. Rather than offering mere reduction of pre-existing ideas, these authors have exposed the intricate reconfigurations of knowledge that occur in graphic design.

In his epilogue, Steadman underlines copying as a fundamental type of work with diagrams. He points to the need to be aware that while the term 'work' carries with it a pervasive semantic of intentionality and control, some of these practices have their own unintentional dynamics. Referring back to foundational studies by Pitt-Rivers, Balfour, Haddon, and others, Steadman provides evidence from his own experiments with copying. He argues that a diagrammatical way of thinking may rest on underlying mental "tendencies toward schematization" that point us toward issues of cognition and conceptualization that inform diagrammatization more broadly.

Lukas Engelmann is a Senior Lecturer and Chancellor's Fellow in History and Sociology of Biomedicine at the University of Edinburgh. His work focuses on the history of epidemiological reasoning in the long twentieth century, and is funded by an ERC starting grant. Recent publications include *Mapping AIDS: Visual Histories of an Enduring Epidemic* (2018) and, co-authored with Christos Lynteris, *Sulphuric Utopias: A History of Maritime Fumigation* (2020).

Caroline Humphrey is a social anthropologist who has worked in the USSR/ Russia, Mongolia, Inner Mongolia, Nepal, and India. Until 2010 she was Sigrid Rausing Professor of Anthropology at the University of Cambridge, and she is currently a Research Director at the university's Mongolia and Inner Asia Studies Unit. Recent publications include *On The Edge: Life Along the Russia-China Border* (2021), co-authored with Franck Billé; *Trust and Mistrust in the Economies of the China-Russia Borderlands* (2018); and *Frontier Encounters: Knowledge and Practice at the Russian, Chinese and Mongolian Border* (2012), co-edited with Franck Billé and Grégory Delaplace.

Christos Lynteris is a Professor of Medical Anthropology at the University of St Andrews. A medical anthropologist investigating epistemological, bio-political, and aesthetic aspects of infectious disease epidemics, he is the principal investigator of the Wellcome-funded project, "The Global War Against the Rat and the Epistemic Emergence of Zoonosis." His recent publications include *Ethnographic Plague: Configuring Disease on the Chinese-Russian Frontier* (2016), *Human Extinction and the Pandemic Imaginary* (2019), and, co-authored with Lukas Engelmann, *Sulphuric Utopias: A History of Maritime Fumigation* (2020).

INDEX

Leadership in the Crucible

Joseph G. Dawson III, *General Editor*

Editorial Board:
Robert Doughty
Brian Linn
Craig Symonds
Robert Wooster

Leadership in the Crucible

THE KOREAN WAR BATTLES OF
TWIN TUNNELS & CHIPYONG-NI

KENNETH E. HAMBURGER

Texas A&M University Press
College Station

The paper used in this book meets the minimum requirements
of the American National Standard for Permanence
of Paper for Printed Library Materials, z39.48–1984.
Binding materials have been chosen for durability.

Library of Congress Cataloging-in-Publication Data

Hamburger, Kenneth Earl, 1941–
    Leadership in the crucible : the Korean War battles of Twin Tunnels and Chipyong-ni /
Kenneth E. Hamburger.—1st ed.
        p. cm.—(Texas A&M University military history series ; 82)
    Includes bibliographical references and index.
    ISBN 1-58544-232-1 (cloth : alk. paper)
    1. Chipyong-ni, Battle of, Chip'yŏng-ni, Korea, 1951. 2. Twin Tunnels, Battle of, Korea, 1951.
3. Korean War, 1950–1953—Regimental histories—United States. 4. United States. Army.
Infantry Regiment, 23rd—History—20th century. 5. Korean War, 1950–1953—Regimental
histories—France. 6. France. Armée. Bataillon de Corée—History. I. Title. II. Series.
DS918.2.C37H36 2002
951.904′242—dc21

                                                                                    2002013307

All photographs except those taken by the author are courtesy of the
U.S. Army Military History Institute, Carlisle Barracks, Pennsylvania.

Contents

Illustrations

Maps

Preface

Acolored print posted in the adjutant's office of the artillery battalion where I began my military service as a lieutenant in the 82d Airborne Division was my first contact with the 23d Infantry Regiment and the battle of Chipyong-ni. It was one in a series of illustrations of famous battles that the U.S. Army distributed to raise soldiers' awareness of their heritage. As I remember it, the scene was a busy and somewhat muddled composition, predominantly blue, depicting a snow-covered battlefield with excited soldiers in hand-to-hand combat. The print was tacked to the wall behind the adjutant's desk, and I looked at it whenever I was summoned to his office, wondering whether all battles were as disorganized as the one it depicted. Almost twenty years later, when I was an artillery battalion commander in Korea, the print was still posted in many offices there. It was not until I began serious study of the Korean War in preparation for teaching an elective course on the Korean and Vietnam Wars at the U.S. Military Academy that I started to connect the print with the accounts of the battle. I discovered that the battle was one of the most famous of the war, and the more I studied it, the more interesting and puzzling the battle became. How did the battle come about? How did the isolated and outnumbered United Nations forces manage to prevail? How did the battle affect the outcome of the war? Even more important to me then and now were questions pertaining to how men summon the resources to face overwhelming odds, and how leaders instill and encourage commitment in their soldiers. The profound bond between leaders and the led, a bond that will cause a man to lay down his life for his comrades and for a cause, is one of the esoteric mysteries of military history that can never be fully explained, even by participants who have experienced the phenomenon. I have sought to probe it in this work.

I studied the battle in as much detail as was available during the time

I was assigned to the Department of History at West Point, and used the opportunity of a sabbatical leave to concentrate on it in some depth. Colonel Robert Doughty, professor and department head, encouraged the project, and a grant from the Association of Graduates of the U.S. Military Academy underwrote the study. Tom Ryan, Eighth Army historian in Seoul, walked the battlefields with me and provided many insights. The U.S. Army Training and Doctrine Command's Paris liaison office assisted me with archival research on the French Battalion, which was attached to the 23d Regiment. Steve and Denise Arata were wonderful hosts during my stay in France, and Steve provided information on the French military that was especially helpful. Cathy Robert performed yeoman duties as assistant and as translator while working at the archives of the École Militaire and the French military archives at Vincennes. Archivists at the U.S. Army Military History Institute at Carlisle Barracks, Pennsylvania, and the National Archives and Records Administration in Suitland, Maryland, were especially helpful. Richard Summers and Dave Keough at Carlisle deserve special mention.

A number of individuals offered to read parts or all of the manuscript, and their observations helped to make the story clearer for military novices as well as for professionals. Steve Arata, Robert Curtis, Serge Bererd, Robert Hall, Mable Hamburger, Jan Jason, Jay Jason, Claude Jaupart, Frank Meszar, Paul L. Miles Jr., Robert Morrison, Roger Nye, Michelle Powers, and Ansil Walker all provided thoughtful suggestions for revision. Dale Wilson, the freelance copy editor contracted by Texas A&M University Press, taught with me years ago at West Point and was especially helpful. My brother Steve was particularly helpful in overcoming technical problems with the maps.

However, the real credit for the stories of the battles at Twin Tunnels and Chipyong-ni goes to the many veterans who shared their stories with me. Because I promised them anonymity if they desired it, I have not cited the specific letters or interviews in the text. I will deposit all of the letters and notes used in the preparation of this manuscript at the U.S. Army Military History Institute for use by other historians. While there were inevitable conflicts in the accounts of events that occurred a half-century before the retelling, most of the recollections agreed with remarkable unanimity. Whatever value there is in this account belongs to them. From the U.S. Army, contributors included Bob V. Andersen, Dewey R. Andersen, Duane L. Anderson, George F. Bammert, Robert Beeby, Bernard A. Bossov, Jack G. Brown, Lloyd Burke, Frank C. Butler, Donald M.

Byers, Wendell Calfe, James Coulos, Robert W. Curtis, G. C. Davis, William D. Devine, Arthur F. Dorie, Earl J. Dube, Kenneth Dumler, Herbert B. Drees, Morris V. Evans Jr., Carroll G. Everist, Emmett Fike, Joe W. Finley, W. H. Francis, Victor L. Fox, Leslie G. Gains, Thomas B. Giboney, George M. Gilbert, Patrick H. Godfrey, Doug F. Graney, William R. Guthrie, Larry L. Hauck, Robert Hall, Seymour "Hoppy" Harris, Thomas C. Harris, Charles Hemauer, Donald W. Herrick, Ralph M. Hockley, Maury Holden, John G. Hoffman, James K. Howell, Ben Judd, Eli Kermmoade, Ira Kesterson, Ralph H. Krueger, Donald H. Larsen, Bob Lozier, Charles A. McCave, John J. McGlue, Glenn C. McGuyer, James F. Malone, Vernon Marquart, Frank Meszar, Albert Caswell Metts Jr., Aubrey Milbach, Arnold E. Mitchell, Sherman Pratt, Richard A. Riley, Ralph R. Robinson, Thomas M. Ryan, Bickford E. Sawyer, Peter F. Schutz, Richard K. Sexton, Samuel G. Shdo, Robert A. Shepherd, Kenneth J. Sisson, Charlie Snow, Keith Stewart, S. J. Sullivan, Richard E. Turner, John J. Vogt, Ansil L. Walker, Robert Ward, Harley E. Wilburn, and Raymond C. Wisniewski.

French veterans who told their stories included Maurice Barthelemy, Serge-Louis Bererd, François De Castries, Pierre Collard, Claude L. Jaupart, Gérard Journet, Jean-Pierre Liron, Michel Rossi, and Claude Tainguy.

I should stress that none of the contributors have approved of the use I made of their accounts and are not responsible for my interpretations, some of which I am sure many would argue against. Any errors of fact or interpretation are, of course, my own.

Finally, I must thank my family, who put up with the tedium of writing with remarkable equanimity and support. Kate and Dan read portions, and their questions spawned further analysis. My wife Jane did every mundane task I asked of her, and provided a congenial environment for my work; her gentle prodding when needed kept the manuscript alive.

The story of the battles at Twin Tunnels and Chipyong-ni offers a stirring and enlightening glimpse of men fighting at the limits of their abilities and endurance. My only hope is to have done justice in recounting the feats of the participants and to have offered some insights that future combat leaders may find useful.

Leadership in the Crucible

Introduction

*Many commanding generals only spend their time on the day of
battle in making their troops march in a straight line, in seeing
that they keep their proper distances, in answering questions which
their aides de camp come to ask, in sending them hither and
thither, and in running about incessantly themselves. In short, they
try to do everything, and as a result do nothing. They appear to me
like men with their heads turned, who no longer see anything and
who are only able to do what they have done all their lives, which is
to conduct troops methodically under the orders of a commander.
How does this happen? It is because few men occupy themselves
with the higher problems of war. They pass their lives drilling
troops and believe that this is the only branch of the military art.
When they arrive at the command of armies, they are truly ignorant, and in default of knowing what should be done, they do what
they know.*

—Count Hermann Maurice de Saxe

*Peruse again and again the campaigns of Alexander, Hannibal,
Caesar, Gustavus Adolphus, Turenne, Eugene, and Frederick.
Model yourself upon them. This is the only means of becoming a
great captain, and of acquiring the secret of the art of war. Your
own genius will be enlightened and improved by this study and you
will learn to reject all maxims foreign to the principles of these commanders.*

—Napoleon Bonaparte

*The history of a battle is not unlike the history of a ball. Some indi-
viduals may recollect all the little events of which the great result is*

the battle won or lost; but no individual can recollect the order in which, or the exact moment at which, they occurred, which makes all the difference.

—*Arthur Wellesley, Duke of Wellington*

The phenomenon of leadership—leaders and their followers together accomplishing given tasks—is the focus of this work. As a way to study this phenomenon, it examines in some detail the actions of the 23d Infantry Regimental Combat Team and the French United Nations Infantry Battalion during the first eight months of the Korean War, with a particular focus on the pivotal battles of Twin Tunnels and Chipyong-ni in February, 1951. The aim of the work is to explore leadership at all levels, from lowest to highest, in search of insights into how leaders and followers acted, successfully or unsuccessfully, during peace and war. The goal is to record the regiment's story and to gain an understanding of the human factors that cause men to follow other men in combat.

A number of sources contributed to this account. The official records and earlier accounts by authors who interviewed participants immediately after the battles gave important insights. Walking the battlefields and examining the fighting positions, many still identifiable on the quiet Korean hills, showed, as only the terrain can, why commanders made many of their important decisions. The most important resources, however, were the accounts provided by the veterans of the battles. More than three hundred veterans gave me their accounts in interviews or letters. They provided a vivid human comprehension of the often-incredible events in which they participated.

The battlefield is an environment alien to the rest of human experience. It is a condition of confusion, of intense stimuli to all human senses, of physical exertion and human suffering. It is a place where strangers try to kill one another to avoid being killed themselves. Success, sometimes simply survival, calls on reservoirs of moral and physical courage that equal any human endeavor. As the great philosopher of war Carl von Clausewitz expressed the phenomenon:

> If one has never personally experienced war, one cannot understand in what the difficulties constantly mentioned really consist, nor why a commander should need any brilliance and exceptional ability. Everything looks simple; the knowledge required does not look remarkable, the strategic options are so obvious that by comparison the simplest problem of higher mathematics

has an impressive scientific dignity. Once war has actually been seen the difficulties become clear; but it is still hard to describe the unseen, all-pervading element that brings about this change of perspective.

Everything in war is very simple, but the simplest thing is difficult. The difficulties accumulate and end by producing a kind of friction that is inconceivable unless one has experienced war. . . . Countless minor incidents—the kind you never really foresee—combine to lower the general level of performance, so that one always falls short of the intended goal.[1]

No laboratory environment can yet replicate the intensity of combat. As we enter the twenty-first century, the U.S. military has accomplished wonders in simulating battlefield conditions. Such facilities as the military services' training centers, where simulators replicate weapons' and environmental effects, are truly impressive in their imitation of the complexities of the battlefield. No training, however, can inspire in a soldier the fear, revulsion, and anger that the wounds and deaths of comrades engender when they occur in his small, close-knit unit—which may well have become more important to him than his family. Nor can it inspire in a soldier the willingness to sacrifice his life for his country or his comrades that one finds throughout military history.

Even in simulated battles, however, no military unit can afford to conduct training that achieves the extremes of fatigue and fatigue-caused errors and danger, or the profound destructiveness that accompanies extended combat. Writers, commentators, and coaches often use the analogy of warfare to sport, but it is no less telling for the repetition. Physical fitness and resistance to sickness have frequently marked great commanders throughout history. Combat makes the strongest possible demands on participants, and the struggle for survival in war is unquestionably a contest to the death between the participants. It was not for nothing that Tom Wolfe called aerial combat over North Vietnam "The Truest Sport," because it was a "sport" in which the loser died.[2]

The factor that often makes the difference between success and failure on battlefields where the extremes of physical conditions and enemy action test the hardiest warriors is often leadership. But leadership is hard to identify as a tangible factor in most such actions, and even harder to define with any degree of accuracy.

Definitions are a critical issue in any discipline, and practitioners of a discipline typically relish debate over definitions in their field. The problem of defining leadership is a complex one, and a detailed examination of the subject could greatly complicate this discussion to no profitable end. For that reason, this work will employ a broad working definition: Leadership is a complex interpersonal phenomenon in which a leader and a group of followers act together and cooperate to accomplish a task. Several advantages accrue to such an expansive definition. It encompasses formal and informal leaders at intermediate levels in addition to the leader at the top of the organizational hierarchy. Additionally, it addresses the relations between followers themselves at intermediate levels and thus the issues of morale and unit cohesion. Finally, it suggests an explanation for the phenomenon of how some units accomplish near-impossible tasks, because many top-performing units function within a compact between the leader and the led. The terms of this unwritten yet profoundly felt compact require each member of the unit to contribute to the accomplishment of the unit's mission. They depend on one another to fulfill their obligation to the shared duty, as only the keen sense of obligation to the brotherhood of the unit can bind each soldier to the compact.

It is my conviction—after having practiced and studied leadership during peace and war for more than forty years—that combat leadership differs in fundamental ways from other kinds of leadership. Men have followed other men into combat throughout history.[3] The circumstances under which leaders and followers have functioned in combat have similarities among themselves. Nevertheless, they differ fundamentally from the circumstances in which some individuals follow others in pursuits unrelated to warfare. Some of these differences involve the techniques of leadership used in a given situation and the intensity of the physical and emotional environment in which combat occurs.

As society defines leaders in venues other than combat—such as the mayor of a city, the chief executive of a corporation, the commander of an army post, or the manager of a baseball team—they usually exert their leadership in an atmosphere of relative order. Although the hyperbole of the marketplace and the sports arena often use images of war to stress the intensity of the experience of these varieties of leadership, it is hard to believe that anyone seriously confuses the relative orderliness of noncombat leadership with the chaos, agony, and death of the battlefield.

Because of the circumstances under which combat leadership is exercised, researchers cannot study it as efficiently through traditional techniques of observing and analyzing human behavior as they can other forms of leadership. Historical studies involving leadership in combat thus must supplement scientific studies of peacetime leadership experiments in order to better understand this complex phenomenon.

Most leadership and management texts and theories rely on codifying techniques for motivation into fundamentals such as rewards and punishments, sanctions against nonproductive behavior, using the followers' self-interest as a way of getting them to follow, and identification of individual goals with group goals. These techniques are then studied and listed so that leadership theory can be at least somewhat prescriptive. While details vary from theory to theory, much of the basic idea remains. Most management and leadership texts and "how-to" manuals imply that the reader has only to follow a checklist to be successful.

Leadership in combat sometimes relies on theories and techniques similar to those of noncombat leadership. Even so, it is usually exercised at a far higher intensity level. The nature of the battlefield has few parallels with the city hall, corporate boardroom, drill field, or baseball dugout. Furthermore, some leadership techniques must be supplemented, modified, or discarded in combat, where the environment restricts or eliminates many commonplace motivational tools. Traditional material rewards can become meaningless, as in the hypothetical case of offering a squad a bonus if its members collectively take a machine-gun bunker, or promising special leave to a soldier if he will stay behind and hold off the enemy as his platoon withdraws.

Often, instead of traditional rewards, the combat leader must rely almost entirely on psychological rewards. There is nothing the leader can offer a corporal manning a machine gun at an outpost except his goodwill, his thanks, and his respect for a job well done. The corporal may stay at his gun until he is killed or he may leave his post at the first strange sound and there is little his leader can do other than reward him with praise and perhaps a medal, or threaten him with punishment that is almost surely less onerous than the danger the corporal avoided by leaving his post. Sanctions in combat, rather than being merely unpleasant—such as being reduced in rank or fined for failing to hold one's fighting position—can be far more intense, extending to the death of an individual or the destruction of a unit. Men must frequently ignore self-interest in favor of group goals, to the point of self-sacrifice for the group. Leaders cannot coerce or demand such behavior; they must build it into the unit in such a way that self-sacrifice flows from the dynamics of its soldiers.

As a result of the uncertainty and individual nature of battlefield conditions, combat leadership has been displayed in an extensive variety of styles. Even when restricting the study of leadership styles to American military history, one can observe every gradation from dictatorial martinet to loving father figure; from profane blasphemer to evangelical parson; from devil-take-the-hindmost gambler to cautious plodder. Almost every category offers both successful and unsuccessful examples. The student discovers all too quickly that there is no single infallible leadership style that will guarantee its practitioner success in combat.

More critical than style to successful combat leadership is the relationship *between* the leader and his followers, and relations *among* leaders and followers. Especially important is the atmosphere of trust within the group. Leaders must build a positive expectation among unit members. This positive expectation must promulgate confidence both up and down the chain of command and laterally across subordinate leaders and followers that convinces them that they can rely on one another. Sometimes a feeling of warmth for the commander inspires this confidence, but warmth is not necessarily the emotion a soldier feels for a commander he trusts. It is about as common to hear a veteran say something like, "Captain Jones was the meanest son of a bitch I met in the army, but he was the best company commander I ever had," as to hear, "Captain Jones was the best company commander I ever had, and I loved him like my father."

However the relationship between the leader and the led is formed, in the best units it becomes a compact into which both parties enter. The leader pledges through his actions to look after the interests of his subordinates as best he can within the limits of mission accomplishment. In return, the followers agree to do their best to accomplish any task the leader assigns them. Although seldom formalized, the compact is as binding as the ethics and morality of the participants can make it.

Military units have a hierarchical chain of command extending from the overall commander through subordinate leaders to the leaders of their lowest organizational components. These leaders usually exercise authority themselves, by virtue of their rank and position. However, "informal" leaders who exercise authority by virtue of their natural abilities, force of personality, or other traits often arise. The more confidence a unit has in its chain of command, the more likely it is that the informal leaders will be the same individuals as the formally designated leaders. For example, senior leaders found it necessary early in the Korean War to commission many qualified noncommissioned officers as lieutenants. In so doing, the army was really investing the informal leaders with rank commensurate with their day-to-day performance, thus strengthening mutual confidence within the unit.

Leaders in good units are confident that their soldiers will carry out any mission they assign them. In return for such obedience—to the death if necessary—followers trust their leaders not to value their lives lightly and to assign perilous missions only when there is no other recourse. That such dangerous and challenging missions would never be assigned for the self-interest or personal glory of the leader goes unquestioned.

Although leaders may display a hard-core attitude disdaining their own austere creature comforts, they must show concern for their followers' well-being. Successful leaders often conspicuously share their men's hardships and discomforts, refusing the amenities authorized them by virtue of their rank and position.

Trust that allows leaders and followers to rely upon one another for their own well-being is the result of cohesion that comes from shared experiences, especially shared hardships and exposure to dangerous situations. Even when such stressful events occur only in training, they nurture cohesion. Moreover, the longer a unit is together under stress, the stronger the cohesion grows. In good units, high morale bolsters this cohesion. The U.S. Army's famous infantry, armor, cavalry, and parachute units, as well as elite units in the U.S. Marine Corps and the French Foreign Legion have proud lineages and distinguished histories. Soldiers take pride in their units' accomplishments and their reputations. They seek harder missions, relish the hardships they endure, and build a character unique to the unit. They often isolate themselves from the rest of their service, feeling that they are not really the same as other units. Even a higher headquarters' failure to properly support a unit can foster a perverse pride in being able to persevere without outside assistance.

Finally, a charismatic or idiosyncratic leader can be the decisive element in lifting such a unit above the merely "good" unit. Such a leader need not have the panache of a MacArthur with his corncob pipe or a Patton with his ivory-handled revolvers, but he must project a presence that makes the soldier feel that his leader is communicating directly with him.

When everything comes together in a cohesive unit with a good leader and followers who trust him, one finds a unit that can accomplish far more than might be reasonably expected. Leaders expect more of their followers and the followers rise to meet those expectations. Followers similarly think their leaders can accomplish anything, and they do, at least in the eyes of the led. This phenomenon builds on and reinforces itself.

9

One of the worrisome questions in studying military operations is the measurement and determination of degrees of success in combat. The historian should be especially careful not to use the advantage of hindsight as a means of second-guessing the leader who had to make his decisions on the battlefield with all its physical and emotional distractions and unforgiving constraints of time and matériel. Notwithstanding this caveat, there is little reason for studying history except to try to gain insights into how other outcomes might have been different—better or worse—than those that are recorded in history. The simplest and most obvious determinant is mission accomplishment. If a commander is assigned a mission and he carries it out, no one can say he failed. However, one may still judge that success was gained at too high a cost, or without the commander's taking prudent precautions to minimize his losses. Some missions are more important than others, and the accomplishment of a minor goal may not be a worthwhile gain for the cost. A mission that carries a high risk of heavy losses—a "suicide mission" or "forlorn hope"—may be essential to attain an important goal. Nonetheless, such missions should never become commonplace, and the overriding importance of the goal in such missions should be clear. Higher commanders are responsible for specifying what loss percentage constitutes a justifiable cost of success. Should they fail to do so, subordinate commanders must seek specific guidance on this matter.

This is a historical study. It does not purport to be rigorous in the sense of rigidly accurate or scientifically precise, or replicable in other circumstances. Combat is a messy and disordered state of human affairs. No two engagements can ever be identical, and many, even when close together in time and space, reveal no similarities. Regarding accounts of the battles of Twin Tunnels and Chipyong-ni, there often were a half-dozen versions of events to choose from, including official journals, after-action reports, eyewitness accounts, and published histories. These accounts frequently contradict one another. Staff agencies properly placed their priorities on directing a battle, not on preserving the historical record. After-action reports have always been as much an opportunity to garner glory and avoid blame as to carefully weigh mistakes and missed opportunities and apportion responsibility for failure. Eyewitness accounts are seldom consciously erroneous, but memories sometimes harbor versions of the "truth" that have been subtly edited by the subconscious over time. In such cases, the best the historian can do is analyze the record, giving added weight to accounts made closer in time to the event, and use judgment in deciding on the most likely course of events.

History provides no "lessons" comparable to such indisputable conclusions as that of geometry concerning the square of the hypotenuse of a right triangle or that of chemistry concerning the composition of a hydrogen atom or that of physics concerning the wavelength of the color indigo. What then, is the merit in studying the actions of one regiment during two weeks of February, 1951, in such detail? Students of human behavior who are satisfied only by scientifically inviolable and irrefutable axioms will profit little from such a study. At the same time, there is no tangible benefit in studying history in any field if the student is merely looking for such lessons. Learning from history should not be merely superficial knowledge that teaches a specific response to a particular situation. Rather, history sharpens the intellect and disciplines the judgment better to analyze any situation within its context.

To study combat is to study the phenomenon of men interacting with other men in an atmosphere of violence and death. Because it is a human phenomenon, it is both unpredictable and *sui generis.* Nonetheless, different engagements show similarities and differences at times, and those similarities and differences can be enlightening. Just as in the study of history generally, the purpose is not to make one smarter for the next time, but to make one wise for all time. No one person is likely to engage in more than a few years of combat in a lifetime, but one can vicariously expand those experiences, however inadequately, through those of others. If this immersion into combat by proxy is to touch the emotions as deeply as the intellect, as it should, the reader should strive to feel a tingle of the exhilaration and a shudder of the despair of the human elements of combat and even to detect a hint of the stench of the battlefield in the participants' descriptions.

Leadership in the Crucible begins with events in 1950 at a verdant army post in America's Pacific Northwest, where the 23d Infantry Regiment was conducting routine peacetime training. With the outbreak of the Korean War, the regiment departed for the Far East with a new commander: Col. Paul Freeman. The desperate conditions on the Naktong River line soon gave all of the regiment's soldiers combat experience, and strengthened the cohesion of an already cohesive unit. Following the successful invasion at Inchon, the war entered a new phase and the regiment participated in the headlong advance of United Nations forces toward the Chinese border. Thanksgiving brought the entry of Chinese Communist Forces (CCF) into the war, and they drove the UN troops in a precipitate retreat down the peninsula.

The new year of 1951 saw a new Eighth Army commander on the battlefield: Lt. Gen. Matthew B. Ridgway. It also brought the only French UN forces to participate in the war, the Bataillon de Corée, and its larger than life commander, Lt. Col. Ralph Monclar. In just two months, the French Battalion and the 23d Regiment built bonds of camaraderie and combat efficiency unsurpassed by any similar units in the war. At the end of January, the units participated in a fierce and dangerous battle with Chinese forces at Twin Tunnels. In mid-February, elements of two Chinese armies cut off and surrounded the regiment and its French allies at Chipyong-ni and battered them for three days before an armored task force broke through to relieve them.

The story of the units and their combat is a story of combat leadership, successful and unsuccessful, at all levels of command. It is a story of men living and fighting together through desperate circumstances that many survived and many more did not. Their stories—stories of men sustaining themselves and one another to the limits of human endurance—are the focus of this work.

Chapter 1

The 23d Infantry Regiment and Col. Paul Freeman

T*here is one cardinal principle which must always be remembered: one must never make a show of false emotions to one's men. The ordinary soldier has a surprisingly good nose for what is true and what false.*

—Field Marshal Erwin Rommel

H*e makes a great mistake . . . who supposes that authority is firmer or better established when it is founded by force than that which is welded by affection.*

—Terence (Publius Terentius Afer)

D*iscipline must be imposed, but loyalty must be earned—yet the highest form of discipline exists only when there is mutual loyalty, up and down.*

—Maj. Gen. Aubrey "Red" Newman

In the summer of 1950, the soldiers of the 23d Infantry Regiment had no inkling of the destiny that awaited them in the Korean War. The regiment would earn two Presidential Unit Citations, the U.S. Army's highest award for achievement in combat by a unit. Individual soldiers would receive the full array of decorations that the nation awards its heroes. Unfortunately, many would be posthumous. The war's horrors and glories would forever change the lives of every soldier in the regiment.

The 23d Infantry Regiment

After the Second World War ended in Europe, the 23d Infantry Regiment returned to the United States and its new station at Camp Swift, Texas, about forty miles east of Austin. The regiment stayed there until its move to Fort Lewis, Washington, in 1947. The regiment was a part of the 2d Infantry Division, the U.S. Army's first division to be reorganized after World War II. Nonetheless, the 23d Regiment wrestled with the same problems that plagued every other infantry regiment in the post World War II army. It was understrength and had equipment left over from the war, much of it in need of rehabilitation. It had the normal "post support" and menial labor details that caused entire companies frequently to have only a few men left for training. It had the postwar army's emphasis on unit athletic competition, which reached semiprofessional standards. To all appearances, it might have been a typical infantry regiment in June, 1950. Nonetheless, its appearance hid some features that made it atypical in many ways.[1]

The regiment resided at North Fort Lewis, remote from Fort Lewis proper. There the troops lived in wooden mobilization-type barracks, avoiding the daily scrutiny of the 2d Division staff, which inhabited new brick buildings on the main post. In army slang, the soldiers were "away from the flagpole," meaning they could conduct their daily activities with a certain degree of autonomy. This separation built esprit de corps by making it seem to the men that they were different from the rest of the division. North Fort Lewis, for example, had its own officer, noncommissioned officer (NCO), and enlisted clubs, all of which were noted for their high-quality food and entertainment.

The one element that most set the 23d apart from the "average" U.S. infantry regiment was that it was a part of the 2d Infantry Division, the only infantry division in the continental United States (CONUS) that functioned as a regular infantry division. Other CONUS outfits were "training divisions" used only to train recruits, as the 2d itself had been until 1948. During World War II, the army had created special organizations outside the combat elements of the force to give basic military training to recruits. In the shrinking postwar army, however, units in excess of its tactical requirements were seen as a costly luxury, and using active army divisions to train recruits was an attractive, if inefficient, solution to the basic training problem. The soldiers in such training divisions provided instruction in close-order drill, individual and crew-served weapons, and other basic soldier skills. Organizations performing training missions did not get to train soldiers to become part of cohesive fighting units ready for war, and it was not a particularly satisfying assignment for the average soldier. Many career NCOs returning from the armies of occupation in

Europe and Japan sought to avoid duty in training divisions by requesting assignment to the 2d Division. Most soldiers preferred to be in a unit that trained together, where soldiers built bonds of camaraderie through shared stressful advanced training.

An additional difference in the 23d Regiment was its high number of seasoned NCOs, many of whom had accumulated extensive combat experience during World War II. Many platoons had NCOs who had received battlefield commissions as reserve officers; at least one platoon had seven. After the war, faced with a reduction in force, most of these "battlefields," as they were known, reverted to the enlisted ranks in order to remain on active duty. At least one NCO was a Medal of Honor recipient. This reservoir of talent and experience would prove crucial when the 23d went into action. It would provide the regiment with leaders who knew how to integrate new men quickly into their units and teach them the survival skills of an experienced infantryman. Just as important, it would give the regiment many soldiers with the potential to become top-notch commissioned officers.

The officers came from all of the various commissioning sources then in use by the army. A minority were graduates of the U.S. Military Academy at West Point, while most were commissioned through the Reserve Officers Training Corps (ROTC) at colleges and universities or the Officer Candidate Schools (OCS) run by the combat arms. A few were battlefields who had been allowed to retain their commissions.

The 2d Infantry Division was relieved of its recruit-training mission in order to become a regular combat division in the summer of 1949. That fall, the division began training for Operation Miki, an amphibious invasion of Hawaii. The training for and execution of this exercise provided the catalyst for a good outfit. The exercise immersed the officers, NCOs, and soldiers in the same sort of activities they would perform in wartime. Even though the tempo and urgency of combat operations could not be fully simulated, the enforced intimacy, hard work, and cooperation required in round-the-clock operations were much the same as in actual engagements with an enemy. The exercise was especially effective at teaching the techniques of combined arms operations, which involve the coordination of infantry, armor, artillery, and close air support on the battlefield. In addition, the soldiers and their leaders learned more of one another's strengths and weaknesses: whom they could trust, and whom they needed to supervise closely. Although most of the draftees departed before the regiment left for Korea, the cadre of officers and NCOs was little changed.

During the spring of 1950, the 23d Infantry Regiment conducted squad, platoon, and company training, including coordination with artillery and tanks. This hard training left the officers and NCOs with a solid grounding in fighting as a combined arms team. The shared stress of simulated combat, both in the Hawaii exercises and in the unit training the following year, was without question the best experience the organization could have had to build the bonds between soldiers that make for a cohesive unit, and it further raised the outfit's esprit de corps. This was important, since the average soldier in the 23d was a good soldier, but came from a humble background with little education. More than a few were in the army because a judge had offered service to them as an alternative to jail. One officer remembered only one soldier out of a hundred that he commanded who was a high school graduate.

When soldiers train hard together, they build cohesion that makes them greater than the sum of their parts. They are no longer just a group of men in uniform, but a unit that functions like a living organism in its cooperation to accomplish the mission. The ultimate cohesion-building exercise is combat. As one perceptive observer of men in combat expressed the phenomenon: In combat, the leaders

> realize that comradeship first develops through the consciousness of an obstacle to be overcome through common effort. A fighting unit with good morale is one in which many are of like mind and determination, unconsciously agreed on the suppression of individual desires in the interest of a shared purpose. . . .
>
> At its height, this sense of comradeship is an ecstasy. . . . In most of us there is a genuine longing for community with our human species, and at the same time an awkwardness and helplessness about finding the way to achieve it. Some extreme experience—mortal danger or the threat of destruction—is necessary to bring us fully together with our comrades or with nature. This is a great pity, for there are surely alternative ways more creative and less dreadful, if men would only seek them out. Until now, war has appealed because we discover some of the mysteries of communal joy in its forbidden depths. Comradeship reaches its peak in battle.[2]

This effect, present to a lesser degree even in simulated combat, though without the stakes and risks of combat, made teambuilding endeavors such as field exercises even more important.

The infantry regiment of 1950 was a unit of 3,781 men organized into three infantry battalions of 919 men each, supported by organic headquarters companies, a heavy mortar company, a medium tank company, and its own medical company.[3] During World War II, the army had recognized the need for a basic fighting unit of all ground arms that habitually worked together. By 1950 this concept had produced the Regimental Combat Team (RCT). By attaching other units to an infantry regiment, which would provide command and control for the RCT, the higher headquarters (usually a division) could construct a unit tailored for any mission. Units that were normally attached included a field artillery battalion, an antiaircraft artillery battery, and a combat engineer company. Other units that might have been attached for special missions included additional infantry, tanks, heavy artillery, signal (communications), military police, and Rangers. An RCT so augmented was a couple of thousand men larger than the basic organization. Such an organization allowed the units to learn one another's abilities, skills, and weaknesses, and its soldiers and leaders to know and trust one another.

The RCT was a self-contained fighting unit of formidable capabilities. Its mission was "to close with the enemy by fire and maneuver in order to capture or destroy him; or to repel his assault by fire and close combat." Its capabilities included furnishing a base of fire and maneuver for other units; seizing and holding terrain; maneuvering in any terrain or climatic conditions; providing antitank protection and support; and providing its own communications, reconnaissance, medical service, and supply and maintenance. Moreover, it could operate independently of its higher headquarters when required.[4]

When Pres. Harry S. Truman decided that the United States would defend South Korean soil at the outbreak of war in June, 1950, he sealed the 23d Infantry Regiment's destiny. On Sunday morning, 9 July 1950, the day after Gen. of the Army Douglas MacArthur was made commander of all United Nations forces in Korea, the Pentagon alerted the 2d Infantry Division that it was being transferred to MacArthur's Far East Command (FECOM). Someone who has not experienced such an abrupt change in mission might expect such a notification of deployment to lower the morale of a unit's soldiers. Such was by no means the case in the 23d. Instead, the morale of many of the regiment's professional soldiers rose, and disciplinary infractions fell to a surprisingly low level as members of the unit prepared to deploy to the Far East. The soldiers went on a round-the-clock duty schedule preparing equipment and personnel for debarkation. Scuttlebutt in the division was that the deployment would be little more than an exercise—a live-fire exercise against another army, albeit a second-rate army at best. Soldiers were ordered to take their dress uniforms for occupation duty after the short war. Unlike World War II, when infantrymen deployed to war with the knowledge that they faced hardship or even death, this overconfidence contributed to a lack of psychological readiness for the intense stress the soldiers encountered upon arrival in Korea.[5]

To bring the regiment to full strength, a call went out for volunteers from other units, personnel were levied from other units, and men were sent directly from basic training. A number of veterans of postwar occupation duty in Korea were among the replacements. More than a few were unwilling transfers from other specialties and units far from Fort Lewis who had no training in infantry skills. Many of the personnel who filled out the regiment were not up to the physical fitness standards expected of the average infantryman.[6]

The attitude a soldier brought to the 23d often related directly to whether he had volunteered or been shipped off by his parent unit to fill a quota. Unwilling warriors provided a challenge to their leaders. One unhappy levy from another unit was Pfc. Carlton C. Kluck:

> I was sent by way of troop train from Fort Riley, Kansas to Fort Lewis to fill up the 2d Division prior to overseas shipment. At the time I was a PFC [Private First Class] and a tanker. During the in-processing at Fort Lewis I was told that tanks weren't needed in Korea because of the terrain and that I was now an infantryman. This came much to my displeasure as I had enlisted in 1948 as Armor. I hadn't asked for much. . . .
>
> Many of us [replacements] were reclassified to fill a slot, not because we were qualified or had the training. We soon found out that this criminal practice not only happened to the lower enlisted grades but also to some NCOs.

Kluck's dissatisfaction was understandable. Partly as a result of his meager infantry training, he would be wounded for the first time less than a week after his arrival in Korea.

In contrast to the reluctant levies from other units, one of the soldiers who volunteered was Pvt. D. W. Hoffman, assigned to an engineer battalion at Fort Lewis. Hoffman enlisted in the army at the age of nineteen after dropping out of high school a year earlier. His company commander addressed the soldiers in a formation in the company street and asked for volunteers to fill the 2d Infantry Division. Out of a 250-man company, more than two hundred volunteered. Hoffman later characterized those who did not as family men or soldiers too old for combat. He remembers the duty motivation at the time as being very strong.

Only two weeks after notification, the 23d Regiment was steaming out of the Puget Sound aboard seven ships bound for Korea. The trip across the Pacific was mostly uneventful. Some units arranged for their soldiers who lacked infantry training to fire their weapons off the fantail of the ship. As the reluctant Private Kluck remembered the exercise:

Officers would throw blocks of wood overboard and this was to be your target. The best way I can describe it is it was like shooting from a moving elevator at another moving elevator going in the opposite direction. We were called to the fantail by compartments. Some men avoided fouling their weapons by wandering into other compartments. Very little control was exercised.

Classes were conducted on the main deck on disassembly and assembly of the M1 rifle, BAR, and .30-cal. machine gun. I soon found out I wasn't the most ignorant infantryman aboard ship.

I don't remember how long it was before the fantail shooting stopped. Rumor had it that some of the guys were shooting at the seagulls, which were reported to be easier to hit than the wooden blocks. As a result the [ship's] crewmen were up in arms. Something about international law and omens of dire future occurrences.

Other units conducted classes, including lectures on how poor the North Koreans soldiers were. Rumor had it that they could not shoot or handle ammunition, and that they were afraid of the dark. For most veterans, however, there was little preparation aboard ship for their coming ordeal; they recall only the boredom of the two-week voyage.

Colonel Freeman

In June, 1950, the army chose Col. Paul Lamar Freeman Jr. to lead the men of the 23d. The son of an army surgeon, Freeman spent much of his childhood in East Asia, where his father served in the Philippines and Japan, and the rest on small army posts in the United States. Just turned forty-three, Freeman was a member of the West Point class of 1929. Reflecting on his career in retirement, he said becoming an army officer "seemed the only natural and normal thing to do. It never occurred to me to be anything else." In 1925, there were two hundred candidates for only twelve Presidential appointments to the Military Academy, and Freeman ranked thirteenth.[7] A family friend recalled: "thus began a frantic search for congressmen with vacancies in the vicinity of Governors Island, where [Freeman's] father was stationed. With ten days left, he received a call from the Third Congressional District of New York, located in Brooklyn, asking if he were still interested. Paul responded, 'Definitely, yes!' When he went to the District, he found out why they hadn't filled any vacancies in several years; no one spoke English! Paul immediately established his residence in a Brooklyn rooming house, and in July 1925 he entered West Point with the Class of 1929."[8]

Freeman did not shine academically at West Point, and he remained a cadet private all four years. In his own estimation, he "led a very undistinguished cadet life." In later years, Freeman said he received a first-rate math and science education at West Point. Nonetheless, he always believed that the academy had not prepared him properly to be a good army officer in terms of writing and foreign language skills, or in general knowledge of the military.[9] One of his classmates wrote of him in the 1929 *Howitzer,* the West Point yearbook: "In a manner characteristic of his placid and pleasing nature, Paul entered Beast Barracks unnoticed by and unknown to many, but it was not long before he was the boon companion of many and well liked by all. He is the possessor of remarkably carefree spirits, but his carefree attitude is not one of indifference. For [he] can and does tackle unpleasantnesses and duties with a dogged determination that is only his."[10]

Although he wanted to enter the Army Air Corps, his eyesight deteriorated during his cadet years and he was commissioned as an infantry officer. After completing infantry training at Fort Benning, Georgia, he reported to Fort Hood, Texas, for his initial assignment: with the 2d Infantry Division's 9th Infantry Regiment.

He began his first Far East tour in 1933: three years at Tientsin, China, with the 15th Infantry Regiment. More than one of his fellow Korean War veterans, along with many observers of Freeman's career, credit much of his success in Korea to his long experience with the Chinese before the war. Following a stateside tour of duty as an instructor at the Infantry School at Fort Benning, he returned to China as a language student. In 1941, he became the assistant attaché at Chungking and was there when the Japanese bombed Pearl Harbor. When Lt. Gen. Joseph W. "Vinegar Joe" Stilwell arrived in the newly created China-Burma-India theater, Freeman served as his supply officer during the early years of World War II.[11] His wartime assignments, as a friend described them, "were like a Frederick

Forsyth novel: a mission to northwest China in an old Ford Trimotor, an investigation of Soviet activities along the Sino-Russian border accompanied by a Chinese graduate of VMI, a meeting with Hemingway in Rangoon, the British Commando School in Maymyo, Burma, driving a car over the old Burma Road from Rangoon to Chunking, liaison to Chennault and his Flying Tigers, working with the British and their long-range Chinese patrols behind the Japanese lines."[12]

After his service in China, Freeman served on the Joint War Plans Committee on the War Department General Staff for a few months. There he prepared plans for the U.S. Army's return to the Philippines. He then became chief of staff of the 77th Infantry Division in the Philippines and carried out some of the war plans he had helped write. After Manila fell he was ordered to report back to the Joint War Plans Committee, where he acted for a time as a liaison officer to MacArthur's headquarters in the Pacific, with the mission of orienting MacArthur on the provisions of the Yalta agreements.[13]

Freeman next went to Brazil, where he spent two years as chief of the Army Section of the Joint Brazil–United States Military Commission. There he met and served under Lt. Gen. Matthew B. Ridgway, then chairman of the Inter-American Defense Board. Ridgway had a profound influence on Freeman, who, looking back on his experiences with Ridgway in Brazil and Korea, rated Ridgway as "my number one combat commander."[14]

Freeman was a handsome officer whose erect posture and slender build made him seem taller than he was. Veterans seeing him again after the war often remarked that "he seemed taller in Korea." One said, "God, I thought that man was seven feet tall, but he turned out only an inch or so above my five feet seven inches." He was utterly without flamboyance. His jeep was unadorned with rank insignia or the flashing lights and sirens adopted by some commanders; no flag flew at regimental headquarters. In Korea, his soldiers would remember his never wearing a helmet, but often having a blue infantry scarf tucked in his collar. He looked to his soldiers "like he just stepped out of a band box." Although he wore rank insignia, "somehow it didn't stand out."

Freeman's command philosophy, as demonstrated by his actions, was similar to that of many good American commanders. He believed that he needed to go where his men would see him. He believed that the American soldier would generally do his best to get the job done, however difficult, if he had faith that his chain of command was doing its utmost to give him the support he needed. As he and his men got used to one another, he gave orders and expected them to be carried out without supervision. Whenever possible, he gave commands in person, often with a grin, a handshake, or a word of encouragement before a dangerous mission. He always gave mission-type orders, and seldom issued formal directives.[15] After the regiment's first few weeks in Korea he abandoned traditional written orders entirely.

Freeman was a friendly and unassuming individual who never held himself aloof from the private soldier, and many soldiers remember him making small talk with them in Korea. Nonetheless, his easygoing manner was neither lax nor careless. He could be firm, brutally so when required. His philosophy on holding ground, for example, was uncompromising: if a unit gave up ground without being overrun, it would take casualties during its retreat. It would then suffer more casualties when the inevitable order came to retake the ground. He could understand one of his units being overrun by a stronger force, but he would not excuse a unit that gave up ground simply because it was under strong pressure. This philosophy caused his subordinate units to be tenacious defenders in Korea, surprising attackers with their determined resilience more than once.

Above all, Freeman understood and devoted himself to his soldiers— a devotion they repaid many times over. One cannot find a 23d Infantry veteran who served under Freeman who does not remember him fondly.

With only a few days' notice that he was being given command of the 23d, he sold his house in Washington, D.C., on the day war broke out in Korea and hurried to Fort Lewis to assume command on the eve of the regiment's departure. It appears that Ridgway may have had a hand in Freeman's selection for command of the regiment. At any rate, Freeman felt that he was taking command of a strong, well-trained regiment with good battalion commanders.[16]

In the hectic days before embarkation at Fort Lewis, Freeman found time to visit each of the regiment's twenty companies. He talked informally with the troops, standing on the mess hall steps or in some similar location. His speeches were never bombastic, but his manner was one that conveyed his sincerity. He was skilled at communicating with soldiers, able to make each of them feel he was speaking directly to him, even in a group. Corporal Leslie Gains remembers Freeman telling him and his comrades that every one of them would be afraid in combat. If they were not, they were either a liar or a fool, and he needed neither in his regiment. He also told them never to get too big to pray. Gains said this speech carried him through his toughest fighting in Korea. No veteran remembers all of the speech, but many recall Freeman's promise to give every soldier three days off to settle his affairs. Given all that had to be done, this was a stiff commitment, but he carried through on his promise.

Just after the regiment received the order to move to Korea, an incident occurred involving an NCO that underlined Freeman's attention to the well-being of all soldiers. Sergeant Frank Butler had planned to get married later in the year. The banns had been published and his fiancée arrived for the wedding the day before the regiment was alerted for Korea. Sergeant Butler contacted the Catholic chaplain and told him that the wedding would have to be moved up. The chaplain refused, saying that he did not perform "gangplank weddings." Devastated, the sergeant took the problem to his company commander, who called Colonel Freeman. Freeman arranged for the wedding to take place that very night in the regimental chapel.

The colonel was affable and at ease with all ranks, but an infantry regiment does not get things done if everyone has a relaxed attitude. Someone must be ready to play the heavy when necessary. As in many good units, that personality resided in the second in command. Freeman's executive officer (initially, his operations officer) was Maj. Frank Meszar, a former enlisted man who graduated from West Point in 1940.

At the academy, Meszar built a reputation for being more a soldier than a scholar, and he kept the reputation of being a first-rate field soldier throughout his career. Not yet thirty-five years old when the regiment left for Korea, Meszar hit it off with Freeman aboard ship. There the two men established the relationship that would carry them through the hard combat of the next six months.

Extremely reluctant to offend anyone, Freeman was not a "hard" disciplinarian. He found his disciplinarian in Meszar, who was never reluctant to tell a soldier that he was wrong, whatever his rank or station. Meszar, who possessed a dry wit, was able to do the dirty work almost gently unless the situation required more stringent measures, from which he did not shrink.[17]

In the combination of Freeman and Meszar, the 23d had one of the finest commander-executive officer relationships in the history of American arms. Freeman, a brilliant judge of subordinates, became his men's benevolent and inspirational father, whereas Meszar was the tough and demanding older brother who kept them in line.

C h a p t e r   2

Baptism by Fire on the Naktong River Line

Here dead we lie because we did not choose to live and shame the land from which we sprung. Nor did they choose to shame their comrades, or themselves.

—A. E. Houseman

I believe that anyone can conquer fear by doing the things he fears to do, provided he keeps doing them until he gets a record of successful experiences behind him.

—Eleanor Roosevelt

The first quality of a soldier is constancy in enduring fatigue and hardship. Courage is only the second. Poverty, privation, and want are the school of the good soldier.

—Napoleon

The 23d Infantry Regiment arrived in Korea to find itself in a war unlike any the U.S. Army had ever fought, in a place it had never expected to fight. Neither the American people nor their soldiers had ever envisioned an American army fighting on the far-off Asian mainland in a country few in either group could have found on a world map, in a cause few would have called vital to America's interests.

The Korean War: Outbreak and Early Action

The Korean peninsula juts from the Asian mainland in an elongated and irregular expanse toward the islands of Japan. The peninsula measures roughly 150 by 500 miles, but narrows to only about 100 miles in width at both Seoul and Pyongyang before it spreads to the 500-mile border along the Yalu River to the north. In 1950, that northern border separated Korea from both the newly established People's Republic of China (PRC) and the Soviet Union. Although it occupies roughly the same latitudes as the United States from Los Angeles to Portland, Korea is anything but similar in geography and climate. The peninsula is very rugged and mountainous, making the few intervening flat areas especially important for agriculture. One GI remarked that Korea "would be a hell of a big place if they ever flattened it out." By 1950, most of the mountains were barren, with at most a few scrubby trees on their slopes. The remaining forests had been cleared during the period when Korea was a Japanese colony. The mountains provide a substantial challenge even for toughened infantrymen. Short, hot summers and long, cold winters characterize a climate of extremes. The annual temperature ranges from far below zero to above one hundred degrees Fahrenheit.[1]

As the portion of the world war in the Pacific came to an abrupt end in August, 1945, the American and Soviet victors almost casually agreed to partition the Korean peninsula along the 38th Parallel. No American at the time saw this arrangement as anything more than a convenience for taking the surrender of the Japanese in Korea. In the years that followed, however, it became a feature of the Cold War. The United States soon became the benefactor of the southern government, while the Soviet Union nurtured the northern regime. Although it did not become apparent until the outbreak of the war, the two patrons of the North and South Koreans had divergent philosophies concerning their charges. The Russians set about building a communist state under Soviet-trained leader Kim Il Sung. The Americans, on the other hand, looked for a way to set South Korea on its own feet as quickly as possible. The U.S. Army was especially eager to return its occupation forces to the United States. The leader of South Korea was American-educated Syngman Rhee, a single-minded and conservative defender of Korean interests as he defined them.

The causes of the war are still emerging from the mists of myth and legend that have enshrouded it on all sides. They are being clarified as scholars gain freer access to the Chinese and former Soviet archives, but will not be entirely revealed until North Korean archives become available.[2] There is little debate over the actual events, however. In the early morning hours on Sunday, 25 June 1950, North Korean units invaded South Korea in a lightning attack by well-trained infantry supported by tanks and artillery. The American-trained defenders, who possessed no

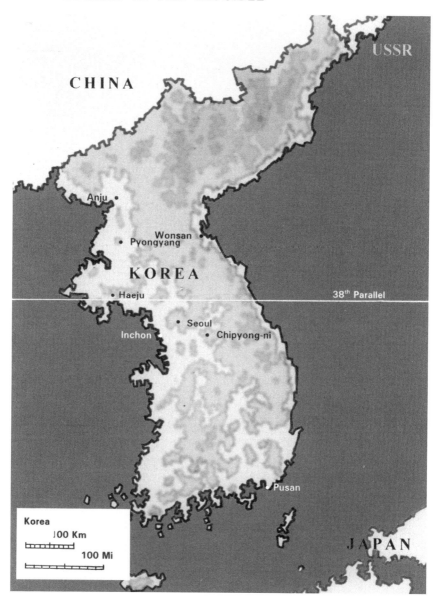

tanks and virtually no artillery, quickly succumbed to the offensive. There was nothing on the peninsula to stop a precipitous defeat of South Korea.

Staff officers in General MacArthur's headquarters in Tokyo and military and political leaders in Washington generated hurried and concerned appraisals of the situation in Korea. Although the Truman administration had placed the peninsula outside America's defensive perimeter in the

26

western Pacific, it seemed unthinkable to let this example of unprovoked and unbridled conquest go unanswered. For President Truman, this clear aggression was, if unanswered, the harbinger of another world war. Without hesitation, Truman told Secretary of State Dean Acheson, "we've got to stop the sons of bitches no matter what."[3]

The Truman administration took the matter to the United Nations Security Council and received UN backing to send forces to assist the South Koreans with their defense against the northern onslaught. The American forces closest to the conflict were those of the occupation army in Japan. General MacArthur, in his role as commander in chief in East Asia, immediately dispatched units to intervene in South Korea.

When the peninsula leapt into American consciousness at the end of June, few in the U.S. Army thought the war would provide much of a challenge to American soldiers. The plans MacArthur's staff developed offer a glimpse at their wishful thinking. The first plans included a preposterously optimistic landing at Inchon, far up the peninsula's west coast, near Seoul. This amphibious invasion was timed to coincide with other U.S. forces entering the fray through the southern port of Pusan. In the event, MacArthur's forces would land at Inchon, but two months later than initially planned. When MacArthur's chief of staff, Maj. Gen. Edward M. "Ned" Almond, dispatched the 1st Cavalry Division to the planned July landing at Inchon, he told its commander to hurry or his men would hit only the tail of the 24th Division as it passed through Seoul on its way north. Reality proved far different.

The American-trained Republic of Korea (ROK) army proved no match for the Soviet-trained North Korean People's Army (NKPA), which routed the ROK forces in the initial days of the war. When American units arrived, the North Koreans pushed them from the initial battlefields as well. By the beginning of August, when the 23d Regiment docked, the NKPA had squeezed the United Nations forces into a defensive perimeter around the essential port of Pusan, an enclave that became known as the Pusan Perimeter or the Naktong River line.[4]

The North Korean People's Army had substantial advantages over the ROK army. Soviet advisers trained the NKPA in the years after World War II, and many were still with units as late as 1950. The advisers did not, however, take part in the invasion of the South. Stalin recalled them on the eve of the war, fearing that they might be taken prisoner and thus provide evidence of Soviet involvement. The NKPA outnumbered the ROK army about two to one in total number of trained soldiers. Additionally, about one-third of the North's soldiers were CCF veterans who had fought in the Chinese civil war. They gave the NKPA a core of experience and training the ROK army lacked.

The Americans who trained the ROK forces had omitted a number of important items that an efficient military force needed in 1950. Foremost among these shortcomings was the ROK army's lack of tanks and heavy artillery. The only artillery piece the ROKs employed was the 105-mm howitzer, with a range of only about seventy-five hundred meters compared to about fourteen thousand meters for the NKPA's 76-mm divisional guns. In 1950, however, neither the South Koreans nor their American advisers appreciated this facet of the NKPA's superiority over the ROK army. Most members of the American military on the eve of the war would, if asked, have expressed confidence that the Republic of Korea could defend itself efficiently. After all, had not the ROK army's senior U.S. adviser described it as "the best Army in Asia"?[5]

The 23d Infantry Regiment Enters the War

After the 23d Infantry disembarked at Pusan on 5 August, it drew equipment and trained during a two-week respite before being committed to battle. Truck drivers became adept at navigating the difficult terrain, while communications men, mess personnel, and maintenance crews practiced the intricacies of full-time field operations. Round-the-clock perimeter security became second nature. Another indicator that leaders in Washington did not view the NKPA as a capable and determined foe was that Pentagon planners had determined the 2d Infantry Division would not be "combat loaded" for the voyage to Korea. This meant that instead of placing all of the men and equipment of a single unit on the same ship, ready for combat on arrival, the division was "administratively loaded," with equipment and personnel dispersed in such a way that cargo space was used in the most efficient manner, with no provision for quick deployment. As a result, the men were in Korea for some time before their heavy equipment arrived. They used the time for training, especially forced marches, to toughen the men and improve their endurance.

Although a number of heat casualties occurred, Freeman credited this fitness regimen with improving the men's combat capabilities. Above all, the soldiers, their officers, and NCOs became toughened to the climate and terrain. Additionally, those soldiers who had arrived in the regiment just before departure became fully assimilated into their units during the training.[6]

Immediately upon arrival, Freeman began transforming the 23d Infantry into a Regimental Combat Team. The 2d Infantry Division had attached the 37th Field Artillery Battalion, a battery from the 82d Antiaircraft Artillery Battalion, and a company from the 2d Engineer Battalion to the regiment. The field artillery battalion had three cannon batteries, each equipped with 105-mm howitzers. The antiaircraft artillery battery had eight gun sections, each equipped with one twin-barreled 40-mm and one quad-mounted .50-caliber automatic weapon. In the vernacular of the soldiers, these World War II leftovers were known as "flak wagons." The quad-.50 was mounted on a half-tracked truck, and the twin-40-mm came on a fully tracked tank chassis. They provided fearsome firepower for the infantry. None of the forces opposing the United Nations Command (UNC) in the Korean War ever used much close air support, so commanders used the antiaircraft weapons for additional firepower in ground operations. The combat engineer company's nine platoons were used to help build or destroy field fortifications and shelters, and their soldiers fought as infantry whenever required. Had all units been at full strength, this would have added almost eleven hundred men to the 3,781-man regiment. In reality, however, all units were understrength.[7]

By mid-August, all of the regiment's leaders understood the seriousness of the situation. For the next month, until succored by the still-secret amphibious invasion of Inchon far to the north, the Eighth Army, at that time commanding all forces in Korea, would be fighting for its survival. On 19 August, higher headquarters ordered the 23d to occupy a defensive position astride the 2d Division's main supply route (MSR) from Pusan to Taegu. At the time, other forces were fiercely engaging a large NKPA force trying to take Taegu, a linchpin on the Naktong River line and the last important road junction between the line and Pusan itself. If Taegu fell, the Eighth Army would have to consider evacuating the peninsula.[8]

Lieutenant General Walton H. Walker, the Eighth Army commander, credited the 23d Regiment's first combat action in Korea with saving Taegu. The NKPA drew first blood with an attack on 22 August. During the night of 22–23 August, Colonel Freeman and Major Meszar went forward personally to control the action. The American regiment counterattacked at dawn. Determined attacks by two battalions took their ground objectives and held on against fierce NKPA counterattacks all day and into the night. The 2d Battalion's Fox Company received a strong all-out counterattack at about 2100 hours, but repulsed it after taking a heavy toll of the enemy. The regimental heavy mortar company coordinated its fires with the field artillery battalion and kept the NKPA from successfully re-forming in front of the 23d's lines. The action was over by dawn on the twenty-fourth—at dramatically different costs to the enemy and friendly forces. The 23d's losses were light, whereas five hundred North Korean bodies lay in front of the regiment's positions, and uncounted others had been killed or injured by indirect fire. An NKPA lieutenant captured later told his interrogator that, after this action, his regiment existed "in name only."[9]

Many of the 23d's senior officers and NCOs had experienced combat before and understood the fears of facing hostile fire for the first time. Most of the junior officers and enlisted men, however, were getting their baptism by fire on the Naktong. D. W. Hoffman spent several weeks with a graves registration detail burying American dead before he was sent to the infantry. He remembers his initiation to combat vividly:

Upon arrival at Fox Company we were introduced to the First Sergeant. There was no company commander at the time. He had been wounded the day before. As I remember it now, there were four officers in the company; all were second lieutenants and were all battlefield commissions. Up until that time and for the next seventeen days and nights Fox Company will take a hell of a beating.

I was introduced to the third platoon leader, Second Lieutenant James D. Currie, who was the platoon sergeant the week before. There was no bullshit and he told it as it is. He assigned me to a foxhole with an experienced man. He took my M-1 [Garand rifle] and gave me an M-2 carbine with double banana clips plus six more double clips.[10] He told me to listen to my partner and I would do all right. My foxhole "buddy" was Stan Ledbetter. He was a corporal and had been in the 2d Infantry Division for two years.

My baptism of fire came at about [0300 hours] the first night I was on the line. The North Koreans hit us with what appeared to be everything they had. It seemed to me that the firefight lasted for hours but in reality it lasted for about 45 minutes.

I never fired a shot nor threw a grenade. I just curled up in a prenatal position in the bottom of the foxhole and begged almighty God to spare me. I awoke at daybreak. Stan was sitting on the backside of the foxhole with his M-1 across his lap. He asked me if I was okay. I said yes, but I felt like a complete ass. He said, "Don't worry about it. You will be okay. It just takes time."

Lieutenant Currie came around and checked every foxhole. He came to our hole and asked if all was okay. Stan said yes. He then asked for my piece. He looked it over and said, "You never fired this weapon did you?" I said, "No." He then, in a very slow deliberate manner began to explain the facts of life to me and what I must do to stay alive.

Thus began a relationship of complete trust and respect. I would follow that man into the gates of hell. He was one hell of a fine soldier. He never yelled, he spoke in a low and matter-of-fact tone. It appeared he feared nothing, nor nobody. I adjusted and became part of the family of the third platoon. . . . I adjusted.

This relationship of trust and respect would take Private Hoffman through many more harrowing experiences, and through the war.

The process of transforming a civilian into a soldier begins when he enters the military, but it progresses through basic training and unit training when he joins an organization, often through months and years of preparing for action without hearing a shot fired in anger. However much leaders may try to inculcate a spirit of readiness for combat during peacetime exhortations and exercises, individual soldiers deal with the actual experience in many ways. Some soldiers are able to harden themselves as they imagine the situations they may face. Many, however, still find themselves surprised by the intensity of the experience. Becoming inured to the experiences of seeing one's friends injured or killed, as well as the necessity of killing other human beings or suffering injury or death oneself, is not a casual metamorphosis. It usually involves an expectation of danger and a determination to take whatever actions may be required to survive. Once a soldier experiences such profound changes in his ethos, a return to "normal" conditions may be difficult. Audie Murphy, the most decorated soldier of World War II, perhaps best expressed the feeling of many soldiers who have experienced combat. When someone asked him how men survive war, he answered, "I don't think they ever do."[11]

Sergeant Doug Graney, the Easy Company communications chief, remembers his feelings in the early days on the Naktong River line:

I can't speak for others but in the beginning when we were first committed on the Pusan Perimeter, survival was everything because of the loss of people you'd known. Maybe not well but people you trained with were either killed or wounded bad enough not to return to the company. The constant rush of adrenaline until you'd be shaking all over for what seemed like eternity. The smell of cordite and the stench of rotting bodies stacked around our positions on the Naktong, which was like sticking your head in a barrel of dead rats and keeping it there.[12]

Later I for one became less nervous or scared and seeing people killed or in pieces bothered me less until it seemed almost a normal human existence. The filth of body and clothes became normal; living in a foxhole of rainwater or digging into frozen ground and living like an animal became normal or seemed so.

At times I felt "bulletproof." At other times I couldn't dig my foxhole deep enough. I was always confident I'd come home in one piece.

The regiment had cause to feel good about its first ordeal by fire in the Korean War, but it could not rest on its laurels. During the next three weeks, the 23d faced some of its heaviest fighting of the war.

As combat continued day after day, casualties mounted among the defenders. More and more junior officers were lost to enemy action in the crucial fighting on the Naktong, and before long the 23d began tapping its reservoir of experienced NCOs. Junior officer leadership is critical in an infantry unit, and hard fighting, by its very nature, takes a toll on good junior leaders. The need for lieutenants soon caused units throughout Eighth Army to begin screening NCOs for those with the potential to perform well as lieutenants. Noncoms who had received battlefield commissions in World War II and later returned to the NCO ranks were reluctant to accept commissions because of the way they had been treated after the war. Many came from rural backgrounds and were used to hard work and individual initiative, but they lacked a strong educational background or the social skills that the peacetime army expected of officers. As a result, when the global war ended, the army summarily told many of them that they could choose either to revert to the enlisted ranks or be discharged. One of these World War II "battlefields" was M.Sgt. Robert W. Curtis of the 2d Battalion, 23d Infantry. He adamantly refused a commission, and accepted it only through a stratagem involving the battalion commander, Lt. Col. James Edwards, and Maj. Gen. Laurence B. "Dutch" Keiser, the 2d Division commander. Edwards told Curtis to report to division headquarters for an award ceremony. When he arrived, General Keiser pinned a lieutenant's bar on him. He took the bar off and handed it back, but was persuaded to keep it to avoid embarrassing the general. As a lieutenant, he played an important part in a number of key actions on the Naktong and later.

Throughout the early part of the Korean War, vexing ammunition shortages caused commanders to ration ammunition, especially for field and antiaircraft artillery weapons. As Freeman put it: "We were always on the brink of running out. Always scared to death that we were going to get caught with no ammunition." For this reason, in contrast to World War II and the Vietnam War, there was little use of harassing and interdiction (H and I) fires, in which the artillery fires on likely or suspected enemy positions without knowing whether enemy soldiers were actually occupying the positions.[13]

The shortage of ammunition placed a premium on ingenious methods of using whatever was available. One time on the Naktong, the 23d's antiaircraft artillery battery commander, Capt. Kenneth Bullion, suggested that Freeman allow him to clear a ridge of enemy soldiers with his flak wagons rather than with field artillery fires. The 40-mm cannon shells then employed were fused to burst at preset times so that they would explode near high-flying aircraft. Using a technique that later became standard, Bullion moved his twin-40-mm cannons into position at a range approximating that altitude and fired toward the crest of the ridge. The shells arrived above the ridgeline at the same time their fuses burned out, causing effective airbursts that saturated the enemy positions with shell fragments. Freeman nicknamed Bullion "the vacuum cleaner" because of the way his guns "cleaned up" the hill.[14]

The NKPA leaders had operations planned for the end of August that they expected to constitute the final offensive of the war. Although the U.S. soldiers in the field knew nothing of this, Eighth Army intelligence had more than an inkling of what was in the plan. Instead of trying for a breakthrough at a vulnerable point in the line, the NKPA planned to attack at several locations on the line in multidivision assaults. General Walker, knowing that he had to have units all along his almost 150-mile front, ordered units to occupy unheard of frontages. As an example, the 23d Infantry's 1st Battalion occupied a sixteen-thousand-meter line, or almost ten miles. This was not a continuous line, of course, but a series of company positions often several miles apart.[15]

Freeman's regiment was now on the southwest portion of the Pusan Perimeter, his fighting strength reduced by one-third when the 3d Battalion was detached to reinforce the 1st Cavalry Division to the north. The regiment deployed with one battalion forward and one to the rear, with the regimental headquarters located between them.

During World War II, the 2d Infantry Division commander, General Keiser, was the VI Corps chief of staff at Anzio in Italy. During this amphibious invasion, American soldiers were much criticized for their lack of aggressiveness in getting out of their foxholes and moving inland from the beachhead. Possibly as a result of this experience, General Keiser had put the word out that his soldiers should not dig strong defensive positions because doing so might weaken their offensive spirit. As a result of Keiser's ill-considered guidance, the soldiers were in weak fighting positions. An hour before midnight on the last day of August, simultaneous attacks hit the left half of the forward battalion's positions. An estimated four battalions of NKPA infantry supported by a heavy artillery barrage hit Charlie Company on the left boundary and a similar force hit Baker Company in the center of the sector. Although both units fought gallantly, the North Korean forces poured around the U.S. positions, attacking Able Company's southern flank and threatening the battalion command post (CP) to the rear. By the early hours of 1 September, all of the forward battalion's elements were under attack and casualties were heavy.[16]

It soon became apparent that Charlie Company could not hold its sector, so Colonel Freeman ordered the 2d Battalion, in the rear, to form a strong blocking position to keep enemy forces from getting through.[17] Major Lloyd K. Jenson, the battalion executive officer, formed a force consisting of Fox Company reinforced with elements of Hotel Company and moved to seize the high ground commanding the main road to Charlie Company's rear. The position was called the "switch" position because it was near the battalion's forward telephone switchboard. Meanwhile, Freeman attached George Company to the 1st Battalion and ordered it to form another blocking position on high ground to allow the battalion's forward elements to withdraw to its rear.

Pending the arrival of George Company, Freeman's emphasis on holding ground came into play. He ordered a Charlie Company platoon to hold the position until George Company showed up. He reinforced the platoon heavily, giving it a section of 75-mm recoilless rifles, a twin-40-mm flak wagon, and a platoon of tanks. The reinforced platoon fought a gallant delaying action against tremendous odds. The heavy weapons—recoilless rifles, flak wagon, and tanks—laid down a base of fire for the infantrymen to maneuver rearward.

As he fought his way to the rear, the Charlie Company platoon leader fired a previously prepared barrel of *fougasse* at the approaching NKPA force. *Fougasse* (French for land mine), as used in the Korean War, was a fifty-five-gallon drum of gasoline mixed with motor oil or other thick flammables. During defensive preparations, soldiers buried the drum at an angle aimed toward an approach to the position. The infantrymen ignited the combined explosives from a remote location using detonating cord to explode white phosphorous grenades or mortar shells or TNT buried under the base of the barrel. When fired, the *fougasse* erupted in a huge inferno of napalmlike flame that engulfed everything over a wide angle to the front with devastating results. In this instance, it disorganized the attackers enough that the platoon could quickly withdraw with no further losses.

The NKPA isolated the rest of Charlie Company from the battalion at the beginning of the attack, and in the hours after midnight the enemy overran it. The remnants of the company made their way to the switch position that Major Jenson had established. The company commander and many of his soldiers were never seen again; only thirty-three survivors made it back to the battalion CP.

At the same time the North Koreans overran Charlie Company, Able Company was under attack from the south, and the battalion commander, Lt. Col. Claire E. Hutchin, ordered it to consolidate near its north flank. Hutchin had assumed command just before the regiment deployed and his officers worried because he had only about a year of experience in the infantry—most of his experience had been as a staff officer. He had an experienced staff, however, and demonstrated that he would listen to their advice. His actions in this defense earned him his first Distinguished Service Cross of the war.[18]

After a hard night of fighting, Lieutenant Colonel Hutchin ordered Able Company to begin withdrawing to the switch position at 0730 hours. By early afternoon, what remained of the battalion was consolidated there. A ring of low hills provided cover for the battalion CP, facilitating a fine perimeter defense.[19] Captain William R. Guthrie, Hutchin's Dog (heavy weapons) Company commander, remembers the defense:

Lieutenant Colonel Hutchin ordered me to the rear, covered by two tanks, to take wounded and [captured] classified documents and to bring ammunition, food, and water back. My trip to the regimental headquarters was interesting. We saw a North Korean battalion advancing well to the rear of the 1st Battalion, passed the 555th Medium Artillery Battalion using maximum rate of fire, and finally reached the 23d Infantry command post. I reported to Colonel Freeman and then collected the ammo, food, and water and started back to the 1st Battalion when a North Korean self-propelled track knocked out the tires of my lead truck. Colonel Freeman told me to find a hole in his perimeter and while I was in the command post, Colonel Freeman talked to Lieutenant Colonel Hutchin authorizing him to withdraw. Colonel Hutchin said, "No, I am going to stay where I am." Colonel Freeman agreed.

During the morning of 1 September, Freeman's CP, defended only by the regiment's Headquarters Company, endured a three-hour attack by about four hundred North Koreans before it withdrew several hundred yards to the rear to the 2d Battalion CP.

Early in the afternoon, Lieutenant Colonel Hutchin sent an Able Company platoon, reinforced with a section of tanks, to reconnoiter to his rear to see whether the mountains to the east were clear. The force soon returned with word that a large mountain pass was held by at least a battalion of North Koreans who had gotten through the lines during the night's fighting. At this, Hutchin decided it would be wise to prepare to hold his position, and he called Colonel Freeman for permission. When Freeman again agreed, Hutchin used the rest of the day to dig in and prepare his perimeter to hold out against further attacks.[20]

That same afternoon, General Keiser formed a task force to consolidate and hold positions to keep the North Koreans from seizing the MSR behind the 23d Infantry. Task Force Haynes, named for the division artillery commander, Brig. Gen. Loyal M. Haynes, who led it, combined the 38th and 23d Regiments with portions of the division artillery and a company of tanks. The force began preparing its positions. That evening, word came down that Generals MacArthur and Walker had ordered that units in Korea would "not surrender another inch and [would] hold regardless of cost."[21]

Freeman and Haynes did not get along. As Freeman later recalled:

Finding himself nearly in the front lines of desperate hand-to-hand combat did not appeal to [Haynes]—to say the least. My first problem with Haynes was his calling me to report to him at his CP some miles to the rear. Twice this happened when we were at the critical stage of repulsing strong enemy attacks. Not only did I have to leave my CP but literally had to fight my way through rear area infiltrators to get to his CP. I finally told him in a *respectful* way that I believed it improper to summon a commander to the rear during a firefight and suggested he send one of his staff forward to *my* CP if he didn't want to come himself. Moreover, he diverted a tank company, sent to reinforce my sector, to reinforce the protection of his own CP.[22]

The relationship deteriorated until Haynes asked for permission to relieve Freeman. The only time Haynes went to Freeman's command post was to deliver a message ordering Freeman to report to division headquarters. Freeman angrily drove to the division CP and fell into a fatigued sleep. The division commander, General Keiser, had been Freeman's tactical officer at West Point, and Freeman had served under Keiser several times during his career. While Freeman slept, Keiser sent his operations officer, Col. Maurice Holden, to the front to investigate the situation. After hearing about the situation at the front from the 23d's officers, Colonel Holden recommended that Keiser not relieve Freeman, and Keiser did not.[23]

The regiment's soldiers became veterans on the Naktong. Sergeant Doug Graney, recalls how Capt. Perry Sager, the Easy Company commander, came to the company on the Naktong River line in an incident involving the difficulty of communicating to headquarters exactly what the situation was at the front:

[The company commander] was a good officer. I was his radio operator. He brought the company to Korea from Fort Lewis. He was a positive thinking type of person. He knew the names of most everyone in the company and was not reluctant to praise men openly for a job well done. We had been taking a beating on the hills the company defended about a thousand yards back from the Naktong River. We'd been overrun and lost one of the knobs we were holding and had been ordered to take it back.

We organized an assault platoon. . . . The hill was similar to the one we'd lost connected by a razorback ridge that ran off to our right. The North Koreans had a machine gun covering the forward slope. The idea was to run across the ridge on the reverse side to avoid that machine gun. The problem began when the attackers started across the ridge. Another machine gun covered the rear side of the slope and we lost a couple of people real quick.

[The company commander] called off the attack while he consulted his map. We were using Japanese maps that did not show a small outcropping where the other machine gun had taken position. [He] tried to explain this to Colonel Edwards. I was relaying most of this conversation via my radio. Colonel Edwards finally ordered the hill taken immediately or [the captain] was to be relieved. [He] chose to be relieved. The Company Exec was ordered to assume command and he ordered the attack to resume. Again the enemy cut down two men after only a few yards. The Exec broke down and began to cry. A sergeant called off the attack.

Colonel Edwards relayed via radio that a Captain Sager would arrive to take command of the company. Not until Sager saw the situation did

Colonel Edwards realize the problem. Sager suggested that Fox Company, which was above the North Korean machine gun, lay down fire on the gun—which they did and we walked across with little trouble. I heard [the former company commander] referred to as a coward—which he wasn't. It was simply a matter of maps and communication and trust.

Captain Sager was the best officer I ever served with. . . . He had a sense of humor and always kept morale up in the gravest of times. He was always the leader and before an attack was careful to point out the disposition of the enemy and what to expect during our attack. He was about six feet tall with a ruddy complexion but seemed taller because he always walked erect even while enemy bullets were flying by. He never showed the slightest fear of the enemy or death. . . .

Sager had been with the 1st Infantry Division during World War II—I believe a Virginia Military Institute graduate. . . . If all commanders were like him we'd have an unbeatable army. He did not hesitate to chew out an officer in front of the men when lives were at stake. We all appreciated him for that. He was cool under fire—always—I never saw him in doubt or nervous. This is of course what made him an excellent officer. . . . He knew infantry tactics and was an excellent map-reader.

On 2 September, airdrops resupplied both battalions. Freeman, now virtually ignoring the task force commander and running the task force himself, sent a patrol out to find a route to the 1st Battalion. When the patrol found an unguarded trail, he sent a battalion from the 38th Infantry to reinforce the isolated battalion. For the next three days, the task force beat off attacks both day and night. On 3 August, the 1st Battalion and its sister battalion from the 38th Infantry made their way back to the rest of the task force and the regiments consolidated, finally digging into strong defensive positions.

About this time, the soldiers began to appreciate their foe's brutality. The North Koreans drove civilians ahead of their attacking formations, forcing the Americans to fire into the civilians. It was an excruciating order to give the soldiers, but it came down to shooting the civilians or being overrun by the soldiers behind them. In other instances, units elsewhere on the Naktong River line discovered dozens of American prisoners who had been murdered by the North Koreans after having their hands bound behind their backs.[24]

By 6 September, Freeman felt confident enough to order a push to return to the positions the regiment had been forced from earlier. That evening, the regiment was again overlooking the Naktong River. During the following day, the regiment received 374 ROK army replacements. These soldiers came to be called KATUSAs, an acronym for "Korean Augmentation to the U.S. Army." Throughout the first year of the war, these "soldiers" were seldom more than dragooned civilians. They were virtually untrained, without equipment, and generally spoke no English. The 23d Infantry paired them up with Americans who taught the Koreans the rudiments of soldiering through sign language. Although the KATUSAs never quite became integral members of the regiment, many became dedicated to their American counterparts and vice versa. More than one soldier recalls his Korean friend with fondness, and a conviction that they would have given their lives for one another.[25]

On 7 September, an enemy buildup was spotted in front of the regiment and artillery was fired at the formation. In the early hours of the next morning, the NKPA launched a savage attack on the regiment, supported by fires from artillery and self-propelled guns. It soon created a breach in Fox Company's positions. As the gap widened and enemy soldiers began to pour through, it became evident that the entire position was in danger unless the opening was plugged. Freeman shifted forces from the 1st Battalion to fill the breach. The unit made its way to the gap in darkness and under fire the entire time, but the soldiers successfully stopped the penetration and held their position until dawn, when the attack abated. The unit then spent the day reorganizing and digging in its positions in anticipation of another attack the next day.[26]

The North Koreans attacked as expected. Although there were no breakthroughs that morning, sharp assaults hit Baker, Charlie, Fox, and George Companies. Casualties were heavy, and by late morning all of the frontline units needed replacements. Freeman had to weaken the perimeter in areas not under attack in order to send men to the hardest hit sectors. The deteriorating situation forced him to muster all the noninfantry soldiers—clerks, cooks, mechanics, and drivers—until the entire regiment was manning the line. At one point, the reserve force dwindled to six men. The situation was desperate, and would become hopeless if the North Koreans were able to sustain their attack unabated. Fortunately, the attack flagged in the early afternoon and the rest of the day was quiet.[27] Had the attackers employed better communications and coordination, they easily could have overrun the American defenders. It was a shortcoming they frequently exhibited during the war and never fully overcame.

Freeman's presence during these actions was a tonic to the men, who were using up their last reservoirs of endurance. One observer described the regimental commander's actions:

> When action was joined, he gave his battalion commanders a free hand to fight their rifle companies as they saw fit. But he was always up there where the killing was going on, moving from hole to hole, standing up straight in the presence of the enemy. He wanted the troops to see him, to know that he was running the same risks as they. Once, riding his jeep on a mountain road that was under mortar fire, he told his driver to slow down to five miles an hour.
>
> "If they see me going faster than that they'll get the idea I'm scared," he said.
>
> Major John Dumaine, his operations officer, was with him. "Aren't you?" Dumaine asked.
>
> "I sure as hell am," Freeman replied. "Are you crazy?"
>
> . . . When a patrol was out on a dangerous reconnaissance or a battalion was under pressure, he couldn't sleep or eat until the patrol was in, the battalion safe.
>
> "I'm going up there and see what the hell's happening to those people," he'd say, bouncing off in his jeep. Then there'd be a growing tension, a gnawing worry, in the CP until he was back again.
>
> "If the word had come back that old Paul was trapped by the gooks somewhere," [Lt. Col. Frank] Meszar said, "every man in the CP down to the last cook would have grabbed a weapon and headed up there to get him."[28]

Freeman's ability to overcome or at least override his fears to show a brave face to the troops on the line was characteristic of many good combat commanders, who know that being present in dangerous spots, sharing the dangers of their men when they could have remained secure in their headquarters in the rear, is critical to maintaining morale. Even when there is nothing a commander can do at the front to influence the action, he is at least undergoing the rigors that he is asking his men to face as well as demonstrating the paternalistic concern that bonds his soldiers to him.

For the next few days, the regiment experienced repeated attacks of lesser intensity and called for artillery and air strikes on the NKPA units to its front. Had the North Koreans been able to sustain the strength of the attacks they had made on 8 and 9 September, the American regiment would have had difficulty surviving. Combat efficiency was down to 38 percent, and there were no reserves.[29] On 11 September, an aerial observer reported fifteen hundred enemy dead in front of the regiment's position; the incredible punishment the 23d had meted out to its attackers had sapped the strength of both attacker and defender.[30]

More than one veteran remembers the air strikes, generally with gratitude for their assistance. Occasionally, however, there is bitterness over friendly casualties and second thoughts about how they could have been more effective. Sergeant Doug Graney recalled an air strike gone awry for lack of ground control:

> Attacking P-51s strafing the forward slope of enemy-held positions seemed a waste of ammo. The Air Force was able to keep the enemy mortars and artillery silent for a while but it would begin as soon as the planes left. Two P-51s killed and wounded many men from Easy Company while we were attacking a hill overlooking the Naktong. I was with the attacking platoon radioing battalion to call off the [air strike] and learned no [air force liaison officer] was there so the attack continued. It's pure luck I'm able to write you about this—most of the platoon was killed outright—no cover—we just sat there and watched the planes firing at us—then came napalm; finally they got word they were killing their own people.
>
> This can leave a bad taste but there's no question the air support was needed. However, Air Force and infantry units should have been trained to work together—as the Marines seemed to do.

Corporal James Cardinal was even more embittered about the bureaucratic turf battle that led to the lack of Air Force attention to the close air support mission and the poor air-ground coordination:

> Totally lost in the acrimonious debate over turf and larger budgets between the Air Force and the Navy was the Army's voice on how best to support ground forces to win the nation's war, if indeed the pre–Korean War Army was even aware of the implications given its ready acquiescence to the Air Force's departure from its parents' house with all the appliances.
>
> The infantry was to pay a high price in the early months of the Korean War for the Army's oversight and the Air Force's neglect. Hundreds of men died unnecessarily due to inadequate air support. It took time for the Air Force to master techniques not practiced since World War II, and that cost many lives, some of whom were victims of strafing and napalm attacks gone wrong. I once saw the remains of eight American infantrymen burned to a crisp by napalm as the result of targeting errors by the Air Force.

The Marine Corps was wise to insist on full control of its own air support. Marine Corps aviators were thoroughly trained to provide close air support to Marine Corps ground forces, primarily their infantry. That was (and still is) the primary reason for the existence of Marine Corps aviation.

The United Nations Shifts to the Offensive

Eighth Army's situation on the Naktong River line was precarious, but its soldiers had at least some advantages. Although there were shortages of war matériel, they were never as great as those of their adversaries. The North Korean forces were at the extreme limits of a logistic system that stretched back through a transportation bottleneck at Seoul to North Korea. MacArthur's Far East Air Force (FEAF) harassed the transportation system during daylight hours. Little got through South Korea's limited road network except what was carried by porters. Above all else, however, General MacArthur had prepared an operation that would dramatically reverse his army's fortunes overnight.

The Inchon invasion is a military operation that will be debated so long as military historians continue to enjoy asking, "What if?" The maneuver was fraught with jeopardy, yet in the face of what the U.S. Marine Corps termed five-thousand-to-one odds, it succeeded. In doing so, it released the North Korean pressure on the Naktong River line's defenders and allowed the units there to advance northward and link up with the invading forces in a matter of days. Within just a few weeks, the UN forces were slashing deep into North Korea.

On 15 September, General Keiser disbanded Task Force Haynes and the 23d Regiment's 3d Battalion returned to its control from the 1st Cavalry Division, restoring the RCT to its full fighting strength. Eighth Army planned an offensive across the Naktong River to coincide with the Inchon landings more than 150 miles to the north. The comparatively intact 3d Battalion would lead the 23d's attack to gain crossing sites on the river.

The NKPA made its final assault against the 23d Infantry on 16 September. The enemy attacked in the early morning hours and succeeded in penetrating Charlie Company's position. After bitter hand-to-hand fighting, the company restored its position, but not without heavy losses. The heavy weapons platoon leader, attached from Dog Company, and all but one of Charlie Company's officers, were killed. After the attack was repulsed, the 3d Battalion, supported by Charlie Company of the 72d Tank Battalion, attacked through positions held by the 2d Battalion at 0715 and

Associated Press correspondent Hal Boyle (*seated at center*) converses with Col. Paul L. Freeman, Jr., the 23d Infantry Regiment commander (*seated to Boyle's left*) and other regimental officers on the Naktong River Line on 15 September 1950. *Courtesy National Archives.*

swept toward the Naktong. At the same time, the badly mauled 1st Battalion attacked to secure a ridge to the left of the regimental sector. The 3d Battalion met resistance, but pushed on rapidly. By midmorning, Freeman was reporting to division headquarters that NKPA forces still in the slower-moving 9th Regiment's zone to the south were threatening his left flank. Enemy resistance in the 23d's sector had collapsed by late afternoon, and the regiment was able to secure defensive positions on the east bank of the Naktong. They estimated the NKPA suffered twelve hundred casualties for the day. Meanwhile, the regiment was ready to cross the Naktong River, which its soldiers had seen to their front ever since their arrival in Korea.

Because of a shortage of bridging materials, Freeman had to improvise a crossing. Soldiers built a sandbag ford for vehicles to cross the shallow river, and planned to use assault craft to transport soldiers making the initial crossing.[31] Early in the morning on 20 September, the 37th Field Artillery Battalion, attached to the 23d RCT, ceased its harassing fires on the enemy across the Naktong and at 0330 hours the men of the 3d Battalion slipped across the river in their assault craft.

There were not enough of the boats, so many soldiers made the crossing by hanging in the water, holding onto their sides. The assault was so successful at achieving surprise that Love Company discovered a North Korean lieutenant colonel and his staff asleep on the company objective. By the end of the day, the rest of the 23d had crossed the river and the regiment consolidated its bridgehead on the west bank the following day.[32]

Unfortunately, the next four days saw more petty friction involving the personalities of senior officers than fighting with the NKPA. General Keiser formed another task force similar to the ill-fated Task Force Haynes for the advance on Seoul. This time he placed his assistant division commander, Brig. Gen. Sladen Bradley, in command of the 23d and the 38th Infantry Regiments.

Freeman had "mechanized" his 3d Battalion so that the unit was no longer restricted to the speed of its foot soldiers. He did this by using his regimental tank company, augmented by an attached tank company, for mobile firepower. At the same time, he consolidated the battalion's organic vehicles for infantry mobility, so that the battalion could move much faster when there was no contact with the enemy. This also meant that his foot soldiers were fresher at the end of a movement because they had ridden all the way. This mechanization let Freeman barrel past the 38th Infantry toward the next objective, the village of Kochang. He was annoyed when General Bradley ordered him to pull his tanks off the road and give priority to the 38th so that it would have the honor of taking the objective. Freeman attributed this intervention to jealousy emanating from Col. George Peploe, commander of the 38th RCT. Soldiers overheard arguments between the colonels and the general, and men of the 23d felt that the task force commander had betrayed them. As the 3d Battalion commander, Lt. Col. Robert "Gib" Sherrard, put it, "Paul Freeman was a superb leader of men; we all felt he had been betrayed by the orders of Sladen Bradley. What a blow to morale—to everyone in that noble 23d Infantry—by such an insolent, vainglorious upstart, showing favorites at a time when men's lives were at stake and teamwork was the order of the day."[33]

Late in the afternoon on 26 September, after the carping among the commanders had abated, Bradley ordered Freeman to take the village of

Anui, a few miles southwest of Kochang. The regiment arrived at dark to find all the rice paddies flooded, unlike the area it had come through days earlier, and the men had no choice except to settle into the village itself. Freeman was suspicious of the only open area, in a schoolyard that was a little too clean and neat, with flowers on the desks in the schoolhouse. Nonetheless, he felt that with the flooded area around the village and the unequivocal order from Bradley to take the village, he had no alternative other than to occupy the village. Events proved Freeman's suspicions to be justified, as the enemy had targeted the schoolyard. Just before dawn the following morning, an intense artillery and mortar barrage fell on Anui, killing the 3d Battalion executive officer and four other staff officers, and wounding twenty-five enlisted men and Lieutenant Colonel Sherrard.[34]

Day-to-day events soon returned to the mundane routine of soldiers moving forward against little resistance. For the next two weeks, until 11 October, the 23d RCT moved north and conducted patrols to mop up groups of NKPA soldiers still in the area. The regiment finally arrived near Seoul for ten days of resupply and training. The training concentrated on problems of small-unit tactics, patrolling, maintaining equipment in combat conditions, and firing individual weapons. Leaders particularly emphasized training for the many KATUSAs who had joined the regiment on the Naktong. Soldiers of all grades attended classes on adjusting mortar and artillery fires.

The speed of the advance following the breakout from the Pusan Perimeter had severely taxed the division's support capabilities, and many items were scarce. All weapons and vehicles needed maintenance and reconditioning. Even the normal exercise of equipment requires routine maintenance, but the 23d RCT's aging vehicles had received far more than normal use—and no attention beyond the minimum required to keep them running. Personnel losses had been appalling, and in early October the number of replacements and returnees finally exceeded the division's losses for the first time since its arrival in Korea.[35]

Chapter 3

Disaster in the North

It has long seemed to me that the hard decisions are not the ones you make in the heat of battle. Far harder are those involved in speaking your mind about some hare-brained scheme which proposes to commit troops to action under conditions where failure seems almost certain, and the only results will be the needless sacrifice of priceless lives. When all is said and done, the most precious asset any nation has is its youth, and for a battle commander ever to condone the unnecessary sacrifice of his men is inexcusable. In any action you must balance the inevitable cost in lives against the objectives you seek to attain. Unless the results to be expected can reasonably justify the estimated loss of life the action involves, then for my part I want none of it.
—Gen. Matthew B. Ridgway

I rate the skillful tactician above the skillful strategist, especially him who plays the bad cards well.
—Field Marshal Sir Archibald P. Wavell

Nothing gives one person so much advantage over another as to remain always cool and unruffled under all circumstances.
—Pres. Thomas Jefferson

By 1 November, the 23d Regiment was stationed near Haeju, a deepwater port on the coast of North Korea southwest of Pyongyang. Soldiers and even their commander, Col. Paul Freeman, thought that the 2d Division, including the 23d Infantry, was likely to be one of the first units to be transferred to Europe at the fast-approaching end of the war. Soldiers could envision troopships picking them up in a few weeks. Of course, this was not to be. Their fate had been foreshadowed in the 2d

Division's Periodic Intelligence Report for 31 October, which estimated that there were 316,000 Chinese soldiers—a force of forty-four divisions organized into twelve armies—massed on North Korea's boundary with Manchuria.[1]

The Chinese military force that intervened in the Korean War in late November 1950 comprised some of the finest light infantry in modern history. They called themselves the Chinese People's Liberation Army, but to their foes they were the Chinese Communist Forces (CCF). Many of its commanders had never suffered a defeat. It was the same force that had been fighting for independence continuously in China since 1927, as well as against the Japanese during World War II.

The armament the CCF used in Korea was neither more modern nor more powerful than that which it had used in the Chinese Civil War, but Mao Tse-tung, the leader of the new Chinese nation, had trained his army in a sophisticated doctrine of mobile guerrilla warfare. Its tactics were neither new nor revolutionary. That is not to say, however, that the Americans were familiar with them when the Chinese intervened. The simple but effective fundamentals the CCF relied on were to perform thorough reconnaissance, concentrate forces at a decisive point, make a surprise night attack, and withdraw quickly after victory.[2]

The CCF carried a variety of light infantry weapons into Korea, but little ammunition, expecting to replenish weapons and ammunition with captured stocks. They had only limited artillery and armor, and virtually no air support. The soldiers' winter gear consisted of a heavy quilted uniform, a padded cap with earflaps, and sandals over layered socks. A cloth tube carried diagonally across the chest instead of a backpack sufficed to carry their Spartan rations.

Food and ammunition supplies were reduced in practical terms to what the soldiers themselves could carry: one hundred bullets, three grenades, and two to ten days of food. Resupply was by means of columns of coolies bearing loads of seventy to one hundred pounds on A-frame packboards. During an offensive, a unit's resources allowed it to conduct one or two short attacks without needing resupply.[3]

This level of logistic support meant that a Chinese soldier required less than ten pounds of supplies per day, whereas an American soldier needed sixty. An eight-to-ten thousand-man CCF division required forty tons of supplies per day compared to its American counterpart's six hundred tons. It is worth mentioning, that this "logistics on the cheap" carried the seeds of its own destruction, for once the CCF came upon American largess

47

efficiently used, the more lavish levels of support would take a toll on the Chinese forces.

To avoid the overwhelming strength of UN airpower and artillery, the CCF customarily hid in camouflaged locations during the day and attacked between midnight and 0300; they made few daylight attacks in good weather. Bad weather—common throughout the war—was an important ally of the Chinese, as it often kept them from being pounded by UN airpower. Their camouflage was so effective that CCF defenders would allow UN patrols to pass by their concealed positions and then spring an ambush. When the CCF was on the offensive, soldiers said the attackers appeared to be "rising up out of the ground." They were also superb infiltrators, and early in the war often made it inside friendly positions before being detected. Communications consisted of noisemakers and light signals—bugles, whistles, shouts, flares, and torches. Telephones were available only at battalion level.

The key to the CCF organization was the squad, composed of three teams of three men each, plus a squad leader. This made for an extremely coherent and efficient organization. The men lived, ate, worked, trained, and fought together. They looked after one another and checked any tendency a team member might have for deviation from expected behavior. Their predominant tactic was to attack in overwhelming numbers, looking for a hole in the lines and pouring through it, or enveloping and cutting supply routes to the rear. The average Chinese soldier was a peasant in his late teens or early twenties: robust, hardy, sober, and alert. To these qualities the discipline of the communist ideology added, for many of them, an enthusiasm touching on fanaticism.

The simplicity of his army's weapons compensated for the Chinese peasant soldier's lack of technical sophistication. The soldiers faced modern weapons and death with a stoicism that was unsettling to their Western adversaries. Attacks bordered on the fanatical, and at times the men in the first wave attacked without weapons. The CCF had surprising mobility; daily marches of ten miles over mountainous terrain were the norm. They were serious adversaries, practicing a war of hate, among other motivations. In short, the Chinese infantry were very light, very robust, very aggressive, and very mobile.[4]

The CCF soldiers respected American weapons. After their first encounter with American forces, one wrote: "The coordinated action of mortars and tanks is an important factor. . . . Their firing instruments are highly powerful. . . . Their artillery is very active. . . . Aircraft strafing and bombing of our transportation have become a great hazard to us . . . their transportation system is great. . . . Their infantry rate of fire is great and the long range of fire is still greater."[5]

They had less respect for the fighting skill of the American soldier, for when cut off from the rear, American soldiers

> abandon all their heavy weapons, leaving them all over the place, and play opossum. . . . Their infantrymen are so weak, afraid to die, and haven't the courage to attack or defend. They depend on their planes, tanks, and artillery. At the same time, they are afraid of our fire power. They will cringe when, if on the advance, they hear firing. They are afraid to advance farther. . . . They specialize in day fighting. They are not familiar with night fighting or hand-to-hand combat. . . . If defeated, they have no orderly formation. Without the use of their mortars, they become completely lost . . . they become dazed and completely demoralized. . . . At Unsan they were surrounded for several days yet they did nothing. They are afraid when the rear is cut off. When transportation comes to a standstill, the infantry loses the will to fight.[6]

The Other Enemy

The intense cold proved to be an enemy as deadly to the United Nations soldier as his North Korean or Chinese foes. Temperatures in the winter of 1950–51 went as low as thirty degrees below zero Fahrenheit, and the wind significantly increased the effects of the chill. It was a pervasive enemy, one the soldiers could not evade. Above all, while many days and nights brought no Chinese, the cold was always present and ever ready to wreak its ill effects, from simple discomfort to permanent disability. At its most benign, the cold merely forced soldiers to wear more clothing and seek shelter. However, when the temperature dropped to twenty degrees below zero Fahrenheit and a thirty-knot wind dropped the wind chill to eighty below, protection from its effects became an all-consuming effort. The cold required the soldier to eat more to fuel his body's metabolism, and protection against the wind was imperative to prevent frostbite. The cold sapped reserves of energy and dulled thinking skills and judgment. In an infantry unit, leaders had to focus their efforts on the not-so-simple task of getting soldiers through the cold with minimal harm.

The cold was an enemy that caused casualties as surely as an enemy bullet, and one that commanders at every level had to deal with constantly.

Medics had to treat any soldier who was frostbitten and, if the injury was severe enough, evacuate him through medical channels. Soldiers from northern climates usually knew how to deal with the cold, but those who had grown up in more temperate climates had to be taught how to avoid becoming casualties. Often, a soldier who had never experienced extreme cold would feel pain and assume it was just part of being cold, rather than the beginning of frostbite. Soldiers had to flex their feet and hands constantly to maintain proper circulation.[7]

The only protection against the severe temperatures was good cold weather gear or shelter, and often neither was available in the United Nations Command during that first terrible winter of the war. Instead of heavy woolen garments, the soldiers usually had to make do with cotton flannel shirts and outer garments worn in as many as seven layers. A typical arrangement would be cotton or wool underwear, wool dress pants, and field pants with suspenders for the lower half of the body; for the top half, an undershirt, then one or more wool shirts, wool sweaters, fatigue jacket, and parka with liner. The difficulties of performing one's bodily functions with multiple layers of clothing on are obvious, and many veterans remember them vividly—especially instances when they were under fire. Gloves were scarce until 1951, and most soldiers preferred mittens with trigger fingers to gloves, although they were awkward when handling weapons. The pile caps were never available in sufficient quantity for every soldier to have one, leaving those without caps to wrap their heads in wool scarves. Either headgear made it difficult to wear a steel helmet, and soldiers often discarded them.

The army solution to the problem of footgear was the "shoepac," a version of the L. L. Bean boot that featured a leather upper portion and a rubber foot. The soldier was expected to wear the shoepac with wool socks, which he would change when they became wet from perspiration. Under combat conditions, however, the soldier often had neither dry socks nor the opportunity to change them. The result was that the men's feet often became wet and then froze, causing frostbite. Frostbite could lead to the loss of toes or even feet when severe. In conditions above freezing, wet feet could cause trench foot. Even in weather that was above freezing but below fifty degrees, the lack of evaporation inside the rubber shoe could cause "macerated feet" or "shoepac foot," a condition that made the saturated soles of one's feet resemble wet blotting paper. Soldiers who could get them preferred wearing rubber overshoes over their regulation leather boots to the shoepac.

Soldiers generally got warm only when exercising, usually walking or digging. When they exerted themselves enough, they sweated and were almost comfortable. When they stopped the activity, however, the sweaty clothes quickly chilled, making them doubly cold and increasing the possibility of getting a cold injury. None of the preventative measures described above really made soldiers feel warm, they merely prevented permanent damage.

Food and shelter were other difficulties. There could be no fires near the forward positions, so there was no way to cook food or warm the body. Soldiers often had to chip at frozen C rations with their bayonets at mealtime. When company mess sergeants made the heroic effort to get hot food close to the front lines, it was usually cold before all of the men had a chance to get through the serving line. Hot coffee often froze within a few minutes, so soldiers learned to drink it quickly. When the contents of canteens froze, they had to be thawed with heat tablets in order to get a drink.[8]

There was seldom shelter at the front, although when they were near a village, soldiers, especially headquarters elements, would move into houses. Usually, though, the soldier's only shelter was his foxhole, laboriously dug in the frozen earth, sometimes by driving steel posts into the ground with sledgehammers to break it up enough to dig. Two men would normally huddle inside the hole so that one could sleep wrapped in one or more blankets while the other remained awake—and hopefully alert. Sleep was not difficult because of the enervating effect of the cold, not to mention a soldier's normal daily exertion. Most men remember being fatigued throughout their tour in Korea. There were few quilted, down-filled arctic sleeping bags (the standard army issue for cold weather at the time) until after the coldest weather of the winter in January, 1951. When they first became available, units allowed one bag per foxhole so that only one soldier could sleep at a time. Later, when sufficient sleeping bags were available for all of the men, soldiers usually sat with their upper torso exposed because they feared being stuck inside during an attack. If a soldier was lucky enough to be in a bunker, he could stay warm by burning a tallow candle between his feet and draping his poncho tentlike around himself to trap the heat.

The cold also affected the soldiers' weapons. Both the Browning Automatic Rifle (BAR) and the M1 carbine would freeze and malfunction in the extreme cold. The field expedient for thawing them was to urinate on the bolt and then fire a few rounds to thaw the weapon entirely. Recoil mechanisms on field artillery pieces malfunctioned when temperatures dropped low enough to thicken the recoil oil. Mortar base plates, the trails of towed artillery pieces, and other heavy steel castings became brittle and sometimes fractured when the weapons were fired in cold weather. Diesel fuel thickened, making it difficult to keep vehicles running. Lead-acid batteries—which became useless even in moderate cold unless taken off the vehicle and kept warm—froze in extreme cold, cracking the housing and ruining the battery.

In retrospect, many soldiers would say that the first winter of the war was memorable to them for the cold as much as for any other aspect of the war.

The Chinese Enter the War

The Chinese had given enough warnings for a prudent commander to take seriously the possibility of their entry into the war. In this matter, MacArthur was anything but a prudent commander. He had a will to disbelieve in the possibility of Chinese intervention. Such action, he believed, would have had to come earlier in the war to have the desired effect. In any event, he assured Washington, the FEAF would slaughter the Chinese if they tried anything. Yet there were abundant intelligence indicators that intervention was not just possible, but probable: diplomatic warnings, reports of CCF formations massing in Manchuria, prisoners of war (POWs) who were unarguably Chinese from many different units, and bitter, bloody encounters with large Chinese forces as early as late October. Nonetheless, MacArthur's sycophantic staff was able to provide an explanation—sometimes tortuous, but wrong in every case—for each indicator. For example, diplomatic warnings were judged to be from unreliable communist or neutral countries; FEAF reports indicated no CCF formations were in Korea; the plethora of units identified merely confirmed to analysts that CCF soldiers in Korea were volunteers from a number of different units; the annihilation of a Korean unit and the mauling of a U.S. regiment in October occurred only because the units stumbled into Chinese positions and not because the CCF had skillfully laid an ambush.[9]

One American who had no illusions about the likelihood of Chinese intervention was Col. Paul Freeman. When the Chinese mauled the 8th Cavalry Regiment in early October, dreams of an early end to the war dimmed, and the Eighth Army ordered the 2d Division north from the port of Haeju. By late November, Freeman had led his regiment to within about sixty miles of the Yalu River, where he and his men celebrated

Thanksgiving with a traditional dinner on 23 November. Meanwhile, MacArthur ordered General Walker to launch his "final offensive" on the following day.

On Saturday, 25 November, Freeman's regiment was in position behind the 2d Division's other two regiments, the 9th and the 38th, on the banks of the Chongchon River. The 23d Infantry was in division reserve, prepared to attack through the 9th Infantry the following morning. The 23d had captured some Chinese prisoners earlier, and Freeman had personally interrogated them in their dialect. It was not the last time his Chinese language skills would prove to be an asset. He had determined to his own satisfaction that the Chinese were in North Korea in force and planned to intervene. He passed his premonitions on to division headquarters where, as far as can be determined, they were ignored. Nonetheless, he convinced his soldiers, through warnings he passed through the chain of command, that Chinese intervention was imminent. Regimental patrols were continuously finding more Chinese, and the 23d's soldiers were alert and apprehensive.[10]

The regiment was positioned astride the division's MSR to the south, with the 1st Battalion to the west, collocated with the regimental tank and heavy mortar companies. The battalion was just behind the 1st Cavalry Division's 61st Field Artillery Battalion. Freeman had warned Lieutenant Colonel Hutchin to be ready for anything, and the 1st Battalion held strong positions. Able, Baker, and Dog (heavy weapons) Companies were dug in facing the river and tied in with the regimental tank and heavy mortar companies. The regimental headquarters was on a small rise at the base of a hill nicknamed "Chinaman's Hat" because of its shape. The position was vulnerable to attack from Chinaman's Hat, but there were no enemy forces on it at the time.

The 2d Battalion was to the south in division reserve, and the 3d Battalion was attached to the 38th Regiment. Both, however, were to revert to regimental control when the next morning's attack began—a little late in the game, Freeman thought. Moreover, the 23d Infantry had a different field artillery battalion attached. Because of a disagreement between the 9th Infantry commander and the commander of his attached artillery battalion, the division artillery commander had ordered a switch, which meant the 15th Field Artillery Battalion was now in position to support the 23d.[11]

The early hours of the bitterly cold evening were quiet, but at about 2200 hours, infantrymen of the Fortieth Chinese Army, the CCF's preeminent combat organization, arrived at the Chongchon River to the northwest of the 23d Infantry's positions and began crossing it. Some of the Chinese removed their clothing and held it above their heads before wading naked into the icy water, while others removed only their sandals and pants, since the river was only about waist deep. Arriving on the southeast riverbank, some did not even put their pants and sandals on before attacking the 1st Battalion's Able Company and smashing into the rear of the 61st Field Artillery Battalion. Many of the CCF soldiers carried no small arms, only satchel charges—packages of explosives the size of a briefcase used to destroy heavy equipment such as tanks and artillery pieces. Bugle calls, flares, whistles, and shouting accompanied the attack. One bugler played U.S. bugle calls, including taps, which many soldiers found macabre.

Accounts differ concerning how many of the artillerymen fled in a panicked rout, but it has been established that many U.S. soldiers ran out of control through the 23d Infantry's positions, some yelling "GI, GI" in hopes the defenders would not shoot them. The artillerymen were particularly angry because their forward observers had detected the approaching Chinese but the artillery headquarters turned down requests to fire on them. Gunfire awakened the Dog Company commander, Capt. William Guthrie, and his first sergeant before panicked soldiers running through the area knocked down their shelter.

In a matter of minutes, the enemy launched an attack on the 1st Battalion's left flank. Hutchin's infantry and tanks opened fire and repelled them, but the attack overran a portion of Able Company's position, including the mess tent. The mess sergeant was successful in organizing a counterattack to retake his kitchen tent, and the battalion held off four more attacks during the night, at fearful cost to the attackers. The regiment captured more than a hundred enemy soldiers, its largest haul of the war, and Freeman again interrogated them. He found that "the Chinese had very unwillingly entered the Korean War, that they were scared to death, that they were really going to be clobbered by we Americans."[12]

Realizing that their initial attacks had failed, the CCF forces turned their attention to Charlie Company, which blocked the approach to Chinaman's Hat. If they could gain Chinaman's Hat, they would be in position to attack the regimental headquarters at its base. Charlie Company beat off the first few attacks, but the Chinese finally ran them off the hill about dawn. Freeman dispatched Able Company to reinforce Charlie in retaking the position. Hutchin, the battalion commander, led the attack.

Sergeant John Pittman volunteered to lead his squad in the counterattack. Although wounded by mortar fragments as they surged forward, he continued the assault until a grenade landed in the midst of the squad. Pittman fell on the grenade and absorbed the blast with his body. When an aid man reached him, his first question concerned his squad and how many of his men had been hurt. He was subsequently awarded the Medal of Honor.[13]

The Chinese were finally on Chinaman's Hat directly above the regimental CP. Hearing of the situation in the 23d's sector, General Keiser returned the regiment's 2d Battalion, reinforcing it with Baker Company of the 72d Tank Battalion.

When the 2d Battalion arrived, Freeman organized a strong force of infantry to counterattack Chinaman's Hat. An air strike showered the hill with napalm and rockets, and all of the regiment's supporting weapons fired on the position as Easy and George Companies jumped off on their attack about dusk. Chinese on the hill fired green and white signal flares as the men neared their positions and lit strings of firecrackers to get the Americans to fire at them and give away their positions. The going was slow on the steep slope, and the Chinese defenders stopped both companies by 1800 hours. When they withdrew from the hill they abandoned two captured wounded soldiers. The Chinese bandaged the Americans' wounds, brought them to the bottom of the hill, and stood guard over them. When firing got close to their position, one of the Chinese who spoke English told them they were leaving and then gave them each a grenade. He told them that if NKPA troops came along they should use the grenades to commit suicide rather than undergo the brutal treatment they could expect from the North Koreans. American soldiers recovered the men the next day.

At 1945 hours, a strong attack from the hill overran Easy Company and then the regimental headquarters. At 2100 an improvised force from the headquarters attempted to retake the CP. The counterattack failed, and the major leading it was killed. The situation remained confused during the night and soldiers were nervous. A recoilless rifle crew saw shadowy figures and, worried that they might be Americans, halted them and asked for the password.

"We're Baker Company," came the reply.

Knowing that English-speaking Chinese had participated in earlier attacks, a soldier asked, "Who won the World Series?"

Even though the response was, "Who the hell played?" the crew decided they were Americans.

Sometime during the hours of darkness the Chinese withdrew, and at dawn the staff returned to the command post. Freeman was astonished to find nothing disturbed. The maps and classified codebooks were where they had been at the time of their hasty departure, the Chinese apparently unaware of their intelligence value.[14]

While the 23d Infantry was defending its sector, the 9th and 38th Regiments were having an even harder time coping with the CCF offensive. The 9th, in particular, had been badly mauled. On the way forward, one of the 2d Battalion convoys met a 9th Infantry convoy stopped on the way to the rear. A King Company soldier asked a soldier standing in a truck how the 9th was doing. The soldier did not answer; he instead made a thumbs-down gesture and pointed to the rear. No one understood what he had meant until the convoy began moving forward and the shocked members of King Company saw that the cargo beds of that truck and many more were filled to top with litters, each holding the body of an American soldier. The casualties were the first indication the 23d Infantry soldiers had of the heavy losses in the fighting that had been going on since the Chinese intervened.[15]

At 0700 hours on the twenty-ninth, the division commander ordered his units to begin withdrawing southward. Because it was in better shape, he designated the 23d Infantry, reinforced by a battalion from the 9th, to fight a delaying action and act as the rear guard until the other regiments moved through it. The 23d established collecting stations for stragglers from the units moving south and fired on enemy positions.

As soon as the 9th and 38th Regiments were clear, Freeman began his own withdrawal, leapfrogging his battalions to the rear. Lieutenant Colonel James Edwards's 2d Battalion was the rear guard for the regiment's withdrawal. The 1st battalion would set up a roadblock at a road junction a few miles to the south at Kujang-Dong and hold the road open until the rest of the regiment got through. The Chinese were pounding the area with artillery when the 1st Battalion reached it, however, causing Hutchin to set up his roadblock a little to the north of the road junction.[16]

The Eighth Army Retreats

When the commanders informed the soldiers that their orders were to withdraw to the south, many wondered why, as they felt they were holding their positions. It was only when word came down describing how badly the flank regiments had been battered and that the II ROK Corps had disappeared on the division's right flank that they began to understand that the war had taken a decisive turn. The Able Company commander called his men together and told them that too many of them were worrying about getting cut off and surrounded. He reassured them that they were completely capable of setting up a perimeter and defending against even greater numbers. With a warrior's bravado, he said he hoped that this might occur "so that I can prove to you that being surrounded is not the end of the world."[17]

The rear guard for the 2d Battalion at Chinaman's Hat was George Company. The last unit out of the area was Lt. Robert Curtis's platoon. His job was to hold off any Chinese threatening to impede the regiment's withdrawal and then clear the area, carrying out anyone who could not walk. Prior to his departure, Curtis received a radio message ordering him to find a trailer with a specific bumper number among the equipment that had been abandoned in the headquarters area and bring it out with his party. When he found it, he discovered it contained the regiment's liquor ration. Before Curtis's force left, a group of Chinese approached his position waving a white flag. The Chinese soldiers were courteous and some, speaking perfect English, wanted to make sure he had gathered up all of his wounded. They told him that he could leave anytime he wanted to, that the units to his rear had been destroyed and the war was over. The Americans asked where the Chinese had gotten their American uniforms and weapons. They replied that the uniforms had originally been supplied to Chiang Kai-shek's Nationalist Army. When Curtis was ready to leave, he loaded his soldiers into trucks in view of the Chinese, who shouted and waved at the Americans. He walked back to the top of the hill and waved back at them before pulling out. Such chivalrous conduct between combatants was almost unheard of in the war.

By dusk on the twenty-eighth, the 2d and 3d Battalions had passed through the roadblock and the 1st Battalion began withdrawing with Able Company as its rear guard. The men were so exhausted from the exertions of the past three days that Lieutenant Colonel Hutchin ordered each officer to move forward to the next officer's vehicle whenever the convoy halted, making sure all of the drivers in between were alert, and then return to his own vehicle when the column began moving again. Hutchin stayed with the rear guard. As the 1st Battalion cleared the roadblock, the Chinese launched a strong attack on Able Company, which withdrew under cover of the tanks that had remained with them. The road was congested with vehicles during the road march to the south, and a pursuit force estimated to consist of two CCF battalions attacked the column at each halt. Hutchin personally led the counterattacks and received a painful facial wound during one of the five separate actions. The 1st Battalion passed through the 2d Battalion, 9th Infantry's, roadblock to its rear at 2230, but at midnight received word that the 9th Infantry troops it had passed through were heavily engaged. They were ordered to stop and set up another roadblock to allow that battalion to disengage and move south. Hutchin's battalion held the road open not only for that battalion, but also for the 24th Infantry Regiment, which had been diverted to the 2d Division route.

In the entire day and night of fighting a flawless rear-guard action, beating back multiple CCF attacks with a combined arms force of tanks and infantry, Hutchin did not lose a man. Freeman again recommended him for the Distinguished Service Cross, but the recommendation came back tersely annotated, "We don't give DSC's for retrograde actions." When the regimental commander himself took the paperwork to higher headquarters it came back approved.[18]

At midmorning on the twenty-ninth, General Keiser again designated the 23d Infantry to be the division's rear guard, this time as it passed through Kunu-ri on the way to Sunchon twenty miles to the south. Because of the severe losses in the 9th and 38th Regiments, the 23d was the last combat-ready regiment in the division. It would accomplish the rear-guard mission by holding the vital road junction at Kunu-ri. When the entire division had cleared his position, Freeman would follow it down the Sunchon road. The division's vehicles and soldiers had clogged the road throughout the night in a massive traffic jam. During the afternoon, the 23d Infantry's 1st and 2d Battalions moved into fighting positions south of Kunu-ri while the 3d Battalion remained north of the village as a blocking force for the division. Although attacked several times during the night, the regiment held its positions as the division streamed through its roadblocks. During the early morning hours, hundreds more United Nations' stragglers—Americans, Turks, and ROKs—moved southward through the regiment.[19]

In the early morning hours on the morning of 30 November, approximately one hundred CCF soldiers attacked Baker Company on a hill southwest of Kunu-ri. Farther down the hill, Chinese soldiers set up a machine gun and fired into the regiment's tanks. The tanks returned the fire, but it went high and into Baker Company lines, driving a number of soldiers off the hill, killing twenty and wounding seventy before Hutchin could get the firing stopped. In the confusion, the Chinese took the hill.

Captain Melvin Stai attacked with Able Company and retook the hill about dawn. In addition to the killed and wounded in Baker Company, nineteen soldiers driven off the hill by the friendly fire were missing.[20]

Unknown to its members, the division was marching headlong into a slaughterhouse. General Walker, with MacArthur's approval, had decided to pull the entire Eighth Army south of the 38th Parallel. He designated the 2d Division as the unit to hold off the Chinese until the rest of the army was safely to the south. In Freeman's view, MacArthur was "sacrificing the 2nd Division to save Eighth Army." During the previous days, strong Chinese forces had raced southward on both sides of the narrow column of retreating UN forces and taken up positions on the high ground on both sides of the valley through which the Kunu-ri–Sunchon road ran. As the division entered this gauntlet, the Chinese attacked it from the heights. Many American units were virtually annihilated. Beginning in the early morning hours on 30 November and continuing throughout the day, the 2d Division lost thousands of men killed, wounded, or captured.[21]

At the same time, Freeman and his regiment, with substantial help from the Far East Air Force, were blocking the northern mouth of the valley. The FEAF gave priority throughout the day to Kunu-ri and flew 287 sorties in support of the regiment. Nonetheless, the CCF forces in the area continued to build up.[22]

Throughout the day, Freeman monitored messages on the division radio nets. He could hear reports that allowed him to construct a disturbing picture of what was occurring on the Kunu-ri–Sunchon road. In spite of the dozens of air strikes, soldiers all around the area could see Chinese moving to the north, west, but especially to the east, some even marching in formation. Freeman contracted his forces ever more tightly as the day wore on until all units were in a single integrated perimeter. At one point, his radio operator was wounded, and he turned around and asked if anyone in the area could operate a radio. D. W. Hoffman, the soldier who had cringed at the bottom of his foxhole during his first night of combat on the Naktong, volunteered.

More than once during the afternoon, things looked and sounded desperate. At one point during an attack, Freeman and his executive officer, Major Meszar, and the soldiers around them laid out all their weapons and ammunition for a last stand. Nonetheless, Hoffman remembers how demonstrably Freeman was in control of the regiment and himself. Throughout the day he spoke in a matter-of-fact tone without hyperbole.[23] It is hard to overrate the calming effect of the equanimity of a senior officer in a dangerous situation. Just as the company commander at the China-man's Hat had reassured his soldiers that being surrounded was not the end of the world, Freeman's even temperament made his soldiers think that things were not as bad as they seemed, and that their commander still had some control over their destinies. Confidence spread as soldiers who had seen Freeman's demeanor told others that "the old man" was working to get them out of their tight spot.

But Freeman still had to get his regiment down the gauntlet.

Colonel Freeman was aware that the road to the southwest leading to Anju had been clear when the last I Corps units traversed it. The corps boundaries put the road in I Corps sector. For this reason, IX Corps, which included the 2d Division, could not use it without approval from I Corps. Freeman had received a secondhand approval to use it from his division commander by relaying messages through the 9th Infantry's commander. In addition, he had a radio conversation with the assistant division commander, General Bradley, in which he told Bradley that the 23d was in a suicidal position and would never get out of Kunu-ri once darkness had fallen.

Finally, when the extent of the disaster that had befallen the division on the Kunu-ri–Sunchon road became clear, Bradley told Freeman, "Do what you have to do—we can't afford to lose any more units." About the same time, a liaison plane flew over and dropped a note telling Freeman to take the 23d out on the Anju road.[24]

Freeman organized the regiment for the march out with Edwards's 2d Battalion in the lead, followed by Hutchin's 1st Battalion, and Kane's 3d Battalion, which would act as rear guard. He put out the word that if the Chinese stopped the regiment and it could not break through, soldiers should take to the hills, maintaining unit integrity as much as possible, and make their way south. The men understood and were determined to comply. Freeman and his artillery commander, Lt. Col. John Keith, discussed whether to try to tow Keith's eighteen howitzers out on the withdrawal. The road was a typical Korean frozen dirt track through the towering mountains, often narrow and with numerous twists and defiles. Both commanders were worried that one of the howitzers might tip over and block the road, so they decided to fire all of the remaining ammunition and abandon the guns. This was no small decision: Keith had 3,206 rounds of 105-mm ammunition. He mustered all the personnel in the battalion area—cooks, clerks, and mechanics—to handle ammunition, and the shoot started at dusk. The battalion's eighteen guns fired all the ammunition in twenty minutes, a rate of fire of almost nine rounds per minute per gun, or less than seven seconds between rounds on every piece. About 160 shells exploded in the impact area every minute. The guns were blackened and the paint was peeling from the heat of the firing, but the artillerymen still used Thermit grenades to destroy the weapons. Forward observers saw one of the large troop formations they were firing on begin digging in as if to repel an attack.[25]

Every soldier in the regiment remembers the ride out. Commanders were determined to carry all the soldiers on vehicles, even if it meant riding on the hoods of jeeps and on tanks and flak wagons. About the time the artillery shoot began, a liaison plane flew over a group of soldiers looting cigarettes and candy from abandoned PX supplies. It dropped a note that Pfc. Morris V. Evans Jr. picked up; the note stated that three Chinese divisions were outflanking the regiment. Evans raced to find Freeman. After reading the note, he told Evans: "Get back to your unit. We're going to be pulling out in a few minutes."[26]

The regiment started moving about dark. The planned order of march was to be 2d Battalion, 1st Battalion, 3d Battalion. When the movement began, however, the departure took on an improvisatory nature of its own. Soldiers clambered onto the nearest vehicle, many riding atop tanks and flak wagons. Within a few hours, the regiment arrived at an outpost line held by the 24th Infantry Division's 5th Regimental Combat Team and was soon moving south toward Seoul. It was the beginning of a journey none of them ever forget. The exodus became a three-day ride south in subzero temperatures. The soldiers had no food except the motley items they had looted from abandoned PX supplies and mess rations—canned fruit, graham crackers, cornflakes, candy, and the like.

Sergeant Don Thomas, then a rifleman in King Company, remembers beginning the ride jammed into the back of a truck. Someone found a can of frozen corned beef hash in the truck bed, opened it, and passed it around "so each of us could tear out a frozen chunk and eat it. Tasted like T-bone steak. The can made two or three trips around the group before it was empty." After a later stop, from which he rode out on a tank, he described the trip as "the coldest ride I ever experienced," adding:

A dozen of us climbed on the tank. I was one of the last ones up and therefore the only space I found was behind the turret over the grate where the air is drawn in by the engine cooling fan. I was so exhausted, cold, and hungry, I just laid down on the grate and went to sleep. The [temperature was] in the minus twenties for this period of the withdrawal. In addition to the wind-chill from the tank movement I had the additional wind from the drawing engine fan. The convoy clanked down the road all night. I was on that grate eight hours. I never knew when the tank stopped. Nor did I get off of it. I was carried off and was walked up and down the road between two guys until I "woke up" or came to.

The ride resulted in severe frostbite of Thomas's fingers and toes, an affliction many soldiers suffered.[27]

Safe Haven in the South

Finally, on the evening of 3 December, the regiment arrived at the village of Munsan-ni, which is in South Korea north of Seoul but behind the barrier of the Imjin River. For the first time in many days, the soldiers were able to catch up on sleep, food, and personal hygiene. Colonel Freeman set to work pulling the regiment back up to the standards it had met when it arrived in Korea three months before. The core of the regiment that came from Fort Lewis still remained, but there had been many casualties. Replacements arrived over the next few weeks, and the quartermaster replaced the bulk of the equipment that had been damaged or abandoned in the North. The regiment began training, spending much of the month integrating the new personnel into the unit.[28]

Freeman's decision to take the Anju road was controversial. Many officers at the time thought he should have fought through to Sunchon, and that had he done so the division would not have been hurt as severely. Others thought he failed to fulfill his mission and that by taking the Anju road he had increased the casualties on the Sunchon road. There was widespread criticism of Freeman throughout the Eighth Army. It was rumored on the division staff that he had withdrawn without authority, and other rumors spread that he would or should be punished for his actions. What might have happened if Freeman had followed the rest of the 2d Division down the Sunchon road can never be known. Even with a half-century of hindsight, however, it is difficult to speculate that things would have turned out differently for those units already in the gauntlet on the Kunu-ri–Sunchon road had Freeman followed them. What is less subject to debate is that the 23d Infantry would have suffered more in doing so.[29]

Freeman himself was aware of the criticism, but never doubted that he had done the right thing. A week after the withdrawal, Freeman wrote:

"[I can state] with every degree of certainty that my force could not have held its rear guard position an hour longer than it did. There is no doubt in my mind that the correct decision was made. I feel that the 23rd RCT made its maximum contribution to the withdrawal of the 2d Division and could have done no more without annihilation."[30]

By taking the Anju road and thereby saving his regiment, Freeman built the legend that lives still in the hearts of those who served under him. The legend and the controversy are built on the myth that Freeman made the decision on his own, without permission. General Keiser, understandably preoccupied with conditions on the Kunu-ri–Sunchon road and the massacre of his division, either did not personally approve the change in route or did not remember relaying approval to Freeman, although both Freeman and Col. Charles C. Sloane, the 9th Infantry commander, whom he relayed it through, clearly understood that Keiser was giving approval.

When Roy Appleman was researching the action for the army's chief of military history, the assistant division commander, Brig. Gen. Sladen Bradley, stated in writing that he had given the approval in the division commander's absence. Frank Meszar remembers the radio conversation. Part of the blame for the confusion over this episode lies with Brig. Gen. S. L. A. Marshall, the military historian who wrote in the first detailed account of the action that Freeman had relied on garbled radio transmissions for approval. Whatever the circumstances, the romanticized action of taking the Anju road cemented a bond between Freeman and his soldiers that is alive in the regiment's veterans more than a half-century after the event.[31]

Chapter 4

The French Battalion and
Lt. Col. Ralph Monclar

The commander must try, above all, to establish personal and comradely contact with his men, but without giving away an inch of his authority.

     —Field Marshal Erwin Rommel

When you set out to war, be not inactive, depend not upon your captains, nor waste time in drinking, eating, or sleeping. Set the sentries yourselves, and take your rest only after you have posted them at night at every important point about your troops; then take your rest, but arise early. Do not put off your accoutrements without a quick glance about you, for a man may thus perish suddenly through his carelessness.

     —Vladimir II of Kiev

On 24 July 1950, Gen. Douglas MacArthur established the United Nations Command in Tokyo. The UN Security Council resolution calling for an end to hostilities and withdrawal of North Korean troops behind the 38th Parallel also pledged member nations to assist in carrying out the resolution. As the first American units were pushed into the Pusan Perimeter in July and August, it became apparent that the conflict would not be a short one. President Truman wanted the UNC to be representative of the United Nations and encouraged participation by as many nations as possible.

The U.S. State Department began to persuade member states to send forces. Although the military leaders preferred to solicit only fully equipped ground combat units, the policy soon evolved into one of accepting whatever a country offered. By the beginning of 1951, sixteen nations had dispatched ground combat units. In addition, a number of countries sent air and naval units, and five countries that did not send combat troops contributed medical units.[1]

In France, as in many UN member countries, public and private debates addressed the question of participation in the UN effort. The question was more difficult for France than for some members of the United Nations, however. At the time, guerrilla warfare with the Vietminh in Indochina was France's greatest international concern, and sending substantial forces to Korea would be difficult. Nonetheless, by 22 July, the French government had decided to participate and immediately placed the frigate *La Grandiere* at the UNC's disposal.[2]

After further debate in August, the French government and service chiefs decided to send a *mission observateur* (observer team) to the war. General MacArthur did not want observers without troops, so on 25 August the French decided to send a battalion of infantry. Initially, they thought that sending a regular army battalion would be the easiest solution. However, the demands of Indochina, along with the ready availability of large numbers of volunteers, led to the decision to send a battalion composed entirely of volunteers.

The decision to send a battalion of volunteers was a delicate one: France would be sending an untested unit of unknown abilities without traditions or lineage. This would be France's first military operation to be observed by its allies since the "French disaster" of 1940, when Germany defeated France's military forces in a single campaign. France's allies would judge its military potential by this battalion's performance in Korea, and a poor showing would be disastrous for the nation's reputation in the military arena. These concerns were unfounded: the French Battalion became a legendary unit whose exploits would come to rival and complement those of the 23d Infantry Regiment, and their destinies would be linked throughout their time in Korea.[3]

The men who volunteered to serve in the battalion came from all walks of life, and for reasons as varied as their backgrounds. About 70 percent of the officers and half of the NCOs were volunteers from the regular army, as were about a quarter of the private soldiers. The nonregular volunteers came from the reserves. Beyond that, the requirement that all volunteers be French citizens limited the number of foreigners in the ranks to about twenty legionnaires of German and Spanish origin who had taken French citizenship. About fifty Algerians, whose homeland the French considered to be part of metropolitan France, responded to the call. They quickly become known for their loyalty and ferocity. Between half and three-quarters of all the volunteers had experienced combat in World War II or Indochina.[4]

Although their motives for volunteering were varied, one thing was common among all the volunteers: they were excited about the prospects of going to war. As one reporter who observed them in action in Korea would describe their attitude, "They truly 'go to war as to a wedding.'"[5]

One motivation that all the men shared was the spirit of anticommunism. In much of the postwar French army, the political outlook was center-left: because of the wartime resistance's communist legacy, much of the army was left leaning. Soldiers who had seen the communist excesses and even atrocities during the liberation could only mention them at the risk of being dubbed fascists. Many of the volunteers saw themselves as lifetime professional soldiers. Furthermore, reserve officers could not yet volunteer for service in Indochina; thus, if a reserve officer wanted to see action in 1950, the only place he could do so was Korea.

Another motive uniting the volunteers was a desire to wipe out the bitter memory of 1940. The humiliation of their precipitous defeat at the hands of the Germans rankled every Frenchman, but especially those who felt in themselves a martial spirit. Many armies performed poorly in the early battles of World War II, the U.S. Army included. Nonetheless, the French people, as well as the rest of the world, held France's army in especially low esteem.

For many Frenchmen in 1950, there was a profound respect for the American military and its role in freeing France in World War II. Many French veterans welcomed the opportunity to serve with the Americans. A tour in Korea would also give men a chance to practice and polish their English language skills. Some volunteers had fought in Indochina with poor weapons and wanted a chance to fight with first-class equipment. Although it is hard to fathom, there also were those who wanted to spend the winter in a warmer climate—some had looked at a map and seen that the 38th Parallel dividing North from South Korea also runs between Naples and Tunis. Finally, there were those rationales that commonly motivate men to volunteer for wartime service: a romantic chance for adventure; the opportunity to test one's limits; the desire for foreign travel; few restrictions on the consumption of alcohol or mingling with native women; a chance to save money; and simply the desire to abandon a dull existence. Some soldiers volunteered for that most noble of reasons: "to fight for the freedom of a country that we didn't even know, Korea, following the example of the young Americans who came to fight for *us* during the two World Wars."[6]

The large proportion of reserves and the diverse motivations for volunteering for Korea gave the battalion a distinctive and unique character that made it different from the French army in France, Indochina, and Africa. The men who volunteered for Korea showed a strong demonstration of resolve and determination through the mere act of volunteering. In addition, they brought diverse civilian backgrounds and skills such as interpreters and mechanics that would not be common in the average regular army infantry battalion.

Many volunteered to serve in ranks lower than those for which they were qualified in order to be part of the French Battalion. For this reason, as one veteran put it, "The battalion was a fake." In saying this, he meant that it was not representative of the French army, that there was no other battalion in the French army with either its qualities or its qualifications. As events transpired, the French Battalion's unique character would soon prove that the gamble of sending a newly formed battalion without traditions or lineage to represent France in Korea was a worthwhile one.[7]

The battalion's official designation was Forces Terrestres Françaises de l'O. N. U., or Bataillon Français de l'O. N. U., but it was usually called the Bataillon de Corée by the French and known to the Americans as the French Battalion. It was organized with roughly the same number of men and types of equipment found in a separate U.S. Army infantry battalion, that is, a battalion not planned to be part of a larger unit such as a regiment or division, and therefore authorized somewhat larger numbers of men and a wider range of equipment. It had a total of 1,017 men organized into a headquarters company, three rifle companies, and a heavy weapons company. The rifle companies had three platoons, each with a .30-caliber machine gun and three BARs, and a support platoon with two 60-mm mortars and two 57-mm recoilless rifles. The heavy weapons company had a machine-gun platoon with eight .30-caliber machine guns and an antitank platoon with four 75-mm recoilless rifles. A four-hundred-man replacement unit provided a replacement pool for the battalion. Beyond that, the French government would prove stingy with replacements during the battalion's first year in Korea.[8]

As the battalion took shape in southern France, it formed into companies of distinctly different character. The 1st Company was made up mainly of old marine veterans, the 2d Company veterans of the old metropolitan infantry, and the 3d Company paratroopers and legionnaires. The headquarters company incorporated artillerymen and specialists, and the heavy weapons company was made up of specialists in the types of weapons it employed. The distinctive makeup of each company caused an atmosphere of healthy competition between them, with each trying always to demonstrate that it was better than the others. The battalion conducted several weeks of training in patrolling and ambush techniques, and on 25 October embarked from Marseille for Korea.[9]

The commander of the French Battalion was an infantry commander unique in military history: General de Corps d'Armée Ralph Monclar, a *nom de guerre* adopted by General Magrin-Vernery. The son of a Hungarian nobleman and a French woman, he bore a hyphenated name that joined his mother's name, Magrin, and that of the French colonel who provided for his education, Vernery. Monclar lied about his age when he was sixteen to enlist in the Foreign Legion, and was already a sergeant when his family took him out to prepare for Saint-Cyr, the French counterpart of West Point. Graduating in the class of 1914, he swore he would enter battle in his Saint-Cyr hat and cockade. A lieutenant in World War I, he was wounded seven times and cited for valor ten times. During the interwar period, Monclar fought wherever he could find action—in Syria and Morocco among other places. He commanded French forces in the Anglo-French invasion of Narvik at the beginning of World War II. After France fell, he escaped to England and took command of the Foreign Legion's 13th Armored Demi-Brigade. In 1941, after taking the key fortress in Eritrea, he accepted the surrender of the admiral commanding the Italian Red Sea fleet, along with several thousand enemy soldiers.[10]

Monclar was fifty-eight in 1950 and, as the inspector general of the Foreign Legion, held rank equivalent to a lieutenant general in the U.S. Army. When the decision was made to form the French Battalion for service in Korea, Monclar volunteered to lead it. The minister of war told him he was too old, but Monclar heatedly persisted and prevailed. He even offered to wear the insignia of a lieutenant colonel to avoid problems of rank.[11]

Monclar was a sophisticated yet profoundly human soldier. Well-educated, he could speak seven languages, and was proud of the fact that he could talk to his soldiers in their native tongues. In Korea, he found a young orphan who had grown up with Roman Catholic monks. Monclar used the boy as an interpreter by speaking to him in Latin and then having the Korean question POWs and translate their answers into Latin. A renaissance man of vast cultural experience, he did everything with style and panache. Monclar had recently married a young woman and had two small children. Aware that at his age—and in his profession—he was un-

Lieutenant General Matthew B. Ridgway, Eighth Army commander, stands in a jeep with Lt. Col. Ralph Monclar, the French Battalion commander, as they pass in review during a parade in March, 1951. *Courtesy National Archives.*

likely to see the youngsters become adults, he wrote them long and philosophical letters sprinkled with Latin and Greek quotations, in the hope that his correspondence would constitute posthumous guidance as the children matured. He possessed both modesty and a sense of humor. On one occasion, as a battalion commander objecting to the micromanagement of his unit, he told his division commander that he had commanded sixteen battalions in his career, "but not at one time."[12]

Monclar was without peer as a leader of men in peace and war. With most leaders, one can discern their leadership philosophy only by inferring it from their actions. In Monclar's case, he made it explicit by carefully typing his "Catechisme de Combat" in the fall of 1940 while serving with the Foreign Legion in Cameroon. This remarkable document, written less than six months after the fall of France, covers in fifteen chapters everything that Monclar had learned in twenty-six years in the military. Chapters three and four are entitled "Morale" and "Cohesion." In these chapters, he records why high morale and unit cohesion are essential, and how it is almost impossible for a unit with high morale and cohesion to perform poorly in combat.[13]

Monclar opens his chapter on morale by quoting Ardant du Picq, the prominent nineteenth century military theorist: "Nothing can be wisely ordered in matters of tactics, organization, instruction, discipline, (all things which go together), if we do not take as the starting point man and his state of morale, at the definitive moment of combat." Monclar then defines morale in combat as the mastery of nerves by the soldier and his leader in the frightful milieu of combat. The soldier must be trained so that explosions, gunfire, and actions of the enemy do not distract him to the degree that he cannot effectively use his weapon. Similarly, leaders must be so inured to the distractions that they can take appropriate action in the chaos. Every soldier and leader is mortal and will experience fear, but he must learn to control it. A battle, Monclar continues, is often a contest between two adversaries who are both afraid. The winner is the one who is most effective at bluffing the other.[14]

Discipline, according to Monclar, reinforces morale. In addition to discipline, morale is built through traditions and esprit de corps; instruction and habit; confidence in leaders; the spirit of sacrifice; and the offensive spirit. Discipline rests on the familiar military axiom that by being forced to comply in often-meaningless detailed minutia, a soldier will be accustomed to comply automatically when stakes are higher. Esprit de corps builds on the heritage of units like the Foreign Legion that have a tradition of bravery, military behavior, and discipline. For Monclar: "The dead continue to fight with us. Our self-esteem and public opinion compel us to compete with them to maintain, intact, the union of the Corps with its heritage of glory."

Action distracts from danger. Monclar stressed that a soldier must be instructed his actions are essential for unit success, so that he will acquire reflexes that will continue to function in combat. For example, a machine gunner who knows that the platoon he is supporting cannot maneuver unless he provides a continuous base of fire will keep firing his weapon in spite of fear or distractions.

Leaders, Monclar strongly believed, give confidence by their presence on the battlefield. "The men say, 'He's here, and he's not saying anything, so everything must be all right.'" For the same reason, soldiers must see them in times of calm as well as crisis. In the spirit of sacrifice, the soldier must understand before combat that he may have to give his life. In coming to this understanding, however, he must resolve that he will give it only for a high price and not through either imprudence or negligence. Leaders must sacrifice also and share the same danger, hardships, and fatigue as the troops.

Some men may lack a spirit of sacrifice and long for the relative security of the rear. Monclar wanted those soldiers to know that "their leaders and comrades will force their obedience, by physical means first, then, if necessary, by extreme coercion. For them, the danger will be greater at the rear than at the front."[15]

Monclar then examines those factors that can play roles in lowering morale: surprise; losses, especially useless ones; the cries and sight of the wounded; bad news and rumors; and enemy maneuvers to the flanks or rear.

He quotes the Athenian soldier and historian Xenophon as saying that whether something is pleasant or unpleasant, surprise doubles the effect. Surprise paralyzes a soldier or leader for a moment and gives the assailant an advantage. The offensive spirit, when joined with surprise, can often bring success by itself. From this came the importance of any measures that increase security and reduce the possibility of surprise: obstacles and fields of fire in the defense, and patrols always. During exercises, he wrote, leaders must train their soldiers to fight in any direction so that they will not be demoralized by an attack on their flanks or rear.[16]

Numerous losses give the soldier the impression that his turn is next. In Monclar's experience, the presence and sight of the wounded always depressed their comrades. These factors increase the importance of efficient casualty evacuation. In addition, efficient medical care contributes its own positive effect on morale. Medical personnel must be made aware that the wounded will naturally be pessimistic and give an exaggerated account of how bad conditions are. They must prevent the aid stations from becoming a source of false rumors. Officers and NCOs must also stop the spread of rumors. Unwelcome rumors always spread faster than positive ones and can quickly demoralize a unit.

Infantrymen had to become familiar with the idea of danger, and Monclar wanted their leaders to inculcate it in them. Good soldiers will learn to accept the aphorism that things are never as good as one hopes, or as bad as one fears. Leaders must provide exercises that get soldiers used to explosions, the firing of artillery and automatic weapons, tanks, and low-flying aircraft. Finally, leaders need to make men dig fighting positions to reassure them and make them not only feel, but in fact be, safer if they are attacked.[17]

Monclar wanted leaders to read passages of war literature to the soldiers so that they will know how other soldiers have reacted to combat. As Plato answered when asked how to make children brave, tell them stories of glory.

A soldier with high morale in a unit with correspondingly high morale should expect, according to Monclar, above all, the satisfaction of duty accomplished. Beyond that, he should expect the respect of his leaders and his comrades: "in combat, man bares himself. There is no more 'big shot' warrior of the barracks or the saloon." A good soldier possesses an inner drive and resilience that will carry him through adversity. As a result of his sacrifices, a soldier has a right to expect decorations and promotions. Leaders must, in spite of fatigue, write recommendations for awards immediately after the battle. Soldiers should receive awards proportional to their losses and their leaders' awards should be proportionate to the results achieved.[18]

As he recorded in his "Catechisme," Monclar believed that awards were another big factor in sustaining morale. Through the first year in Korea, he maintained a spirited exchange with the War Ministry over the question of awards. A typical expression of Monclar's outlook is found in a letter he wrote to the French war minister in Paris in February, 1951. After describing the actions of recent battles in some detail, Monclar wrote:

> I have permitted myself to expose these considerations to you, because I know I will be criticized and it will be said that I award too much and that I should "limit and block citations."
>
> All the wounded were hurt during active operations, six officers were wounded twice, three of the wounded are dead, two from a second wound. Three officers who could have been evacuated remained or returned to their combat post. Many of them carried back their friends or leaders who had been hit. [Regulations] award soldiers who brought back wounded comrades or superiors the Military Medal. . . .

If we accept the principle of blocking the award of war medals, we would have to decide that two wounds received in one month counted as one. I've always regretted the fact that I was not able to give the Legion of Honor to Lt. Nicolai, dead of a second wound . . . because I feared he would be killed before obtaining it. . . .

Others would point out to me that since 1948, in Indochina and Madagascar citations were limited. I spent eleven months in Indochina . . . at the moment where we were fighting the most. Even there, the men had some time and place to rest and shower and two hours after my arrival I was present with the Foreign Legion members, dressed in impeccable uniforms with blue belts. Here, neither our men nor the Americans from our tactical group have any relaxation. They [have just] received their first Arctic sleeping bags. They rarely get to wash up, either themselves, or their clothes, and are covered with more filth than with underwear. At Madagascar, I'm familiar with the number of citations accorded, in particular to the battalion that had one killed in action. . . .

I repeat, the men are beginning to lose their nerves, and I support their morale as best I can. I demand that this letter be personally submitted to the Secretary of Defense, War Department for a decision.[19]

Unfortunately, the secretary's answer is not preserved, but we can infer that it was negative and that it deprecated Monclar's position in Korea as merely a battalion commander. Monclar responded that the tone of the letter was unfortunately the same as an earlier reply, and continued:

Of course I have a fictitious rank *only* in the U.N. Army. In the French Army, I remain "General of the Army Corps, Great Cross of the Legion of Honor" whom you named, and under no circumstances am I to be expected to stand at attention in front of all the colonels and generals on the Boulevard St. Germaine.

I have nothing against serving under an American colonel or sleeping outside, without, not *under* a tent, in holes and at temperatures of minus twenty degrees (I said *minus* twenty degrees) and colder.

But I have the honor to demand that I not be considered as a "minor" General in the French Army and to conserve within this army all my rights and prerogatives, General of the Army Corps and Superior Commander of Operations. . . .

It is not my intention to elude any control. However, this control should consider the present situation in Korea. Is it proper to compare us to the situation in Madagascar?

In Madagascar, the Battalion of the Foreign Legion only had one killed and its enemies carried only spears.

Here, in less than a month of operations, we have suffered 275 losses: 40 killed, 131 wounded. . . .

In the eyes of the Americans, the Battalion proved the eternal combat qualities of the French. . . . I attach a copy of the letter, written by General Ridgway, Commander-in-Chief, showing the esteem in which, outside of Paris, we are held.[20]

Despite Monclar's entreaties, the minister of war never resolved the situation with respect to awards to his satisfaction.

In his short chapter on cohesion, Monclar calls it one of the principal reasons for success in infantry units. He says it consists of the way the men live, work, eat, and sleep together so that, if necessary, they will stay together to the death. Cohesion builds on a trust between soldiers and their leaders so that they know that as a group they will do whatever has to be done to accomplish the mission. Cohesion builds confidence. As Ardant du Picq wrote, twenty men who do not know one another will flee before a lion, whereas four men who know one another will attack one.

Cohesion is the best means of avoiding the "contagion of fear" that Monclar knew could otherwise destroy a unit. This contagion is most rapid in dense formations, at night, when soldiers have nothing to do, when they are fatigued, or when they have no confidence in their orders. A unit must be kept together, and when outside units such as artillery or machine guns are attached for support, the units should habitually be the same ones.[21]

Monclar credited his soldiers with their success in Korea. They, on the other hand, maintain that the extent of their success would not have been possible under anyone but Monclar. Much of the high level of performance that the French Battalion demonstrated in Korea came about because of the bond built between Monclar and his men. They knew that he would not order them to do the impossible; that he only accepted and passed along orders he thought reasonable. As both a company commander and battalion commander in World War I, Monclar refused orders that he considered suicidal when he thought they would accomplish nothing. As he put it to a journalist after Korea:

It's just that, you see, at a certain rank in the hierarchy—that doesn't apply of course, to young officers or to the soldier (because then, what army would be possible?); there is a moment when you must assume your responsibilities and if you judge that an attack is impossible, you must know how to say "No." Of course someone else will replace you and, who knows, maybe win a victory. It's a risk to run, a personal risk, a risk which can have repercussions on your career. What matters this risk if you have made your decision with a clear conscience? It's nothing in comparison to the risk the men would have run, they who could lose their lives.[22]

In Korea, Monclar was fond of saying, "There are two things which keep up the morale of soldiers—meals, including wine, and the mail." He took every opportunity to taste the quality of the soldiers' food, sometimes irritating the mess sergeant, who said, "The general's always on my back, but I think it's really because he likes to eat." The officer in charge of the mail once provoked Monclar's anger when he briefed him on mail delivery. He told the general that there was a rapid service for mail from France costing twenty-six hundred francs per bag and a slower one for seventeen hundred francs, concluding, "So it's understood, we'll take the slower service." Monclar's face turned purple with rage as he exploded: "What do you mean, it's understood? *What do you mean, it's understood?* What gives *you* the right to decide all by yourself? *I'm* the commander of French Forces in Korea, and responsible for morale. So—if I hadn't called you here, you wouldn't even have sent me a report to attract my attention to the problem? Well, now *you're* going to find a solution, and if *you* don't find the funds, *I* will! I consider that rapid mail service is essential for the morale of the troops, and I will not compromise over it. We'll see if it's *'understood'!*"

Monclar's fearlessness was legendary. As he stated in his "Catechisme," he thought it was important that the soldiers see their leaders both in combat and during quieter times. In combat, he made sure the men saw him by visiting them in their fighting positions. He walked upright behind the line of foxholes and stopped by each one to pass a few moments of conversation with the soldiers, reassuring them. As he explained it: "I must be where I can reach them quickly if they are attacked, so that I may walk among them speaking cheerfully. It serves to steady them and give them the cool blood." Some soldiers with a sense of humor said that Monclar had merely calculated how many seconds it took for a Chinese mortar crew to aim and fire a round, and stayed less than that amount of time at each hole so that the mortar shell fell immediately after he stepped away.[23]

An affectionate joke in the French Battalion was that when Monclar got the hiccups, he had them for a long time because nothing could scare him enough to cure him of the disorder. Lieutenant Colonel Meszar, the 23d Infantry's executive officer, who owned his own solid reputation for bravery, once accompanied Monclar on a tour of the line. After some near misses, he told the French commander, "This may work for you, but it's too much for me," and left the general to continue alone.

At the general's headquarters, the men customarily dug some holes for protection from incoming fire. On one occasion, the staff took cover in the holes while the headquarters was being harassed by enemy fire. Monclar, however, sat imperturbably writing letters throughout the shelling, with a small smile for his staff. Several of those who were close to Monclar in Korea believed that he wanted his career to culminate with a soldier's death.

Although Monclar did not demand that all of his officers adopt his own consummate standards of fearlessness, he set higher standards for them than for his soldiers. After one tough battle he held an officers' call in which the participants reviewed every action in detail. Monclar was silent throughout the meeting but took notes. At the end, he said: "There should have been one officer killed for every five non-officers. The count doesn't show it. I'm not saying that the officers didn't do their duty, but I just wanted to point it out."

Monclar was technically commander of all French forces in Korea. Before the battalion and its replacement pool left France, there had been talk of sending additional forces later to increase the size of the French command to a regiment or possibly even a division. Thus Monclar did not directly command the French Battalion, but rather had a staff that was superimposed over it. The staff consisted of thirty-one personnel, including his chief of staff, the normal aides and secretarial personnel, and an officer-observer from each branch of the army. The effect of this was that the battalion's actual commander constantly had Monclar, the senior general of France, looking over his shoulder, as well as an independent staff observing his staff's actions in detail. This was a difficult situation at best. Monclar developed a reputation for controlling the battalion with an iron hand, even when physically and mentally fatigued. That the battalion compiled the record that it did in these conditions is a commentary on its soldiers and documentation of what a truly remarkable individual Monclar was.[24]

The French Battalion departed Marseille for Korea on 25 October 1950. During the voyage to Pusan, many of the soldiers expressed disappointment that the war seemed to be almost over and worried that they would miss out on the adventure they had anticipated. Meanwhile, a few weeks before they embarked, a disaster had occurred in Indochina. During the first week of October, Vietminh general Vo Nguyen Giap began his first offensive against the French in North Vietnam. Employing an overly ambitious plan that never had a chance of success, the French army blundered into an ambush. The battle turned into a slaughter of about six thousand French soldiers and caused the abandonment of tons of military supplies at Cao Bang and Lang Son, the greatest French colonial defeat since Montcalm had been killed at Quebec in 1759. Those losses closed the book on plans for a larger French force in Korea. Although enough volunteers had been raised for a second battalion for Korea, the government instead sent the soldiers to Indochina.[25]

On arrival at Pusan, soldiers began organizing their equipment, finding a number of inexplicable shortages in matériel that had not been abundant to begin with. Nonetheless, they were happy finally to be in Korea. They felt little fear, and were eager to get to an American unit as a way to get into action.[26]

The Eighth Army commander, Lt. Gen. Walton Walker, sent the French Battalion to Taegu for training and acclimatization. There the battalion filled its days with exercises emphasizing patrolling and night defensive perimeters, and familiarization with American weapons. The heavy weapons company received its four American 75-mm recoilless rifles to supplement its machine-gun and mortar platoons. The battalion was still training at Taegu when the Chinese intervened in late November. Many of the soldiers were happy to hear of the reversal, as it meant they would get into the fighting after all.[27]

During its stay at Taegu the French Battalion was assigned to the 2d Infantry Division. When it joined the division in early December, it spent time with each of the other regiments before finally being attached to the 23d Infantry Regiment. The soldiers resented being, as they put it, "waltzed around" the division in this manner. They felt unappreciated and even repudiated.

Several reasons why the American regimental commanders rejected the offer of the French Battalion are fairly obvious. The simple fact was that most American soldiers held a low opinion of French military capabilities in 1950, and that alone is probably enough to explain the rejections. In addition, everyone knew that "Lieutenant Colonel" Monclar was in reality a French lieutenant general and the first soldier of France. This was undoubtedly somewhat intimidating to the American commanders who declined the French Battalion. Finally, the thirty-one man staff that accompanied the French Battalion appeared to be, and in many respects was, an unwieldy imposition on the battalion that would cause any regimental commander to consider whether he wanted to live with a foreign staff of "experts" looking over his shoulder.

Lieutenant Colonel Ralph Monclar (General de Corps d'Armée Magrin-Vernery) presents the French Croix de Guerre to Col. Paul Freeman, Jr., at the French Embassy in Washington, D.C., on 3 July 1951. *Courtesy National Archives.*

Finally, in mid-December, the French Battalion settled in with the 23d Infantry Regiment. "Lieutenant Colonel" Monclar and Colonel Freeman hit it off from the start. The two men formed a relationship of mutual respect that would grow for the next two months and last through both soldiers' lifetimes. Freeman always addressed Monclar as "General Monclar," although Monclar objected that he was only a lieutenant colonel in the United Nations Command. Monclar even insisted that Lieutenant Colonel Meszar walk on his right because, as the regiment's second in command, he was "senior" to a battalion commander. The troops got along equally well, and the Americans paid their French counterparts the compliment they most wanted to hear: As one French veteran said many years later, "The 23rd treated us like just another unit."

As demonstrated by his "Catechisme" and by his actions with the French Battalion in Korea, Monclar profoundly grasped why men follow other men into desperate straits. He had the quality of "heart" that allowed him to read his soldiers' feelings and respond to them. He knew his soldiers and called them by name when he saw them. In doing so, he built a little conspiracy between himself and his soldiers, so that each man felt he had a special bond with the general—a feeling that, as was often the case with Napoleon and his soldiers, he acknowledged them as comrades in arms. "We are in this thing together, you and I," Monclar told them. During the next two months, the remarkable synergy of the American regiment and the French Battalion would lead each to be awarded an unprecedented two Presidential Unit Citations—the highest recognition a unit can receive for action in combat.[28]

Chapter 5

Matthew Ridgway and a New War

The job of the commander was to be up where the crisis of action was taking place. In time of battle, I wanted division commanders to be up with their forward battalion, and I wanted corps commanders up with the regiment that was in the hottest action. If they had paper work to do, they could do it at night. By day their place was up there where the shooting was going on.

I held to the old-fashioned idea that it helped the spirits of the men to see the Old Man up there, in the snow and sleet and the mud, sharing the same cold, miserable existence they had to endure.
—Gen. Matthew B. Ridgway

The real reason why I succeeded in my own campaigns is because I was always on the spot.
—Arthur Wellesley, Duke of Wellington

When Lt. Gen. Walton Walker was killed in a vehicle accident just before Christmas, 1950, Lt. Gen. Matthew Bunker Ridgway flew to Korea to take command. On the way to the Eighth Army in Korea, he stopped in Tokyo to be briefed by General MacArthur. While there, he asked whether he could go on the offensive if the opportunity arose. MacArthur, in a remarkable display of confidence in Ridgway's abilities, told him, "The Eighth Army is yours, Matt. Do what you think best."[1]

When he arrived in Korea at the end of December, Ridgway began touring the frontline units. He found a defeated and dispirited army, one that he immediately began rebuilding. He did not blame the soldiers for their condition, for they were not responsible for their predicament or their leadership. He held the leaders responsible for the road-bound army he found, an army that had, in large part, forgotten how to soldier.

Ridgway began by stressing the elements of basic soldiering through the chain of command. He wanted the army off its vehicles and on the hills. He wanted the troops to construct tight defensive perimeters for night fighting, while expanding the perimeters during daylight. Although the United Nations Command had total air superiority and a strong advantage in tanks and artillery, he did not think his commanders were using the tools available to them efficiently. For example, Ridgway wanted his units to defend themselves at night, destroying the attackers with artillery and flak wagons, and using tanks to support the infantry, then call in air strikes during daylight hours. He particularly wanted to punish the Chinese by killing as many as possible, not just fighting for real estate. There would be no more "bug outs."[2] Units would stay in position and fight surrounded if need be, holding out until a relief force could get to them the next day. He ordered commanders to leave no unit to be overwhelmed and destroyed, and promised to send as much force as necessary to relieve an encircled unit.

Ridgway found that many commanders in Korea believed the United Nations Command was in danger of being driven from the peninsula. He did not believe this, but he fully understood that political factors might require UN forces to be withdrawn. For this reason, he asked that if the situation required such a decision, that it be kept secret long enough to plan for an orderly withdrawal. President Truman had always been resolute in upholding the principle that the United States would leave the peninsula only if forced out by military necessity. In the first week of December, just after the Chinese intervention, Truman told Prime Minister Clement Atlee of Great Britain: "We did not get into this fight with the intention of getting licked. We will fight to the finish to stop this aggression." Whatever happened, UN forces would not voluntarily withdraw from the peninsula. "I don't want to get out if there is any chance that we can stay."[3] In spite of this, however, MacArthur continued to warn that his forces might not be able to hold the line in Korea. Finally, in a message to MacArthur, Truman made his position clear: "We recognize, of course, that continued resistance might not be militarily possible with the limited forces with which you are being called upon to meet large Chinese armies. Further, in the present world situation, your forces must be preserved as an effective instrument for the defense of Japan and elsewhere. . . . In the worst case, it would be important that, if we must withdraw from Korea, it be clear to the world that that course is forced upon us by military necessity and that we shall not accept the result politically or militarily until the aggression has been rectified."[4] With this message, planning for withdrawal from Korea became moot and Ridgway was able to get on with his own agenda for going over to the offensive against the Chinese.

Ridgway's greatest challenge was not in getting the material necessities for fighting the war, although he gave attention to getting good winter uniforms and hot meals to the soldiers. His challenge was to rebuild the fighting spirit of the army,

> a spirit that cannot be imposed from above but that must be cultivated in every heart, from private to general. It is rooted, I believe, in the individual's sense of security, of belonging to a unit that will stand by him, as units on both sides and in the rear stand by all other units too. Good training should help a soldier get rid of that awful sense of alone-ness that can sometimes overtake a man in battle, the feeling that nobody gives a damn about *him,* and that he has only his own resources to depend on. Americans, I think, are often more self-sufficient than soldiers of other nations. But still they need help in cultivating that assurance that they belong to a group that will return their loyalty no matter what danger threatens.[5]

The new attitude that Ridgway wanted to instill in the Eighth Army percolated down to the individual soldier surprisingly quickly. William Guthrie, then a captain, remembers Ridgway visiting the 2d Infantry Division headquarters and saying, "I don't want to hear your withdrawal plans—I want to hear your attack plans." Guthrie, along with some of his acquaintances, was happy with the change in attitude, and similar statements went down the chain of command and through the rumor network equally swiftly. In some jaded souls such an aggressive spirit inspired derision, but not for long. Captain Roger Nye, then a division staff officer in another division, remembers the black humor of staff officers who made remarks about how the new Eighth Army commander simply did not understand the situation in Korea if he expected them to go on the offensive anytime soon. Captain Albert C. Metts, who commanded the heavy weapons company in the 23d Infantry's 3d Battalion, remembers that his soldiers were glad to hear that the new orders were to "Clear the road and establish the line." The days of abandoning the high ground to the enemy and clearing the valleys only to the shoulders of the roads were over. The soldiers were tired of retreating and needed the kind of leadership Ridgway brought. The new orders encouraged everyone that the war was going to be fought by taking to the hills and clearing them one by one, the way they should have been in the first place.

Ridgway's own style of leadership was to set the example in every aspect of his conduct and appearance. In this way, he inspired every commander and soldier who saw him—and by rumor and word of mouth, every soldier in the Eighth Army. He was every inch a warrior, with a grenade always taped to his right shoulder strap in a theatrical but soldierly gesture. Soldiers sometimes joked about the grenade, calling Ridgway "Old Iron Tit" and speculating as to whether the grenade had powder in it, but it had the desired effect. When Ridgway visited units, he wanted to talk to soldiers and see the action, not merely receive a briefing at the regimental or battalion headquarters. Like Monclar and Freeman, Ridgway knew how to talk to soldiers and express his sincere involvement in their welfare. They reciprocated with the same kind of devotion they gave to Freeman and Monclar. Ridgway had tremendous reservoirs of personal courage. Lieutenant Robert Curtis remembers seeing him drive through mortar fire to reach the 23d Regiment, then walk along the line of riflemen through mortar and small-arms fire, talking to individual soldiers. Captain Ansil Walker, the 1st Battalion's heavy weapons company commander, saw Ridgway striding erectly across a valley through a hail of small-arms fire, and was impressed that a general would take such risks.

Ridgway had a rare combination of talents. He was a tested soldier and parachutist, but also an officer who understood the political dimensions of making war. As the army's senior paratrooper in World War II, he was used to taking action under perilous conditions. For him, the Chinese were no different from other opponents. Even before Truman clarified his policy to stay in Korea unless pushed off by force of arms, Ridgway wanted to stay and fight—but without putting his Eighth Army at risk of destruction. Before the theorists had begun to call the conflict a limited war, Ridgway made it clear he understood the new concept of fighting for limited goals, with limits on his forces and weapons, in a theater that was geographically limited. He was prepared to fight on in Korea to prevent the spread of a hostile ideology without necessarily rolling back that ideology to where it had existed before hostilities commenced. In this, he was profoundly unlike MacArthur, who saw no reason to continue to fight in Korea if communism was allowed to survive anywhere on the peninsula. Ridgway was content to duel for a limited objective such as the status quo antebellum— the situation prevailing before the war—as MacArthur could never be. Ridgway intended to first destroy his soldiers' feelings concerning the invincibility of the Chinese soldiers, the invulnerability of the guerrillas in the rear, and the fear of encirclement. Then he would proceed to destroy the CCF, one unit at a time.[6]

Finally, after Ridgway had assessed the state of Eighth Army's military abilities and begun turning the army in the direction he wanted it to move, he had to address his soldiers' inner needs. He found in the UN soldiers under his command what he described as "a bewildered army," unsure of either why they were there or for what they were fighting. In a letter dated 21 January 1951 directed to every man in his command, he answered both questions. They were in Korea because their respective governments had decided to commit them there. The loyalty they gave to their governments precluded any "slightest questioning of these orders." To Ridgway, the second question, what they were fighting for, was far more significant:

> To me the issues are clear. It is not a question of this or that Korean town or village. Real estate is, here, incidental. It is not restricted to the issue of freedom for our South Korean Allies, whose fidelity and valor under the severest stresses of battle we recognize; though that freedom is a symbol of the wider issues, and included among them.
>
> The real issues are whether the power of Western civilization, as God has permitted it to flower in our own beloved lands, shall defy and defeat Communism; whether the rule of men who shoot their prisoners, enslave their citizens, and deride the dignity of man, shall displace the rule of those to whom the individual and his individual rights are sacred; whether we are to survive with God's hand to guide and lead us, or to perish in the dead existence of a Godless world.
>
> If these be true, and to me they are, beyond any possibility of challenge, then this has long since ceased to be a fight for freedom for our Korean Allies alone and for their national survival. It has become, and it continues to be, a fight for our own freedom, for our own survival, in an honorable, independent national existence.
>
> The sacrifices we have made, and those we shall yet support, are not offered vicariously for others, but in our own direct defense.
>
> In the final analysis, the issue now joined right here in Korea is whether Communism or individual freedom shall prevail; whether the light of fear-driven people we have witnessed here shall be checked, or shall at some future time, however distant, engulf our own loved ones in all its misery and despair.
>
> These are the things for which we fight. Never have members of any mil-

itary command had a greater challenge than we, or a finer opportunity to show ourselves and our people at their best—and thus to do honor to the profession of arms, and to those brave men who bred us.[7]

The 23d Infantry Regiment after the Chinese Intervention

If Ridgway was to be able to go on the attack, he had to have units that were cohesive and effective when the opportunity for the offensive arose. The 23d Infantry was one of the few regiments left relatively unharmed and with most of its fighting strength intact after the Chinese hit the Eighth Army. The Chinese had mauled the 2d Infantry Division's other two regiments in December, but the 23d's escape on the Anju road brought it out intact. Although many of the soldiers in its sister regiments blamed the 23d at least partially for their own losses, there were no second thoughts about Freeman's decision within its own ranks. The regiment received 833 replacements and had 127 personnel returned from hospitalization during December. In addition, the French Battalion joined the regiment in the middle of the month. Under Colonel Freeman, the 23d was a healthy unit not only in terms of its light losses, but the soldiers and the units had a healthy attitude as well. Commanders at all levels had faith in one another and there were strong bonds between the men and their leaders. The soldiers had fond nicknames for Freeman that showed their respect: "Tall Paul," "The Great White Father," and "Colonel Paul." The remaining presence of a core of veterans also was significant. By 1951, there was still a nucleus of troops who had been with the regiment at Fort Lewis and who could pass on the regiment's pride, skills, and experience to the new soldiers.

One of the other things that strengthened the unit in December was the result of the GIs' inveterate scrounging during the withdrawal from Kunu-ri. Abandoned equipment was abundant in the area during the panicked withdrawal, and, like all good soldiers, the men of the 23d grabbed whatever they could use. Consequently, the regiment had more automatic weapons, radios, spare parts, and even vehicles than they were authorized. This would give them capabilities greater than those envisioned by the planners in the Pentagon.

Another factor that promoted a feeling of confidence in the 23d Infantry was excellent medical care. The medical system used in the Korean War grew out of the policies that had evolved through both world wars. The system's goal was to treat the wounded soldier according to his needs from the time and place he was wounded or became ill, although the combat environment and lack of optimum treatment facilities limited this, of course. Treatment began with the platoon aidman on the front lines who acted as the "family doctor" for the unit he accompanied. The aidman saw to it that proper measures were taken by soldiers to prevent disease and cared for those who became sick or wounded. Each aidman accompanied his platoon's patrols; when there were shortages of qualified aidmen, they accompanied the patrols of other units.[8]

After the aidman administered emergency treatment, vehicles or litter bearers would evacuate the wounded to the battalion aid station. There, the battalion surgeon, a physician, treated them and gave lifesaving treatment to stabilize the more seriously wounded men's condition. The overriding concern was to evacuate the wounded, injured, or sick soldier no farther to the rear than that point at which he could be treated and returned to duty with his unit.[9]

From the battalion aid station, vehicles or helicopters could, if necessary, evacuate casualties to the regimental or divisional collecting station. This was usually a blacked-out tent that could be heated and where lights could be used to examine and treat patients. About one in ten casualties needed to be rushed to a Mobile Army Surgical Hospital (MASH), where surgeons could perform lifesaving surgery. In 1950, the air force and Marine Corps performed all helicopter evacuations; the first army helicopters arrived in January, 1951.[10]

Although there were a few self-inflicted wounds in the 23d Infantry when it first arrived in Korea, there were virtually none after the breakout from the Pusan Perimeter. Any soldier who shot himself in the hand or foot to get out of combat got no sympathy from his fellow soldiers and, in fact, experienced considerable resentment. Private First Class Robert Beeby saw a soldier being carried away on a litter after shooting himself in the foot and remembers soldiers cursing him and trying to hit him. "It was a very emotional and pathetic scene," he recalled. "I think most of us would rather be dead than to be in that guy's shoes." Private Carlton Kluck, who was present when a soldier shot himself in the hand on the Naktong, said that his squad leader threatened to kill anybody who helped the man.

The French Battalion was well served by its medical services. The surgeon quickly integrated his activities into those of the Americans. The only complaint Monclar had was that when a casualty reached a hospital, orderlies stripped him of his clothes and put him in a hospital gown or pajamas. In the process, the wounded soldier often lost money, papers, and souvenirs. This particularly distressed the relatives of soldiers who later died of their wounds. Monclar proposed assigning a French NCO accountant to the aid station, who would take charge of the personal effects of the wounded, but he could not get the proposal implemented during his time in Korea. He also considered the Americans to be obsessed with preventive medical measures, especially latrines. Even so, he admitted that the American latrines seemed better than those built by the French. "French Sociability tends to multiply them everywhere," he observed, "as well as the debris and detritus of every kind." He even published rules for the French soldiers to observe around the Americans. In addition to admonishing his men to remain calm, not to joke on duty, and to observe fire discipline, the rules had a section on "Hygiene, Cleanliness, Security." In it, Monclar wrote: "The latrines must remain absolutely clean. Use only the special paper provided. Absolute hygiene must be maintained in the kitchens, infirmaries, etc."[11]

Despite these positive developments, an unhealthy attitude began to affect the 23d Infantry's relations with the rest of Eighth Army. This attitude was a feeling that the regiment was a unit that could depend only on itself to get through the war. The paragraphs on the last page of the regiment's Command Report for December, 1950, entitled "EVALUATION," capture this attitude:

> The 23rd RCT was shaken by its action at Kuni-ri, therefore, the first weeks of the month of December were devoted primarily to training activities which would integrate the replacements and returnees into the units, and restore the combat efficiency of the 23rd Regiment.
>
> There was a definite lack of confidence on the part of the 23rd in the rest of 8th Army. The feeling persisted that the 23rd was fighting on its own and couldn't depend on any support.[12]

Someone has lined through the last paragraph of the copy of the report held in the National Archives. Nonetheless, the fact that such a statement appears on an official document evaluating the unit in December, 1950, is remarkable. This, then, was the state of mind of the 23d Infantry Regiment as General Ridgway began the process of rebuilding the Eighth Army.

Chapter 6

Wonju and Patrols to Twin Tunnels

Some people seem to think that an army can be whipped by waiting for rivers to freeze over, exploding powder at a distance, drowning out troops, or setting them to sneezing; but it will always be found in the end that the only way to whip an army is to go out and fight it.
—*Ulysses S. Grant*

The history of famous armies is the history of great generals, for no army has ever achieved great things unless it has been well commanded. If the general be second-rate the army also will be second-rate. Mutual confidence is the basis of success in war, and unless the troops have implicit trust in the resolution and resources of their chief, hesitation and half-heartedness are sure to mark their actions. They may fight with their accustomed courage; but the eagerness for the conflict, the alacrity to support, the determination to conquer will not be there. The indefinable quality which is expressed by the word moral will to some degree be affected.
—*Col. G. F. R. Henderson*

By January, 1951, three UN corps were responsible for roughly the western half of the Korean peninsula. From west to east, I Corps was on the left; IX Corps next, south of Seoul; and X Corps was on the right. Republic of Korea units and the U.S. Marine Corps were responsible for the mountainous eastern half of the country, the most rugged and therefore the most difficult for North Korean or Chinese operations. Ridgway's plan for his first offensive was to have I Corps and IX Corps clear their sectors of enemy and close on the Han River. By the end of January, the river had again become a major obstacle to enemy movement because of the early thaw following the brutal weather earlier in the month. To begin the offensive, X Corps would attack, simultaneously extending its lines to the east to prevent enemy movement around Eighth Army's right flank.[1]

At the same time, a struggle began between the United Nations Command and its Chinese and North Korean opponents over who would control the north-south corridor that channeled all transportation routes east of Seoul. In the Taebaek mountain range forty miles east of Seoul there is a network of roads that look like an inverted Y. To the north is Chunchon, at the juncture of the Y is Wonju, and Andong and Taejon are at the southern ends of the roads after they split. The force that held Wonju, therefore, could control traffic into central South Korea. As the People's Liberation Army began its Fourth Phase Offensive on New Year's Day, several new North Korean divisions moved toward Wonju. Becoming aware of the threat, General Ridgway quickly moved the 2d Infantry Division from Eighth Army reserve and dispatched it to Lt. Gen. Edward M. "Ned" Almond's X Corps. He ordered Almond to seize and hold Wonju.

General Almond was a character of some controversy. Veterans hold strong and differing opinions of him. Nonetheless, his reputation as an aggressive corps commander is unquestioned. As one of his contemporaries put it, "When it pays to be aggressive, Ned's aggressive, and when it pays to be cautious, Ned's aggressive, and he wouldn't step two paces to the rear for the devil himself." Almond had a distinguished combat record in World War I, and in World War II he commanded one of only two black divisions committed to combat as divisions. There are, however, reasons to question his generalship of that division, particularly on the issue of racism. Almond treated his black soldiers with the paternalistic attitudes of the Jim Crow South, where he had been raised. The soldiers of the 92d Infantry Division compiled an uneven combat record in Italy, and critics blame Almond's policies for its performance. Later, in Korea, he ordered that a valor award be withdrawn from Capt. Forrest Walker because he was black. Almond never lost the conviction that black soldiers were less capable and valiant warriors than white troops.[2]

In X Corps, Almond was known for bypassing division headquarters and issuing orders directly to regiments and even battalions. When his orders resulted in unfortunate outcomes, he blamed subordinate commanders for failing to execute them properly rather than admitting bad judgment and taking the blame himself. Among veterans of the 2d Infantry Division and the 23d Regiment, Almond had a reputation as a martinet who often commanded by instilling fear in subordinates. More than once he relieved subordinate commanders and placed his favorites in "plum" positions that would qualify them for promotion. He was a stickler for detail, and sometimes the attention paid off. For example, he required the chain of command to submit daily reports that soldiers had changed their socks. Squad leaders initiated the reports, which were passed up the chain of command to reach Almond before midnight. Observers credited this practice with dramatically reducing cases of frostbite. His headquarters was immaculate, and field soldiers were not welcome there in their dirty vehicles and ragged uniforms. Sergeant Frank Butler remembers visiting X Corps headquarters:

> The First Sergeant put me in charge of a quartering party to go to X Corps Headquarters along with others from the regiment. We went there in our old, battered, dirty jeeps. We, too, were battered and dirty. Corps Headquarters, far to the rear, was spick-and-span. Tents all aligned in rows, paths and driveways marked with whitewashed rocks, everyone in clean uniforms. Upon our arrival, a Lieutenant rushed out of one of the tents and told us to "get those dirty jeeps out of sight." That did not sit too well with us, but we did as we were told and went about our quartering party business.[3]

The 23d Regiment had operated under a new chain of command since mid-December. General Walker had relieved General Keiser after the debacle on the Kunu-ri–Sunchon road, and placed Maj. Gen. Robert B. McClure in command of the 2d Infantry Division. At about the same time, Walker's death brought General Ridgway in to command Eighth Army. When Ridgway ordered the 2d Division transferred to X Corps, the 23d came under Almond's command. Colonel Paul Freeman and his regiment would perform well for General Almond, but they would never come to love him.[4]

The Battles around Wonju

The first two days of January, 1951, saw the 23d Infantry ordered to the Wonju area, where Lt. Col. Charles F. Kane's 3d Battalion engaged a North Korean roadblock twenty miles north of Wonju. In attacks later supported by Lt. Col. James W. Edwards's 2d Battalion, the regiment destroyed an estimated division of NKPA soldiers. The regiment then held blocking positions on the road north of Wonju through 5 January while the II ROK Corps withdrew through it. It was bitter cold, and the temperature plunged as low as twenty-five degrees below zero Fahrenheit. The operation was significant in slowing the withdrawal to the south.[5]

During the action north of Wonju, Sfc. Junior D. Edwards demonstrated the kind of courage and intrepidity that every infantryman admires. When a North Korean machine gun forced his platoon off a hill, Edwards personally charged the position and drove the enemy away with hand grenades, only to have the crew return when he ran out of grenades. Returning with a fresh supply of grenades, he again charged the position, destroyed the machine gun, and killed the crew, but small-arms fire drove him back. When the North Koreans replaced the machine gun, Edwards got more grenades and returned a third time, neutralizing the weapon and killing the new crew, but this time fell mortally wounded. He was posthumously awarded the Medal of Honor.[6]

The 23d and 38th Regiments held Wonju on 6 and 7 January. There, French Battalion joined the 23d Infantry in action for the first time. On the morning of 7 January, North Korean soldiers infiltrated the town and there was sharp fighting. The Chinese were massing for another attack and General McClure, a good tactician in Freeman's opinion, was worried that they might cut his supply line at a mountain defile eight miles to the south. McClure tried repeatedly to contact Almond for approval to withdraw. Freeman, recalling the action years later, said: "Almond, as usual, was out playing company commander or battalion commander. Nobody in the headquarters could give the authority for this retrograde move. My regiment was exposed on all sides and fighting hard in Wonju. We were told to break contact and to withdraw eight miles to the rear. We were told to booby trap and scorch everything, every possible approach to Wonju. We were back there in another little village and we got the word that night that the movement had been disapproved."[7]

Almond himself had approved the withdrawal to the southwest, but the distance the division pulled back was about twice as far as he had intended. As a result, the X Corps commander was furious when he found out how far the 23d had withdrawn, and ordered McClure to send one battalion back to retake Wonju on 8 January. Edwards's 2d Battalion made this attack. Fresh snow had covered the mines and booby traps, making the approach hazardous. Nonetheless, the battalion moved quickly, surprising an enemy outpost south of Wonju. The NKPA regiment in the area reacted swiftly and began enveloping the unit. Edwards ordered his battalion to fall back to high ground south of Wonju and set up a defensive line. By 1500 hours, Edwards was requesting reinforcements or permission to withdraw. General McClure, who was at Freeman's headquarters, approved the withdrawal. That night, Almond ordered another attack on Wonju for the following day.[8]

On 9 January, McClure attached the 38th Infantry to Freeman's 23d Regiment and ordered the next attack to take Wonju. He ordered Lt. Col. Jim Skeldon, commander of the 38th's 2d Battalion, to lead two battalions in the attack and Freeman to stay in the rear with the remaining forces. The attack began in the morning with Skeldon's 2d Battalion on the left side of the road and the 2d Battalion, 23d Infantry, on the right. The attackers again encountered stiff opposition from the enemy forces on the high ground south of Wonju. A hard-fought battle ensued throughout the day, with the two battalions finally taking the hill at dusk. Because of the hill's size, Freeman ordered the French Battalion to join the assault force, placing two companies on the left flank of the hill and holding the other two in reserve.[9]

Almond visited the battlefield with McClure that afternoon, and dressed Freeman down on a number of points he did not like. Freeman's radio operator, Pvt. Wendell Calfee, remembers Almond telling Freeman that he was to hold Wonju at all costs, to the last man if necessary.[10] Freeman's recollection of the meeting gives some insights into the personalities of both himself and Almond:

> I could hear all the fire and a hell of a mess up there so I went up there. And I'm not sooner getting up there and the snow is coming down thick and here comes this convoy of McClure, Almond, Ruffner, Almond's staff—some of them—Al Haig, the aide to Almond, climbing up on this little hill where I was. I'd never seen Almond before. "Who's in command here?" I said "Colonel Skeldon." He said, "Where's he?" I said, "Over on that next hill." "Who are you?" "I'm Colonel Freeman." "Aren't you in command?" "No, sir. I'm in command of the [unit] back to the rear." "What are you doing up here?" "I came up to see how I could help." And he said, "Well, why isn't a stronger force being used to go back to Wonju?" "Sir, we were told to use two battalions." He said, "McClure, who said to use two battalions?" By that time, fortunately, here comes a big attack; everybody yells, "Banzai, hit the ground." We did. So that question never got answered right then. And he said, "Where are we?" I says, "You're about three miles south of Wonju." He says, "Show me on a map." . . . Somebody finally brought up an old pocket map. He said, "Show me where we are." I says, "Here." He says, "Put the pencil on it." I said, "Who's got pencils?" That was my first meeting with Almond.

Well, then they had another attack coming, so they decided to get off the hill. In the meantime, Almond asked some poor, bedraggled sergeant, he said, "Good morning sergeant." The sergeant said, "Hello." He said, "It's goddamned cold, you know." Sergeant said, "Yes sir." He said, "It's so cold a basin of water froze in my trailer this morning." That was a stupid remark for someone to make. The sergeant said, "You're goddamned lucky to have a trailer and a basin of water."

So then we start down the hill; Almond slides and falls on his butt. And I'm right behind him and offered a hand, and he turned around and said, "If I need your help, I'll ask for it." Great first meeting.

Then down at the bottom of the hill, here's some soldier clumsily chopping at a piece of firewood. Almond says, "Look out, young man, you'll chop your foot off." He said, "I hope to hell I do; maybe they'll send me out of this goddamned place."

We go a little further on and here's another soldier. He'd dug himself a foxhole right behind a big tree. Almond says, "Get out of that hole, soldier." So he gets out. "Give me your rifle." So Almond jumps in there and he gets the rifle on this side of the tree. On this side of the tree, you can't see anything. So he raises hell about that. By that time I'm ready to pack my bags— I'm through.

So, off we went, the whole party trudging along. They never did answer the question about the two battalions, you know. I could see that McClure hadn't done what he was told to do about retaking Wonju. [If asked] do I say I was only told to use two battalions or let McClure answer that or remain silent? Well, it never got to that. But I was sure I was going to be relieved. . . . And the next day McClure was gone and Ruffner was the new division commander and nobody told me to go so I stayed on.[11]

By 1100 hours on 10 January, the situation was precarious. Freeman briefed McClure that he was continuing to attack as ordered, but that very strong enemy forces were threatening both flanks. The French Battalion and the 2d Battalion, 38th Infantry, were in special danger. He considered the continuation of the attack unsound and requested instructions. McClure responded that he could not withdraw, then authorized Freeman to use his judgment in changing his dispositions, but to "do nothing that would appear as a withdrawal." By early afternoon Freeman's reserve was reduced to one platoon. Finally, at the end of the afternoon, the division chief of staff authorized Freeman to withdraw to defensive positions south of the hill—but no farther. On the afternoon of 11 January and through the next morning, fighter-bombers arrived on the scene and concentrated on the North Korean positions to good effect. The artillery filled the sky with shells during the lulls when no flights were inbound.[12]

By 12 January, McClure had attached the 38th Infantry's 1st Battalion, the Dutch Battalion normally attached to the 38th, and the 1st Ranger Company to the 23d Infantry. Freeman also had two extra artillery battalions. That afternoon, Freeman sent his 2d Battalion and the French Battalion on a strong attack that finally took the hill. The attackers found many enemy dead there who were clearly the victims of air strikes and artillery fire.[13]

During this attack, the French made the first of the bayonet charges that would make them famous. Reporters observed one of these charges and the story was soon a part of the battalion's lore. To the French, fixing bayonets before a firefight was standard procedure, and using the bayonet when fighting became hand-to-hand was second nature. The French also thought that the North Koreans, and later the Chinese, were more afraid of the bayonet than of bullets, partly from the psychological effect. They believed that the peasants who largely made up the CCF were more afraid of the bayonets they could see than the bullets that they could not. This "spirit of the bayonet" was what Ridgway wanted in his entire Eighth Army, and he used it to inspire U.S. soldiers, telling them to follow the example of the French. Bayonets were not designed for opening C rations, Ridgway declared, but for fighting. Monclar, for his part, felt that the importance of the bayonet in this case was overstated and that machine guns, grenades, recoilless rifles, and bazookas were far more important in the victory. Nonetheless, he admitted the positive effect the publicity had on the morale of his soldiers as well as the intimidating effect a bayonet charge had on the Chinese.[14]

The action at Wonju cemented the bonds between the soldiers of the French Battalion and the 23d Regiment and their leaders. These bonds would remain strong for the rest of Freeman's time with the regiment. After the battles at Wonju, General Monclar made a speech to his men in which he congratulated them for their outstanding showing in their first battle alongside the Americans. "Now you are prisoners of your glory," he said, "for you must continue to live up to your reputation in future battles." As one of his officers put it in a speech in France after the war, the French Battalion had "opened its book of gold and blood" at Wonju. The French had demonstrated the proper mind-set for expeditionary forces, that is, units fighting with another army. Commanders easily motivated their soldiers by telling them they must do well because they were representing France: "The Americans are looking at you as at all of France." The same attitude motivated the Americans when they were operating with the French, and leaders of both groups often had to rein in their soldiers because they were taking foolhardy chances in an effort to impress the other group.[15]

In addition to the rapport between the French and American soldiers, a similar relationship had taken root between Freeman and Monclar. The two had profound esteem and admiration for one another and total confidence in the other's decisions. Monclar thought that Freeman treated the French Battalion with the respect it deserved and that the American commander was always concerned with their difficulties and dedicated to minimizing their losses. In Monclar's eyes, Freeman never gave the French the worst jobs or less than they deserved. Monclar and Freeman were always on an equal footing, not only impartial but also friendly. Both of them treated the war with passion and drama, not as a scientific exercise. They both wanted to address not only the physical needs of their soldiers, but their moral needs as well, and strove to see that they were met. In Monclar's words: "Freeman always spared us as much pain, sweat, and blood as possible. He never gave us the impression that we were his guests, to whom he would give the unpleasant tasks to do or the rough jobs from which he would benefit. We were on equal footing with them when it came to distribution of goods. When it concerns warm clothing, shoes, or trucks, that counts!"[16]

In January, the French asked for and received their first group of ROK soldiers. Unlike the Americans, who doled the ROK soldiers out to each company, the French instead organized them into a ROK company within the French Battalion. They did this in the same way they had with the indigenous soldiers in their colonies: by placing French officers in charge. The ROK army's officers were known for their unreliability early in the war and for their brutality in disciplining soldiers throughout the conflict. For this reason, the fair treatment the French officers gave their ROK troops went far toward winning them over. The company eventually had 176 ROK soldiers assigned. In spite of their lack of training, typical of the ROK enlisted soldiers at that time in the war, and the language difficulties, the company became an important addition to the French Battalion.

About this time, General Ridgway began implementing what the French came to call his "lure and kill" tactics. It made sense to go on the offensive as soon as Eighth Army had rebuilt itself to the point that it was capable of doing so. Ridgway had made it clear—from his first meeting with MacArthur in Tokyo through his many journeys to frontline units in Korea—he intended to seek out the Chinese as soon as the American units were rebuilt. For this to happen, Eighth Army had to find the enemy, regain the initiative, and ward off enemy counterattacks while protecting its lines of communications. At some point, the Chinese would undoubtedly manage to surround a UN force, most likely at an important transportation hub. When this happened, Ridgway would get relief forces to the scene while the enemy attack developed and the surrounded unit fought off its attacker.[17]

Almond relieved McClure as the 2d Division commander on 14 January and replaced him with his own chief of staff and fellow Virginia Military Institute alumnus, Maj. Gen. Clark L. Ruffner.[18]

Patrols Search for the Enemy

By the last week of January, in accordance with Ridgway's guidance, the 2d Division's new commander was emphasizing combat and reconnaissance patrols as a way to find and fix the enemy in the division's sector. In an annex to the Operational Instructions for 24 January, Ruffner's operations officer, Lt. Col. Claire Hutchin, who had commanded Freeman's 1st Battalion, wrote:

1. Combat and Recon patrols are for the purpose of establishing contact with the enemy and determining enemy locations where practicable. Small parties of enemy should be engaged and destroyed, and wherever possible, identification should be made by taking POW's and by searching enemy dead for documents.

2. At the same time, it is not intended that patrols become cut off, but rather that units generate succeeding patrol impulses wherein each patrol can extricate itself, or be assisted by other patrols and units in supporting distance. Recon patrols should advance from base units upon which they can retire. Successive elements should move into unswept areas rather than a single small group patrolling at a distance from its base.

3. Strong aggressive patrols can achieve a second purpose: They can create an impression of a strong northward movement of our forces in these areas.[19]

In carrying out the spirit of these instructions, the 2d Division's units would be going far to demonstrate the spirit of the offensive that Ridgway had been laboring to engender during the month he had been Eighth Army commander. In compliance with these directives, all of the division's regiments began patrolling to their front, looking for the enemy.

Both platoon- and company-sized units conducted patrols. They usually were motorized—meaning that jeeps and three-quarter-ton trucks would carry the soldiers through the area of interest. If a patrol encountered any enemy or suspicious circumstances, the soldiers would dismount and engage the enemy or search the area. A two-seat army liaison aircraft usually accompanied the patrol overhead, providing additional security. The aircraft could scout for routes through the mountains, relay radio messages to higher headquarters, and, most importantly, warn of enemy concentrations to the patrol's front or flanks. If there was reason to expect trouble, commanders could reinforce patrols with weapons from the heavy weapons company or even flak wagons or tanks. Generally, however, tracked vehicles were too unwieldy for the constricted Korean trails and bridges and proved to be more trouble than they were worth.

At first, patrols only went a few miles, but as they ranged farther without finding either NKPA or CCF units, the patrols gradually extended until they were covering fifty to one hundred miles in a day. When they went that far, the time consumed employing prudent safeguards left them hard-pressed to complete their mission in the short days of midwinter. Bad weather complicated circumstances. Snow and fog meant that aircraft could not cover the patrol, increasing the danger. An unseasonable late-January thaw forced streams over their banks, washing away sandbag fords and weakening bridges. Vehicles could no longer drive across the Han River ice, as they had been able to earlier in the month, but dismounted soldiers could still pick their way over the ice in places.[20]

The Eighth Army offensive began on 22 January. A crucial area for the success of the offensive was the boundary between IX and X Corps: the Han River. The coordination of such matters as firing artillery, maintaining consistent rates of advance, and securing rear areas across boundaries is difficult in units of any size. For this reason, military organizations take it as a given that attacking into a boundary stands a better chance of success than an attack into the center of a coherent organization.[21]

The X Corps's intelligence staff had reason to expect an attack along the east bank of the Han sooner or later. At the moment, however, they had not located the CCF's Forty-second Army, which they suspected was between Seoul and Wonju. At all costs, it had to be prevented from moving to the southeast and threatening Wonju. Key to preventing this was success in seizing and holding the road junction at the village of Chipyong-ni, forty-five miles southeast of Seoul. Accordingly, Almond ordered the 2d Division to begin patrolling in that direction.[22]

Patrols to the Twin Tunnels

About three miles southeast of Chipyong-ni, the Seoul–Yangpyong–Wonju railroad abruptly turns from south to east and tunnels under two ridgelines before turning again to the south and east. The terrain in the tunnels area consists of two ridgelines running generally north to south and rising to about a hundred meters above the valley floor. The ridgelines curve toward one another in the north, where they close into a horseshoe with a single constricted road leading to Chipyong-ni. As this road leads out of the valley, it crosses over the east-west railroad between the tunnels that give the area its name. The valley's flat floor is about five hundred meters from east to west and a thousand meters from north to south. Rice paddies and a few poplars break its monotony. A stream runs beside a road in the center of the valley, and there are small villages in the northeast and southwest corners. Sinchon, the largest village in the tunnels area, lies just southeast of the valley. At the south end, the valley is dominated by a steep, 453-meter-high hill that is itself overshadowed by a 543-meter-high hill to the southwest, to which it is connected by a saddle. All of the hills were barren in 1951, with nothing but brush and a few scrubby pine trees scattered on the steep, rocky slopes.[23]

The first patrol to the tunnels area moved out on 28 January. Led by Lt. Maurice "Fendy" Fenderson of Baker Company, the patrol saw enemy soldiers several miles south of the tunnels and took them under fire, but returned without incident.[24]

That night, General Almond ordered another patrol for the following day. It would be a joint one with the unit directly across the Han River from the 23d: the 24th Division's 21st Infantry Regiment, the right flank unit of IX Corps to the west. The patrol would range twenty miles from the nearest friendly unit and a distance of forty miles from its base. Major George H. Russell, the new 1st Battalion commander, gave this second mission to Charlie Company's Lt. James P. Mitchell. Lieutenant Mitchell reported for his briefing at 0600 hours on the morning of the twenty-ninth. Major Sammy Radow, the battalion operations officer, told him to meet the contingent from the 21st Infantry at the village of Iho-ri at 1030 hours, patrol the tunnels area, and return, avoiding contact with any large enemy force.[25]

The patrol was to leave at 0700 hours, but delays in getting organized set the departure back about an hour. A pair of 57-mm and 75-mm recoilless rifles and two heavy machine guns and their crews from Dog Company, the battalion's heavy weapons company, augmented Charlie Company. They also borrowed two radios from other units. As finally organized, the patrol consisted of forty-four officers and men who set out in two three-quarter-ton trucks and nine jeeps. Five of the jeeps were for 21st Infantry soldiers, as the Han River had thawed enough that they had to cross on foot.[26]

At the last minute, Capt. Melvin R. Stai, an assistant operations officer, joined the patrol to help coordinate with the 21st Infantry patrol. He was an experienced officer, having commanded Able Company in the fighting at Chinaman's Hat. He intended to return to battalion headquarters when the composite patrol departed for the tunnels area. The patrol finally left about 0800 hours and proceeded to a rendezvous with the soldiers from across the Han. A liaison airplane circled overhead to assist with security and communications. The patrol advanced slowly during the morning hours, hindered by patches of snow and ice on the mountain roads. The morning fog in the valleys, typical of winter mornings in Korea, meant that the airplane could not always see the patrol, and it was soon forced to leave.[27]

They reached Iho-ri a little before noon, where they met the soldiers from the 21st Infantry, commanded by Lt. Harold P. Mueller. Captain Stai then decided not to return to the base camp, but to accompany the patrol, keeping the only radio that could communicate with the liaison airplane in his jeep. As it moved out from the village, the patrol consisted of four officers and fifty-six enlisted men armed with carbines, rifles, eight BARs, two heavy and four light machine guns, a rocket launcher, a 60-mm mortar, and 57-mm and 75-mm recoilless rifles. Their objective, the Twin Tunnels, was still about fifteen miles away.

The patrol was uneventful until it reached the tunnels area. Lieutenant Mitchell halted at a ford at the south end of the valley leading to the tunnels and waited for Lieutenant Mueller and Captain Stai to arrive. Mitchell had instructed his men to keep at least fifty meters between vehicles and for the trucks carrying the heavy weapons to lag several hundred meters behind the jeep-mounted infantry so they could deploy and support the infantrymen with their machine guns and recoilless rifles if necessary. From the ford where Mitchell stopped, the road leads north to the tunnels; Sinchon is to the east. Because the patrol was late, Captain Stai offered to check out the village himself while the main body proceeded a mile north to check out the tunnels. Leaving his driver with the vehicle, Captain Stai walked alone into the village. He was never seen again.[28]

As the lieutenants and their men headed toward the tunnels, "Murphy's Laws" began taking effect as things started to go wrong. The liaison aircraft rejoined the patrol about the time of the conference with Captain Stai. Major Millard O. Engen, the battalion executive officer, was riding in the plane and saw enemy soldiers on the slope of Hill 453, the large hill mass that dominates the valley south of the tunnels near where the jeeps stopped. He radioed instructions for Lieutenant Mitchell to get out of the valley as soon as possible. However, because Captain Stai had the only radio that could communicate with the aircraft, Mitchell did not hear the message.[29]

When the patrol reached the railroad tracks between the tunnels at the north end of the valley, Lieutenant Mueller's men from the 21st Infantry saw enemy soldiers running and began firing at them. At about the same time, a few mortar shells landed near the patrol. Lieutenant Mitchell tried to get the vehicles turned around and out of the valley, but it was too late. He could see enemy soldiers running down the slopes of Hill 453 and setting up a roadblock at the ford where the patrol had stopped.

Major Engen, in the liaison aircraft, again tried to communicate with Lieutenant Mitchell—this time to order him to get to the high ground east of the road—but his message again went unheard. The liaison aircraft then departed to refuel, and Major Engen notified regimental headquarters at 1245 hours that the patrol was in trouble.[30]

Lieutenant Mueller realized that the patrol's only chance was to gain the high ground to the east of the road. Seeing Chinese heading for the hill, he called to his men and to Lieutenant Mitchell: "We're going to have to get to the top of that hill. The Chinese are coming up from the other side. This is our only chance!"

The two lieutenants then had to abandon most of their heavy weapons in the valley, carrying only their individual weapons, a rocket launcher, and one machine gun up the hill. The north side of the hill, where the American force was climbing, was covered with brush and about a foot of wet snow. It was an agonizing climb for the men, slipping and tripping in the snow, all the while under fire from the Chinese. The soldiers from the

21st Infantry had an advantage: they wore new white parkas that gave them some camouflage, while the 23d Regiment men had on dark outer garments that stood out on the snowy slopes.[31]

Twenty of Mitchell's men were seeing their first action. They were replacements, mostly technicians with little infantry training or experience, who had joined the unit only a few days before. Seven of them, frightened by the firing, took cover in a ditch near the road and refused to follow the platoon up the hill. None of the patrol leaders took strong enough action—such as threatening them with punishment or physically dragging them along—to compel them to seek safety. The Chinese attackers killed them in the ditch later that afternoon. With Captain Stai missing, fifty-one men were left to make their way up the hill.[32]

Lieutenant Mueller and his men were the first to reach the top of the ridge. They were on a tiny knob no more than twenty feet across, with Chinese-held knobs to the north and south. There was not enough space on the knob for all of his troops, so Mueller put some of the men in a saddle to the north. His most critical area, however, was to the south, where a Chinese machine gun fired from another knob a little higher, giving the gun a large beaten zone on the knob held by the Americans. Under fire from this gun, the Chinese would be able to move along a saddle that was difficult for the Americans to hit, being much lower than the two knobs. Mueller's only hope was to hit the Chinese with grenades as they approached. His men repelled the first Chinese assault only a few meters from the crest, and things were quiet for about twenty minutes.[33]

In effect, Mueller was now commanding the defense, as Lieutenant Mitchell was having trouble making his way up the hill. Mitchell had suffered a spinal injury in World War II and he did not have the stamina expected of an infantryman. About three-fourths of the way up the hill, he had to stop and rest. One of the new men stopped with him, urging him to move on, then offered to stay until he was able to continue. During their half-hour there, Lieutenant Mitchell killed three Chinese soldiers about fifteen feet away.[34]

Just after the threat from the south died down, a machine gun on the knob to the north opened up and wounded several GIs. Men lay still on the knob to avoid attracting enemy fire—except for Cpl. LeRoy Gibbons, an intrepid eighteen-year-old squad leader who had already been wounded six times in the war. He stood erect and walked over to report to Mitchell. When his soldiers called for him to get down, he said, "Aw hell, they couldn't hit the broad side of a barn." He continued walking as tracers sliced through the air around him.[35]

At about 1300 hours, when Colonel Freeman heard that the Charlie Company patrol was in trouble, he began taking action to retrieve it. From division headquarters, he requested liaison aircraft to drop ammunition and medical supplies, and any close air support that the Far East Air Force could provide. He warned the 2d Battalion to prepare a rescue force to go to its aid. Armored vehicles, either tanks or flak wagons, would have strengthened the rescue force, but a damaged bridge on the route to the tunnels area precluded their use. Instead, Lieutenant Colonel Edwards gave Capt. Stanley C. Tyrrell's Fox Company the mission. Captain Tyrrell arrived at the battalion CP for his briefing at 1415 hours. Colonel Edwards told Tyrrell that his mission was to rescue the Charlie Company patrol and bring back the bodies of any casualties. He told Tyrrell to put up a defensive perimeter and hold out until morning if he could not get the patrol out that night. Edwards reinforced Fox Company with a section of 81-mm mortars, a section of heavy machine guns, and an artillery forward observer section with radios to communicate with aircraft. The patrol, consisting of 167 officers and men, was on its way by midafternoon.[36]

The Americans inside the cold mountaintop perimeter were not optimistic about their chances of surviving the night. By late afternoon, medical supplies were exhausted, ammunition was running low, and about a third of the men had been wounded. Their first assistance came in the form of a Mosquito aircraft. The Mosquito was a World War II–era training aircraft, the North American AT-6 "Texan," a low-wing, propeller-driven aircraft that carried an air force pilot and a combat-experienced army officer or NCO observer. The air force used Mosquitoes to spot targets for the fighter-bombers delivering ordnance. Ground support aircraft at this point in the war had to come from bases in Japan or from the few carriers the navy had stationed in the Sea of Japan. Whether propeller planes like the F-51 Mustang, or new jets like the F-80 Shooting Star, they consumed so much fuel flying to their targets that they had little time in which to expend their weapons. The fighter aircraft would orbit high over the target area to save fuel while the army observer located targets. He would then radio instructions to the fighter-bombers, which descended and attacked the targets he had identified. John Collins, who served as an observer, recalled after the war that their mission was "to do for the jets what they couldn't do for themselves. Blinded by their own speed and rushed by their tremendous thirst for fuel, the jet bombers could not pick out ground targets. So the heavy slow T-6 Mosquitoes preceded them in flak-heavy enemy territory, dropped down to tree-top level to spot the gun emplacements and tanks and pinpoint them with smoke markers for the kill."[37]

Two flights of four planes each hit the hill at dusk. The men cheered as the first jets roared in firing machine guns and rockets. The planes came in so low the GIs thought they could have touched them with their bayonets. The second flight blackened the Chinese positions with napalm. Following the air strikes, an army liaison plane came over and dropped ammunition and a message. The pilot made four runs across the position, only fifteen feet over their heads. He dropped two cases of machine-gun ammunition, thirty bandoleers of rifle ammunition, and some carbine ammunition. Only one case of machine-gun ammunition landed inside the tiny perimeter, but the Charlie Company men defied the Chinese and retrieved everything that was close. The message, retrieved from a can trailing a long yellow streamer, read: "Friendly column approaching from the south. Will be with you shortly." Lieutenant Mitchell crawled around the area showing it to the men and raising their spirits, especially when they heard firing in the vicinity of Hill 453 and assumed it was the relief column.[38]

Mitchell and Mueller moved from one soldier to the next, talking to each man, telling them not to cry out if they were hit, because they did not want the Chinese to know how many wounded they had. Both expected an assault on their encircled force as soon as it was dark. The Chinese attacked under a barrage of mortar fire early in the evening, wounding many more Americans inside the packed perimeter. Lieutenant Mueller, hit earlier in the leg, was hit again—this time in the head. Most of the soldiers' clothing was wet, both from the snow and from sweating during the climb up the hill. Now, as the temperature plunged, many began to suffer from the effects of frostbite in addition to their injuries from the fighting.[39]

Captain Tyrell and his rescue company were even closer than the embattled soldiers in their mountaintop perimeter suspected. The gunfire they had heard at dusk was indeed Fox Company arriving in the area. The first two vehicles had been stopped by machine-gun fire from Hill 453, near the ford where Captain Stai had disappeared that morning. Captain Tyrell, in the third jeep, decided that he had to clear Hill 453 before moving on to rescue Charlie Company. He had good intelligence regarding the company's location, because the aircraft that had dropped supplies to the men in the beleaguered perimeter later flew over Tyrrell's column and dropped a message giving its grid coordinates as well as information on other Chinese troops he had seen in the area.

Captain Tyrrell organized a hasty attack, placing his 2d Platoon on line and having the men lay down a base of fire to cover an assault on Hill 453 by his other two platoons. Meanwhile, the mortar section he had brought along dropped shells just ahead of the attacking infantry slogging up the hill. In the dark, the mountain became an enemy to be dealt with. The steep, snow-covered slope delayed the 1st Platoon more than two hours in its ascent. The two platoons conducting the assault finally made contact at about 2030 hours, and cleared the hill. Captain Tyrrell ordered the 2d Platoon, still fresh, to move north to be ready to fight through to the Charlie Company patrol. One of the platoons on Hill 453 returned to the road while the other moved to a position lower down on Hill 453 from which it could support the attack on the crowded knob.

At about 2100 hours, a medic from the surrounded patrol stumbled into one of the platoon positions on Hill 453. He explained that the situation in the patrol's position was desperate, with three-fourths of the men now casualties. He had left the perimeter hoping to get to the vehicles and return with more medical supplies, but became lost. Captain Tyrrell immediately ordered Lt. Albert T. Jones to move his platoon north along the ridgeline toward Charlie Company's position. The GIs moved out silently, as the air filled with the sounds of another firefight coming from the surrounded patrol's area. Lieutenant Jones's platoon slowly made its way to the perimeter, reaching it at about 2300 hours. The enemy had vanished.[40]

The Charlie Company men were happy to be relieved. It took more than three hours to carry all of the survivors down the hill, back to friendly lines. At 0330 hours, certain that he had all the surviving patrol members in his trucks, Captain Tyrrell ordered the column to move out, with one of his platoons walking ahead and one behind the convoy. Dawn broke as the column reached Iho-ri.[41]

The patrol's survivors were so grateful for Tyrrell's initiative—in what Colonel Freeman considered one of the finest small-unit actions in the Korean War—that they presented him with a banner inscribed, "When in peril, send for Tyrrell." Only about a dozen men escaped unscathed. In addition to about thirty wounded, thirteen men were dead and five missing.[42]

The patrols the 23d Infantry sent into the tunnels area had established that there were unquestionably enemy in the area who were willing to contest possession of the region. The action that would allow Ridgway to launch his first offensive against the Chinese had commenced.

Chapter 7

The Battle of Twin Tunnels

*An extraordinary situation requires extraordinary resolution. The
more obstinate the resistance of an armed body, the more chances it
will have of being succored or of forcing a passage. How many things
apparently impossible have nevertheless been performed by resolute
men who had no alternative but death!*

— *Napoleon Bonaparte*

*There is no human affair which stands so constantly and so gener-
ally in close connection with chance as War.*

— *Carl von Clausewitz*

A vaincre sans peril, on triumphe sans gloire. [*When there is no
peril in the fight, there is no glory in the triumph.*]

— *Pierre Corneille*

O n the morning of 30 January 1951, Lieutenant Colonel Edwards
reported to the regimental headquarters that Captain Tyrrell
estimated there were two enemy companies on Hill 453. Receiving this information, Lt. Gen. Ned Almond, the corps commander, ordered the regiment to take the high ground in the tunnels area, clear out
enemy forces, and take prisoners to identify what enemy units were in
the area. The regimental operations officer, Maj. John Dumaine, promptly
directed the French Battalion and the 3d Battalion to move to the Twin
Tunnels, taking antiaircraft flak wagons along. A few minutes later, given
the distance to the tunnels, he modified the order to move into an assembly area six miles to the south of them. The corps commander further
directed that an air strike destroy the vehicles the Charlie Company patrol
had abandoned at the Twin Tunnels. By evening, the 1st and 3d Battalions

and regimental headquarters had moved into the assembly area. The 2d Battalion was in division reserve and so did not accompany the regiment.[1]

Brigadier General George C. Stewart, the assistant division commander, accompanied the patrol. A member of the West Point class of 1923 with considerable combat experience in World War II, Stewart saw his job as being the division commander's eyes and ears. When he arrived at the 23d Regiment's CP, Stewart found Freeman angry at the order to move to the Twin Tunnels area, ten miles beyond the division's front lines and out of range of divisional artillery support. "They're going to murder my regiment," Freeman said. Stewart replied that Freeman had his orders. Moreover, Stewart announced that he was going to accompany the regimental patrol. Nonetheless, Freeman was in command of the operation. Stewart considered Freeman "one of the best fighting commanders you ever saw, but kind of temperamental." He also knew that Almond often bypassed the chain of command with orders that were not well thought out, and he knew Freeman resented it when those orders affected his regiment, as they had at Wonju.[2]

The two battalions, along with the regimental headquarters, the regimental mortar battery, and an attached tank and medical company, moved out at 0630 hours on 31 January. Two additional artillery units that were attached to the 23d, the 37th Field Artillery Battalion and Baker Battery of the 82d Antiaircraft Artillery Battalion, accompanied the column. On the way to the tunnels area, Freeman placed the field artillery battalion in a firing position about three miles south of the Twin Tunnels. He left all the accompanying vehicles with the artillery, and gave the drivers the mission of strengthening the artillery battalion's defenses by fighting as infantry. The 1st Battalion held key positions along the road from the artillery position to the rear to insure that the regiment's supply route remained open.[3]

Freeman's plan was dictated by the terrain. In Korea, proper utilization of the crests of hills or mountains often determined the success of a unit's actions. The Chinese had proved adept at hiding units in villages, caves, and tunnels during daylight hours and attacking at night. As a result, UN forces were forced each night to construct tight perimeters on high ground, as impregnable as possible, in anticipation of an attack during the hours of darkness. To go on the offensive, as Ridgway wanted, units had to take a defensive perimeter on the hills in one area, and then advance to another hilltop defensive perimeter within a day or two. It was a slow procedure, but the only relatively safe one. An ideal hilltop position exposes attackers to fire on all avenues of approach. The high ground constituted both a physical and moral obstacle to the attacker while at the same time boosting the defender's morale.[4]

Hill 453 commanded the south end of the valley. For this reason, Freeman had to anchor his perimeter on it before moving into the valley itself. He used French forces for this task. As soon as they had made the hill impregnable, the rest of the French Battalion could occupy the western ridgeline while his own 3d Battalion secured the eastern one. The forces would curve in to meet in the northwest, where the road led out of the valley a half-mile north of the tunnels.

If one moved to the center of the perimeter and stood on an imaginary clock face with twelve at the north, Love Company would hold the position from eleven to two o'clock, Item Company from two to three-thirty, and King Company from three-thirty to five. In the French Battalion sector, 1st Company occupied the commanding Hill 453 to the south, isolated and not tied in to any other unit. The 2d Company held the line from eight to nine, the ROK Company held a small sector from nine to about nine-thirty, and the 3d Company filled in from nine-thirty to about eleven. There were two gaps in the line: to the north, a tank-mounted roadblock covered the territory between the French 3d Company and the 23d's Love Company; to the south, the French heavy weapons company covered the gap between King Company and the French 2d Company. In placing the heavy weapons company there, Freeman and Monclar were giving it the mission of holding and defending terrain—one that is not included in a heavy weapons company's task list, and a mission that most tacticians would consider questionable. The French later explained the gambit by saying that they did not expect an enemy to attack across the "firing range" of flat ground in front of the company and, at any rate, they had no other force to place there.[5]

As finally conceived, the perimeter was not a tightly closed one, but composed of three sectors. The 3d Battalion would hold the ridge on the east side. The French Battalion would hold the ridge to the west with three companies, while its heavy weapons company and Monclar's staff held the valley. Half a mile to the south and a thousand feet above the valley floor, the French 1st Company would hold Hill 453. As in the overall concept, terrain dictated company frontages. At the Twin Tunnels, company fronts varied from a few hundred meters to over a thousand.[6]

This scheme stretched Freeman's forces as far as they could go. It left him without a regimental reserve, although the French Battalion kept a platoon from its ROK Company and its engineers out of the line.

Nonetheless, the terrain around the Twin Tunnels left Freeman with no alternative. Giving up any of the ridgelines or Hill 453 would provide the enemy an open entryway into his perimeter. The rugged terrain dictated where he had to place his infantry while at the same time limiting the effectiveness of his tanks and artillery. It meant that the soldiers must be prepared for hand-to-hand combat, because their abundant supporting weapons—mortars, recoilless rifles, tanks, artillery, and flak wagons—could not assist them as much as in more open terrain. The movement of reinforcements to beleaguered units would also be slower and more difficult. Finally, it meant that evacuating the wounded, especially from Hill 453, would be a nightmare.[7]

Movement went slowly throughout the day. Freeman observed that the "temptation to barge ahead was tremendous." The greatest delay was in taking Hill 453. Although military convention labels it a hill, no soldier who climbed it that day would be satisfied with describing it as anything less than a mountain. The steep pinnacle was covered with ice and snow, and progress up its slopes was agonizing for the soldiers of the French 1st Company, who were assigned the mission of securing it. Captain François DeCastries, the company commander, remembers slipping and climbing up its slopes all through the morning before securing the crest in the early afternoon. Monclar insisted on accompanying the unit, and Freeman later blamed his slowness in climbing for the delay in taking the hill. DeCastries, however, insists that his soldiers, a generation younger than the general, could have gone no faster without him.

Monclar made a proud figure and was an example for his men. Private Gerard Journet, assigned to the section charged with protecting the general and his chief of staff, remembers how the general's endurance impressed him. During the arduous climb in the presence of the general, the men did not complain the way they normally would have. When Monclar left the mountaintop to join the rest of his battalion on the lower ridgeline to the north, DeCastries and his company were alone. The soldiers began digging into the frozen, rocky ground. Their only contact with the rest of the force would be by radio or runner, although it would take a "runner" hours to move down the hill to regimental headquarters, especially after dark. In the event of an attack, they knew that no one could come to their aid in time to be of assistance.[8]

Freeman later recalled his actions and the reactions of his men. His comments underline the hardships of the infantryman's war during this first winter of the Korean War:

with proper coordination between the two forces, each commenced the tiresome climbing and ridge-running that was so characteristic of the Korean campaigns. Characteristic, too was the total absence of enemy both from ground and air observation. But our troops had learned—learned months ago—that the enemy seldom appeared in daylight in conventional formations and positions where he would be at the mercy of our artillery and air, but that unless he had a tremendous preponderance of force, he would pull back and remain hidden until darkness, or until we walked into a trap. We weren't walking into traps these days.

That was why there were no grumbles from the men when they were ordered to the painful task of climbing the slippery, snow-covered hills, rather than to march up the peaceful looking road. That was why many were willing to forego a can of rations [so] that they might load themselves down with all the cartridges and grenades that they could possibly carry. That was why no thought was given to leaving behind coats and blankets though they knew it meant a bitter cold night—at least, it was insurance against survival if not against temporary misery. On this occasion all realized that it was inconceivable that they could poke their necks out twenty miles beyond friendly units into the area of the recent ambush without provoking a violent reaction. The enemy would materialize sooner or later—the hope of all was that he would be discovered in daylight.[9]

If anything, Freeman understated the arduous task that the infantryman had in that most challenging of terrain and weather. The soldier's standard load of battle gear at the time was a full ammo belt with shoulder straps, first-aid packet, bayonet, entrenching tool (a folding shovel), canteen, one blanket, and a poncho. Each soldier carried five bandoleers of ammunition for the machine guns and four fragmentation grenades. All this was in addition to his personal weapon—a carbine, BAR, or M1 Garand rifle—and any other ordnance he had scrounged during his time on the peninsula. Many soldiers carried more if they were able.

For the rest of the afternoon, the 3d Battalion and the remainder of the French Battalion advanced northward along their respective ridges. Adjusting artillery concentrations ahead of them, they coordinated their movement so that their rates of advance would be approximately the same. Although slow, they thus rendered the advance secure. Terrain restricted the tanks and flak wagons to moving along the valley floor. During the approach, the 3d Battalion's soldiers passed Captain Stai's jeep, now a burned-out hulk overturned by the roadside. The grisly and blackened corpse of the captain's driver, still at the wheel, was a macabre portent to the more impressionable soldiers. Throughout the afternoon, a liaison plane circled the area, but saw no trace of enemy forces. By late afternoon, the soldiers were in position, digging in for the cold night ahead. The air strikes that General Almond had ordered to destroy the abandoned vehicles of the earlier patrol had proved ineffective, and some of the French Battalion's mechanics spent the afternoon stripping them of usable spare parts. Freeman placed his headquarters along the road, approximately in the center of the perimeter. Monclar's headquarters was a few hundred meters to the southwest, across the road from Lieutenant Colonel Kane's 3d Battalion headquarters.[10]

Staff Sergeant Thomas C. Harris spent the late afternoon hours in front of Item Company, firing in mortar concentrations with his radio operator. Assigned to the regiment only that day, he was a forward observer for Mike Company, the 3d Battalion's heavy weapons company. His company commander had ordered him to take his equipment and get acquainted with the forward observers from the field artillery and the heavy mortar company who were on duty with Item Company. When he had the defensive concentration from his mortars where he wanted it, he told the fire direction center (FDC) to mark it for firing on his call. At the same time, observers in the artillery position two miles to the south were adjusting the fires of the regimental heavy mortar company to defend their position. Both positions thus could count on timely and accurate indirect fires in any battle to come.[11]

Both Monclar and Freeman walked much of the perimeter during the afternoon. The commanders were keenly appreciative of the importance of knowing the terrain they were holding, and shared the belief that if they were properly to control their fires and maneuver their forces, they must be intimately familiar with the ground they expected their soldiers to hold. In addition, their visits to the front lines had an indisputably positive effect on the morale of the soldiers who saw them striding through their positions, stopping occasionally to give a word of encouragement or admonishment.[12]

The Night at Twin Tunnels

General Almond visited the 23d Regiment's command post on the afternoon of 31 January. Surprised that the regiment had not yet made contact with the enemy, he was impatient and expressed dissatisfaction with Freeman for not having moved directly through the tunnels area and taking Chipyong-ni. Stewart tried to explain that the regiment had to move with caution given the known enemy presence and the lateness of the day. Finally, Almond ordered General Stewart to "put Chipyong-ni under fire." The assistant division commander immediately commandeered a tank and rode in it to Chipyong-ni. There was still no sign of the enemy. Reluctant to shoot at a village housing only noncombatants, he fired several bursts from the tank's machine guns and cannon over and on each side of it. He then returned to the regimental CP and reported that he had "taken the village under fire."[13]

Freeman was angry with Stewart for firing on Chipyong-ni and furious at General Almond for giving such an order. Although artillery had been firing in the area all day, it could have come from miles away, but the machine-gun fire meant that any Chinese within hearing distance now knew UN infantry forces were in the Twin Tunnels vicinity. Already uneasy about what he judged to be an overextended perimeter, Freeman considered the firing to be an invitation to wipe out his force. One of his company commanders remembers Freeman saying: "I don't mind the corps commander being around and there's no problem either with him telling me what to do. He should as a courtesy go through the division commander, but that's between those two. What I can't accept is his telling me how to do it, especially if I think his way is dangerous to my command and mission. If Almond wants to be a regimental commander, damn it, let him take a reduction to bird colonel and come down and be one." Stewart himself, in retrospect, considered the action unwise. His compliance with what he later called a "ridiculous" order was probably motivated in part by the knowledge that Almond had previously bypassed the chain of command and relieved officers who did not precisely carry out his orders, however ill-advised they may have been.[14]

Almond's dissatisfaction with Freeman for not pushing on to Chipyong-ni gives further reason to question the corps commander's judgment. Even a simple map reconnaissance shows that the Chipyong-ni basin, although about the same size as the Twin Tunnels valley, is poorer defensive terrain. Whether the regiment could have held out that night at Chipyong-ni with only two battalions against the kind of onslaught it suffered at the tunnels is doubtful.

The night was quiet and cold. A thick fog developed in the early morning hours, combining with the snow to muffle sounds. Many of the soldiers there remember an eerie, ghostly feeling as they anxiously awaited the enemy's next move. In the French Battalion, Maj. Maurice Barthelemy was worried that the men were tired from the previous day's exertions. He was afraid they would not be alert for an attack. As early as 0200 hours, there were sounds of skirmishes from Hill 453, and, for the rest of the night, faint sounds of bugles in the mist. Then, a little before 0500 hours, soldiers in the headquarters heard small arms and mortar fire to the north. One man remembers hearing Chinese bugles and a new soldier asking what the sound was. "You can bet your ass it's not Harry James," was the hard-bitten response from the next foxhole. From that moment on, there was continuous action somewhere in the area until late in the afternoon. A veteran of many battles said it was "the oddest infantry battle I ever saw, fighting from before daybreak until after 1600 hours nonstop, just blasting away."[15]

When the firing began, Freeman thought it was the inevitable outcome of General Almond's order to General Stewart to fire on Chipyong-ni the night before. "I told you this was going to happen. What do you want me to do now?" he asked Stewart. Stewart's laconic response was that their only choice was to stay and fight. "Let's kill as many Chinese as we can," he added.[16]

Freeman was especially apprehensive because of the late hour of the attack. After the initial fighting on the Yalu, the Chinese had customarily attacked by about 0300 hours and withdrawn by daylight. After conferring with his intelligence and operations officers, Freeman concluded that the Chinese were desperate to deny the Americans the vital road net at Chipyong-ni. To forestall its capture, they had rounded up a force large enough to overrun the American position and intended to continue the attack throughout the day if necessary.[17]

The initial sounds were the CCF attacking the armored roadblock to the north between Love Company and the French 3d Company. The Chinese marched toward the tanks and quad-mounted .50-caliber half-tracks and were almost upon them before the enemies saw one another in the fog. The American gunners opened up on the CCF force and killed a number before the Chinese deployed to their flanks and damaged both vehicles with rocket launchers. Fifteen minutes later, the vehicles were limping back to headquarters with their wounded. The Chinese then turned their attention to Love Company at the north end of the perimeter, accompanying the attack with the unnerving sounds of bugles, shepherd's horns, and whistles. Some of the Chinese wore American uniforms, causing the defenders to hesitate before firing on them until they were sure they were

Chinese. Other forces attacked Item Company on the east side of the perimeter. Both companies were under heavy attack for the next hour.[18]

The Chinese attacked the 3d Company at about the same time. Lieutenant Ange Nicolai, who commanded a section to the front of the company on the heights to his rear, directed his machine-gun's fire against the most threatened point before a Chinese grenade wounded him. The attackers wounded six other soldiers in the initial assault, including three NCOs. While Nicolai was ordering his section to retire to the company's main line, another grenade exploded nearby, wounding him severely. Before the soldiers could fall back, the Chinese were on them and fighting became hand-to-hand. The machine gunner took on a trio of Chinese, whom he fought off with kicks and punches. The platoon sergeant then carried out Nicolai's order to fall back.

When the 3d Company's commander learned that Lieutenant Nicolai was still in the forward position, he regrouped the soldiers and led a counterattack, reinforcing the platoon with men from the main position. The counterattack surprised the Chinese, who fell back. Although Nicolai's soldiers managed to get him to the aid station, his wounds proved to be mortal.[19]

Meanwhile, at 0545, Monclar had ordered the heavy weapons company to send reinforcements to the embattled 3d Company. Captain André LeMaitre, the commander, sent twenty-four men supported by three machine guns and a recoilless rifle, leaving him with only forty-five men to hold his position on the valley floor. Less than an hour later, Chinese hit his weakened position in the valley and overran it. The fighting in the valley went on until 0730, when the heavy weapons company received the engineer platoon as reinforcement, counterattacked, and retook the position. The Chinese killed Captain LeMaitre while he was giving orders to a machine-gun crew.

The Americans and their French comrades responded with everything at their disposal. The artillery concentrations that had been fired in the previous day were ready, and the mortars added their punch. Artillery illumination rounds gave the foggy battlefield an eerie glow that all the participants remember. In spite of the UN forces' murderous fires, a number of Chinese got into the defensive positions, and fighting was hand-to-hand in several portions of the line. The defenders repulsed the Chinese attack after a stiff struggle, and a lull in the fighting that lasted through the early morning hours followed. Commanders took this opportunity to consolidate their units' positions and redistribute ammunition.[20]

The Daylight Battle

During the initial assaults, Colonel Freeman put out the word for everyone not actually involved in the fighting to form a second line in the valley in case units on the perimeter were overrun. Corporal Serge Bererd, a soldier in the intelligence section of Monclar's headquarters, found himself on a combat line for the first time—and scared. A few days before, sent to awaken the staff, Bererd had done so with gusto. In so doing, he unintentionally woke up General Monclar, who, he discovered to his dismay, was sleeping in an adjacent room. "To be awakened by Corporal Bererd!" Monclar shouted, his voice muffled by the wall between them. "When we need to sleep! A general is awakened by Corporal Bererd!" Years later he remembered being on the line, as well as awakening the general:

> I didn't like that too much, my military education being sufficient to know that it's one thing to be on a line in a dominating position, with friends from the section who won't let you down and with heavy arms well placed in a company which can maneuver under a captain who can ask for support. It's another thing entirely to be on a line with people you don't know, with no support and no command and on top of that to be in a position which is dominated by high ground on all sides. While I'm thinking about that, General Monclar comes to see us, stopping behind me and says, "So, Bererd, you're looking a little pale!" Taken aback and not being in a very comfortable position lying on the ground, I didn't know what to answer. It was Captain Michelet who came to my rescue by responding for me, "Oh, Bererd is always pale, that's his natural state." In fact they were both right, Michelet because I'm anything but the ruddy type and Monclar because I was, in fact, a little tense.
>
> You have to understand that even if I had been bombarded by the Flying Fortresses in France and had done a year in Indochina, . . . I had never been involved in a serious battle. Of course, I had to ask myself if the general was putting me on the spot as revenge for the fanfare wakeup call I had treated him to a few days before. And then I abandoned the idea because Monclar, like Napoleon, liked to call people by their name with a wink in his eye, which meant to say, "We know each other, we two." It's good for the morale of the troops.

Sergeant Harris, the forward observer who had joined Mike Company the day before and adjusted his mortar concentrations in front of Item Company, began firing them at about 0400 hours. A couple of hours later, about 0630, his radio operator, Pvt. James Strickland, was hit just above the left pocket of his field jacket. Harris took over the radio and called for medics, who carried Strickland out a half-hour later. During the wait, Harris himself was hit in the foot. His company commander crawled to his position to tell him that the field artillery and heavy mortar forward observers had also been shot and that he was the last observer in the Item Company sector. After looking at Harris's wound, the captain told him to stay and adjust fires until a replacement arrived. The company commander remained at the observation post and helped Harris adjust the fires of all three supporting units. Harris's relief arrived by midmorning and he made his way first to the French aid station and then to the regimental aid station. There he found that his radio operator was dead. Less than forty-eight hours later, Harris was in a hospital in Japan.

The Chinese had not neglected the French company on Hill 453. They had probed the French outposts as early as 2300 hours the night before and had renewed the attacks throughout the night. The only good approach into the 1st Company perimeter was along a saddle that ran northeast into Captain DeCastries's position. The saddle connected Hill 453 to Hill 543 a little over a mile to the southwest. The most damaging attack came between 0200 and 0300 when the Chinese attacked with small arms, grenades, rocket launchers, and blocks of explosives. This attack ran the easternmost platoon, commanded by Sergeant Girardot, off its position. Although many of the French soldiers' weapons were frozen and would not fire, the attack stalled when the platoons holding the flanks hit the Chinese with 57-mm recoilless rifle fire and grenades.

At the height of the action, Captain DeCastries called in defensive fires from the heavy mortar company in the valley and then rallied his men, who counterattacked with bayonets and restored the position after hand-to-hand fighting. The company suffered about ten killed and many more wounded in its isolated position. It also captured a badly wounded Chinese soldier, one of only two taken by the regiment that day. The Chinese left forty-three corpses in the 1st Company position and thirty-nine more outside of it.[21]

By daylight, the fighting on Hill 453 was over for the day. With victory almost in their grasp, the Chinese had failed to take the position critical to their success. As they pulled back, Captain DeCastries began the daylong task of carrying his wounded down the hill to the aid stations. About noon, an army liaison plane flew a few feet over the company and free-dropped ammunition. The drop was accurate, but it broke a soldier's ankle. The failure to take Hill 453 may have been a factor in delaying the CCF attack on Freeman's positions in the valley until so late an hour.[22]

The day dawned with a haze that thickened into solid overcast. This was bad news for the soldiers in the perimeter, since there could be no close air support until the weather improved. There was no way of knowing how long the fog would cloak the battlefield, and it was imperative that fighter-bombers be on station to exploit any break in the weather. For this reason, as dawn lightened the dull overcast, the regimental operations officer, Maj. John Dumaine, asked division headquarters to send all available aircraft as soon as possible.[23]

About dawn, the French experienced their first crisis of the day as the Chinese mounted almost simultaneous attacks against the 3d Company and then the 2d Company. Captain LeMaitre, commanding the French heavy weapons company, ordered Lt. Claude Jaupart to take one of his 75-mm recoilless rifles and reinforce the 3d Company, which was in danger of being overrun. Major Barthelemy, the battalion's third in command and the officer whom Monclar most often relied to handle dicey situations, immediately rescinded the order when the Chinese overran the heavy weapons company. The attack mortally wounded Captain LeMaitre while he was trying to emplace a weapon on the flank of his position. As the machine guns were about to be overrun, the gunners were forced to fend off the attackers with their fists.[24]

The heavy weapons company was positioned to cover the gap at the south end of the perimeter. If the Chinese mounted a successful attack through it, they would threaten both the battalion and regimental CPs. Barthelemy ordered Jaupart to lead a counterattack with the platoon from the French ROK Company and the engineers that had been held out of line. Supported by recoilless rifles in the King Company sector, they counterattacked and retook the position. The retreating Chinese left twenty-three corpses behind.[25]

Enemy mortars fired on the perimeter throughout the day, although the barrages were not as heavy as those the regiment had withstood on the Naktong River line. By 0800 hours, the Chinese had renewed their ground attacks against Item and Love Companies on the north and east sides of the perimeter, and against the French 2d Company to the southwest. The situation was becoming desperate in both locations. When a gap of four hundred meters developed between Item and Love, the Chinese seized the ground and set up machine guns that could fire on the command posts on the valley floor. Freeman ordered Lieutenant Colonel Kane to drive the Chinese off and retake the hill. At the same time, he ordered the 1st Battalion units guarding the road to the south to move to the tunnels area to assist the regiment in its fight.[26]

Baker Company, the 1st Battalion company closest to the tunnels, started north immediately. However, when it reached the position occupied by the 37th Field Artillery Battalion to the south of the regiment, it observed Chinese on the ridge above it. Freeman, who considered the artillery's supporting fires to be vital to his success at the Twin Tunnels, consequently reversed his order for the company to join the tunnels battle, and instead ordered it to stay with the guns. The soldiers formed a perimeter around the artillery unit and—supplemented with the regiment's drivers, who had been left to help the artillerymen—beat off an attack on the position.[27]

At this point in the battle, Freeman began to worry about his ammunition supply. Some companies had not been completely resupplied with all types of ammunition since the heavy fighting at Wonju a week and a half earlier. At the rate the soldiers were expending all types of ammunition, they could not last through the day. He radioed for the rear CP to send ammunition of all types forward. At about the same time, division released his 2d Battalion from its reserve mission and it started moving to the tunnels area.[28]

The Chinese renewed their attack on the French 3d Company at dawn. Major Barthelemy considered this area his most critical for the moment, and positioned himself there. Soon the heavy fires wounded him and killed Capt. Leon Serre, the company commander. The fighting did not slacken.[29]

At 0900 hours, Lieutenant Colonel Kane reported that the situation was critical in Item and Love Companies. He asked Freeman to send any help possible. Kane had the reputation of being a conscientious and combat-experienced commander who never exaggerated his situation, and everyone in the headquarters understood the gravity of his report. Freeman sent an improvised force and personally directed the fires of a twin-40-mm cannon against the Chinese holding portions of the 3d Battalion's line. When Love Company was on the verge of running out of ammunition, drivers, telephone linemen, and French and American stretcher-bearers climbed the hill to resupply them. Kane ordered a platoon from King Company, which was not engaged by Chinese infantry at the moment, to the aid of Love Company. Item Company, on the highest ground except for the French on Hill 453, beat off wave after wave of attackers, stacking Chinese bodies in piles as barriers in front of their position and on the steep slopes leading toward it.[30]

The Crisis in the Afternoon

At about noon, the Chinese intensified their attack on the French Battalion positions at the northwest end of the perimeter. After a period of heavy fighting, they managed to drive the 3d Company off the ridgeline. At 1400 hours, Major Barthelemy gave the survivors permission to fall back to the south. During the intense hours of what both Freeman and Monclar later remembered as their most desperate fight, the regimental commander did everything in his power to retake the hill. With ammunition stocks lowering every minute, he poured all the firepower he had available on the hill. He had no reserves—every driver, clerk, cook, and mechanic had long ago been put into the battle somewhere. He finally radioed Monclar and said, "Dammit, we need that hill."

Monclar went to Freeman's CP and together they planned the last counterattack they were capable of mounting. Freeman put two tanks and a twin-40-mm flak wagon—which he called "the sweetest weapon possible for vacuum cleaning a ridge"—in position to fire on it, along with all available mortars and artillery. Major Olivier LeMire, the French Battalion commander, under pressure from regimental headquarters, ordered the 3d Company to hold the ground it was on to the last man, no matter how hard the Chinese might hit them. Barthelemy, who had been wounded earlier in the day but was continuing his mission, organized a counterattack force with the remnants of the 3d Company and a platoon from the French ROK Company. He designated the ROK Company commander to lead it and ordered the 3d Company's only surviving officer, who knew the ground, to accompany the assault. Barthelemy's terse instructions were to retake the hill at any cost. For ten minutes all weapons fired as much ammunition as they could before the French attacked. The soldiers then fixed bayonets and raced up the hill, screaming like madmen. The Chinese had had enough; they turned and ran, pursued by small arms and mortar fire.

The anonymous author of the official French account of the action describes how General Stewart sat calmly observing it, smoking his pipe. After the French ROK Company's successful attack, he murmured, "Mag-

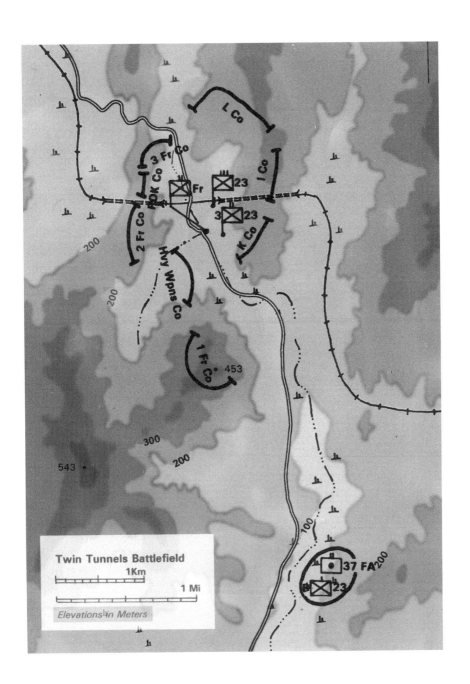

Twin Tunnels Battlefield

1Km

1 Mi

Elevations in Meters

nificent" to himself. Stewart himself remembers being so "calm" that he bit the stems off three pipes that day.[31]

The division commander, General Ruffner, had been calling Stewart just about every half-hour since early morning to check on the situation at Twin Tunnels. One time Ruffner asked if things were really as bad as the reports sounded. Hearing a note of skepticism in the division commander's voice, Stewart replied that he was standing in the blood of the radio operator, who had just been shot, and then held the handset out the window so the general could hear the firing. General Ruffner replied that help—presumably Freeman's 2d Battalion, recently released from division reserve, and his 1st Battalion, which had been sent from the rear earlier—was on the way.[32]

By early afternoon, both the French Battalion and Item and Love Companies were under severe pressure. The Chinese were now pushing the French 2d Company from its position. On the other side of the valley, Lieutenant Colonel Kane had reinforced Love Company with men from King Company, but could do little for Item Company. One platoon was down to eighteen men, fighting desperately to hold their ridge. Chinese soldiers had returned to the gap between Item and Love and were again in position to fire directly into the valley.[33]

In Item Company, M.Sgt. Hubert L. Lee performed heroic actions for which he would receive the Medal of Honor. When Chinese attackers forced his platoon off their position and wounded his platoon leader, Lee assumed command. Regrouping his surviving soldiers, he led them in repeated attacks to retake their position. Grenade fragments wounded him painfully in the leg when they were twenty meters away, but he continued the attack. Lee renewed the assault five times. On the fifth attempt, another grenade exploded nearby, knocking him to the ground and seriously injuring both his legs. He continued to crawl forward, rising to his knees to fire, before finally reaching the position with his men. During the fight, which occurred a few hours before his thirty-sixth birthday, Lee's men killed eighty-three Chinese.[34]

By midafternoon, the final crisis had arrived. The Chinese were preparing to push the remnants of the two UN battalions back into the valley and annihilate them. Freeman, Monclar, Stewart, and their staffs gathered all the ammunition they could find and prepared to make a last stand near Item Company, over the east tunnel.

The air liaison officer, standing near General Stewart in the inner perimeter, said: "General, I don't like this. What's going to happen?" Stewart replied that he thought they would all be dead in about twenty minutes.

The Twin Tunnels battlefield, looking east over the King Company positions on a ridge, as it appeared in November, 1992. *Photo by author.*

Stewart then asked the air liaison officer about air support. The officer replied that several flights were stacked up over them as they spoke, but the cloud cover prevented them from delivering their ordnance. The two looked up and saw a small patch of blue directly over their position. The general asked if the air force could do anything with that. The liaison officer radioed the aircraft that there was a break in the clouds over their position, "We are directly below the break, and we need help." The flight leader replied, "Here we come." In one of the most dramatic rescues in military history—Freeman later said it was too unbelievable even for a Hollywood scriptwriter—a flight of Marine Corps F4U Corsairs zoomed through the break in the clouds and swept down over the battlefield, loaded and eager for the kill. It was a valiant act on the part of the pilots, because the battlefield was ringed with mountains that they could not see from above.[35]

The Tactical Air Control Party directed the aircraft first to the Item Company position. The experienced marine pilots circled the target four times to make sure they could distinguish the intermingled friendly and enemy formations. As Freeman described it:

> then climbing for the dive they came in. They didn't waste one round! First, 500 pound bombs, daisy cutters, right in the middle of the closely packed Chinese who went up in pieces; next, back to work with rockets—"gook goosers," our infantry facetiously called them, then, with the .50 calibers against the now disintegrating enemy. What beautiful air support! The next flight coming in before the Marines had barely started was laid on the Chinese in front of the center of the French position. This mass of Commies on the bare ridge went down like prairie grass in a wind storm. The pressure was immediately relaxed on the defenders as the enemy tried to rally or to dig in. Flight after flight came in up to a total of twenty-four and what was left of the enemy began to "bug out."[36]

Tanks and quad-mounted .50-caliber machine guns rushed to cut off and kill the fleeing enemy. The Chinese, about eight thousand strong when they began the battle, left twelve hundred corpses around and inside the perimeter. Intelligence estimated total Chinese losses at thirty-six hundred, or almost half the starting strength of the enemy division. Freeman's losses were 225 casualties of all types: killed, wounded, and missing.[37]

Aftermath of the Twin Tunnels

The battle was over, but the day's work was not. Two army liaison planes dropped ammunition and rations to the still-isolated French 1st Company. After the fighter-bombers finished, fourteen cargo transports—C-119 "Flying Boxcars"—dropped supplies of all types into the valley. The pilots displayed masterful skill. They approached the valley from the southeast, following the road at an altitude below the peaks on either side of the narrow valley. After the planes dropped their loads to the west of the road, the pilots fire-walled their throttles and climbed sharply out to the north, using all their power to clear the 319-meter-high hill at the valley's north end. The supply drop included the regiment's first arctic sleeping bags, a most welcome comfort to the soldiers.[38]

After dark, the 1st Battalion began arriving, having marched all after-

The Twin Tunnels battlefield, looking west over the French 2d and 3d Company positions, as it appeared in November, 1992. *Photo by author.*

noon. Baker Company stayed at the artillery position where it had helped defend the guns throughout the afternoon. Freeman gave the rest of the battalion the mission of defending the northern portion of the perimeter, with Charley Company to the west of the road and Able Company to the east. This allowed the 3d Battalion and the French Battalion to contract and tighten their perimeters. When the 2d Battalion's Easy Company arrived, Freeman took a platoon for regimental reserve and placed the rest of the company in the valley near the French heavy weapons company. Together with the tank platoon still there, they would cover the southern entry into the perimeter. The remainder of the 2d Battalion arrived at the artillery position about midnight and was ordered to stay there until morning.[39]

The only prisoner to survive the day's fighting was the badly wounded one taken by the 1st Company. During the afternoon, the French Battalion's intelligence officer, Captain Michelet, sent Corporal Bererd to bring the prisoner back, giving him two French-speaking Koreans to interrogate the man and help carry him down the mountain. Bererd, from France's Alpine country, raced up Hill 453. Finding the prisoner in bad shape and unconscious, Bererd doubted whether the Chinese soldier could survive the trip down the hill. He searched other corpses in the area and found nothing but a diagram of the attack route to Hill 453.

Bererd decided to have the Koreans carry the prisoner down while he moved ahead to a French outpost to search more corpses. He told the Koreans that when they reached the outpost he would relieve one of them. Unknown to Bererd, the Koreans abandoned the prisoner and followed him to the bottom of the hill. Bererd was angry, but, after deciding there probably were many more prisoners and that this one was not too important, he returned to headquarters empty-handed.

When Bererd reported to Captain Michelet without the prisoner, the intelligence officer blew up. The X Corps was pressuring division, division was pressuring the 23d, and the 23d was pressuring the French Battalion to deliver the man for interrogation. Bererd volunteered to return immediately, but Michelet was so angry he went himself. It was after dark when Michelet got back with the wounded prisoner. He took the man to Freeman's headquarters, where a medical officer revived him and Freeman interrogated him in Chinese. Freeman spoke very slowly to make sure he was understood, and the soldier finally admitted he was Chinese and gave his regiment. He was from the PLA's 125th Division, a part of the Forty-second Army that Eighth Army had been trying to locate. The force that had attacked the 23d at Twin Tunnels was composed of three regiments from that division.[40]

Everyone expected the Chinese to make another all-out effort to overrun the regiment that night. Weary soldiers tried to remain alert for probes, but none came. After a quiet night, there was no sign of the enemy at daylight.[41]

At dawn, patrols ranged into the surrounding hills looking for the enemy. Neither ground nor aerial patrols found any sign of the Chinese. The 23d's 3d Battalion and the French Battalion had gone into the battle at Twin Tunnels at about 80 percent of their authorized strength. After tallying their losses they determined that they would be going into the fighting ahead at about 70 percent strength.[42]

With the arrival of the 23d RCT's other elements, Freeman felt confident of its ability to fight off further Chinese attacks so long as his ammunition held out. Supplies had run perilously low in only one day of hard fighting. He knew that unless the 2d Division and X Corps resupplied the unit every day, particularly after night engagements, the Chinese could emerge victorious merely by surviving and outlasting the defenders' ammunition. The regiment was dangerously far from friendly lines for resupply by ground vehicles to be a sure thing, and the weather was sufficiently unpredictable for aerial resupply to be assured. Fully appreciating this dilemma, General Ruffner ordered an all-out effort by his logisticians to move the regimental supply base to Yoju, no matter how much it taxed the support units. Additionally, he ordered the 9th Regiment to keep the 23d Infantry's supply route open and to serve as a rescue force in an emergency.[43]

Following the success at Twin Tunnels, the 23d received a new mission: "Dominate the road center of Chipyong and occupy the high ground in the vicinity so as to protect the right flank of the IX Corps and establish the western anchor of a X Corps line of departure for the offensive." This mission would support the X Corps plan for Operation Roundup, which envisioned the 23d Infantry holding the corps' left flank while the 38th Regiment held Hoengsong, twenty miles to the east. To the right of the 38th Infantry, the 187th Airborne Infantry Regiment would protect the division's right flank. The corps' right-flank unit was the 7th Infantry Division, at Pyongchang, forty miles east of Chipyong-ni. As soon as the American forces were in place, the 5th and 8th ROK Divisions would attack north and take Hongchon, fifteen miles north of Hoengsong. The operation would jump off on 4 February.[44]

On Saturday morning, 3 February 1951, after another welcome but unexpected quiet night, the 23d Infantry set out for its rendezvous with destiny at Chipyong-ni.

Chapter 8

Prelude to Chipyong-ni

Campaigns and battles are nothing but a long series of difficulties to be overcome. The lack of equipment, the lack of food, the lack of this or that are only excuses; the real leader displays his qualities in his triumphs over adversity, however great it may be.
                                                        —Gen. George C. Marshall

Unity and confidence cannot be improvised. They alone can create that mutual trust, that feeling of force which gives courage and daring.
   Pride exists only among people who know each other well, who have esprit de corps, and company spirit. There is a necessity for an organization that renders unity possible by creating the real individuality of the company.
                                                        —Ardant du Picq

The battle of Twin Tunnels gave the Americans and their French comrades confidence in their ability to absorb anything their foes could muster against them. The battle had been a close call in which the defenders were saved by airpower at the last moment before disaster struck. Nonetheless, the UN forces had prevailed.

On the day following the battle, the 23d Regimental Combat Team patrolled the area around the tunnels and the road to Chipyong-ni. The patrols found Chinese troops in the village of Sindae, about three kilometers north of the tunnels and halfway between the tunnels and Chipyong-ni. They engaged the Chinese with artillery as well as fire from the tanks accompanying the patrol.[1]

The 23d Infantry continued to the north and entered the village of Chipyong-ni on 3 February. The village was at a road junction about two and a half miles northwest, or about four miles by road, from the tunnels.

There was nothing to distinguish the village from countless others in that part of the peninsula. Dirt streets led between small buildings with mostly thatched roofs. Rice paddies took up all the flat ground around the village, and on the west, came right up to the buildings themselves. On the other three sides, low hills formed the edges of the town, and from any spot in the village one could look toward the horizon and see high, almost treeless mountains dominating the site. Freeman was cautious after the battle at the tunnels, and ordered a watchful approach march. The 1st Battalion followed the high ground to the east of the road, while the French Battalion scoured the high ground to the west. Both battalions ranged far out to the flanks of the main body, which was moving slowly up the road. The 1st Battalion saw enemy soldiers on Hill 506, east of Chipyong-ni, and directed air strikes on them. Otherwise, the approach was uneventful and the regiment arrived at the placid village by late afternoon. By 2000 hours, the regiment had occupied the line of low hills closely surrounding the town to the north, south, and east.[2]

It was a busy day for the regiment as the entire Eighth Army chain of command visited the headquarters. Generals Almond and Ruffner were the first to arrive just after lunch. Then, at 1500 hours, General Ridgway, accompanied by Assistant Secretary of the Army Earl D. Johnson, arrived. Ridgway presented the Presidential Unit Citation to the regimental headquarters, the 3d Battalion, and the French Battalion for their victory at Twin Tunnels. He also decorated Colonel Freeman with the Distinguished Service Cross. Freeman later recalled that the large number of Chinese bodies scattered throughout the area impressed Ridgway.[3]

Freeman's mission was to deny the enemy the use of the road net and hold the area that would become the left flank of the 3d ROK Division when it maneuvered into line before attacking to the north. His experiences at Wonju and the Twin Tunnels had impressed upon Freeman the importance of having a perimeter as tightly integrated as he could make it. He especially wanted to avoid any gaps like those that had given the Chinese an opportunity to attack between units at the tunnels. As a result, he and Lieutenant Colonel Meszar decided to occupy the largest ring of low hills they could man while keeping a small reserve—the largest ring they could afford in order to fully man the perimeter without any breaches.[4]

The final perimeter was an irregular oval measuring about a mile and a half from west to east and about a mile from north to south. It assured the continuity of defense needed to avoid infiltration into weak areas or the breakthrough of even a strong enemy force. It also was large enough to

Major General Clark L. Ruffner, 2d Infantry Division commander *(left)*, confers with Maj. Gen. Edward M. "Ned" Almond, X Corps commander, at Chipyong-ni. *Courtesy U.S. Army Military History Institute.*

accommodate the regimental and battalion CPs, the reserve force, motor pools, artillery positions, airdrop zones, and a short airstrip. It was not, however, large enough to keep enemy mortars out of range or to prohibit effective enemy observation of the area.[5]

Freeman and Monclar had learned important lessons at Wonju and Twin Tunnels. The Chinese were skillful at probing defensive lines at night, finding areas of weakness or gaps in the lines before flowing through with a speed that was difficult to counter. When this happened, only immediate counterattacks by a determined force could retake the positions overrun by the Chinese. Especially in the mountains, dug-in Chinese troops could stand up to almost any weapons the Americans and French had available. As a result, it was always better to hold ground than to have to retake it with the meager reserves that were available. Freeman knew that the attacking units could be expected to be weaker than the defending forces, but he had to be ready for anything, as he was beyond the range of supporting artillery and too far away from the Eighth Army's front lines to expect help in a tight situation. Another lesson the commanders had absorbed was that sufficient ammunition stocks had to be on hand to continue to fight without resupply. At Twin Tunnels, the regiment had so depleted its ammunition stocks during a single day's fighting that a second effort by the Chinese in the same strength as the first would have wiped the defenders out. When counterattacks became necessary, forces had to be immediately available. For this reason, in a perimeter as large as at Twin Tunnels or Chipyong-ni, reserve forces had to be dispatched to the area to launch a counterattack before the situation became desperate in order to arrive in time to be effective. This made the job of the senior leader on the spot a life-or-death matter, since someone with the authority to commit the reserve had to be at the critical location to make the decision. In the French Battalion, this was Major Barthelemy; in the 23d Regiment, Lieutenant Colonel Meszar.[6]

Field artillery and mortar fires were crucial in each engagement. Fires had to be planned in advance on as many locations as possible in order to speed up the fire, since if it arrived more than three minutes after requested, it was probably too late. Accuracy was important because both the Americans and the French tended to bring supporting fires in close to their own lines and short rounds were deadly. Mortars validated their effectiveness in this type of combat. Often they were the only indirect fires available, as would be the case many times at Chipyong-ni. As Monclar wrote, "In the bass singing of the artillery support, it is the alto of the infantry's 81-mm. mortar which leads the song."[7]

Tanks were important weapons in support of the infantry. They could accompany some patrols, but they were best used to reinforce portions of the perimeter that were inherently weak or threatened. At Twin Tunnels they had become, in effect, mobile blockhouses that Freeman could quickly dispatch to shore up the defenses. They had played an especially important role helping the French hold the valley in the south, and firing machine guns in support of the 3d Company's desperate defense in the north.[8]

Mountains, designated hills in military jargon, dominate the valley around Chipyong-ni in every direction. Hills 248 and 345 to the west, 348 and 411 to the north, 506 and 319 to the east, and 397 to the south were two to three hundred meters higher than the hills closer to the town. To occupy

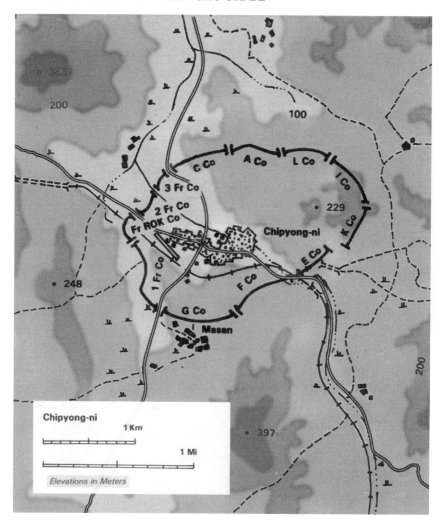

the higher hills, however, would have meant a perimeter about ten miles long, requiring the forces of at least a division. Freeman's perimeter would be only about four miles long, but it would have no dangerous gaps between units.[9]

Picture a clock face with north at twelve: the final dispositions were 1st Battalion from twelve to one, 3d Battalion from one to five, 2d Battalion from five to seven, and the French Battalion from seven to twelve. Most of the positions were on hills rising from twenty to eighty meters above the frozen rice paddies that surrounded Chipyong-ni. Hills 248 and 345, more than a mile away, were the only hills on the west side of the valley. This

Chipyong-ni, looking southeast with the French positions in the foreground, as it appeared in November, 1992. *Photo by author.*

meant that the French Battalion had the poorest defensive area: frozen rice paddies. The soldiers of the French Battalion joked among themselves that they could not decide whether this meant that Freeman was discriminating against them by giving his American units the best positions, or that he had so much confidence in their fighting abilities that he knew they could better handle the poor terrain. In reality, the French positions had good fields of fire, just no high ground to slow attackers down.[10]

At first, the soldiers expected to move on to another position soon, as they generally had in the past. However, after staying in position for two days and then three, word got around that they were twelve miles from the nearest friendly troops. Their commanders selected positions with the best fields of fire they could find. The fighting positions were usually on the "military crest" of the ridge, the place on the forward slope where a defender can see to the bottom of the incline and thus bring any attacker under observed indirect as well as direct fires. They ordered the soldiers to dig in and to prepare positions that would hold up against any attack. The weather had turned cold again. Although it seldom went below ten degrees Fahrenheit, it never rose above freezing. As a result, the ground was frozen, making digging defensive positions hard labor. The standard procedure was to use steel bars and sledge hammers to break up the soil and shovels to dig out the positions. On occasion, however, the soldiers spread gasoline around and ignited it to thaw the ground, or they buried explosive charges and blew them up to make a cavity.

For the next ten days, the men improved their positions during the daylight hours when they were not patrolling. Commanders located foxholes within whispering distance of one another whenever possible. They emplaced machine guns to cover likely approaches to the positions, and BARs on the flanks. Everyone preferred two-man foxholes, which measured about two by five feet and were waist deep. At Chipyong-ni, most platoons established an ammunition dump in a bunker or trench on the reverse slope behind the fighting positions, close enough for a quick dash from the foxholes for resupply. Forward observers laid in mortar concentrations so that they could be called in quickly when needed, without the need to adjust fire. The only bunkers with overhead cover were those built by the engineers. They were about six feet square and covered with six-inch timbers or limbs crisscrossed to make a foot-thick roof that was then covered with two or three layers of sandbags.

The French invariably constructed better fighting positions than the Americans. Their individual fighting positions were deep foxholes with floors of rice straw. Some had trenches connecting them with adjacent positions or positions to the rear. As a journalist who observed them in action described it, they made themselves at home in their fighting positions: "[In his foxhole] he cuts a shelf in one side and here, as neatly arranged as a grocery display, he lays out his grenades and extra ammunition so that it will be close at hand. Lower down he cuts another shelf and here he builds a little fire and warms his food. . . . He places a poncho over the top to keep out the rain and through the poncho he puts a cardboard container which serves as a stove pipe."[11]

Freeman and Monclar did everything they could to provide the means for the soldiers to improve their positions. Barbed-wire barriers across the best avenues of approach into the perimeter reinforced the defenses. The soldiers also constructed outpost lines forward of the fighting positions that were manned during daylight hours. At dusk the defenders constructed booby traps and placed trip flares that could be detonated by wires running back to the main line of defense before they withdrew to their nighttime positions. Barrels of *fougasse* were buried in front of some positions. Communication specialists strung wire between positions and back to headquarters, sometimes triply redundant so that the telephones would be more likely to continue to function even during an artillery barrage.

At this point in the war, infantrymen were often reluctant to improvise positions with overhead cover for fear they would collapse. Infantry soldiers had received no instruction in building such positions during their basic training. Additionally, they usually lacked the engineer equipment such as saws, picks, and shovels that were needed to construct such emplacements. At Chipyong-ni, soldiers from the engineer company built some permanent fighting positions with reinforced overhead cover. In addition, some vehicles and guns were dug in to half their height. This not only prevented rounds from exploding under them, it protected the tires from being punctured by shell fragments.[12]

Freeman and Monclar constantly walked the lines, stopping to talk to soldiers and reassure them that things were going well. Additionally, Freeman was stockpiling the provisions he would need to hold out if his supply lines to the rear were cut. He stockpiled more ammunition than the regiment had seen since arriving in Korea. It reached the point that he began to worry he might get in trouble for hoarding so much if a battle did not occur.[13]

By the time the 23d RCT arrived at Chipyong-ni, it had been reunited with all the elements normally supporting it. It had all its organic units— three infantry battalions, a heavy mortar company, a medium tank company, and a medical company. Reinforcing and supporting the organic units were a number of attachments. These included the French Battalion; the 37th Field Artillery Battalion; Baker Battery, 82d Antiaircraft Artillery Battalion; Baker Company, 2d Engineer Combat Battalion; and the 1st Ranger Infantry Company. However, the regiment's heavy artillery, Baker Battery, 503d Field Artillery Battalion, had not yet joined it.[14]

Supporting Weapons

The 37th Field Artillery Battalion was a 574-man organization equipped with eighteen 105-mm. howitzers. It had been a part of the 23d RCT since its departure for Korea, except for a short period before the Chinese intervention, when the 15th Field Artillery Battalion supported the regiment.

The unit had a good reputation for planning fires in support of the infantry and delivering them quickly when needed. Lieutenant Colonel John Hector, the commander, was known for calm and effective leadership under fire. His command presence and disdain for enemy fire set the example for his subordinates. At Chipyong-ni, Hector located the battalion headquarters with Charley Battery, behind the French 1st Company in the southwest portion of the position; Able Battery was behind the French 2d Company just to the northwest corner of the village; and Baker Battery was behind George Company south of the village.[15]

The other artillery unit attached to the regiment was the 503d Field Artillery Battalion's Baker Battery. It was a 155-mm howitzer battery that arrived in the perimeter on 9 February. A segregated black unit with white officers, it had a good reputation with the men of the 23d Infantry. Known as the "nickel-oh-trey," its soldiers often competed for speed in delivering fires, and they were accurate. They had their own psychological warfare ploy that involved removing the bottom of an empty C-ration can and jamming it over the fuse of a projectile before loading it. When fired, air rushing between the loose can and the round would create a horrendous scream that sent chills down the spines of soldiers all around. There were few who judged Baker Battery by the color of its soldiers; the men of the 23d merely wanted them to provide the most accurate and timely fire support possible.

Baker Battery of the 82d Antiaircraft Artillery was armed with quad-.50 caliber machine guns mounted on half-tracked vehicles and twin 40-mm. guns mounted on tracked chassis. Because virtually no aircraft were used against UN forces, these antiaircraft weapons became efficient infantry support weapons. Although the battery had an authorized strength of 198 men, it had only a hundred men and six quad-.50s and four twin-40s at Chipyong-ni. It did, however, have twice its authorized amount of ammunition. Captain Clyde C. Hathaway, commanding Baker Battery, located his headquarters near the center of the village, as he had to anticipate calls for his guns to move to any portion of the perimeter.

Baker Company of the 2d Engineer Combat Battalion should have had 168 men, but at Chipyong-ni only about 125 were present for duty. Its mission was to perform combat engineering functions such as mine emplacement and clearing, barrier construction and breaching, and light construction tasks in support of the regiment. As with all combat engineer units, it could fight as infantry when necessary. Its primary tasks at Chipyong-ni included constructing defensive protection for the regimental collecting station, where the wounded would be treated until they could be evacuated or returned to duty; building a small runway for light planes and helicopters; and assisting infantry units with the construction of fighting positions and barriers. The engineers "hardened" the collecting station's tents by building walls around them made of salvaged railroad ties topped with sacks of rice they found in the village. They blocked the entrance with barriers made of more railroad ties so that soldiers carrying wounded GIs on litters could get into the facility, but shell fragments from nearby impacts could not. The engineers had neither the time nor the materials to provide overhead cover, so the tops of the tents remained vulnerable to shellfire.[16]

The Rangers

The 1st Ranger Infantry Company joined the regiment in December, 1950. At full strength a unit of 105 men, its mission was infiltrating enemy lines and attacking key positions such as command posts, support units, and communications centers. The Rangers had been trained at Fort Benning, Georgia, where they were strongly indoctrinated with the conviction that they were an elite "hit-and-run" unit that should not be used for traditional infantry missions such as defending terrain. Even though their armaments were about the same as those of conventional infantry units of comparable size, and their organization's doctrinal capabilities included "seizing and holding terrain," the Rangers strongly objected to being assigned defensive missions. Unless augmented, the company had to be attached to another unit for all support functions: administration, mess, supply, and maintenance.[17] Some of the regiment's senior officers, including Freeman, disagreed with the concept of the Ranger organization. According to Freeman: "This was a very admirable organization, but one in which I didn't believe. . . . They were highly talented long range patrol individuals made up into teams in a company group. They could go for miles on skis or on foot or by air and do all those things, yet they didn't have any logistic increment in their organization. They could barely cook their own meals. They couldn't maintain their vehicles. They couldn't even deliver their mail if there was any, or distribute their rations or go to the rear for additional ammunition. They were a parasite."[18]

Freeman designated Baker Company, the Ranger Company, and the Engineer Company as his reserve forces, to be committed in that order if needed.

In spite of the best efforts of the leaders and their soldiers, the situation at Chipyong-ni had several inherent weaknesses. The perimeter lent itself poorly to defense at several points. Particularly worrisome were the locations where saddles or ridges led into defensive positions, as they did from Hill 397 into the George Company position in the south and from Hill 506 into Item and King Companies in the east. The high hills all around the perimeter provided excellent observation posts for the enemy to adjust fire into the position. The command posts, artillery positions, and ammunition dumps had little protection. There was no friendly artillery within range of the perimeter, and the pieces located inside the perimeter could not fire the short ranges—less than a mile—necessary to provide direct support close to the front lines. This meant that the mortars, especially the 4.2-inch heavy mortars, would have to serve as artillery, and that plentiful supplies of mortar ammunition would be critical. Finally, there were few reserves, and the commanders could expect to use them up quickly if there were heavy losses.[19]

Medical Support

The medical personnel at Chipyong-ni also prepared to operate on their own, without depending on resources outside the perimeter. Their success in doing so, however, depended on the understanding and support of the commanders inside the perimeter. These commanders supported the medical mission in every way they could. Colonel Freeman respected his medical personnel, welcomed advice from his medical staff, and acted on it quickly and decisively. Even though Freeman and the commanders over him increasingly expected the regiment to have to operate on its own resources for an unknown period of time, the medical units had no reinforcements from outside the regiment. If the unit were to become cut off and unable to evacuate casualties as necessary, the battalion aid stations and regimental collecting station would be inadequately staffed to provide the nursing and other care required. In spite of these shortcomings, the medical personnel would successfully support operations throughout the coming siege at Chipyong-ni.

Shortly after the regiment arrived in the area, soldiers discovered two dead Chinese soldiers in a small, one-room building near the regimental collecting station as its tents were being erected. Both men wore the quilted uniform of the Chinese forces and neither had been wounded. There were no rashes or other abnormalities on their exposed skin, and no cause of death was apparent. Captain Robert M. Hall, the regimental surgeon and medical company commander, placed the building under guard to prevent anyone entering it and went to discuss the matter with Freeman and Meszar.

Louse-borne typhus was endemic in some areas of Asia, and epidemics had occurred in both China and Korea in the years since World War II. In addition, flea-borne diseases such as plague also existed in Asia. If the soldiers had died of typhus, lice that had fed on the bodies would be present in their clothing and in the building. If they had died of a flea-borne disease, fleas and rats in the building would also carry the disease. Hall recommended burning the building and its contents to avoid the possibility of an outbreak of disease inside the perimeter. Although the fire would illuminate the area and give away the position during the coming night, Freeman ordered the building burned as a preventive measure.

According to army doctrine, the division medical battalion was responsible for evacuating casualties from regimental collecting stations to the divisional clearing stations. In spite of this responsibility, the 2d Division's medical battalion had established a policy that the ambulance company would not send ambulances into forward areas to evacuate casualties because the vehicles might be lost to enemy action. This meant that instead of being evacuated in the heated three-quarter-ton "box" ambulances, the wounded had to be evacuated in the medical company's quarter-ton "litter jeeps" or larger trucks belonging to the infantry units. As a result, the wounded were more uncomfortable during their evacuation, and the 23d Infantry had to designate men and vehicles to evacuate casualties that should have been evacuated by their higher headquarters.

The regimental surgeon described this absurd policy to Colonel Freeman and recommended that the regimental collecting station be redesignated as a "clearing" station so that the casualties could be evacuated in three-quarter-ton ambulances. Never one to let rear-echelon bureaucrats and their policies interfere with the way he ran his regiment when the welfare of his soldiers was involved, Freeman grinned and, with tongue firmly in cheek, said that from then on the regimental collecting station would be known as the regimental clearing station. When this semantic solution was explained to the division medical battalion, its commander declined to challenge Freeman on the policy and provided ambulance service for the regiment. Four of these ambulances were with the regiment when it was surrounded and cut off.

The presence of the division's ambulances would prove to have ramifications far beyond the extra comfort of the wounded being evacuated.

When the regimental collecting station tents became filled and there was no more room for the casualties that kept pouring in, the ambulances were a haven for the less seriously wounded. By occasionally running their engines and heaters, the ambulances furnished heated areas where a number of soldiers could be kept warm. Although the 2d Medical Battalion's 2d Clearing Platoon was later cited as part of the 23d RCT, the only soldiers from it who served at Chipyong-ni were the four ambulance drivers—who served courageously and well.

Patrolling

Patrols were a key part of Freeman's plan for the defense of Chipyong-ni. For however long the regiment remained there, it had to be ready for a Chinese attack. The more he knew about the whereabouts of Chinese forces near him, the better he could prepare his soldiers, mentally and physically, to meet them. An isolated American regimental combat team operating outside the range of artillery and beyond the supporting distance of other units was simply too ripe a plum for the Chinese to resist. In effect, the defenders expanded the perimeter by pushing enemy forces away from it. This retarded the tightening of the Chinese encirclement until only a day or two before they attacked. At the same time, the patrols would destroy any supplies they found and thus diminish any sense of security the Chinese might have. When accompanied by a liaison aircraft, it was difficult for a superior force to take a patrol completely by surprise.[20]

The first patrols into the area around Chipyong-ni moved out the morning after the regiment arrived in the valley. Wounded ROK soldiers in the village reported that groups of Chinese had been passing through the area for several days and that a large group had passed through only the night before. Beginning a pattern that would continue until the Chinese struck their first blow on the perimeter, Freeman ordered each battalion to send a platoon-sized patrol with a radio out to the high ground to its front. The patrol's mission was to explore the hills, look for signs of enemy activity, destroy supplies, and engage any enemy in the area with their own weapons as well as indirect fire and air strikes.[21]

About an hour after starting up Hill 345 to the south, the 2d Battalion's patrol fired on a half-dozen Chinese soldiers and the aircraft overhead reported occupied foxholes on the west side of the hill. A little later, a King Company patrol got into a firefight with an enemy force on Hill 506 to the northeast. The GIs withdrew and called in indirect fire and air strikes on the Chinese. As evening approached, the regimental intelligence officer reported to division that a patrol had observed a hundred soldiers marching in a column about six miles east of Chipyong-ni. At the same time, civilians in the area reported that more than three hundred enemy troops had passed by on the same road each of the previous two days.[22]

A patrol sent out on 5 February to contact a patrol from the nearest infantry unit to the southwest relayed a report from that unit of an estimated six-thousand-man enemy force about seven miles to the west. That same day, another patrol fought a skirmish with a twenty-five-man enemy force about four miles west of Chipyong-ni. The following day, patrols reported twenty-five contacts with enemy forces within five miles of Chipyong-ni; several resulted in friendly casualties. An air observer reported the largest concentration of forces, estimated at five hundred to six hundred, in and around the village of Sanggosong just two and a half miles to the east. The area was very rugged and contained a number of abandoned gold mines that provided protection for the remnants of the Chinese 125th Division. This was the unit that had attacked the 23d RCT at Twin Tunnels while operating from its staging area near Sanggosong. A patrol from the regimental Intelligence and Reconnaissance (I&R) Platoon tried to reach the village that day, but was stopped by several large craters only a mile and a half from the perimeter. A company-sized patrol tried to get to the top of Hill 506, between Chipyong-ni and Sanggosong, but was pinned down in knee-deep snow near the crest and needed air strikes to help extricate it. Freeman ordered the 2d Battalion to send a reinforced rifle company into Sanggosong the following day. That night, soldiers saw a number of enemy flares in all directions around and over Chipyong-ni.

Lieutenant Colonel James Edwards, the 2d Battalion commander, assigned the patrol mission to Easy Company. The company commander, Capt. Bickford E. Sawyer, was an experienced officer who had joined the regiment in 1949. Nicknamed "Buz" after the hero of a popular comic strip, he had previously been the battalion intelligence officer and later the mortar platoon leader. He had taken command of Easy Company in January when Capt. Perry Sager became the assistant operations officer. Edwards reinforced Sawyer's company with a section of machine guns from his heavy weapons company and asked the regimental operations officer for a tank and twin-40-mm and quad-.50-caliber flak wagons. The battalion commander also sent a squad from the battalion's Pioneer and Ammunition (P&A) Platoon—essentially a light combat engineer squad—to help the vehicles over the craters reported on the earlier patrol.

The Easy Company patrol moved out about an hour after sunrise, 0900 hours, on 6 February. The support platoon from Fox Company moved into key positions in Easy Company's sector of the perimeter during its absence. An hour or so down the road, Captain Sawyer halted his column and he and the artillery observers registered the artillery and lobbed a few mortars at possible enemy locations.

The company moved down a trail that paralleled the road to the south and was in sight of it, with the P&A Platoon accompanying the tanks on the road to provide close-in protection. Captain Sawyer had reasoned that his biggest threat was likely to be enemy infantry astride the road. If his troops stayed off of it, they would be in position to flank any enemy formation that fired on the tanks.

Although only two and a half miles from the Chipyong-ni perimeter in a straight line, Sanggosong is about five tortuous miles away by road. There are two mountain passes, the first only a few hundred meters long, and the second centered in about a mile of high switchbacks. The hills were not heavily forested, but they had more trees than usual—clumps of small scrub trees interspersed with pine—and a great deal of dead grass and brush. The patrol got through the first pass without incident and Sawyer again halted it.

The second pass was a saddle between the crest of Hill 506, a half-mile to the north, and Hill 363, only a few hundred meters to the south. The pass is at about 340 meters elevation, so Sawyer thought it important to clear the hill to the south before trying to go through the pass with his vehicles. His plan was to keep his 1st Platoon and his supporting weapons near the first pass to provide a base of fire for his 2d and 3d Platoons, which would maneuver through the valley and take the hill.

When the maneuvering platoons reached the base of Hill 363, they came under small arms and mortar fire from a force hidden in the scrub brush covering the hillside. The two platoons deployed and returned fire as the company commander ordered the supporting weapons—heavy machine guns, 57-mm recoilless rifles, and 60-mm mortars—to fire on the hillside. At the same time, the artillery observer accompanying the patrol began adjusting fires from Chipyong-ni on the area. After a half-hour, at about noon, the enemy fire stopped and the company began moving again. The plan was for the 2d Platoon to attack toward the pass while the 3d Platoon seized the northern part of Hill 363 and the 1st Platoon took the southern portion.

When the forces were about halfway up the hill, an artillery observation plane flew over at fairly high altitude. A few minutes later the plane was back, this time almost buzzing the unit. The observer dropped a canister with a long, black streamer attached. It landed only a few feet from the soldiers. Inside was a message: "Long column enemy troops headed up hill in your direction." Captain Sawyer did not know how far the enemy troops were from the top of the hill, but he knew that his men were now in a foot race for the summit.

The 3d Platoon reached the north part of Hill 363 by 1330 hours without incident, but when the GIs turned south to link up with the 1st Platoon, they ran into a hail of small arms and machine-gun fire from the crest. At about the same time, other fires stopped the 1st Platoon as it worked its way up the more heavily wooded southern slope. The Chinese defenders had won the race for the hilltop and had both platoons pinned down. The 3d Platoon leader ordered two bayonet charges, but made little progress at the cost of several wounded soldiers. The company commander ordered both platoons to withdraw a hundred yards so he could pepper the hill with direct fire from his tanks and recoilless rifles, and indirect fire from his mortars and the artillery at Chipyong-ni.

By 1530 hours, forty to fifty Chinese were coming down Hill 506 to join the fray when the 2d Platoon opened fire from its position behind the 3d Platoon. Half an hour later, the Americans could see more Chinese approaching from both Hill 506 and Sanggosong. An aerial observer was adjusting artillery on five hundred to six hundred enemy troops in the village at the same time. When Lieutenant Colonel Edwards received word that the patrol was taking fire from the north, south, and east, he ordered Sawyer to withdraw. The 3d Platoon and the tanks covered the withdrawal of the rest of the reinforced company, and it returned to Chipyong-ni without incident. The patrol had cost three dead and eleven wounded, but it had shown that Chinese were in force only a few miles from Chipyong-ni.

The same day, the other regimental patrols were finding evidence of enemy units within striking distance of the 23d Infantry. The French Battalion's patrols reported three different groups of enemy soldiers less than three miles west of the perimeter, and they could not reach their patrol objective because of enemy fire. The 3d Battalion reported enemy dug in to the northeast of the perimeter. Its patrol received mortar fire and broke off to return with its wounded. The 1st Battalion's patrol to the northwest could not get beyond Kosan, only about a mile from the perimeter.

That night, after reviewing the day's action and getting a report from Captain Sawyer, Freeman ordered the 2d Battalion to patrol to Sanggosong on 7 February and return to Chipyong-ni by dark. Lieutenant

Colonel Edwards was to leave Easy Company behind to man the 2d Battalion's perimeter. Edwards's plan was much the same as the one Sawyer had used on the day before, except expanded to battalion size. Reinforced by four tanks, the battalion, minus Easy Company, would move out at dawn and advance to the first pass, then lay down a base of fire while one company advanced to take Hill 363 and secure the second pass. After the craters between the two passes were filled so that tanks could accompany the patrol, the battalion would proceed into the Sanggosong valley.[23]

The "Fighting Foxes" of Capt. Stanley Tyrrell's Fox Company led the battalion as an advance guard, with two tanks attached. Lieutenant Thomas Heath's George Company (less one platoon to serve as the battalion's rear guard) would follow, then the other two tanks, the battalion headquarters element, the heavy weapons company, and the rear guard. The action went according to plan, and Fox Company took Hill 363 by 1030 hours without a fight. The P&A Platoon estimated that it would take two hours to fill the craters and adequately revet the road in places to make it passable for the tanks. Lieutenant Colonel Edwards requested that a platoon of engineers be sent from Chipyong-ni to speed the process, but none was available. Instead, regimental headquarters sent another P&A Platoon from the 1st Battalion to assist.

Lieutenant Colonel Edwards was a cautious commander, wary of risk-taking. He was reluctant to advance far from his tanks and, more importantly, the heavy weapons company's weapons carriers, which had hauled his extra ammunition. Nonetheless, if the mission were to be completed and the return trip begun by dusk, the battalion needed to get moving. Edwards ordered the heavy weapons company's soldiers to dismount and carry as much ammunition as they could, and the battalion—less the tanks and weapons carriers and the pioneers repairing the road—moved out on foot. They had gone less than a mile when the final curve in the road opened onto the panorama of the valley around Sanggosong. Mindful that several hundred Chinese had recently put up a stiff fight in that valley, Edwards decided to halt and wait for his vehicles. The soldiers ate C rations while they waited.

The vehicles arrived by 1300 hours. The plan for clearing the valley was for Tyrrell's Fox Company to take and clear Sanggosong, covered by the rest of the battalion from the south end. When Sanggosong was secure, George Company would move off to the northwest to Hill 506 and then parallel to the valley until it was above Hagosong, half a mile up the valley from Sanggosong. Fox and George Companies would then envelop

Hagosong. Fox Company began its advance at 1310 hours, moving cautiously, and took Sanggosong without opposition. There were no enemy troops to be found in the village, but plenty of evidence that a large body of soldiers had recently been there.

George Company began its arduous climb of Hill 506 as Fox Company's lead elements reached Sanggosong. They found the bodies of several Chinese soldiers and searched them for documents; they also found the body of a GI killed in an earlier action.

At 1430 hours, Edwards ordered Tyrrell to send a cautious probe toward Hills 320 and 218 on the eastern side of the valley above Hagosong. About this time, as mortar shells began falling on the soldiers in Sanggosong, Tyrrell moved his men to the west, out of the village. The firing then stopped, either because the Americans had moved out of range of the mortars or out of visibility of their observation posts. It was now clear that because of its slow progress, George Company would not reach Hagosong before dark. As a result, Edwards changed his plan and ordered the two Fox Company platoons moving toward Hills 320 and 218 to stop and support by fire the 2d Platoon, which he ordered to go directly toward Hagosong.

Fox Company's 2d Platoon leader moved his squads by rushes across the valley floor. When they had covered about half the distance to the village, a storm of fire from Hills 320 and 218 and from Hagosong itself stopped them and pinned them down. Feeling that he had accomplished the mission of this patrol, Edwards ordered Fox Company to withdraw from the valley. His radio went out at that moment, however, and he had to pass the order through the artillery forward observers at battalion and company level. To cover the withdrawal, the artillery, tanks, and mortars began firing on the hills from which the enemy was firing. At the same time, Edwards ordered Lieutenant Heath to abandon George Company's mission and descend directly to the valley floor and rejoin the battalion by the most expeditious route. By 1730 hours, as dusk fell, the patrol was retracing its route.

Edwards ordered one George Company platoon and two of his tanks to remain behind and act as a rear guard, lagging two hundred meters behind the main body. The regiment had sent enough trucks to the first pass to transport the battalion back to Chipyong-ni. In the darkness, however, the rear guard closed on the main body before it had loaded into the trucks. This lapse in security could have proved disastrous had a hostile force been following the rear guard, and there were a few anxious moments before the battalion was loaded and moving with blackout-drive lights to

Chipyong-ni. They reached the perimeter at 2015 hours. Four soldiers had been wounded by mortar fire, but only one was seriously injured.

That same day, 7 February, the 1st Battalion had again sent a patrol to the north—and again it had not been able to go beyond Kosan. From Kosan, however, the patrol could observe a steady stream of soldiers moving about two miles farther north. The Chinese were determined not to let the 23d Infantry's patrols go very far north of their perimeter. Other patrols made contact with the enemy only a few miles to the west and northwest of the perimeter. Division informed the battalion an enemy headquarters was located about seven miles to the northeast. Freeman warned all battalion commanders to be especially vigilant as he expected an attack that night or the next.[24]

During the night of 7 February, division headquarters ordered the 23d to send a battalion to clear out Sanggosong and contact a patrol from the 9th Regiment approaching from the opposite direction. Freeman ordered Lt. Col. Charles Kane's 3d Battalion to carry out this mission. The patrol was to return by 1600 hours; the 2d Battalion would man the 3d's positions at Chipyong-ni until it returned.[25]

The 3d Battalion, reinforced with a platoon of tanks and a section of antiaircraft artillery, moved out at dawn on 8 February, equipped only for a one-day patrol. As events turned out, the patrol would last four days and encounter, as Freeman put it, "every adversity of climate and weather." The sky was low and snow began falling before the lead elements reached the Sanggosong Valley at 1015 hours. The column was fired on from Hill 444 before it reached the village. By noon, Lieutenant Colonel Kane was reporting that elements of his patrol were pinned down in the valley. The enemy did not seem to be too numerous, but they were well dug in and camouflaged. Kane requested instructions on how fully he should commit his forces. Freeman's laconic reply, recorded in the S3 journal, was to "continue to develop the situation." In other words, continue with the mission to take Hill 444 and link up with the 9th Infantry Regiment.[26]

At 1310 hours, Lieutenant Colonel Kane got the bad news that unless the 3d Battalion succeeded in contacting the 9th Infantry patrol, division headquarters had ordered that it stay in the valley overnight and continue with the mission the next day. By then, Kane had companies on the slopes on both sides of the valley, receiving heavy small arms and mortar fire from the Chinese. The 9th Infantry's 1st Battalion had departed its position about twelve miles south of Chipyong-ni and begun moving up the north-south valley east of Hill 444. The soldiers expected to meet the 23d Infantry patrol near Hill 444, but reported that they were still more than two miles away. It was unlikely they would be able to link up before dark.[27]

Kane decided that he would have to clear Hill 539, which dominated the valley from the south, before he could successfully attack Hill 444. He sent King and Love Companies to clear the steep hill while Item Company moved against Hill 506 to the west. Both attacks met stiff resistance, and by dusk, Kane was withdrawing the battalion into two perimeters. The two companies on Hill 539 stayed where they were, while Item Company moved to the pass and set up a perimeter with the armored vehicles and battalion headquarters element. The 9th Infantry's Baker Company was in the valley east of Hill 444.

Kane wanted to pull back to Chipyong-ni because the soldiers had no sleeping bags and had not brought enough heavy shovels to dig in properly, but headquarters ordered him to stay in position and continue the attack the next morning. After a miserably cold but quiet night on the hills, the 3d Battalion and the 1st Battalion, 9th Infantry, began their operations at 0830 hours. The two battalions had coordinated their plans through regimental headquarters. Instead of attacking Hill 539 from the valley, Kane was sending Love Company to Hill 401 to the southwest of Hill 539 so that it could attack through the saddle that connected the two hills. Meanwhile, King Company would move down the valley toward Hill 444 while Item remained in reserve.

By midmorning, Love Company was on Hill 401 and could observe enemy positions on Hill 539. The soldiers could also hear firing to the east coming from the 9th Infantry. King Company, now positioned in the valley, was in a firefight south of Sanggosong and had taken casualties. Because of the terrain, it would take eight hours for four-man litter teams to evacuate the wounded back to the regimental clearing station.

On 9 February, Freeman sent his reserve company, Capt. Sherman Pratt's Baker Company, to Hill 506. This hill dominated the northwest end of the Sanggosong Valley, and with Pratt on it, Kane would not have to worry about clearing it. Pratt's force occupied the crest that afternoon.[28]

The 3d Battalion moved slowly throughout the afternoon, encountering resistance from the entrenched enemy on Hill 539. The 9th Infantry patrol in the valley to the east also made slow progress. By late afternoon, the battalion was again consolidating into perimeters for another night of cold survival, with Love and King Companies on Hill 539 and the other elements back at the entrance to the valley. At 1930 hours, division head-quarters gave operational control of the battalion to the 9th RCT for the duration of the operation.[29]

Near midnight, Kane received his orders for the following day by radio from the 9th Regiment. The attack would go at 0700 hours, with the 1st battalion, 9th Infantry, attacking Hill 442—over a mile south of Hill 444—while Kane's battalion attacked Hill 539. The first battalion to take its objective would assist the other, and then the two would jointly attack Hill 444.[30]

On 10 February, Love and King companies had no trouble getting to Hill 539 as the enemy had abandoned it overnight. Needing resupply, they had requested an airdrop for the morning. Although they delayed their departure for Hill 442 almost two hours waiting for the drop, when it came, the airplane dropped the supply bundles into the 9th Infantry position. Although still short on ammunition, Love and King Companies could wait no longer for resupply, so they moved out to the east. By 1330 hours, Item Company was in Sanggosong. At 1530 hours, the 9th Infantry's battalion commander reported that King and Love Companies were attacking Hill 444 with two of his companies against small arms and automatic weapons fire. At dusk, Kane again closed into his defensive perimeter with Item Company and the vehicles. He also received permission to bring Baker Company down off the mountain into his perimeter for the night. His other two companies remained alongside the 9th Infantry units, skirmishing for control of Hill 444. They moved into their own four-company perimeter late that night.

On the morning of 11 February, King and Love Companies remained on Hill 444 and fired in support of a 9th Infantry attack on Hill 412, half a mile to the northeast. Kane received permission to begin moving Baker and Item Companies back to Chipyong-ni with the vehicles at 0900. On the way back along the twisting mountain road, a tank fell off the shoulder and lay on its side. After requesting a bulldozer to retrieve it at 1300 hours, the crew began stripping it of equipment. Regimental headquarters delayed in calling back with instructions, but finally ordered the patrol to leave a security element to guard the vehicle until 12 February. By that late hour, as the important equipment—radios and weapons—had been removed, Kane recommended that the patrol abandon it until the next day and regiment concurred.

The 9th Infantry released King and Love Companies at about 1530 hours, and the battalion was intact back in its positions at Chipyong-ni by

1700 hours. The one-day patrol planned on 8 February had turned into a four-day ordeal, but now, more by accident than by design, the entire 23d RCT was inside the Chipyong-ni perimeter.[31]

The last unit to join the regiment at Chipyong-ni was Baker Battery, 503d Field Artillery Battalion. It had towed its six 155-mm howitzers through the southern entry into the perimeter between the French Battalion and George Company. Freeman emplaced it near a battery of the 37th Field Artillery Battalion at the southern edge of the perimeter. There the black gunners were in a bowl with high ground on three sides, just north of the hill where George Company was located. In fact, their arrival caused George Company to have to move farther south of its original position, and was one of the factors that resulted in George Company having poorer fighting positions and fewer barbed-wire obstacles to its front than most companies at Chipyong-ni. This development would have unforeseen and unfortunate consequences.[32]

The regiment's other battalions had not been idle while the 3d Battalion was fighting in the Sanggosong Valley. Patrols went out every day in all directions, and reported many observations of enemy soldiers and formations. Patrols brought back reports from civilians of numerous Chinese troops moving through the area, especially north of Chipyong-ni. On 10 February, division forwarded a report of a large enemy formation with twelve hundred horses only six miles north of Chipyong-ni with the apparent mission of enveloping the 23d Infantry there. Air observers reported sighting troops in all directions from the perimeter. A group of UN prisoners released the same day reported seeing five thousand to eight thousand Chinese with pack animals and howitzers seven miles west of the perimeter. On 12 February, 1st Battalion's I&R Platoon patrolled to the north and discovered the Chinese massing in large units. When the patrol returned, Lt. Col. George H. Russell, the battalion commander, had its leader show on the map exactly where they had seen two thousand Chinese in a small valley.[33]

Because of the dark night that was expected on 11 February, the Ranger Company planned a raid on Changdae, a little over a mile west of the perimeter. Recent patrols had observed enemy in and near the village, and Freeman was always eager for prisoners to interrogate. The Rangers planned to station a platoon at one end of the town and then attack the other end it, expecting to capture some of the enemy as they fled. A French journalist, Jean Marie de Premonville, was visiting the French Battalion looking for a story and Capt. François DeCastries encouraged him to accompany the elite American force. The patrol left the perimeter at about 2000 hours. Less than two hours later, soldiers at Chipyong-ni heard shooting to the west and the Rangers reported that they were engaged. They had stumbled into an enemy force well short of Changdae. The enemy, who were dug in, engaged them with burp guns, 82-mm mortars, machine guns, and small arms. The Rangers sustained five casualties, including the French journalist. Having taken no litters, they used the doors from houses to evacuate their wounded. At 2355 hours, they requested ambulance support. One Ranger and the journalist died during the evacuation.[34]

Final Preparations

Both the 23d Infantry and the French Battalion received a number of new personnel during their first ten days at Chipyong-ni. The quality of the soldiers, as well as the reception they received from their units, differed. Replacements for the American regiment were primarily reservists mustered from the inactive reserve and draftees just out of basic training. The Pentagon had decided to call up only inactive reserves. This policy was designed to save the trained reserve units in case the conflict in Korea turned out to be the first gambit of World War III. This decision had unexpected and unfortunate ramifications for the Korean War. Many of the reservists were overweight and unfit, and few were highly motivated. Although by no means a requirement for a good soldier, fewer still were educated—except among the officers, high school graduates were rare, and college degrees were almost unknown. The draftees were little better. Many thought they were "fresh meat" for the war. As a result of these unenlightened replacement policies decreed far away in the Pentagon, units in the field had to try to put men where they were fit to serve. Thus, overweight infantrymen who could not keep up on patrol might find themselves in the mortar company or in the mess hall. Inventive first sergeants always found a niche for every new man somewhere.

Some units had a solid reception program that put new men with experienced soldiers to teach them the ropes, while other units were more haphazard in their treatment of replacements. The worst receptions bordered on hazing. But however they were received, they became veterans and were accepted after they survived their first battle.

The French Battalion, on the other hand, had the luxury of choosing from a pool of carefully screened volunteers. The battalion had brought a replacement pool of about four hundred soldiers, many with combat experience, and all highly motivated. Officers roamed among the volunteers choosing the men they wanted, trying to match them to the distinctive personalities each company had built in France and maintained in Korea. Once in a unit, it was not long before a soldier's chain of command got to know him like a son—or at least a younger brother.

When it became obvious that the regiment was likely going to be surrounded and unable to evacuate its wounded quickly, the regimental surgeon, Dr. Robert Hall, procured stocks of type O "universal donor" whole blood with which to treat the wounded. Blood plasma had been used in World War II and early in the Korean War, but physicians had found that it often contained and transmitted a virus that could cause hepatitis. Whole blood was superior to both plasma and Dextran, a synthetic substance available later in the war, for treating and preventing shock. Whole blood had been used in some instances by surgical teams attached to division clearing stations in World War II, but had not been used as far forward as a regimental area at this time in Korea.

As might be expected, such an unprecedented initiative as stocking whole blood at regimental level met resistance in the bureaucratic world of military medicine. Although the procurement of the blood was the regimental surgeon's idea, much credit should go to Colonel Freeman and his executive officer, Lieutenant Colonel Meszar, whose relationships with the staff allowed such initiatives to surface. They were willing to use their considerable talent for cutting red tape to get the blood, without which unknown numbers of wounded might have died.

On the night of 11 February, the Chinese began the offensive they had been massing for in the area north of Wonju. Four CCF divisions and two NKPA divisions attacked two ROK divisions and routed them about twenty miles east of Chipyong-ni. Several American units in position behind the ROK forces were overrun or abandoned their equipment. Division immediately canceled a reconnaissance that had been planned for the 23d RCT's 2d Battalion. The first indications that something big was occurring reached the 23d's CP at 0215 hours. At about 0545 hours a truly alarming warning arrived:

Fr[om] Div: 3d Bn 38th Inf being attacked from N[orth] & W[est]. 21st ROK coming down to the S[outh] hit a roadblock and are in a mess. Dont know the results. They have wounded. 21st ROKs is falling back 2000 yds. 23d ROK Regt also falling back thru 187 RCT. Higher HQ putting out the order to 9th Inf to be prepare on 3 hrs notice to assemble at YOJU. A similar order is given to the 38th Inf to assemble at WONJU. They might be two reasons for this order, to support us or to establish blocking psn along line MUNMANG-NI to HUNGHO-RI. This is only a warning O[rder].[35]

The rest of X Corps had received a hard blow. Now, every soldier in the 23d Infantry was wondering how long their luck could hold.

Chapter 9

Isolated and Encircled
at Chipyong-ni

*The commander must show by his behavior that the "old man" is
always on the job, that he sees that the rations come up in time, that
the mail is never delivered late, and that he is always looking for
better conditions so as to improve the lot of his men. If on all sides
there is this common tie of service—of the commander serving his
men, of the men serving the commander—this will be a unit truly
formidable in battle.*

—Gen. Maxwell D. Taylor

*Courage, however, is that firmness of spirit, that moral backbone,
which, while fully appreciating the danger involved, nevertheless
goes on with the undertaking. Bravery is physical; courage is mental
and moral. You may be cold all over; your hands may tremble; your
legs may quake; your knees be ready to give way—that is fear. If,
nevertheless, you go forward; if in spite of this physical defection you
continue to lead your men against the enemy, you have courage. The
physical manifestations of fear will pass away. You may never experience them but once.*

—Maj. C. A. Bach

Since his assumption of command in late December, 1950, the Eighth
Army commander, Lt. Gen. Matthew Ridgway, had wanted to go on
the offensive against the North Korean Peoples Army and its ally, the
Chinese Communist Forces. At Wonju in January and at the Twin Tunnels in February, he had experienced limited success. His goal was never so
much holding ground as it was killing the enemy: He wanted to punish
them with paralyzing losses through his strong advantage in artillery and
aviation. On the other hand, the NKPA and CCF had not mounted an

offensive in the five weeks since 4 January 1951, when the UN forces had given up Seoul, but they had now launched a strong offensive in the Wonju region.

On the eve of this Chinese onslaught, Ridgway had the advantage of having received the most thorough intelligence appraisal of Chinese and North Korean capabilities since taking command. In an Eighth Army estimate of the enemy situation dated 10 February 1951, his intelligence officer had predicted that the lull in Chinese offensive operations would end when the enemy remedied their logistical problems. When their forces had reorganized their supply and transportation operations they would be ready to resume the offensive; that time now seemed to be approaching. In none of their statements had the Chinese ever backed away from the goal of driving the UN forces off the Korean peninsula.[1]

In this context, both Ridgway and Lt. Gen. Ned Almond, the X Corps commander, appreciated the 23d Infantry's precarious position at Chipyong-ni. Even before the CCF offensive at Wonju, X Corps intelligence officers were speculating that the enemy's Forty-second Army was in a position "to drive southeast past Chipyong-ni through the gap between the 23rd Infantry Regiment and elements of the 8th ROK Division." Intelligence also indicated that the Chinese had "the capability of either turning southwest and enveloping the Chipyong-ni salient, or of continuing to the southeast to strike at Wonju." In a separate report dated 11 February, the intelligence staff noted that the CCF forces northeast of Chipyong-ni had been further reinforced and were ready to start driving south. "It is becoming increasingly apparent," the report continued, "that the enemy has noted the gap between the 23rd Infantry Regiment and elements of the 8th ROK Division and has decided to take advantage of this situation before the gap is closed."[2] After the strong attack at Wonju, the intelligence report became even more somber:

The initiative has temporarily been taken over by the Chinese Forces. Although his divisions are inferior in size and strength to those of the United Nations, he has found gaps in friendly lines and has been able to penetrate and outflank positions on both sides of the X Corps salient. In order to give weight to this attack, he is employing elements of three [CCF armies], one attacking south from the Hongchon area, and two attacking to the southeast from the Chipyong-ni area. . . .

The enemy capability of eliminating the X Corps salient is now a "fait accompli." The decision to continue his attack to the south remains with the enemy. Since he has been able to penetrate the salient and has additional [CCF armies] available as reinforcements, he definitely possesses the capability to continue the attack.[3]

The Decision to Stay at Chipyong-ni

The 2d Division commander, Maj. Gen. Clark Ruffner, had ordered a battalion-sized patrol to the huge mass of Hill 583, three miles to the southwest of Chipyong-ni, on 12 February. When the Chinese attacked Wonju he canceled that order and began considering plans to withdraw the 23d RCT from its exposed position to its supply base at Yoju, fifteen road miles to the south. It was probably too late for the regiment to withdraw without a fight, however, for on 11 February aerial observers had seen large numbers of enemy troops moving even before the Wonju offensive began. Many of the movements were near the 23d RCT's perimeter at Chipyong-ni, and a division-sized force reportedly had passed east of the 23d's position, moving south. The regiment's supply line to the south was cut on the same day.[4]

The feeling that the regiment would be withdrawing soon was so strong that the commander of the antiaircraft artillery battery worried he might be unable to evacuate all his ammunition, as he had accumulated twice the amount he was authorized to stock. When he requested permission to fire some of it at the surrounding hills, Lieutenant Colonel Meszar, Freeman's executive officer, told him there would be plenty of time the next day.[5]

On the morning of 12 February, General Almond approved the withdrawal, and ordered that it take place on the thirteenth. Ridgway, however, had other plans. He did not want to abandon the key road junction at Chipyong-ni because it blocked the Chinese from easy east-west movement across his front. He could not quickly restore the continuous X Corps front that the Chinese attack had dismantled, but he could move units into positions from which they could come to the 23d RCT's aid in the event of a major battle. He moved the 27th British Commonwealth Brigade, then in reserve at Yoju, and the 6th ROK Division from IX Corps to the west, and gave control of them to X Corps. He ordered a regimental task force from the 1st Cavalry Division and the Commonwealth Brigade to begin moving up on two roughly parallel routes to Chipyong-ni.

Ridgway then made the key reversal: he canceled Freeman's permission to bring his regiment out of Chipyong-ni.[6] At 1610 hours on the

From left: Major General Ned Almond, X Corps commander, confers with Col. Paul Freeman, 23d Regiment commander, and Maj. John Dumaine, the regiment's operations officer, at the regimental headquarters at Chipyong-ni in February, 1951. *Courtesy U.S. Army Military History Institute.*

afternoon of 12 February, the 23d RCT's operations officer recorded this laconic message: "G-3 [Division operations] to Inspire 6 [Freeman]. Our forces are executing a withdrawal except for us. We are to remain. By order of Scotch [Ridgway]."[7]

The Calm before the Storm

During the day it had become clear that the Chinese were conducting major movements in the Chipyong-ni area. Aerial observers reported movement of a major unit—possibly as large as a division—north of Chipyong-ni, just out of range of Freeman's 105-mm howitzers. The CCF column included artillery and animal pack trains, and the longer-ranged

155-mm guns fired on it, causing many casualties—as did fighter-bomber strikes later in the day. Patrols brought in the first Chinese prisoners since the 23d RCT had arrived at Chipyong-ni. Under Freeman's interrogation, they identified elements of five Chinese divisions in the area. The enemy continued moving through the night, under flares and in spite of artillery fire and even radar-controlled bombing. Except for a couple of light probes, the night of 12 February was quiet.[8]

During the daylight hours on 13 February, it became clear to everyone in the perimeter that an attack was inevitable. The soldiers' mood was grim but resolute. According to Lt. Robert Curtis, then serving as a general assistant to Lt. Col. James Edwards in the 2d Battalion, "There was nothing humorous about Chipyong-ni, but morale was high." Captain Glenn C. McGuyer, who commanded Able Company at Chipyong-ni, remembers the determination of the soldiers, the tired but steely look of men who knew they were out in front of the whole X Corps—isolated—and who, if attacked, would be fighting for survival. Bickford Sawyer, the Easy Company commander, recalled: "When Colonel Freeman said at Chipyong, 'We're surrounded, but we'll stay here and fight it out,' we supported him with enthusiasm. There was never a doubt in our minds. We knew we were going to succeed."

The men of the 23d RCT used the bravado and denigration of their enemies that soldiers have always employed to brace themselves for battle. A sergeant in George Company, who was killed less than forty-eight hours later, after telling his men they were surrounded, concluded his squad briefing by saying: "Those stupid slant-eyed yellow bastards! They don't realize it but they have just started to dig their own graves."[9]

On 13 February, Freeman called his commanders together and told them that the regiment was probably surrounded but that he intended to stay and fight it out. He had about fifty-four hundred soldiers inside the perimeter. By dusk, massive numbers of CCF soldiers would be leaving their marshaling areas several miles away and moving into assembly areas near the perimeter. How many units would be involved in the attack will never be known with certainty unless reliable historians can someday gain access to the CCF archives, but estimates range from eighteen thousand to seventy thousand enemy troops. The official U.S. Army history estimated no more than six regiments were involved, whereas Freeman figured he went up against a five-division force. Roy Appleman, a generally reliable and careful combat historian of the war, believes the CCF force consisted of four divisions and a regiment.[10]

Private Seymour Harris was one of the men on the last truck carrying replacements into Chipyong-ni from division. Lieutenant Colonel Edwards briefed the new men, telling them not to leave their fighting positions until ordered out. Edwards impressed Harris as being a competent commander who cared about his men, calling them "son" when he addressed them.

Harris remembers being in a bunker with a recalcitrant misfit of a "foxhole buddy" in the freezing cold, waiting for the attack his squad leader had told him to expect that night. For the individual soldiers, the night was one of waiting and wondering what would come—and when. New soldiers wondered how they would react if the Chinese hit. Although Harris had been a marine in World War II, he had seen little action. Harris later described the night and his thoughts:

> Again it is bitterly cold. The snow creaks loudly underfoot. Even the tree limbs crack and make strange noises. The word is out. Tonight we will have 100% alert. Tonight is the night. There is no place to run, no place to pull back to. Our backs are to the wall. Colonel Freeman and Lieutenant Colonel Edwards have checked and rechecked our positions. They have personally checked fields of fire and made corrections where necessary. "Sleepy Jim" Edwards has said tonight will be "Powder River, let her buck."
>
> Jesus I am praying. Not for my life, but for the guts it will take to see me through this. I pray that I will not let anybody down. That I will be able to do what I came here to do. . . .
>
> I keep thinking I may be killed but not without a fight. I will not lie down like a whipped dog anymore than I had in fistfights at home. If the chinks get me I promised myself they were going to have to work at it. The night drags. I wonder from time to time if I am the only one awake. I cannot yell out to find out because we have been ordered to keep quiet.
>
> Suddenly off to the southeast I hear automatic weapons fire. I do not recognize what kind of weapon that is firing. . . . I see the tracers arcing through the night sky and hear the sound of bugles and shepherds' horns. I am so engrossed that I do not hear [Corporal] Ambrose as he comes up to the bunker and sticks his arm in to touch me on the shoulder. Christ, I jump a foot! "You awake?" he asked. "Hell yes, but you damned near scared me to death! I was watching that firing over there." We discuss the firing and Ambrose says he hopes it is someone trying to get in the back door. He tells me to look sharp; someone is going to drive the chinks right into our lap.

Ambrose asks me about [Harris's foxhole buddy] Minnick. Tells me to make him get the hell up and watch too. I said to hell with him. He's a pain in the ass. Let him sleep. I'll wake him up when the chinks come. . . .

Ambrose starts to leave. He stops, turns to me and says, "Harris!" I say, "Yeah!" He says, "Good luck, man!" I say, "Same to you, pappy. See you in the morning." He says, "Yeah, man."

All over the perimeter, soldiers used similar simple expressions of confidence to bolster one another's courage for the ordeal they expected.

The First Night

As soon as darkness fell, flares lit up the sky in all directions around the perimeter. Although there was a "Firefly" aircraft on call to drop parachute flares, these were not friendly flares. They were used by the Chinese to mark the perimeter destinations for the units marching to attack Chipyong-ni. Until 2207 hours, there was no activity other than the flares. At that time, small arms and mortars abruptly opened up on the positions in the 1st Battalion and French Battalion sectors. The Chinese were blowing horns, whistles, and bugles as they began their assault on Able Company. Division had the flare aircraft overhead within the hour, lighting the battlefield with a ghostly yellow glow.[11]

Freeman and his commanders had stressed to the chain of command that soldiers must be trained not to fire at noises and give away their positions. Mortar fires pinned Charley Company down, but fire discipline was good among the defenders. The soldiers did not shoot at sounds or shadows, but waited until the Chinese soldiers bumped into the trip flares, antipersonnel mines, and booby traps in the dummy positions to the company's front. Then they opened up with the artillery and mortar concentrations that had been preplanned and fired in during the previous week and a half. After falling back in the face of the initial artillery barrage, the Chinese regrouped and attacked again at a little after 0100 hours on 14 February. Moving along a finger of high ground that led into the boundary between Charley and Able Companies, the CCF forces attacked into Charley's flank. The GIs in the foxholes fired no small arms until the Chinese reached the wire in front of their fighting positions, then they opened up with their machine guns, supported by quad-mounted .50-caliber machine guns from the antiaircraft artillery battery. Tanks in the low ground to the right of the French position supported the defense as well. Again the Chinese fell back.[12]

Early on, Freeman's staff arranged for air strikes and the airdrop of supplies for the next day. Should their communication to division fail, they agreed to mark their position with panels in the shape of an A. Freeman knew that if the attack lasted through the night, his soldiers would be low on ammunition by morning. He and Meszar were particularly worried about mortar ammunition, as the mortars were the infantry's primary indirect fire support in the absence of artillery within range of the perimeter.[13]

Captain Sawyer, the Easy Company commander, was ready for anything, with reliable communications both to his platoons and to battalion headquarters. He was in a good position, stretching from King Company on the high ground to the left to Fox Company on the right. Before midnight, the 2d Battalion was receiving flat-trajectory artillery and mortar fire from Hill 397. The battalion was also receiving small-arms fire from the railroad tunnel less than a hundred meters in front of Easy Company's 1st and 2d Platoons. From his position on the high ground in the right center portion of his line, Sawyer could see most of his defensive positions. A platoon-sized enemy force advanced on Easy Company from the mouth of the tunnel, soon followed by a company-sized element. Sawyer called for previously registered mortar concentrations and illumination rounds over his position. Machine guns and the quad-.50-caliber flak wagons opened up on the massed infantry with grazing fire. The first wave advanced through the antipersonnel mines, trip flares, and booby traps heedless of casualties, only to be stopped at the barbed-wire entanglements in front of the position. The defenders halted each attack before the Chinese were able to penetrate their lines.[14]

Shortly after midnight, Easy Company began receiving machine-gun fire from a Chinese gun set up in the tunnel. It posed a problem until a bazooka knocked it out. Finally, in the early morning hours, when another Chinese unit came out of the tunnel, Captain Sawyer ordered soldiers to detonate the *fougasse* container they had dug in, pointed toward the tunnel, in preparation for the battle. It went up with a tremendous explosion and the Chinese never used the tunnel as a departure point again. The next morning, Captain Sawyer found half a dozen corpses piled in front of the barbed-wire barrier in the gully between his 1st and 2d Platoons. They had managed to push a bangalore torpedo, a long pipe filled with explosives used to demolish obstacles, under the barrier, but were killed before they could detonate it.[15]

Seymour Harris's machine-gun squad, which was attached to Easy Company, looked out over a dry creek bed that had been cleared of brush and blocked with a barbed-wire barrier. Covering the approach were two .30-caliber and two .50-caliber machine guns in addition to the infantrymen's small arms. Observers had previously fired in mortar and artillery concentrations as close as possible to the friendly positions.

As darkness fell, Harris was more scared of freezing to death than of the Chinese hiding to his front, but an incident occurred that drove home his commander's earlier admonition to stay in his hole. Before heavy firing began in the Easy Company area, two soldiers asked permission to go to the rear for more carbine ammunition, with the real intent of bumming a cup of coffee from the artillery unit behind their hill. Told to stay in their positions, they started over the hill anyway. They had gone only a short distance when a mortar shell burst nearby, killing one man instantly with a shell fragment that entered the back of his head and exited out his eye. The other soldier was shaken but unhurt. Edwards's earlier admonition to stay in his hole rang in Harris's ears.

The Chinese did not neglect the French Battalion. The 1st Company began receiving mortar fire more than an hour before midnight. A short time later, a machine gun opened up on the railroad station and a bazooka hit one of the American tanks positioned between the French ROK Company and the 1st Company. Major Maurice Barthelemy was, as usual, the eyes and ears of the battalion commander, moving to critical positions and taking action as necessary. At 2315 hours, another attack hit the area near the railroad station, where a pioneer section and a recoilless rifle and heavy machine-gun section from the heavy weapons company were in position. The French had found a hand-operated siren in a machine shop at Wonju. When the Chinese attacked, they cranked the siren into a wail. It was not only a morale builder for the defenders and a psychological blow to the attackers, it also made it harder for the attackers to hear the whistles and bugle calls that they used as signals.

As the enemy slid along the railroad track, the pioneers defending the railroad station awaited the attack with discipline, not firing a shot until the attackers arrived at the foot of the raised gravel railroad embankment. When the Chinese finally launched their screaming assault, the French soldiers opened up with all their weapons and slaughtered the attacking unit. The Chinese left twenty-two dead and eleven wounded who surrendered at dawn. Just before midnight, Barthelemy reinforced the 2d Company and pioneers defending the station with a section from 3d Company, which he had held in reserve. Barthelemy also was worried

An M4A3E8 Sherman tank burns inside the perimeter at Chipyong-ni after a Chinese attack. *Courtesy U.S. Army Military History Institute.*

about the high ammunition expenditure and warned all units to economize on their usage.[16]

After midnight, the 23d RCT experienced its heaviest artillery bombardment ever, even heavier than on the Naktong River line. This included 120-mm Soviet mortars and 76-mm guns. Early on, the fires were not particularly accurate, but soon a shell hit a flak wagon and set it ablaze and another started a fire near the 1st Battalion CP. Although the artillery illumination ammunition and the flares being dropped by the flare aircraft from midnight on could be adjusted to illuminate the enemy outside the perimeter without revealing friendly positions, the Americans were now clearly silhouetted by the fires inside the position. This allowed the Chinese to adjust their fires much more accurately, and at times the interior of the perimeter was as dangerous as the fighting positions surrounding it.

Shells fell with increasing accuracy on command posts and artillery and mortar positions as well as on supply dumps and aid stations, causing numerous casualties. The irony of the headquarters personnel in relatively clean, safe jobs receiving more artillery than the soldier in a foxhole was not lost on the infantrymen, one of whom admitted that, "One way, we kinda liked that." During the shelling after midnight, a round hit the regimental CP tent, killing the regimental intelligence officer, Maj. Harold Shoemaker, instantly, and knocking Lieutenant Colonel Meszar down.[17]

The most critical portions of the perimeter after midnight were the sectors occupied by the 2d Battalion—George Company in particular—and the French. Although the French had the poorest positions, they had the best fields of fire. The flak wagons had a field day, killing hundreds of Chinese as they tried to make their way across the open ground from Hill 248, which dominated the French lines. The French had reevaluated their tactics after the battle at Twin Tunnels, where they had found most of their dead in foxholes. As a result, they made a dummy defensive line forward of their main positions at Chipyong-ni. When the Chinese attacked, the men in the forward line abandoned their foxholes and fell back as the defenders in the primary positions jumped out of their holes and attacked the Chinese with fixed bayonets. Some of the French soldiers preferred other weapons to the bayonet for close-in fighting, and they launched wild attacks with whatever they had at hand: machetes, axes, clubs, and fighting knives. Few Chinese attackers persisted when they encountered these wild men.[18]

The topographic feature that made George Company's position so dangerous for the defenders and so attractive as a target for the Chinese to concentrate on was the saddle that connected it to the dominating Hill 397 to the south. This saddle was really a fingerlike ridge that stretched forward of the center of the George Company position to meet a finger extending north from Hill 397. It thus constituted a natural approach for the Chinese on Hill 397 to use to guide into George Company's position. Additionally, of the American positions, this was the weakest. George had been forced to move farther south late in the occupation of Chipyong-ni when the 155-mm battery arrived, thus putting it on a low ridge that was not as dominant as most of the other American hills. Additionally, the move meant that George Company had less time to prepare strong defenses than the other companies.

Lieutenant Thomas Heath, commanding George Company, put his 1st Platoon on a knob on his right flank, and tied it into the French Battalion's 1st Company at the road leading out of Chipyong-ni to the south. This platoon held about 150 meters until a small saddle connected it to the 3d Platoon. The 3d Platoon stretched a little farther, to where the ridge dropped off into rice paddies, where the 2d Platoon's line began and continued on until it tied into Fox Company on the left. The finger of ground connecting the position to Hill 397 led directly into the 3d Platoon's lines. The company had good observation to the front, with only one bit of dead space, a dry creek bed a few hundred meters to the front. Beyond the creek bed were a dozen or so huts that made up the village of Masan. The GIs dug fighting positions slightly forward of the crest of the ridge.[19]

At about the same time that the northern perimeter was being hit, soldiers in George Company heard whistles and sounds of digging to their front. About 2300 hours, two CCF squads probed the line, one crawling along the saddle from Hill 397, the other into the point where the 1st and 3d Platoons joined, taking advantage of the dead space in front of the line. The squad that hit the 3d Platoon crawled close enough to Cpl. Eugene Ottesen's machine-gun position to throw grenades at him before opening up with rifles. Ottesen returned their fire.[20]

Hearing his machine gun firing, the platoon leader, Lt. Paul J. McGee, called Lieutenant Heath and his squad leaders to keep them informed. To conserve ammunition, he warned his squad leaders to fire only at targets they could see. Shortly thereafter, a grenade wounded one of the squad leaders, Cpl. James Mougeat. After calling out, "Lieutenant McGee, I'm hit!" Mougeat crawled out of his foxhole and ran toward McGee's foxhole. This action attracted more enemy grenades, one of which knocked the corporal's rifle out of his hands before his soldiers shot the Chinese. When he arrived at McGee's hole, he crawled in and Lieutenant McGee spent a few minutes quietly talking to him and reassuring him that he could carry on. Recovering his composure, Mougeat said, "I'm not hit bad," and then returned to his squad.[21]

Two George Company soldiers were killed and ten more wounded in the attacks before midnight. Shortly after the 155-mm guns arrived, Lieutenant Heath had coordinated with their commander for assistance in defending his position should it become necessary. The battery was situated in a rice paddy about a hundred meters or so behind Heath's lines. Now, because of the losses that had thinned his lines, he asked for a machine gun from the segregated artillery battery. The commander responded with a .50-caliber heavy machine gun and crew. Four black artillerymen and their sergeant occupied a position in the 1st Platoon line and defended it through the rest of the night.[22]

George Company received its strongest ground attack at 0230 hours 14 February. Two white flares went up from the village of Masan, which apparently served as the headquarters for CCF forces south of Chipyong-ni. A few minutes later, six separate squad-sized attacks hit the line. At the same time, a platoon-sized attack again hit the area between the 1st and 3d Platoons and managed to penetrate some of the positions before being repulsed. Finally, at about 0330 hours, George Company repulsed the last Chinese attack from Hill 397 that night. This attack again broke through the 3d Platoon position and Heath had to request help from nearby tanks to plug the hole. Major Lloyd K. Jensen, the 2d Battalion executive officer, committed the reserve platoon he had held out of Fox Company's line, and it restored the position. Also joining the fray was the Baker Battery machine gun that had been sent to shore up George Company's defenses. The gun fired fourteen hundred rounds in the early morning hours of 14 February.[23]

Ammunition shortages were almost as worrisome as the Chinese. At 0147 hours, before the heaviest combat of the night occurred, the heavy mortar company reported that it was down to only 649 rounds. Major John Dumaine, the regimental operations officer, ordered the company to fire only with his staff's approval. He notified all battalions of the situation and instructed them to rely on their own 81-mm and 60-mm mortars instead. Unfortunately, those stocks were dwindling as well.[24]

The main attack on the railroad station in the French 1st Company sector hit at about 0130 hours. The Chinese were probably hoping to overrun the artillery position behind the French lines. The French had received no ground attacks since repulsing the initial attack on the station before midnight. A number of mortar rounds had hit inside their lines, however, causing several casualties. By 0215 hours, Capt. François DeCastries, the 1st Company commander, had to request reinforcements. The attacking force came in two company-sized rushes from the west and the southwest. Although the automatic weapons and flak wagons killed dozens of Chinese in the open ground in front of DeCastries's position, the attackers hit with enough force to penetrate his lines. Major Barthelemy immediately ordered two squads from the reserve company to reinforce DeCastries. This was his last reserve, and at 0253 hours the French intelligence officer had to report to regimental headquarters that they were hard pressed, with no reserves left. Regimental headquarters ordered George Company's heavy machine guns, to the east of the 1st Company, to fire in support of the French unit. Regiment also sent four tanks to assist the 1st Company. Finally, at 0424 hours, the 1st Company could report that it was again secure.[25]

There were other strong attacks that night against Charley and King Companies. King Company was on a comfortably high hill facing southeast. Lieutenant Colonel Kane had checked all the positions, which were forward of the crest but not on the military crest, where they could have seen the base of the hill. He felt that putting the foxholes on the military crest would have sacrificed too much of the advantage the height would give them by tiring the Chinese as they climbed the hill. After the fighting at Twin Tunnels, King Company was at only about 60 percent strength, causing the line to be a little thin—"drafty," as soldier slang expressed it—with fewer soldiers to hold the hill than he would have liked.

In spite of their reduced numbers, they had an advantage in armament. King Company soldiers were notorious scroungers, and one soldier said, "It seemed like every other soldier had a BAR, and those not carrying a BAR carried BAR ammunition." The soldiers carried more ammunition than most: every man was packing four bandoleers of machine-gun ammunition and as many grenades and as much personal ammunition as he could carry. They also had extra communications capability. Although a company was authorized only two SCR-300 radios, King Company had seven. The only problems this caused were that they had to get rid of them for inspections, and the battalion supply staff could not understand why the company went through so many more batteries than other units. Fighting positions were good, two to four feet deep so that soldiers could get out of them quickly, but none had overhead cover.

The heaviest attack on King Company came in the early morning hours. It had been hit with artillery and probed before midnight, when barrages shook the hill and soldiers experienced a "rain" of artillery unlike any they had known before. The Chinese got close enough to lob grenades, but generally overthrew the foxholes, while the Americans could gently toss their grenades and let them roll into the attackers. When the Chinese were hit, they would scream and then let out a chilling laughing sound the King Company soldiers found unnerving. When the Chinese kept coming, Lieutenant Colonel Kane sent two platoons from Item Company, which was on the left and not being hit, to help King. The company held out and did not relinquish a single position. By 0310 hours, the situation was again stable in King Company's sector.[26]

From about 0420 hours until near dawn, the Chinese again hit Charley Company, trying to get the high ground so that they might "roll up" the 1st Battalion line in the north. Their hearts were no longer in the fight for that night, however, and the company held.[27]

At 0530 hours, a final Chinese assault hit the French 1st Company. The soldiers were getting sleepy after a hard night, but an alert machine gunner saw Chinese moving into position to attack and the whole company opened fire. Two 75-mm recoilless rifles were near the CP and added to the carnage. The Chinese retreated behind a small ridge for a few minutes before the French jumped out of their holes and charged the surprised enemy with fixed bayonets. They scattered the formation, but not before grabbing fourteen hapless soldiers by the scruffs of their necks and dragging them back as prisoners. Under Freeman's interrogation, the prisoners, including an officer, confirmed that the perimeter was being attacked by elements of five divisions with a total strength of about thirty thousand.[28]

Daylight and Freeman's Injury

The regiment had made it through the night surprisingly well. As Freeman put it in retrospect: "We had had a rough night but had not really been in grave danger at any point. No [regimental] reserves had been committed and we had not suffered too many casualties. Our principal difficulty in our cut-off position was, again, ammunition replenishment and evacuation of about 200 wounded."

Near dawn, while there was still fighting going on, Colonel Freeman was trying to get a little rest in the ragged tent he shared with Lieutenant Colonel Meszar when a 120-mm mortar shell hit nearby. A fragment of the shell smashed into Freeman's left leg just above the ankle. Meszar called the regimental surgeon, Capt. Robert Hall, and he arrived quickly to treat the wound. When Hall arrived, Meszar and Freeman were discussing how lucky Freeman was. Moments before the round landed he had reversed his position, so that his ankle was where his head had been a few minutes earlier. Had he not done so, the shell fragment would have given him a severe and possibly fatal head wound. As it was, the wound was painful but not serious. Hall removed the shell fragment and dressed the wound. Freeman was upset that the round that had wounded him had shattered the regiment's last bottle of bourbon. He had promised it to the first patrol to bring in a live Chinese prisoner for interrogation.[29]

Freeman's injury, although minor, would have caused his evacuation in normal circumstances. But these were not normal circumstances, and Captain Hall did not recommend his evacuation. Later that morning, Col. Gerald Epley, the 2d Division chief of staff, called Hall and asked about Freeman's condition. Hall described the wound and told him that he believed evacuating Freeman was not only unwarranted but also unwise. Everyone expected the Chinese to attack again and knew that the ammunition supply was critically low. Hall stressed that morale was high and said he believed that this was because of the great respect and confidence the soldiers had for Freeman. He said he thought Freeman's presence was the main reason the perimeter was still intact. Finally, he reiterated that Freeman's wound was a relatively minor one and that there was no medical reason for evacuating him and that there was every tactical reason for keeping him at Chipyong-ni. Nonetheless, when word of Freeman's injury reached General Almond, he acted immediately to replace the regimental commander. Without consulting General Ruffner, the division commander, Almond ordered his operations officer, Lt. Col. John H. Chiles, to fly to Chipyong-ni and take command.[30]

When Freeman heard that he was to be relieved, he became furious. He refused to give up command or to be evacuated. When Chiles arrived, Freeman told him to stay out of his way until he decided to leave. Freeman argued with the division commander on the radio until Ruffner turned the matter over to his assistant division commander, Brig. Gen. George Stewart, to settle. Stewart had a long talk with Freeman by radio. Freeman argued that being relieved of command while his regiment was in combat was the worst disgrace an officer could suffer. Stewart argued that he had to comply with the corps commander's order, and that Freeman would undoubtedly be decorated and promoted. Finally, after Stewart had convinced him that no one questioned his performance, Freeman agreed to come out—but at a time of his own choosing.[31]

Daylight revealed scenes of carnage in and in front of all sectors of the perimeter. The Chinese had been beaten off, losing many soldiers to the regiment's fires. The soldiers had set about repairing what damage they could and preparing for another night. As Freeman described it:

all hands that could be spared from improving their positions on the hills were set to protecting interior installations. The frozen ground was difficult to dig in, but fortunately there was an abundance of railroad ties and bags of rice in the vicinity to use for revetments, and [aid] stations, [command posts], fire direction centers, and supply dumps were protected as well as possible, but without overhead cover.

Ammunition was distributed, weapons cleaned and readied, routes reconnoitered by the reserve commanders so as to be able to lead their units to any point in the darkness, wires spliced, armored vehicles serviced, trip

General Ruffner arrives at Chipyong-ni in an Air Force helicopter. *Courtesy U.S. Army Military History Institute.*

flares and mines reset, and numerous other tasks accomplished during the day's lull. Patrols were sent out as far as necessary to provide early warning of any daylight attack. Good, hot meals were served and the garrison, with fine spirit, determination, and confidence, waited for the next move.[32]

During the day, Capt. Albert Metts Jr., commanding Mike Company, the 3d Battalion's heavy weapons company, visited one of his heavy machine-gun positions. The .50-caliber piece was solidly sandbagged for stability, and the crew had a twenty-power spotting scope at the position. A soldier said they could see Chinese soldiers crossing a road about a thousand meters away. Metts watched the action, first timing the interval between soldiers. Then the crew fired a burst at the location and measured the time of flight of the projectiles. After a few experimental rounds, they decided to fire just as each enemy soldier hit the ditch at the far side of the road. The round hit the next soldier to cross, and this was repeated time after time. Soldiers gathered with binoculars and watched the action, cheering when hits were made. One said it was more fun than the shooting gallery at a carnival.

Colonels Freeman and Monclar used the day to visit fighting positions and talk to their soldiers. Seymour Harris, who had survived his first night of combat the night before, remembers the only time he saw Freeman:

> I had just got back to our position and stood talking to [Sgt. Stewart] O'Shell when I saw this guy coming toward us walking with a limp, and using a staff about five feet long as an aid. I called O'Shell's attention to him. He said, "Oh, that's Colonel Freeman, the regimental commander." As he drew closer I could see he was frowning as if in pain when he made his way toward us. Stew said, "Hi colonel, what's the situation here?" Freeman said, "Hi Stew. Oh the silly bastards have got us surrounded. By God I hope they try to come in here tonight. We'll bloody their damned noses good."
>
> Now the colonel is alone. Not even a radioman is tagging along let alone another officer. That impressed me. All he had on was a .45 and a short fur lined jacket. You have to understand that when a high-ranking officer came up on line or mixed with the troops he had a radioman with him armed to the teeth. We used to call him the "bodyguard." And he usually had a train of brass with him that to us resembled a bunch of sissies. . . . Lots of times they'd have scared looks on their face. Other times they'd try to act macho. But we saw through that behavior in a hurry. On line you get to be a keen judge of people. Instinct tells you how much is for real.
>
> If an officer came up we enlisted men watched him like a hawk. His demeanor, does he act nervous. How does he talk. Does he pay attention to a sergeant when a sergeant tries to tell him something or does he act indifferent. . . .
>
> Freeman got down the best he could to check our fields of fire. When he saw the machine guns couldn't be depressed far enough to hit chinks if they got within eight to ten yards of the embankment we were on, he told O'Shell to make sure we had plenty of grenades just in case, and to warn ammo bearers like me to be ready to get out of the bunker and make with grenades and rifle fire.
>
> I know he wanted to get in the bunker to see what he could see for himself, but his gimpy leg prevented that. This gives you a good idea of how thorough Colonel Freeman was in making sure everything was just right. He left nothing to chance.
>
> As he started to leave that morning he turned to Stew and wished him

luck. Stew said, "Good luck to you sir." As he passed me I'm sure he recognized me as a new man. He looked me hard in the eye and said, "Same to
you, soldier." I nodded and said, "Same to you sir."

Colonel Freeman—I would have followed him into the deepest part of
hell. He was a soldier's soldier.

In less than five minutes, Freeman had imprinted his brand of leadership
on a new soldier and given him inspiration that would stay with him not
only through Chipyong-ni, but also through an army career.

Resupply

The X Corps was winning a great victory at Wonju on that Valentine's
Day, massacring about five thousand Chinese in a tremendous display of
artillery firepower and air strikes. Because of this, however, there was little
close air support available in support of the fighting at Chipyong-ni.
Fighter-bombers flew only three sorties all day.[33]

The major need during the daylight hours on 14 February was ammunition resupply. Although snow in Japan delayed their arrival until 1515
hours, twenty-four C-119s parachuted pallets of supplies into the perimeter. The Chinese were still observing, however, and kept up a steady rain
of mortar shells on the drop zone during the recovery operations. The Chinese also sniped at soldiers who were out retrieving supplies, but they were
so far away that the sniper fire was ineffective. Seymour Harris remembers
being on the retrieval detail and hearing an occasional buzzing sound.
When he asked an experienced veteran what the sound was, he was told it
was a sniper's spent round and not to worry about it. Later he discovered
that even a spent round could cause a serious wound.[34]

There was great disappointment when the GIs opened the containers.
Logisticians in Japan had sent the sort of supplies an average army regiment might need and not what the 23d RCT specifically needed at that
time. The drops included food, water, gasoline, and artillery ammunition.
However, the regiment had a source of clean freshwater inside the perimeter and needed none from outside; it was not moving, so it needed no gasoline; and the artillery inside the perimeter could not fire at close-in targets,
so there was no critical need for artillery ammunition. What was critical
was mortar and small arms ammunition, but the drops included no mortar ammunition, and the .30-caliber ammunition was loose, not packed in
clips for the M1 Garand rifles the soldiers carried. A small sheet-metal clip

The sky is dotted with parachutes laden with supplies for the beleaguered garrison at Chipyong-ni during an aerial resupply mission in February, 1951. *Courtesy U.S. Army Military History Institute.*

was used to hold eight rounds together, which the rifle forcefully ejected several feet after the last round was fired. The clips were meant to be expendable, and they were difficult to find around a foxhole, especially at night. Because they were not intended for reuse, they were flimsy and difficult to reload, unlike the sturdy magazines used by the carbine and BAR.[35]

Already angry at being relieved of command, Freeman was enraged by the bungled resupply drop. He called General Almond and berated him for not sending his regiment the ammunition it needed, telling him it was his responsibility as corps commander to ensure the beleaguered garrison received what it needed. At one point he asked, "Why don't you drop me a parachute-load of bourbon—I could do more fighting with it than with the stuff you're sending me." The soldiers would have to ration their ammunition use through another night.

Although most of the ammunition parachutes fell inside the perimeter because of their great weight, some of the parachutes carrying lighter

A U.S. Air Force C-119 "Flying Boxcar" drops a load of supplies to the Chipyong-ni garrison on 13 February 1951. *Courtesy National Archives.*

loads of supplies drifted outside of it, and the soldiers could observe the Chinese retrieving them. Captain Metts, the 3d Battalion's heavy weapons company commander, remembers a pallet with cans of water that fell about half a mile outside the perimeter. Soldiers spotted a Chinese patrol moving to retrieve the cargo and opened up on it with mortars and machine guns, killing and driving off the members of the patrol. An hour later, a second Chinese patrol headed toward the parachute. This time the artillery joined in the firing. The process continued until dark. The next day the cans of water were gone, leaving the soldiers wondering what the Chinese thought of the prize they had gained at such cost.

There were some positive outcomes as a result of the parachute drop. Even though they did not deliver the badly needed ammunition, the sight of the huge cargo planes dropping parachute-loads of supplies raised morale and lessened the sense some of the soldiers had of being isolated and forgotten. The parachutes were color coded by the type cargo they were dropping, and the soldiers gathered them and lined their foxholes with them. For the rest of their time at Chipyong-ni, many of the foxholes were brightly colored instead of dirty. One observer remarked that the French sector, with gaily-colored chutes displayed over the positions, resembled a gypsy encampment. Other soldiers used white parachutes to camouflage their fighting positions in the snow.

As the 23d RCT continued to dig in and recover from the night's punishment, General Ridgway was pushing units forward to relieve Chipyong-ni. To the southwest, a tank-heavy task force from the 1st Cavalry Division was trying to break through the Chinese forces that had cut the main supply route, while the Commonwealth Brigade was trying to get through on the road through the tunnels area. Soldiers heard a rumor that one of the forces might get to them that day, but by sunset, neither was close. The men were forced to prepare themselves mentally and physically for another night of punishment.[36]

Chapter 10

Fighting and Surviving on the Second Day

The fighting man's confidence must rest on three things—his leader, his weapon, and himself. His leader can often do little to guide him once battle is on. His weapon cannot make him a smaller target to the aimed or unaimed fire of the enemy. Only the man by himself, through knowledge of what a trained fighter must do to live and fight, can handle himself as he must if battles are to be won.
—Infantry Journal, *1942*

The soldiers of the 23d Infantry Regiment and its French Battalion went into the second night of their siege with a mixture of confidence and foreboding. The word of Freeman's injury had rippled through the command on the rumor network at the same time it was being relayed down the official chain of command. Freeman's reputation for cool assessment and reaction to tactical situations had buoyed the soldiers' self-assurance in their ability to outlast the enemy at Chipyong-ni, but this quality had its negative aspect. With Freeman injured and a new commander already on the scene, the soldiers wondered whether Freeman would stay—and, if not, whether the new colonel would have "the right stuff" to carry them through the ordeal. Freeman's refusal to be evacuated or relieved inspired his units at the same time it made them feel that maybe Freeman had judged his replacement to be the wrong man at the wrong time.

The last airdrops were still coming in as darkness fell. In the waning light, soldiers could see the Chinese coming out of their daytime hiding places and forming into assault units all around the perimeter. The 2d Battalion observed them forming up on Hill 397 and the 3d Battalion saw them gathering in villages to the east. They engaged them with artillery and tank fire, but mortar ammunition was so short that the regimental headquarters withheld the authorization to fire the heavy mortars.[1]

Meanwhile, relief forces continued to approach Chipyong-ni. The 1st Cavalry Division's 5th Cavalry Regiment reported that it had crossed the Han River, although Chinese forces had engaged it and were trying to slow it down eight miles to the southwest. The commander intended to continue to move toward Chipyong-ni during the night. The Chinese also were hitting the 27th British Commonwealth Brigade to the southeast, but it was continuing as well.[2]

Freeman continued to hold Baker Company, the Rangers, and the engineers in regimental reserve. Major John Dumaine, the regimental operations officer, ordered each battalion to designate one man to stand by as a guide for the reserves as required during the night. Division notified the regiment that a Firefly aircraft would be on station throughout the night to drop illumination flares as required, an invaluable tool for illuminating the battlefield on call. The light from the flares was sufficient to prevent large concentrations of Chinese from surprising the defenders, and Freeman said the illumination "helped save our skins as much as any other gadget of the grim business of night fighting."[3]

The Chinese had not pulled back far from the perimeter during the day, so their approach marches were shorter and their attacks began earlier that evening. They launched an hour-long concentration of artillery and mortar fire at dark, hitting most areas inside the perimeter. Several UN soldiers had found bugles on dead Chinese during the day and they blew them when they heard bugles outside the perimeter, causing occasional confusion among the attackers that night. George Company heard whistles in front of its position at 1915 hours, and the Chinese launched the first attack of the night in the King Company sector at 2025 hours. There were further attacks and indirect fire in all sectors before midnight, but it soon began to appear that the Chinese were going to concentrate in the sectors that had seemed most vulnerable the first night: those held by the 2d Battalion, especially George Company, and the French Battalion.[4]

At 2100 hours the regiment got bad news from both relief forces. Neither was closer than six miles to the perimeter, and both were stopping for the night. The forces inside the perimeter were on their own for another night. Everyone's biggest concern was the ammunition supply. Other than rifle ammunition, the French Battalion had a total of only 750 machine-gun cartridges, eight 60-mm mortar shells, and twenty-five grenades. The situation was the same in the American battalions, although the regiment had some extra bazooka rounds stockpiled. The only ammunition that had not been depleted was the artillery's. Those supplies remained plentiful because the short distance from the guns to the perimeter was less than their minimum range, making it impossible for the gunners to provide protective fires close to the defensive positions. The foot soldiers, who had been fighting for more than twenty-four hours, were disgusted by the ammunition situation and worried about the night ahead.[5]

The Chinese attacked at many points on the perimeter. They also rained mortar and artillery fire on the defenders, and generally made things uncomfortable. It became obvious that the Chinese had observed the perimeter carefully during the day, as they brought accurate fires on the command posts in and around the village. The Chinese were using captured American 105-mm and 155-mm artillery pieces and ammunition. Fortunately for the defenders, the CCF gunners failed to unscrew the nosepieces from the 155-mm shells and insert fuses. As a result, the projectiles did not explode, thus causing little damage—nonetheless, the incoming artillery fire was still unnerving.[6]

The most dangerous attacks were in George Company's sector. During the daylight hours, soldiers from the company and the artillerymen to their rear had made additional preparations after the difficult time they had the previous night. Half a mile west of the road that cut between George Company and the French 1st Company was a house that the French suspected the Chinese were using as a command post or mortar fire direction center. Captain John Elledge, the battalion's artillery liaison officer, ordered the 503d Field Artillery Battalion's howitzers to destroy it with white phosphorous rounds. White phosphorous rounds are incendiary rounds that explode and burn with a huge cloud of white smoke, setting fire to any combustibles in the area. Sergeant James Webb cranked his howitzer down and sighted it through the tube at the target, then put three rounds on the house. When the hut began burning, about fifteen Chinese ran from it and eight were cut down by machine-gun fire.[7]

Lieutenant Thomas Heath, the acting George Company commander, visited the artillery battery and coordinated defensive plans with Captain Elledge and Lt. Arthur Rochnowski, the battery commander. All agreed that the most likely target of attacks that night would be the 3d Platoon area in the center of the line, where the Chinese had experienced their greatest success the night before. In addition to the two machine guns Rochnowski's black artillerymen were already manning in the 3d Platoon sector, he now agreed to set up two BAR positions and three other outpost positions behind it. He also agreed to furnish up to forty additional personnel to bolster the company's defenses if it became necessary that night.

The 3d Platoon conducted a short patrol forward of its position. The men found a number of Chinese corpses as well as wounded soldiers. They checked the corpses for weapons and documents. Wounded enemy troops who cooperated were evacuated to the regimental aid station and treated; those that did not were killed. A man whose leg had almost been blown off tried to kill Lieutenant McGee before he shot him. Another time, as the lieutenant tried to turn a corpse over, another body a few feet away turned out to be a very alive and combative soldier who rolled over and tried to shoot McGee with a burp gun before an alert corporal killed the man with a bayonet.

Although the first night had been one of hard fighting, George Company had taken surprisingly few casualties. This made the soldiers confident—perhaps, as events would transpire, overconfident—and some were not psychologically prepared for the night that lay ahead.

The first attack on George Company began as a probe in the saddle between 1st Platoon on the right and 3d Platoon in the center just after 2000 hours. At the same time, a second small force moved against Corporal Ottesen's machine gun in the 3d Platoon. A machine gun on Hill 397 fired at the top of the hill in support of the attack. The Chinese were successful in taking two foxholes at the left end of the 1st Platoon position. From there they moved to the right against the rest of the 1st Platoon line, using pole charges. They crept to the next fighting positions and extended the explosives into the holes, killing four men in the next two holes. With those positions in hand they held the entire left half of the 1st Platoon sector. The Chinese quickly set up a machine gun and began firing into Lieutenant McGee's 3d Platoon line to the east.

When McGee began receiving fire from his flank, he suspected that the 1st Platoon had lost some of its positions. He called the company commander on the field telephone and asked if the 1st Platoon was still holding its line. Lieutenant Heath called the 1st Platoon leader and asked if his line was intact. At this point, things began to become fatally muddled. Unknown to Heath, the 1st Platoon leader was not on the hill with his platoon, but in a hut to the rear of it, maintaining only telephone contact with his platoon sergeant on the hill. The platoon leader called his sergeant who, from his position at the right end of the line, knew nothing of the losses that had occurred. By the time the sergeant had wrongly certified to the platoon leader that the line was holding and the platoon leader had relayed this misinformation to Lieutenant McGee, the Chinese had followed up the machine-gun fire from his right with a ground attack on McGee's positions. By then it was 2200 hours.

In retrospect, Lieutenant McGee was particularly bitter concerning the lack of initiative and integrity shown by the 1st Platoon leader on the night of 14–15 February. He attributed it to poor leadership by the company commander, who was not at Chipyong-ni. (Lieutenant Heath was the acting company commander while the captain was on a rest-and-recreation pass in Japan.) He felt that the commander and a clique of key NCOs had been running the unit in "a partial fashion," apparently playing favorites and not exerting strong supervisory control of the company. He said that key NCOs stayed in the rear with the 1st Platoon leader during the action.[8]

The 1st Platoon leader's ignorance of the Chinese in his position had more serious consequences than those affecting Lieutenant McGee. Had the true situation on the hill been known in the first hour or so after the line was broken, a determined platoon or even squad-sized counterattack could probably have restored it. After that, counterattacks up to reinforced company size would fail throughout the day. The timing of any counterattack is crucial: if one is launched too soon, it will meet a determined enemy with momentum, not yet weakened by the defenders' fires. Too late, and the enemy will have consolidated the position, making it nearly impregnable.

Lieutenant McGee looked to the right and saw a group of four Chinese crawling toward his right squad leader's position, approaching it from the rear. His sound-powered radio was out, so he yelled for the squad leader to throw a grenade to his right rear. The Chinese machine gun was keeping the squad leader down in his hole, so it was left for McGee and his runner, Pvt. Cletis Inmon, to kill the soldiers with rifle fire.

Lieutenant McGee looked down the hill and saw a group of Chinese leave the dry creek bed and launch a frontal attack on his right squad. Again he called the information to the squad leader, but again the fire from the sergeant's right kept him from reacting. The Chinese began lobbing grenades toward the squad leader's three-man hole, and one of them wounded him. The squad leader jumped from his hole, along with another sergeant, and ran and jumped into McGee's hole, landing on top of him and Private Inmon, yelling "Lieutenant McGee, I'm hit, Lieutenant McGee, I'm hit." McGee ordered the men back to their position, and then had to repeat the order. The squad leader was hit twice more as he crawled back. McGee arranged for their evacuation under fire.

At some point during the melee, Private Inmon was also hit. McGee reassured him while at the same time desperately fighting off further attacks on his position. McGee had now accumulated his runner's M1 Garand rifle as well as a BAR and his own carbine. He kept trying to use the BAR because of its greater volume of fire, but the airdrop had crimped some of the cartridges and the weapon jammed every ten or fifteen rounds. For a while he used his penknife to extract the jammed cartridges, but he dropped it and could not find it in the dark. Inmon handed McGee the knife from his mess kit, but it was too large and the lieutenant had to abandon the BAR.

McGee realized he needed help. He sent another runner to find Lieutenant Heath at the command post on the next knoll behind the front line to tell him he needed men, ammunition, and litter teams. Lieutenant Heath called to the artillery commander who quickly rounded up fifteen men. As the runner led them up the hill and over the crest, enemy fire hit them, killing one man and wounding another. McGee watched helplessly as the others ran back down the hill.

Stopping them at the bottom, Lieutenant Heath reformed them and led them back up the hill only to have the group disintegrate again. Angrily he followed them down the hill and tried to humiliate them into following him again, yelling, "Goddammit, get back up on that hill! You'll die here anyway. You might as well go up on the hill and die there."

The black artillerymen serving as machine gunners fought well throughout the night. However, every attempt to organize them for a counterattack failed. Although some soldiers criticized them in personal and other accounts of Chipyong-ni, it should surprise no one who considers the circumstances. These were, after all, artillerymen who had not been trained as infantry, who were thrown together in the worst sort of circumstances, and who were led by white officers not in their chain of command whom they neither knew nor had reason to trust. It is unlikely that any other artillerymen untrained as infantry would have performed better. Even competently trained infantry units, including the elite Rangers, had trouble retaking George Company's abandoned positions.

Meanwhile, the Chinese on the hill were methodically consolidating their defenses. They moved from one foxhole to the next, either killing the defenders or driving them off the hill. Most of the defenders who made it safely down the hill were wounded and wandered back to company headquarters or on to treatment at an aid station.

Sometime before 0200 hours, Lieutenant McGee's spirited resistance began to waver, not because of any lack of determination but from the steady pressure of the Chinese and the losses they were causing. He sent Private Inmon to find the company commander and ask for any help that he could send to ease his desperate situation. Lieutenant Heath called the battalion commander, who immediately committed a portion of his reserve—a squad from Fox Company's support platoon. The squad arrived at 0200 hours and attacked into the saddle that had formed the boundary between George Company's 1st and 3d Platoons. After a brisk ten-minute firefight in which every man in the squad was killed or wounded, the Chinese ran the last of the defenders off the hill.

Some time during the next hour, the rest of the hill fell. When Lieutenant McGee's last machine gun jammed, he and his platoon sergeant threw their last grenades and, with five other men, all who were left of his platoon, crept down the hill. As they withdrew, the little party had to fight its way through Chinese who had gotten behind them.[9]

At 0300 hours, Lieutenant Colonel Edwards committed his last reserve, the remainder of Fox Company's support platoon, and called Colonel Freeman to ask for more soldiers for an attempt to retake the hill. It is not clear if Edwards admitted to Freeman that the Chinese held the entire George Company line. The operations journal merely reads: "0315 From CO 2d Bn: G Co pushed back. [Machine gun] shut-up. Lots of wounded. Call for help. CO [Freeman] ordered G Co to counterattack. G Co tie in 503d [artillery] perimeter." As late as 0340 hours, an entry in the intelligence journal merely reads, "Slight penetration in G Co lines." If Edwards dissembled on the desperate situation in George Company's sector, he did the units at Chipyong-ni a tremendous disservice. Had Freeman had an inkling of what it would cost the regiment to restore the line, it is unquestionable that he would have committed whatever he could at that moment. On the other hand, mindful of the other attacks that were still going on at that hour, particularly in the French sector, and unaware that the situation in George Company was as desperate as it was, Meszar cautioned against committing the reserve too quickly.[10]

Freeman agreed to send a platoon of Rangers and one tank to reinforce the George Company counterattack. He also attached the two tanks and the quad-.50-caliber flak wagon then in the cut between George Company and the French Battalion to the 2d Battalion.[11]

As early as 0100 hours, the French had been concerned with the resumption of particularly violent firing in the area between them and

George Company. The situation in George Company threatened the 1st Company's ability to hold its hillock. If George Company's 1st Platoon fell back, the French 1st Company's flank would be vulnerable to attack. At 0305 hours, receiving fire from the American positions, the 1st Company commander demanded to know "with the greatest urgency" what the situation in George Company was. The reply to his message went unrecorded. At 0338 hours, he observed that the integrity of the defensive line appeared to be broken in George Company's sector. He could see no personnel on the crest, and the Chinese appeared to have infiltrated as far as the 155-mm battery. Battalion headquarters then instructed him to be prepared to send a section of his reserve to assist George Company.[12]

It was a night of carnage almost everywhere in and around the perimeter. Between 0100 hours and 0400 hours, there were attacks on Able, Charley, Item, and King Companies, as well as the French 1st Company. In Item, the Chinese got into some of the defensive holes, but Lieutenant Colonel Kane dispatched two squads from Love Company to help out. The French heard bugles all along their front, and the 1st Company repelled a ground attack. During a lull in the fighting, the French observed soldiers with flares in front of their positions. The Chinese, using sleds pulled by large dogs, were methodically retrieving their wounded and dragging them off. The French soldiers had observed the same phenomenon the night after the Twin Tunnels battle. Neither time did the French fire on them. Whether the indulgence of the French infantry was due to chivalry or a shortage of ammunition is unclear, although most of the participants believe it was the ammunition shortage. The soldiers were aware of atrocities committed by the Chinese in previous days—just after Twin Tunnels, the regiment had come upon prisoners executed in a kneeling position, and they had seen a Chinese soldier approach a wounded American on the George Company hill and place a grenade under him that blew him to pieces—so they had little in the way of gentlemanly compassion for their opponents.[13]

Lieutenant Colonel Edwards had earlier designated Lt. Robert Curtis to guide the Rangers to their position should it become necessary. He was to lead them to the position where they would be attached to the counterattack force and then return to battalion headquarters as quickly as possible. As Curtis walked down the road to meet the Rangers, he could hear and see enemy and friendly fires intermingling in all directions. He had been monitoring the radio and knew from reports to the battalion CP that

George Company had had a rough time of it that night. Before he met the Rangers, he heard them coming down the road complaining loudly about something.[14]

When he finally linked up with the Rangers, he told their company commander, who had accompanied the platoon, that they were to join the counterattack force and attack immediately to restore the George Company line before the Chinese further consolidated it. After the attack, they were to remain in the position and help the defenders. The Rangers already knew about the mission; that was what they had been arguing about when Curtis heard them earlier. The Rangers explained that they could retake the hill, but they were not equipped to defend a static position after it was retaken. Curtis explained that there were no forces left to replace them in the line but that they could probably work out a relief later in the morning after the position was secure.[15]

When he arrived at the George Company position with the Ranger platoon, Curtis found a desperate situation: most of the key leaders were wounded and a sense of confusion prevailed. Lieutenant Heath was trying to reorganize the remnants of George Company and integrate the partial platoon from Fox Company into the organization. Lieutenants Curtis and Heath discussed the situation. They decided that since there were elements of several units in the counterattack force—the remnants of George Company, the reduced platoon from Fox Company, the Rangers, and some hastily assembled soldiers from the battalion headquarters—it would be better if Lieutenant Curtis led the counterattack. As a staff officer, most of the NCOs knew and trusted him and so could be expected to follow him. Lieutenant Heath offered to do anything necessary, including leading the charge up the hill.[16]

Lieutenant Curtis recounted what happened next:

All of the George Company and Fox Company leaders and their men were ready and willing to attack. At that time, we had three 60 mm mortars, three tanks, and light machine gun fires to support the attack, plus the possibility of a quad-.50 caliber weapon that was sitting at an angle on a nearby trail but was inoperable in that position. I couldn't find the 81 mm mortar observer and the company had lost contact with the [heavy] mortar fire direction center. The crew assigned to the quad-.50 had left the area but I knew the tankers would know how to fire the weapon. I was told we had some artillerymen forward of the command post but that they were guarding their howitzers and I did not count on their assistance in the attack because I didn't know how effective they would be as infantry, especially under the conditions that we were in.

I informed the Ranger Company commander and his platoon leader that he would attack on the right flank guiding on the cut in the road and tying into George Company on the left. During a heated discussion with the Ranger Commander the question of rank came up and when the Ranger found out that both he and his platoon leader outranked me he said that he couldn't take orders from me. He again pointed out that he was attached directly to Colonel Freeman and that he would take no orders except directly from Colonel Freeman. I informed him that since he was senior commander on the ground he was welcome to take charge of all the forces in the area and lead the attack and that George Company and the platoon from Fox Company would follow his commands. I told him that I could put him in touch with Colonel Freeman but all it would get him was an ass chewing for delaying the attack. The Ranger Company commander still insisted that he could attack and take his portion of the objective faster than the infantry but that he couldn't hold it with the weapons he had available to him. He said in no uncertain terms that his mission did not allow him to take charge of the counterattack.

Time was critical and the situation was growing desperate so I called Colonel Edwards and explained to him that the Rangers wanted a direct order from Colonel Freeman before they would attack and that they refused to attack under my command since he and his platoon leader outranked me. I told him I had taken command of the breakthrough area and asked him to send a senior captain or a major to the area as soon as possible, either to take command, or to back up my orders. I coordinated with the commanders on the ground and explained that a senior staff officer was on the way and we would attack as soon as he got there.[17]

Captain John Ramsburg, the battalion intelligence officer, arrived a few minutes later. "Christ, John, am I ever glad to see you," Curtis said, "I can't do a damn thing with the Ranger Company commander." Curtis explained the situation and asked whether he would lead or whether he wanted Curtis to lead the attack. Captain Ramsburg said he would lead, but for Curtis to stay and assist. The two had worked together in a similar situation on the Naktong and trusted one another's reactions. As Curtis recalled:

Captain Ramsburg and I proceeded to the George Company CP where he called a commanders meeting and laid out his plan of attack. This still left the Rangers on the right flank of the attack. The Ranger Company commander still didn't believe the defense of the area was a suitable mission for his men but Captain Ramsburg straightened him out with a few choice words that left little doubt of who was in command and what was going to take place. At no time did the Rangers object to the attack, only their defending the area with the weapons and personnel available to them and to the supporting fires we had available to help hold their positions.[18]

In reality, there was little in either numbers or armament that lessened a Ranger platoon's ability to defend as well as any infantry platoon at Chipyong-ni. Considering their lack of fighting up to that time, the Rangers' freshness and lack of fatigue should have made them a better defensive unit than most in the perimeter. The 1950 Ranger company Table of Organization and Equipment (TO&E; the official document specifying the mission, capabilities, and authorized quantities of personnel by rank, specialty, and numbers, and of equipment by type and quantity) lists as a capability, "Seizing and holding terrain"—exactly the same wording as the comparable capability listed in the TO&E for a standard rifle company. The Rangers had a tradition and lineage dating back to World War II, when they had been organized as the American counterpart to the British Commandos. In World War II, however, they were generally used as specialized raiding units designed to strike behind enemy lines, cause destruction and disruption, and withdraw. At Fort Benning, Georgia, they had been very much indoctrinated in this traditional role and they resented being treated like ordinary infantry units. This attitude was also, of course, why many infantrymen at Chipyong-ni saw them as prima donnas who did not pull their share of the load.[19]

There was a half-hour of confused organization as the commanders tried to get more men and support weapons for the attack. Mortar ammunition was critically low, so there would be none available after the attackers arrived on the hill. Ramsburg was firing the mortar concentrations he wanted when Chinese mortar fire hit in the assembly area, wounding several soldiers, including some of the Rangers. The Ranger Company commander, thinking it was friendly fire from George Company, began screaming for the mortars to cease firing. He was screaming so loudly that Captain Ramsburg thought he would demoralize the other soldiers and endanger the attack. Having had enough of this particular Ranger officer, who had already demonstrated singular deficiencies in setting the example to defenders in the area, Captain Ramsburg raced over and ordered him to escort the wounded to the rear.[20]

The attack force finally began assaulting the hill about 0500 hours, more than two hours before sunrise. The men started trudging up the hill, through knee-deep snow in places. The Rangers made a spirited attack, giving motivational Ranger yells as they went. As they had promised, they took their portion of the line before the others. The Chinese in the old George Company positions on the south side of the hill held their fire until the attackers crested it, and then opened up with all their weapons. Soon the Rangers were shouting that they needed litter bearers, medics, and ammunition or they could not hold their positions. "We're on top! Come on up! Get some men up here!" they yelled. About this time, fire from the knob marking the left portion of the French 1st Company began raking the Ranger positions. Thinking it was the French firing on Chinese, one of the tanks opened up on the area as well. To Curtis, it appeared to come from just forward of the French lines. The fire wounded several Rangers and further demoralized them all.[21]

Attackers who were wounded and others who were merely disheartened began straggling back down the hill. About this time, a Chinese grenade exploded near Captain Ramsburg, wounding him in the foot. At first he thought he had squeezed off a round from the .45-caliber submachine gun he was carrying, and wondered how he would explain the wound to Lieutenant Colonel Edwards. When Curtis arrived, Ramsburg was sitting in the snow examining the wound. The lieutenant pointed out that the captain's submachine gun was set to fire full automatic and thus would have blown his foot off. Ramsburg was relieved. Meanwhile, Lieutenant Heath, seeing that Ramsburg was wounded, had gone on up the hill to take charge of the attack. After resting a few minutes, Ramsburg began hobbling on up the hill on his painful ankle. He met a man dragging a wounded GI down the hill. Not wanting to lose an able-bodied man, Ramsburg stopped him and said he could not afford to let him go any farther. The soldier explained that he too was wounded and turned to show an arm hanging only by a piece of flesh. Captain Ramsburg waved him on down the hill and asked who the wounded man he was dragging was. "It's the lieutenant," came the response. "Lieutenant Heath. He got it in the chest." Heath was seriously but not fatally wounded. At about the same time, Chinese killed the Ranger platoon leader, leaving no officers on the crest. Curtis suggested that Ramsburg make his way back to the CP and get things organized for another counterattack while he went up the hill and took charge.[22]

Curtis found little but chaos and disorganization when he reached the

top. All the men were wounded, the less seriously assisting the more critical down the hill. He realized that the talking he heard from the Ranger
portion of the line was coming from the bottom of the hill, not the top.
Convinced that there must still be wounded on the slope, he made a thorough search, but found only three wounded Fox Company soldiers who
assured him that they were the last off the hill and that there were no more
Americans.[23]

Back at the George Company CP, Captain Ramsburg was having a
hard time organizing a counterattack force. He ordered Curtis to get
whatever men he could round up and establish a defense on the knoll in
front of the command post. Meanwhile, Ramsburg began arguing with
the Ranger Company commander, who had returned after evacuating his
wounded, and was now trying to take the rest of his soldiers back to the
rear. Ramsburg finally became so disgusted with the elite unit that he ordered all the Rangers to the rear, depriving him of a substantial amount of
his remaining fighting power. Curtis could find only the squad leader and
five men from Fox Company and eight men from George Company. He
supplemented these with any warm bodies he could find—mortarmen,
wiremen, cooks, and radiomen—and placed them on line. Still puzzled as
to how the twenty-five men he could account for—including the depart-
ing Rangers—could be the only survivors of the attack, he set out for still
another search of the hillside.[24]

On the way to the base of the hill the Rangers had attacked, Curtis was
surprised to find artillerymen and officers still manning their guns in the
155-mm battery. He asked if they knew there was no infantry in front
of them and that they were now the front line. Lieutenant Rochnowski
replied that he had no intention of going down in history as the battery
commander who had abandoned his guns at Chipyong-ni, and that under
no circumstances would his artillerymen leave their pieces. Curtis asked if
they could set up a defensive line in front of their guns and Rochnowski
agreed to do so. As the artillery lieutenant started to position his soldiers,
Curtis departed to check the hillside for casualties.[25]

All of the men Curtis found on the hill's lower slopes were dead. If the
sounds of digging he could hear on the crest were an indicator, it suggested
that the Chinese were not going to abandon the position as dawn approached, but that they were there to stay. Finally, hearing Chinese talking
all around him, he realized that he must be the only American left on the
hill and beat a hasty retreat. He fully expected that the Chinese, whom he
could hear digging in the old George Company positions, would soon be

attacking into the thinly defended company rear area. When he reached the right flank, he coordinated with the tanks, briefing the commanders on the situation and placing them were they could best support in defending against a Chinese attack down the hill. The defense of the bowl behind George Company would not be a robust one—a couple of tanks and a flak wagon, a few dozen men, and some 155-mm howitzers that could not fire in their most efficient mode, indirect fire. There was no 60-mm mortar ammunition left, and the unit had no contact with the medium or heavy mortars.[26]

The ammunition situation was the same in all of the units. There were only a few hundred mortar rounds of all sizes left, and machine-gun ammunition was critically low. The only ammunition available in adequate amounts was for small arms, but none of it was in clips for the M1 Garand. Major Dumaine requested urgent airdrops of all types of ammunition at first light the next morning. In Japan the Japan Logistical Command loaded waiting planes throughout the night. Unfortunately, the logisticians again neglected to provide the types of ammunition most needed.[27]

Curtis returned to the CP and discussed the situation with Captain Ramsburg. Ramsburg's ankle was throbbing, and as they talked, a number of Chinese appeared on the skyline and started down the hill. Thinking they were the lead elements of what would develop into an attack on the newly established line, Curtis told Ramsburg that he had better take the wounded to the rear or they would not be able to get back later. To Curtis's surprise, Ramsburg shouted, "Come on everyone, we're going back to establish a new defensive position." Before Curtis could stop them, everyone at the CP was loping to the rear, including Ramsburg and most of the able-bodied men in the vicinity. Curtis returned to his line, now reduced to about fifteen men from Fox and George Companies, and the artillerymen. He reassured them, and then put the squad leader from Fox Company in charge on the line. The sergeant said that if it looked like they were not going to make it, he would prefer to return to his company and go down with his comrades. Curtis reassured him that they were going to survive and told the sergeant he could go back as soon as the line was shored up.[28]

Curtis moved on to the artillery position, where he talked to the tank commander and artillery officers. In a surprisingly light-hearted exchange, the artillery commander asked if there was anything they could do to help out. In a half-kidding response, Curtis said it would be nice to have some fire on the crest of the hill—the reverse side of George Company hill—less than a quarter of a mile away. Without hesitating the officer assembled a volunteer crew. The men turned one of the big howitzers around and cranked it down until the tube was pointed directly at the hill. They then proceeded to fire half a dozen rounds of white phosphorous into the hillside. Because of the almost point-blank range for a weapon of that size, the sound of the explosions came almost before the crack of firing had stopped reverberating. The hill was bathed in flames and acrid white smoke that drifted over the crest. Not to be outdone, the tanker cranked his turret around and fired low down the frozen valley to the south, skipping his projectiles against the frozen ground like flat rocks on water. The echo off the surrounding hills was formidable even to the defenders, and they hoped the display of firepower at their command would prove intimidating to the attackers. For whatever reason, the valley around George Company remained silent until dawn, except for the ominous sounds of Chinese digging in on the slopes of the hill to the front. When dawn began breaking at about 0700, the artillerymen abandoned their position. Just before daylight, Chinese infantry entered the position and blew truck horns, started motors, and shot out windows.[29]

After the failure of yet another counterattack, Freeman ordered Baker Company, his last reserve except for his engineer company, to try to retake the George Company hill. Before they could do so, ten soldiers from the French Battalion's 1st Company gave the mission a try. Supported by the three tanks holding the cut between the old American and current French lines, they dashed toward the top. Twenty meters from the crest, they got into a grenade fight with the Chinese in George Company's old foxholes. Three more French soldiers and the American artillery liaison officer, Captain Elledge, arrived to support them. Pinned down by Chinese machine guns, they shouted for reinforcements, but when none came they withdrew at 0820.[30]

Before midmorning, Capt. Sherman Pratt arrived with Baker Company to make the next counterattack. After being briefed by Lieutenant Colonel Edwards, he moved forward and coordinated tank support with Lt. Arthur Junot, commanding the tanks that would support his attack. Junot thought two of his tanks would be able to climb the ridge into the old 1st Platoon positions and support the attack with cannon and machine-gun fire. The two-platoon attack pushed off at 1000 hours. Pratt's infantry made it almost to the objective before heavy fire from the Chinese on the south side of the hill drove the attackers back. Meanwhile, Junot's

From left: Major General Clark Ruffner, 2d Infantry Division commander; Lt. Gen. Ned Almond, X Corps commander; Lt. Col. John H. Chiles, the new 23d Regiment commander; Maj. John Dumaine *(behind Chiles);* and Lt. Col. Ralph Monclar, the French Battalion commander, confer at Chipyong-ni in February, 1951. *Courtesy U.S. Army Military History Institute.*

tanks could not get up the hill because of the snow. After that, Baker Company withdrew part way down the hill's north slope.[31]

Sometime around noon, Freeman finally left the perimeter. Some of the lieutenants in the French Battalion near the airstrip saw him, his eyes glistening with tears as he moved to the helicopter that would cleave him from his regiment. After Freeman's departure, Lieutenant Colonel Chiles, displaying uncommon good sense, told Lieutenant Colonel Meszar to run the operations for the rest of the siege, as he was more familiar with what was going on.

Baker's next attack went in after the first air strikes of the day hit the hill. F-80 Shooting Stars were the first in, strafing the old George Company positions with machine-guns, then dropping napalm on them. After a few passes, Lts. Richard Kotite and Maurice Fenderson led their platoons up the two small hills. The Chinese were firing on them with small arms as they moved toward the base of the hill, then began dropping mortars on them about two-thirds of the way up. The attackers got to within five meters of the crest and began lobbing grenades over the top. Within a few minutes, Chinese troops began flanking Lieutenant Kotite's platoon on the right. His soldiers threw grenades until they ran out, and then withdrew.[32]

The situation remained confused throughout the rest of the day on 15 February. At least two more ground attacks and several more air strikes hit the hill during the afternoon, killing many Chinese, but not dislodging them. Nonetheless, the air strikes lifted morale. The soldiers watched the pilots bring their planes in so low that they disappeared behind the hill, then climbed out doing victory rolls before making another pass. All of the strikes on the U.S. positions were directed from the observation post in Fox Company's sector, as it was the only place within the perimeter that had a view of the George Company lines. The first napalm drop did not hit the Chinese squarely because they used captured U.S. marker panels to make the pilots of the attacking aircraft think their positions were friendly. As soon as the ground controller informed the aircraft of the problem, the pilots adjusted and plastered the hill. At the same time, Major Barthelemy was directing strikes in front of the French sector from an observation post on the flat ground behind their lines.[33]

The recollections of "Mosquito Spirit," the close air support controller in the air over Chipyong-ni are revealing:

The next day ... was a day I'll never forget. We departed our riverbed airstrip, just missing a tank at the far end, and reported on station to Major Smith. Apparently Air Force and Navy ground crews had been working all night and fully loaded fighters and bombers checked in.

We had F-4U Corsairs, F-51s, Douglas A. D. Skyraiders (our favorite), F-80s, F-9s, A-26s and of course our own T-6. I can still remember a few call signs: *Cherrytree, Onionskin,* and *Wolfhound.* I squeezed the mike button to call the fighters in and I talked for hours it seemed. When I wasn't talking a flight on target, George was. We had never then and never since had so many aircraft to control in one day.

At times mid-air collisions were almost a problem. Normally the attacking aircraft flight path was a recommendation of Mosquito and decision of the fighter. At Chipyong with so many aircraft it was necessary for us to specify and require the fighters to follow our lead or orders.[34]

The bodies of Chinese soldiers lying just outside the perimeter at Chipyong-ni bear mute testimony to the intensity of the three-day battle. *Courtesy U.S. Army Military History Institute.*

It is hard for one who was not a participant to appreciate the feeling of joy, relief, and even exhilaration that the air strikes inspired among the soldiers in the perimeter. As one man put it:

> One major feeling at Chipyong-ni was the *tremendous* lift I got from the air force making napalm bombing and strafing runs on the surrounding hillsides. Apparently their method was to have the jets drop the napalm to flush the enemy and then the following plane would be a propeller driven unit for strafing. The jets would merely get a couple of very short bursts off during a run whereas the prop planes could fire nearly continuously and actually chase fleeing enemy. The tremendous lift in spirit mentioned above came when they were finished. They would make a very low-level "barrel-roll" run through the valley. The speed, the noise, the barrel-roll victory symbol all added to waving and indeed there was spontaneous cheering by us in the perimeter.

It is hard to imagine that the air strikes were not having a commensurate, but opposite, effect on the Chinese attackers.

Airdrops of supplies began early in the morning. They included litters and blankets needed by the medical personnel, but again no mortar ammunition. An army liaison plane dropped small-arms ammunition for the BARs and M1 Garands, this time in clips for fast reloading. The Chinese kept the drop zone under fire, but did not appreciably hinder the resupply operations.[35]

Although the situation was more critical than it had ever been at Chipyong-ni, the soldiers kept up their spirits with faith in the relief forces and by demonstrating the bravado shared by confident soldiers throughout history. The Duke of Wellington said that the only thing he was afraid of was fear, and many soldiers feel the same—to lose one's courage in a dangerous situation is to have given up the battle.

The 1st Cavalry Division relief force, Task Force Crombez, reported by lunchtime that it was nearing Koksu-ri, less than four miles from the perimeter, and moving. The 27th British Commonwealth Brigade reported that it was still eight miles away and meeting stiff resistance. Both expected to reach Chipyong-ni that day. During the day, soldiers brought a captured Chinese major to Maj. Perry Sager, the 2d Battalion operations officer. The major said he had been educated at Harvard, and he spoke better English than the soldiers who escorted him to the CP. He told Major Sager that it had taken only fifteen minutes for the defenders to kill every soldier in his company. Sager's laconic response, to the delight of the soldiers who related the story was, "Hell, it shouldn't have taken that long."[36]

Helicopters arrived on the morning of 15 February to evacuate the first wounded soldiers since the siege began. These were some of the first helicopter "medevacs" of the war. Bell H-13s and underpowered Hiller H-23s evacuated twenty of the most seriously wounded men. Both aircraft carried so little fuel that they had to shut down and refuel before making the return trip. When reports began coming in that the armored rescue column was nearing the perimeter, the medical personnel began loading the wounded needing evacuation into trucks for the trip south when the tanks arrived to escort them.[37]

The armored column came through the cut south of the perimeter just before dusk. The soldiers did not know it yet, but the siege of Chipyong-ni was at an end.

Chapter 11

Task Force Crombez Runs the Gauntlet

Unity and confidence cannot be improvised. They alone can create that mutual trust, that feeling of force which gives courage and daring.

—Ardant du Picq

Duty is ours; consequences are God's.
—Lt. Gen. Thomas J. "Stonewall" Jackson

When Task Force Crombez, the armor-heavy rescue column from the 5th Cavalry Regiment, entered Chipyong-ni, everyone inside the perimeter and the chain of command up to Ridgway himself breathed a sigh of relief. A United Nations force had won its first victory over the Peoples' Liberation Army in the Korean War. Ridgway had demonstrated that properly equipped and led, the ground soldiers of the United States and its United Nations allies could absorb any Chinese blow and the Far East Air Forces could provide the margin of victory over the seemingly limitless manpower of its Chinese adversaries. There were 164 infantrymen and engineers in and near Chipyong-ni who were not cheerful, however, for they had ridden the tanks of the task force on its relief mission. Only twenty-three soldiers were still on the tanks when they pulled into the perimeter, and of those twenty-three, thirteen were wounded and one of them would die of his wounds that night. The other 141 soldiers who had started out riding the tanks in the column were strung out along the five-mile road over which the task force had raced to the relief of the besieged 23d Infantry Regiment. A dozen of them were dead or dying, nineteen were missing and probably already prisoners, and about forty were wounded. Their story began more than a year before, at Fort Carson, Colorado.[1]

The 3d Battalion, 5th Cavalry, and Edgar Treacy

The 1st Cavalry Division was on occupation duty in Japan when the Korean War broke out. Before it could be committed in combat, however, it had to be brought up to full strength. In the years since the end of the war with Japan in 1945, budget and personnel cuts in the peacetime army had caused military leaders to economize in every area. For reasons that made sense for a unit on occupation duty, the army's leaders had cut units in the divisional organizations in Japan. This meant that instead of three regiments in the 1st Cavalry Division, three battalions in a regiment, and so forth, every organization had two full-strength units (in theory only, as there were shortages in all units in the summer of 1950) rather than three units at reduced strength. Unfortunately, this solution, though logical for an occupation force, made no sense if the unit were to be committed to action, since military doctrine is built on the concept of threes, with three smaller units organized into a larger unit, and so on. In this way, a battalion, for example, can have two companies on line in the defense or offense and hold one in reserve to commit when needed.

To fill the 1st Cavalry Division with a third regiment, the Department of the Army designated three battalions in the United States as provisional infantry battalions and alerted them for immediate deployment to Korea. One was at Fort Devens, Massachusetts, and one at Fort Benning, Georgia. The third was the 3d Battalion, 14th Infantry, at Camp Carson, Colorado. The latter was the infantry unit that participated in the relief of the siege of Chipyong-ni. At the time it deployed, it was one of the more combat-ready units in that generally unready army. It had its full complement of men and equipment and was highly trained. At Camp Carson, it specialized in winter warfare. The battalion had undergone mountain climbing and ski training, and many of its soldiers participated in Operation Sweetbriar in the Yukon learning techniques of winter warfare in the spring of 1950. Thanks to this training, the men were in excellent physical condition and the unit was one of the only organizations to enter the Korean War with knowledge of how to fight in its extremes of climate.

The commander of the 3d Battalion, 14th Infantry, was Lt. Col. Edgar J. Treacy Jr. A member of the West Point class of 1935, he was a conscientious and humane officer whose soldiers were devoted to him. His grades caused him to be ranked in the bottom third of his class, but, as with many cadets who rise to success in the army such as both Freeman and Meszar, his classmates saw qualities in him that his grades did not take into account:

"Brilliant guard-house lawyer and suave master of subtle ridicule, [he] shatters the most fool-proof arguments with the unanswerable logic of his vigorous 'So what?' Wintry evenings passed pleasantly when, amid the cozy intimacy of barren walls and icy radiators, the sage of 'de clique' expounded with carefree idiocy his philosophies of life, love, and text-book absurdities. Reconcile this character with one who possesses unassailable ideals, the soul of a poet and dreamer, and the masterful ability to lead others."[2]

During World War II, Treacy had proven his ability for high-level performance. He rose to the temporary rank of full colonel before he was thirty years old, and became the head of the XIV Corps intelligence section in the South Pacific. At the end of the war, he reverted to his permanent rank of lieutenant colonel, as did many other officers.[3]

The battalion initially was told that it would train in Japan for three to five months before moving to Korea, but the exigencies of combat on the Naktong River Line made it necessary to send the battalion directly to Pusan. The shipboard trip to the Far East gave the leaders an opportunity to polish their skills before combat. Captain Norman F. J. Allen, the Item Company commander, recalled the voyage:

> During the trip over we were pretty much left to our own devices as to what training should be conducted, whatever each of us thought our particular men needed most. 37% of the men in I Company wore the combat infantry badge and I knew that I had good experience there, but they had been off on all sorts of details, so I decided that we would concentrate on weapons, every man would learn to handle, assemble, and disassemble each weapon in the company. Then I got the artillerymen on the ship to teach us all how to call for and direct artillery fire, we didn't have that training previously. Ammo was short in the army like everything else in those days and only artillerymen got to fire artillery. There was so little space that could be used on the boat that we rotated men through training. Once I had gotten the officers through I decided we would do something else. Only two of the six of us had combat experience, and finally we hit on sitting there in a gun tub and talking out combat situations, like for instance, sudden fire from the right at close range, rifles and automatic weapons. What should we do if we were mounted in vehicles, dismounted in column formation, etc. Everyone would make their suggestions and we'd tear each one apart and then settle on the best solution. We were able to spend more time on the proper solution than we would ever have time for when it happened for real. I think this helped us immensely initially in combat.[4]

Cadet Edgar Joseph Treacy, Jr,. U.S. Military Academy class of 1935.

This was admirable mental preparation for leadership in combat. Additionally, such discussions undoubtedly gave the officers a sense of one another's abilities and increased their confidence in themselves and in the group. It was analogous to a sports team going through plays on the chalkboard.

The 5th Cavalry Regiment and Marcel Crombez

Upon arrival in Korea, the 3d Battalion, 14th Infantry, was redesignated as the 3d Battalion, 5th Cavalry Regiment, and assigned to the 1st Cavalry Division. In spite of the cavalry designation, both the regiment and the division were standard infantry units, identical in organization to like units in infantry divisions.

The 5th Cavalry Regiment's new commander was Col. Marcel Gustave Crombez, then forty-nine. Born in Belgium and possessed of a thick accent he would never lose, he had enlisted in the U.S. Army in 1919. Two years later, he was appointed to the West Point class of 1925. His class standing at graduation was almost exactly the same as Treacy's: that is, at the breaking point between the middle and bottom third of the class. His classmates nicknamed him "Machine Gun," and they appear to have detected a trace of hardheadedness in him: "Marcel is possessed of those qualities which one naturally looks for in a soldier. Like all good soldiers, he has an eagle eye, . . . Serious minded, painstaking and conscientious, Marcel has laid his own course and then stubbornly followed it, in spite of criticism, to its conclusion. We cannot fail to respect him for always having the courage of his convictions."[5]

During World War II, Crombez had missed out on the top combat assignments. He served in stateside training assignments until almost the end of the war, when he finally made it to the Pacific. He saw little action, however, and received no awards. After temporary promotion to colonel, he, too, reverted to lieutenant colonel at war's end. In the interregnum before the Korean War, he had commanded two regiments in the 7th Infantry Division on occupation duty in Korea, so he was no stranger to the peninsula when war broke out. In 1949, he again was promoted to colonel, this time permanently.[6]

Men who served under him in Korea remember his flamboyance. Of medium build, he was never without a yellow cavalry scarf around his neck and had an oversize eagle, the insignia of his rank, painted on his helmet. He wore a grenade on his suspenders in the same manner as Ridgway.[7] Wherever he went, he carried a blue poker chip that he would flip in the

Cadet Marcel Gustave Crombez, U.S. Military Academy class of 1925.

air while talking to his soldiers and philosophizing about when it was best to play their "blue chip." To Cpl. Victor Fox, who remembered seeing Crombez only once, about the time of Chipyong-ni, his appearance conjured up the image of an old Roman army commander: "Crombez was dressed in an immaculate winter parka with the hood down. A pile cap had the earflaps tied over his steel helmet. I was a Roman history buff at the time, so it would not have surprised me to see a standard bearer decked in wolfskin with Colonel Crombez. Even his jeep and tires were about spotless on this snow-filled and slushy roadway."

Opinions of veterans concerning Crombez vary widely, and are divided between those whose contact was with him through the 1st and 2d Battalions and his staff, and those who were in Treacy's 3d Battalion. A positive yet balanced assessment was offered by Capt. Keith M. Stewart, Crombez's assistant operations officer and, after Chipyong-ni, his operations officer:

> Colonel Crombez has his critics—few give him credit for the rather successful commander he was. Certainly, he was no great tactician—but he knew with a certainty that in Korea, at least, one would do well to stay to the high ground—a number of commanders never learned that lesson. (To the best of my knowledge, Colonel Crombez had no prior combat experience and also to the best of my knowledge, the unit never found itself in any serious trouble because of a poor tactical decision he may have made.)
>
> He was an arbitrary, stubborn, opinionated individual but he was devotedly loyal to his command. He listened to those he had confidence in and let his battalion commanders do their jobs once a mission had been assigned.
>
> He was extremely proud of the 5th Cavalry and would drive attached unit commanders to distraction by telling them if they couldn't accomplish a job he wanted done and/or when he wanted it done then they should leave their equipment (tanks, bulldozers, or what-have-you) and he would have his troopers do it. Infuriated, the attached unit commanders would get that job done which they had initially advised Colonel Crombez could not possibly be accomplished.
>
> By no means was he devious—he was in fact straightforward and honest. Ego-driven, he wanted to be a general more than anything else in this world. Unfortunately, by his own actions, he was often, to his detractors, the object of derision. He was of high moral character—his conduct was based almost solely on "Duty, Honor, Country." . . . . There was no question about his courage. . . . Colonel Crombez was considered by some to be somewhat of an amusing, slightly incompetent character who somehow or another got through this thing without being relieved. In my judgment, those who had this opinion were wrong—true he was no tactical genius nor was he an outstanding leader—but in his own way he did get the job done.

Another officer who remembers Crombez positively is Capt. Joe W. Finley, the Fox Company commander. Finley, who had served with Crombez during the Korean occupation before the war, recalled:

> Some people had various opinions of Crombez. Having been born and raised in Belgium, he spoke with a very distinct accent that many people did not like. He did not have an outgoing or warm personality. He was, however, very mission oriented. During my pre-war duty in his 32d Infantry Regiment in Korea, there was also a degree of unpopularity concerning him. Our mission at that time was 38th Parallel border patrol. He established a firm policy that no officer could leave his border duty area to visit the socially active Seoul area without the clearance of the battalion commander and then clearance by Crombez himself. Keeping the border properly controlled and supervised was his mission and top priority even if many officers did not like being isolated in the boondocks. During the combat days, I did not have much contact with him, but it appeared that the same conditions existed: unpopular but mission oriented. Before I departed, Colonel Crombez personally contacted me and thanked me for having been a member of his organization and wished me well.[8]

It is not hard to uncover divergent opinions on Crombez. He had a reputation for commanding from the rear and worrying about minutia. Captain Thomas Giboney, the 2d Battalion operations officer, remembers that Crombez visited his command post only once, and then it was with Ridgway in tow. Lieutenant Lloyd "Scooter" Burke, a platoon leader for sixteen months and later a Medal of Honor recipient, says Crombez was "a lousy commander." He never saw him except in the rear and remembers his obsession with such trifles as the alignment of tent pegs.

It is when one encounters veterans of the 3d Battalion, however, that recollections turn from impressionistic memories of a successful but slightly inept and single-minded officer to the character traits that involve the ethical foundation of the U.S. Army and the officer corps. These allegations are that Crombez held a grudge against Treacy going back to World War II. Some claim that Treacy sat on a board that identified colonels who should revert to lieutenant colonel as part of the postwar reduction in force; others simply understood that Colonel Crombez resented the twenty-eight-year-old Colonel Treacy, ten years behind him at West Point, who had far outshone him during the war. Whatever the motive, there can be little doubt that Crombez, now Treacy's commanding officer, found it impossible to lay aside resentment of the younger officer in favor of a professional relationship.[9]

The 5th Cavalry on the Naktong

The first major confrontation between Crombez and Treacy occurred during the desperate fighting to hold the Naktong River line a week before the Inchon landings. The 1st Cavalry Division was fighting to hold Eighth Army's northern shoulder, which included the key transportation center of Taegu, without which General Walker could probably not hold the Pusan Perimeter. The North Koreans were pressing hard, and Hill 174, crucial to holding the sector, changed hands several times. In the early morning hours of September 13 (two days before D-Day at Inchon), the North Koreans captured the hill from Treacy's Love Company, marking the seventh time the hill changed possession. When afternoon counterattacks failed to retake it, Crombez gave the mission to Treacy's Item Company. Earlier, Treacy had objected when Love Company had been ordered to make its three unsuccessful attacks on the hill, and now he objected again. "The enemy knows that we'll be coming, and no matter how [Captain] Allen tries to attack it, it went that way at least once before and the gooks will be ready for them. Item Company is the only company of good strength in the regiment, and probably Eighth Army, and if they get chewed up, that will be the last strong company, gone to hell."[10]

In spite of Treacy's premonitions, Item Company made a successful attack, but enemy forces chased it off the hill the next morning with heavy losses. The next day, one of Captain Allen's squad leaders approached him and, as he recalled the events, the sergeant said:

> "Captain, I think I'm in bad trouble." I asked him why, as we all had all the trouble we could stand and what on earth was he talking about, and he told me, "Sir, I was moving my squad up 174, and we were trying to move fast using as much cover as possible, one of my guys was not bent over like he should have been and was not moving out as fast as I wanted, so I yelled at him to get lower and move out, and then moved up and kicked him right hard in the ass—he turned around and looked at me and, Jesus Christ, it was the colonel [Treacy]."
>
> The same afternoon, Treacy brought orders from regiment for Allen to attack again to retake Hill 174. Allen was incredulous; he refused the order, "Colonel, I never thought I would ever have to do this, least of all to you, but you can report to regiment that Captain Allen of Item Company refuses the order!"

[Treacy] just sat and looked at me, then wearily said, "That's okay, Norm, I understand, I refuse the order too!"

He made no effort to move off, and we just sat there and looked at each other. I never felt closer to him than at that moment. I took the opportunity to ask him, "Colonel, will you please tell me what the hell you were doing up on Hill 174, just before I jumped off on the attack yesterday?" After a long pause, he replied, "Norm, Hill 174 [and one other hill] have just eaten this battalion up; four days ago we numbered almost nine hundred, today we are about 292! If I had been ordered to take Hill 174 again I was going to refuse the order, and I wanted to insure there would be no basis for a charge of personal cowardice!" Several days later I learned that he had indeed refused the order to retake Hill 174, and the regimental commander yelled at him in front of the other battalion commanders and their [operations officers] and others, called him coward and yellow.[11]

Treacy's flaw, if such a positive and humane element of character can be called a flaw, was that he cared for his soldiers too deeply. He was a devout Catholic and, at Camp Carson, had often acted as altar boy for the priest during services. Before Task Force Crombez, his company commanders noticed his devotion to those who had perished under his command. At night in the tent Treacy shared with some of his commanders:

We stood around talking and Colonel Treacy would manage to produce a bottle of whiskey. He would tell us to have a couple of drinks.

He would crawl into the sack, and Ralph [Curfman, the King Company commander] and I would be very quiet because we were sitting right there by him. I would hear him, Curfman is also Catholic, I guess I heard him mumbling and we went out the tent. I said, "What is he doing? What are those prayers? Are those all Hail Marys?" Curfman said, "No. He's reciting the names of the men in the battalion that have been killed."

So, he knew practically every man's name that had been killed. If he didn't know the man by name before, he knew it when the guy was a KIA. He was asking God for forgiveness for the responsibility for the death of that soldier. That, to me, was the most touching living memorial that I ever heard of.

He recited the names, and he didn't have any goddamn notebook and flashlight in that sleeping bag either. Maybe he missed a couple, I don't know. But to hear him rattle off sixty names, seventy names, something like that—it was a very touching thing.[12]

Task Force Crombez and the Gauntlet to Chipyong-ni

The 5th Cavalry Regiment had been in IX Corps reserve until 13 February 1951, after seeing heavy action in January and early February. On 13 February, 1st Cavalry Division headquarters ordered it to cross the Han River to the east and move toward Yoju, prepared to protect IX Corps's right flank. By midafternoon, however, Maj. Gen. Bryant E. Moore, the IX Corps commander, called Colonel Crombez to tell him there was a change in plans and that he should instead prepare to move north from Yoju to Koksu-ri and then northeast to Chipyong-ni.[13]

At about dusk, General Moore called Crombez again and told him, "You'll have to move tonight and I know you will do it." He went on to inform Crombez that the British were moving up from the east on a better and more direct route, but that they were facing heavily entrenched enemy forces and were unable to make a rapid enough advance to relieve the garrison at Chipyong-ni in time.[14]

It was obvious that this was a high-priority mission, possibly as important as any since General Ridgway had taken command of Eighth Army. Ridgway had made it clear that if an isolated unit could hold out against the Chinese, he would send the entire army to rescue it, if necessary. Now fifty, Crombez was the oldest regimental commander in Eighth Army, and Ridgway had been replacing the older commanders with younger officers. Success in this mission would not only protect his position as commander, it would preclude his replacement by Lieutenant Colonel Treacy, his obvious successor. Crombez, uncharacteristically by the standards of his previous engagements, elected to lead the operation himself.[15]

There is no question that Crombez was under constant and distracting pressure to get to Chipyong-ni as soon as possible, regardless of the consequences. The X and IX Corps headquarters, as well as those of both the 1st Cavalry and 2d Infantry Divisions, were calling to check on his progress. Staff officers at the embattled 23d Infantry Regiment's headquarters were reporting their casualty figures and describing the desperate state of their wounded. The emphasis was on speed—the surrounded regiment was in a grave position and might be lost if not immediately relieved.[16]

Some of the 5th Cavalry soldiers were in a somber mood, aware that something big was in the works. It was not unlike their feeling when the last "something big" had transpired: the Chinese intervention. The soldiers knew that the 23d Regiment was surrounded at Chipyong-ni. They

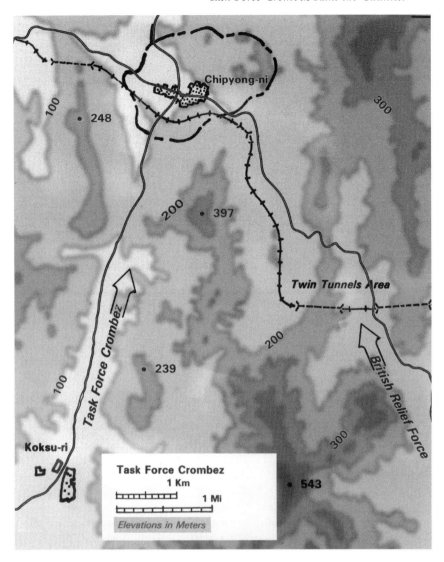

had heard rumors that the Chinese were out to take revenge on the 23d for eluding them in November, when it had escaped the destruction wrought on the rest of the 2d Infantry Division by taking the road to the west rather than following the rest of the division down the gauntlet.[17]

Task Force Crombez, as he organized it before moving out on the evening of 14 February, consisted of the 5th Cavalry Regiment's three organic infantry battalions, to which he added a combat engineer company, two field artillery battalions, and two medium tank platoons plus another medium tank company. Crombez had the tankers paint their vehicles to make them look like tigers so they would appear ferocious to the Chinese in the newly launched "Year of the Tiger." The tankers painted claws on each front fender with a toothy, gaping maw between them, and eyes on each side of the main gun.[18]

All of the task force's elements were across the Han River by early evening and a CP was set up about three miles short of Koksu-ri. Task Force Crombez was then about seven miles short of Chipyong-ni. Enemy mortar fire forced it to displace about a half-mile. From that position, Crombez monitored the task force's movement to a creek just short of Koksu-ri, where a blown bridge forced it to stop for the night.[19]

The task force got an early start on the morning of 15 February. Ridges dominate both sides of the four-mile-long valley from Koksu-ri to Chipyong-ni. The road up the valley runs to the west of the rice paddies on the valley floor, so the ridges to the east are more than a half-mile away and thus posed little danger to an armored force. The ridges to the west, however, abut the road throughout much of its length. A little over a mile from Chipyong-ni, the road passes through a cut in a saddle connecting the western and eastern ridges. Inside the cut, cliffs rise abruptly to as much as fifty feet above the road surface for about a quarter of a mile. Crombez's original plan was to advance from Koksu-ri to Chipyong-ni by clearing the ridges on both sides of the road with infantry before the tanks advanced up it. Accordingly, Crombez sent his 1st Battalion up the ridge to the east of the road and the 2d Battalion up the western ridge. Treacy's 3d Battalion was in reserve.[20]

The attacks proceeded slowly through the morning hours. Chinese dug in on both ridgelines offered stiff resistance. During the morning, three generals visited Crombez's headquarters. General Moore, the IX Corps commander, was first, then General Ruffner, the 2d Division commander. Ruffner asked Crombez if he was going to try to reach Chipyong-ni that day and Crombez assured him that he would get there before nightfall. Finally, Maj. Gen. Charles D. Palmer, the 1st Cavalry Division commander, arrived in his helicopter. Palmer had graduated from West Point a year before Crombez, and the two had been friends there. Known as "Charley Dog" Palmer for his initials in the phonetic alphabet, he had a reputation for being a cantankerous commander who pressured his subordinates, "scaring everybody to death." In Korea, Palmer did what he could to help his friend. That afternoon, Palmer let Crombez use his helicopter to recon the route to Chipyong-ni. Seeing the numbers of Chinese along the ridges, Crombez decided that only an audacious dash by an armored column could reach Chipyong-ni that day. His conviction was bolstered by a message from Lieutenant Colonel Chiles, now in command at Chipyong-ni, stating that the situation there was desperate. As recorded in the 23d Regiment's operations journal, the message sent at 1238 hours read: "Reach us as soon as possible, in any event reach us."[21]

Crombez ordered his twenty-three tanks to form up for a dash to Chipyong-ni. Four engineers would ride on the second tank and clear any mines found on the way. Then, in his most controversial decision, he ordered the 160 men of Treacy's Love Company to ride on the rest of the tanks and defend them against the Chinese on the ridges. He specifically ordered Lieutenant Colonel Treacy not to accompany his soldiers, but to stay behind and bring a supply column forward on call. Crombez intended to send his tanks back down the road that evening to escort the supply column forward.[22]

Crombez ordered Capt. John C. Barrett, commanding Love Company, to have his soldiers riding the tanks man their own weapons as well as the pedestal-mounted machine gun on top of each tank. If it became necessary, the tank column would stop to let the infantry fight off the Chinese before they would remount the tanks and proceed. Neither the infantry nor the tankers had ever practiced such tactics. Both Barrett and Treacy protested the decision, considering it near suicidal, but to no avail. Treacy finally told Crombez that he could not in good conscience order his soldiers to carry out such a mission unless he accompanied them, but Crombez denied his request.[23]

Captain Barrett coordinated with Capt. Johnnie M. Hiers, the commander of D Company, 6th Tank Battalion. They agreed that if it became necessary to stop and deploy the infantry, the tank commander would radio the infantry when to remount the tanks before they proceeded.[24]

Lieutenant Colonel Treacy sensed a disaster in the making. He instructed Barrett to leave behind one man from each squad to serve as a nucleus around which Love Company could be reorganized after the operation. All the infantrymen were ordered to write home and enclose any personal effects, such as the contents of their billfolds, in the letters. Additionally, Treacy arranged for a truck with a South Korean crew to follow the column and pick up any Love Company stragglers. Captain Barrett instructed his men that if anyone became separated from the tanks, they should make their way to friendly lines if possible. Otherwise, they were to defend themselves near the road and wait for the tanks to return later that day.[25]

Crombez organized the column with the newer M46 Patton medium tanks to the front, followed by World War II–vintage M4A3E8 Sherman tanks in the rear. The Pattons mounted a 90-mm cannon, whereas the Shermans had only a 76-mm gun. The Pattons could also pivot around in place (neutral steer), while the Shermans had to make as many as a dozen small turns with the driver shifting from forward to reverse each time in order to change direction 180 degrees. This was not a minor consideration on the constricted road they were about to traverse.[26]

With a fifty-yard interval between tanks, the column stretched out more than three-quarters of a mile. Colonel Crombez climbed into the fifth tank and locked the hatch above him. The infantry mounted the tanks, about ten men to a tank, with the four engineers on the second tank. Riding ten men to a tank is a miserable way to travel, as only the men directly behind the turret can get a grip on it. The other men had to hold onto them to keep from falling off. If the tank fires its main gun, the back blast from the muzzle brake is hot and uncomfortable. Lieutenant Colonel Treacy jumped aboard the sixth tank with Captain Barrett at the last minute, and they rode together huddled against the turret. The column began moving at 1545 hours.[27]

When the column entered Koksu-ri, it was met with a hail of fire from the high ground above the village. The tanks stopped and some of the infantry on the forward vehicles dismounted. Other soldiers were hit by the Chinese or dismounted to take cover from the hostile fire. Some were knocked off the decks as the tanks swiveled their turrets. The tanks opened fire on the Chinese, who were clearly visible on the hills. "We're killing hundreds of them!" Colonel Crombez shouted elatedly over the tank intercom. Then, without giving notice to the dismounted infantrymen, he ordered the column to resume its movement. About thirty infantrymen failed to get aboard the tanks as they moved out.[28]

About a mile beyond Koksu-ri is an outcropping that forms almost a cliff over the left side of the road. They found the Chinese there in force, armed with small arms and satchel charges, ready to attempt to knock the tanks out. Again the column halted and the infantry deployed to fight off the Chinese. This time they deployed farther from the tanks, and when Crombez again ordered the column to resume its advance, more of them were unable to regain their vehicles. How many were abandoned at this second halt is a matter of dispute, but it was between seventy and one hundred soldiers. Among them were Lieutenant Colonel Treacy and Cpl. Carroll G. Everist, both wounded. Treacy had a flesh wound near his mouth, and Everist had been hit in the left knee. Treacy, who could not use the bandage in his first-aid packet on his mouth, dressed Corporal Everist's knee with it. Before the soldiers could evade the enemy, the Chinese were on them and took them prisoner.[29]

The armored column proceeded to the north under continuous enemy fire. The infantry discovered an unfortunate feature of the Patton tanks on the way to Chipyong-ni: even though the deck space was larger than on the Shermans, intense heat from the exhaust grill left less usable space on which the infantry could ride. When soldiers laid an unconscious man with a head wound on the deck of one tank, his clothing soon caught fire. He suffered severe burns before they could extinguish it. Traversing turrets knocked several men off the tanks. This was a greater problem with the Pattons, which had a projection on the rear of the turret that swept men over the side. The concussion of firing the 90-mm gun blew others off.[30]

The most severe fighting came at the road cut south of Chipyong-ni. The Chinese occupied the cliffs in force and made a last-ditch effort to halt the column. A bazooka round hit the lead tank, disabling its radio but not harming the tank itself. The enemy then exploded pole charges near the second tank, on which the engineers were riding, but failed to stop it. Their biggest success came on the fourth tank, which they hit with a bazooka round that penetrated the ring mount beneath the turret. The explosion detonated the rounds in the ready rack, killing all of the crewmen inside except for the driver. Although seriously wounded, the driver had the presence of mind to gun the tank through the cut and off the road to avoid blocking the advance of the rest of the column.[31]

The soldiers inside the 23d RCT's perimeter could hear the firing down the road and knew that rescue might be nearing. Counterattacks continued on the George Company positions. Lieutenant Colonel Edwards had finally organized a counterattack with elements of Baker Company, the remnants of George and Fox Companies, and the Rangers. Meanwhile, the 23d's tanks had begun moving south of the perimeter after the P&A Platoon cleared the road of mines, covered by the Rangers and the tanks. Just as the counterattack appeared to be succeeding, Task Force Crombez's tanks burst into view. The psychological and physical blows were too much for the Chinese, who began to break and run from the hills in all directions.[32]

Thousands of Chinese on all the close and distant hills could now be seen running in long files away from the perimeter. Every available rifleman and

The Task Force Crombez route looking northeast toward Hill 281 as it appeared in November, 1992. Visible in the distance is the road cut where the Chinese tried to stop the armored column. *Photo by author.*

weapon on and inside the perimeter began firing and there were more targets than weapons. Two Chinese Armies were in complete panic! The Chinese ran like terror-stricken deer and stumbled over their own dead and wounded in their wild desire to get away from the perimeter. [The hills all around the perimeter] were swarming with frightened Chinese whose only thought was to get as far away from the perimeter as possible. At 1700 hours, Easy Company again trapped a large group of fleeing Chinese in the draw south of its third platoon area and killed most of them by fire. Air, artillery, tanks, and AA had a field day hitting the more distant targets. The riflemen, machine-guns, recoilless rifles, and mortars hit the close in targets. The din was terrific with all weapons firing. It was like shooting ducks on a pond. Thousands of Chinese were killed during this one "mad hour" of firing.[33]

208

The Task Force Crombez route looking north toward Hills 248 and 281 as it appeared in November, 1992. The road cut leading into Chipyong-ni is visible in the distance. *Photo by author.*

In spite of the hyperbole, it was probably more like ten or twenty minutes of heavy firing before the operations officer gave the order to cease firing and conserve ammunition. Soldiers remember being shocked at how many of the enemy they saw running over the barren hills around Chipyong-ni. Corporal Aubrey Milbach remembers it being like "kicking over an anthill," and being scared when he finally realized just how many Chinese they had been facing.

Why was the rout so dramatic and so sudden? The interrogation of prisoners of war confirmed that as the bodies relentlessly piled up around the Chipyong-ni perimeter, political commissars in the Chinese units were finding it increasingly difficult to force men forward to what they clearly saw was their doom. By the afternoon of the fifteenth, the Chinese peasant soldiers were ready for any excuse to avoid attacking, and Task Force Crombez's arrival, rather that any punishment it inflicted on the Chinese, was the catalyst that broke the siege. As Monclar later said, when both the defender and attacker are in peril, the winner of the battle may be the one who can bluff five minutes longer than his opponent.[34]

The defending infantrymen were more than happy to see Task Force Crombez, even though the tankers brought no ammunition and Crombez would decide not to evacuate the wounded that night. Still, their situation was serious—critical, should the Chinese decide to attack for a third night. In the 2d Battalion, for example, the heavy weapons company had only eighteen rounds of 81-mm mortar ammunition for its tubes, and there were only seven rounds per company for the 60-mm mortars. There were two hand grenades per frontline foxhole. After searching glove compartments, trailer beds, and the pockets and packs of the wounded and dead, there were two clips—sixteen rounds—of rifle ammunition per man in the 2d Battalion's defensive lines, and one clip for those in rear areas. The BARs had two magazines—forty rounds—and machine-guns each had five hundred rounds. The regimental mortar company had about forty rounds for its 4.2-inch mortars. Only the artillery had a plentiful supply of ammunition, as more had been dropped that day. If the Chinese had attacked with the same fury they had on the two previous nights, many of the defenders likely would have died in hand-to-hand combat.[35]

The Chinese, however, had shot their bolt. Except for some flares around the perimeter, the night was quiet and neither small arms nor mortars disturbed Chipyong-ni's defenders that night. Ridgway, understandably relieved that the 23d RCT had not been wiped out, called Crombez's decision to break through with armor when infantry proved too slow one of the best local decisions of the war. Nonetheless, he did not mention Task Force Crombez in his book on the Korean War.[36]

The Aftermath

Colonel Crombez visited the 23d Regiment's CP about dusk, basking in the accolades of the defenders. Since he had decided not to return to his own headquarters that evening, the medical personnel began the disappointing task of unloading all the wounded from the vehicles on which they had been placed for evacuation.[37]

One who observed the arrival of the Love Company infantrymen was

From left: Lieutenant General Ned Almond, X Corps commander, and Lt. Col. Ralph Monclar, French Battalion commander, view the bodies of Chinese troops outside the Chipyong-ni perimeter while Lt. Col. John H. Chiles, the new 23d Regiment commander, confers with an unidentified captain on 17 February 1951. *Courtesy National Archives.*

Sgt. Frank Butler, a tank commander at Chipyong-ni who had been wounded and was in the regimental collecting station:

> This was a very large tent. As I recall, there was more than one tent, for we had a great many wounded. Railroad ties had been stacked up around the outside of the tent in lieu of sandbags, for protection against incoming fire. The tent was heated by a couple of oil-fired small tent stoves and the heat had caused the frozen ground in the tents to melt and turn to mud. Rice

straw had been spread on the ground, and the wounded were sitting or lying in the muddy straw. There were not enough litters to go around. . . .

Outside the tent there was a lot of shouting, and since there had been a
lot of heavy firing just before this, we were concerned. A bunch of people
came into the tent. Among them was Captain Barrett, who I learned later
was commander of Love Company, 5th Cavalry. His company had ridden
into the perimeter at Chipyong-ni on the Task Force Crombez tanks. Barrett was wearing a steel helmet with his name stenciled in black on the bottom of the back of the helmet. He was also wearing a field jacket with a 1st
Cavalry patch and a pistol in a shoulder holster. I don't know if he was
wounded or not, but he was shouting and there was a lot of noise back
and forth. It went something like this: "That son of a bitch got my whole
company killed." Also: "Him and that God Damn Blue Chip." Also, at
that time, there were some wounded Chinese soldiers lying there. I heard,
but did not see this, that Barrett tried to pull his pistol on them, but was
stopped.

Next, some more wounded were brought in. These were three or four enlisted men from the task force. Later that evening, in talking with them, I
saw much bitterness with the whole operation. I heard that Crombez was
thought to be a flamboyant show-off who had gotten a lot of men killed
needlessly. It was said . . . that he carried a blue poker chip that he flipped
in the air while talking. He was called "Blue Chip Crombez" by these
men.[38]

Another soldier who remembers the infantrymen's anger toward
Crombez is Lt. Robert Curtis, whom Lieutenant Colonel Edwards sent to
escort the tanks into the perimeter. His recollections are not so vivid as
those of Corporal Bererd of the French Battalion, who got no response
from the infantrymen on the tanks when he tried to talk to them. Bererd
thought that they were in shock, and that their hatred of Crombez was
only outweighed by their exhaustion: "They were just too tired to kill
him."

Sergeant James Cardinal encountered the anger of the soldiers against
Crombez in the days following the action:

The anger throughout the 3d Battalion at Crombez as a result of what was
widely perceived to be his callous misuse of the men of L Company for his
self-aggrandizement was so intense that it was almost palpable. In the weeks
following [the linkup] I spoke with and listened to numerous men in all of
the companies of the 3d Battalion, including some in what was left of L

Company. I was able to do this because the [Intelligence and Reconnaissance] Section was constantly on the move, and we came into frequent contact with all 3d Battalion units and occasional contact with other 5th Cavalry units. Everyone in the 3d Battalion knew about it, and everyone talked about it with great passion. Feelings about Crombez were so negative that officers were not reluctant to express their contempt for him in front of enlisted men. This serious violation of Army Regulations and the [Uniform Code of Military Justice] I know personally to be true because I heard a number of such comments on various occasions in the presence of other enlisted men. . . .

[Crombez's] spitefulness and inability to set aside old grievances prevented him from acting in a professional and detached manner toward Treacy and the 3d Battalion, with its inevitable adverse effect on morale within the battalion. . . .

I can think of no more contemptible conduct on the part of an officer who accepts, even insists upon, the responsibility to lead men in combat, than to abandon those men to capture by the enemy without making every effort to rescue them.

Captain Barrett tried to persuade Crombez to return down the road that night to pick up his men who might be waiting as they had been instructed to if separated from the tanks. Crombez refused. "No, I'm not going back," he replied. "There's too much enemy fire."[39]

On the road to the south, the infantrymen who had been abandoned by the armored column on the way to Chipyong-ni were making their way one by one to friendly lines to the south, or were learning firsthand the not-so-tender mercies of their Chinese captors.

Lieutenant Colonel Treacy and Corporal Everist were in a group of seven captives whom the Chinese led about three miles to the north before stopping. Corporal Everist's knee injury kept him from being able to walk, so Treacy carried him on his back. When they arrived at a small building in a clearing, the group halted and the Chinese took all of the prisoners' personal belongings. They allowed Everist to keep a small prayer book he had been given by his home congregation in Mason City, Iowa.

After they had taken the other prisoners away, a soldier tried to get Everist up and walking. His knee prevented this and the Chinese soldier raised his rifle to shoot him. Everist became hysterical and the Chinese abandoned him. He used a belt and stick to improvise a tourniquet on his leg and loosened it every few minutes as he had been taught at ski school in Colorado. After three days of eating snow and icicles, he spotted an American patrol. Suspicious of a trap, the patrol leader sent his sergeant to check Everist out. After confirming that he was an American, the patrol fed him his first meal in three days, a can of C-ration beans and franks.

When the patrol had carried Everist back to the unit and he was lying on a litter ready to be evacuated to the rear, Colonel Crombez came to see him. Everist related his story to the colonel, concluding with his assessment that Treacy was the best officer in the regiment. Crombez did not respond.[40]

Several things are worthy of note in the Task Force Crombez after-action reports, all of which it may be assumed were approved, if not written, by Crombez personally. First, Crombez signed the cover sheet of the regiment's report, which is a departure from the custom of these being anonymous documents. Each description of action includes "Comments by the Commander" highlighting positive aspects of the action, and every time the report mentions Task Force Crombez, "commanded by Col. Marcel G. Crombez" is appended. In none of the reports are there any second thoughts or regrets concerning the order for the infantry to ride atop the tanks. There are, however, several negative remarks concerning Lieutenant Colonel Treacy's disobeying orders to accompany the column. Personal criticisms like these are unusual in such a report: "Lt. Col. Edgar Treacy, who had been designated to bring up the supply train and ambulances for the 23rd Inf RCT disobeyed the instructions and joined L Co, riding the tanks. He was later reported missing in action."[41]

In the etiquette of official documents, such a remark without extenuating comments amounts to an official reprimand. Finally, on the overlay accompanying the map, there is the annotation "TOTAL LOSSES—10 KIA." Considering the final tally of thirteen killed or died of wounds, nineteen missing, and more than fifty wounded, this seems to be a deliberately misleading remark.[42]

Among the survivors of Love Company, demands for proper recognition of Treacy's heroism and self-sacrifice soon emerged. Captains John Barrett and Norman Allen, at the request of a number of the soldiers, began collecting statements and preparing a recommendation for award of the Medal of Honor to Treacy. A newspaper article described the effort:

> The GIs who survived the bloody cavalry dash to the rescue of the surrounded Chipyong garrison have petitioned for the award of the Congressional Medal of Honor to their battalion commander, Lt. Col. Edgar J. Treacy.

Ed Treacy, a rifle-toting, West Point-graduated foot soldier, has long been a hero to enlisted men and officers alike of the 5th Cavalry Regiment, 3d Battalion. The fact that he was a lieutenant colonel didn't seem to matter.

Treacy is believed to be a prisoner of the Chinese Communists. He was captured Feb. 15 while carrying a wounded man to relative safety as his task force of 24 tanks and a company of 5th Cav infantrymen ran a 15-mile gauntlet of fire to break the trap around the Franco-American garrison at Chipyong.

In an hour of hell, while Chinese lining the road poured machine-gun and rifle fire into the column, Treacy sustained a light face wound but refused the safety of a tank's interior to fight beside his exposed infantrymen.

Out of the confused memory of the battle, his men remember seeing the colonel manning a machine-gun, picking off Chinese with his M-1 rifle, dashing under fire from squad to squad to hold his outnumbered force together, administering first aid, carrying wounded men on his back to safety, and finally compiling a list of the men taken prisoner with him to send back to the regiment.

The full account was related here Sunday by the infantry company commander, Capt. John C. Barrett of Omaha, Neb. Barrett is recovering from a minor wound.

Immediately after the action, enlisted men who survived the rescue operation started the movement to nominate their colonel for the "highest award a man can get"—the Congressional Medal of Honor. The recommendation is now going through official channels. But whether Ed Treacy becomes the Korean war's sixth winner of the Congressional Medal or not, he has already won a tribute rarely paid by soldiers to an officer.

Barrett said "Colonel Treacy is the best that America can produce. He always put the interests of the men first. He never sacrificed the life of a single man by a tactical blunder or a snap decision. He was the only man in the battalion who never had a bad word said about him."[43]

In fact, the recommendation never left the 5th Cavalry Regiment. When the regiment's executive officer took the packet of recommendations and statements to Colonel Crombez, he threw it on the ground and crushed it with his boot. "Medal of Honor, no goddammit, no," he said, "If he ever returns to military control I will court-martial him."[44]

Treacy died in a North Korean prison camp less than three months after his capture. One reason for the illness that killed him was that he gave his food to other sickly prisoners.[45]

Colonel Crombez was convinced that the commander of a successful regiment in combat deserved a valor decoration and promotion to brigadier general. After dictating his own recommendation for the Distinguished Service Cross, he submitted it through channels. When it got to Eighth Army, the chief of staff, Brig. Gen. Henry I. Hodes rejected it saying, "No sonofabitch earns a DSC inspiring his men buttoned up in a tank. I know, I am an old tanker!" Later, Crombez called on Ridgway and asked that his recommendation for the Distinguished Service Cross be reconsidered. After he left, Ridgway instructed Hodes to approve the award, saying he knew it was questionable, "but he did bust into Freeman's 23rd Regiment, and I told the entire Eighth Army that if any unit could hold against heavy Chinese odds, I'd put the whole Eighth Army in to relieve them, and Crombez did that." Crombez was later promoted to brigadier general and retired at that rank in 1956.[46]

Crombez's decision to have the Love Company infantrymen ride the tanks into Chipyong-ni was much criticized in subsequent army analyses of his task force's performance. At least as open to criticism was failure to have artillery or fighter-bombers subdue the Chinese on the ridges along the route to Chipyong-ni. The guns at Chipyong-ni were capable of firing on targets even beyond Koksu-ri, and they had plenty of ammunition. Air strikes also were available. As early as three weeks later, a training bulletin criticizing the operation was being circulated in Korea:

> In situations such as this Infantry should not have been included in the task force. The surrounded force had plenty of doughboys; all that was needed was a powerful punch to break through with resupply of rations and ammunition. Lacking the armored personnel carriers essential for transporting Infantrymen, the force would have been better off without this additional burden. To insure absolute success, a relieving task force in such a situation should be self-sufficient—as a Combat Command in an Armored Division. Lacking this in an emergency, the force should be small, compact, and strong enough to break its way through. . . .
>
> Infantrymen should ride on tanks only as a last resort and should never let themselves be taken under fire while aboard tanks. . . .
>
> The task force would probably never have exposed itself to such a withering close-range ambush had a liaison plane been overhead picking up the enemy positions. Once in such a situation, the force would not have suffered so many casualties had it been provided with adequate air cover.[47]

Left: Major General Charles D. Palmer, 1st Cavalry Division commander, congratulates Col. Marcel G. Crombez, 5th Cavalry Regiment commander, after presenting him the Silver Star with first oak leaf cluster on 13 July 1951. *Courtesy National Archives.*

Although there is no gainsaying that Task Force Crombez was crucial in breaking the Chinese stranglehold on Chipyong-ni, there can also be no denying that it could have been done at a lower cost in human lives and even earlier on the same day with better planning, judgment, and leadership than Crombez demonstrated.[48]

Chapter 12

Aftermath and Reflections

So ends the bloody business of the day.

—Homer

Battles decide everything.

—Clausewitz

I hope to God I have fought my last battle. It is a bad thing to be always fighting. While in the thick of it I am too much occupied to feel anything; but it is wretched just after. It is quite impossible to think of glory. . . . Next to a battle lost, the greatest misery is a battle gained.

—Wellington

To teach the art of war entirely by historical examples . . . would be an achievement of the utmost value; but it would be more than the work of a lifetime: anyone who set out to do it would first have to equip himself with a thorough personal experience of war.

Anyone who feels the urge to undertake such a task must dedicate himself for his labors as he would prepare for a pilgrimage to distant lands. He must spare no time or effort, fear no earthly power or rank, and rise above his own vanity or false modesty in order to tell, in accordance with the expression of the Code Napoleòn, the truth, the whole truth, and nothing but the truth.

—Clausewitz

The arrival of Task Force Crombez brought the battle of Chipyong-ni to a dramatic end late in the afternoon on 15 February 1951, although the leaders could not be sure of that at the time. Ammunition stocks were critically low throughout the 23d RCT, and the task force's tanks did not add enough firepower to the regiment to make up for those shortages. If the Chinese had regrouped and attacked that night, they would have had a good chance of overrunning and destroying the encircled defenders. For this reason, Lieutenant Colonel Meszar, whom the new commander had effectively put in charge of the defense, demanded emergency aerial resupply of ammunition, and nineteen aircraft made parachute drops of small arms and mortar ammunition, the last at 2340 hours.

The Chinese had no fight left in them, however. Except for more flare activity as they searched the battlefield for wounded, there was no activity through the remainder of the night. On the sixteenth, only a few rounds of artillery fire fell inside the perimeter, and patrols to reestablish contact with the Chinese found no enemy within a mile of the village.

The 5th Cavalry Regiment supply convoy arrived at 1630 hours on the sixteenth and, as soon as it was unloaded, the wounded were loaded on the trucks and they began their evacuation through medical channels.[1] On 20 February, General MacArthur flew in from Tokyo and presented a second Presidential Unit Citation to the 23d Infantry Regiment and to the French battalion.[2]

Battle Appraisals

In some ways, the battle of Chipyong-ni resembled the Duke of Wellington's appraisal of Waterloo: "a damned nice thing—the nearest-run thing you ever saw in your life." Just as Prussian field marshal Gebhard von Blücher's cavalry arriving late in the day saved that victory for the British, so had Crombez's arrival saved the UN forces. Certainly there are many ways that the battle could have turned into a disaster for Ridgway's forces. Probably the greatest factor in the final success at both the Twin Tunnels and Chipyong-ni was the attackers' shortcomings. If the Chinese had possessed the ability to command, control, and communicate within their forces, they could have better coordinated their attacks in each case and overrun the defenders. If, for example, the Chinese unit that took George Company hill at Chipyong-ni could have gotten word of their success to the Chinese high command, their leaders could have rushed more forces to the area and penetrated the perimeter decisively.

If the Chinese had possessed better intelligence-gathering means, they could have ascertained just how desperate the ammunition situation was by the second day of fighting at Chipyong-ni, and then exploited that vulnerability. Anyone using high-powered binoculars from the hills surrounding the isolated force could have observed how desperate the mortar ammunition situation was, as the stocks of that ammunition were continually depleted throughout the siege without replenishment. Had they possessed the ability to monitor radio conversations, they would have been able to hear Freeman's pleas for better coordination of resupply drops.

If the Chinese had brought in fresh units on the third night, it is unlikely that the 23d RCT would have been able to hold out against a final strong attack, even with Task Force Crombez present.

Nevertheless, the American soldiers and their French comrades prevailed. What was it that brought them through? The command was a strong one, with high morale and superb leadership. Colonel Paul Freeman and Lt. Gen. Ralph Monclar were outstanding leaders with a synergism between them like few others in military history. They got along personally and professionally and shared an aggressive, no-nonsense command style. They demanded and received absolute loyalty and competence from their subordinates. This often was accomplished through their strong subordinates, outstanding leaders themselves—including Lt. Col. Frank Meszar, Maj. Maurice Barthelemy, and the competent battalion and company commanders, who all performed superbly during the battles.

Because of this leadership throughout the command, the soldiers were ready to rise to whatever superhuman efforts were asked of them. The men trusted their leaders not to hazard their lives without good cause, and this trust made the leaders confident their orders would unquestionably be carried out. This quality of trust—the compact between the leader and the led—is less evident between the leaders and the led in Task Force Crombez.

The compact between the leaders and the led generated high morale throughout the 23d RCT despite the appalling cold, enemy action, and inevitable losses. It fostered trust between units, and a healthy competition for each unit to outperform its sister units. The men were confident that casualties would get the best possible care at all times, and that their leaders would do all in their power to get them the rations, ammunition, and equipment needed to accomplish the mission.

The Dilemma of Questioning Orders

The soldiers knew that their commanders—especially Freeman and Monclar—would not unquestioningly comply with orders that did not make sense in light of the tactical situation. The question of when and at what level of command the commander has the right—one might say the responsibility—to question orders rather than carry them out automatically is a difficult and sensitive one. Many good officers would answer that a subordinate should never question orders. General Ridgway said that on more than one occasion, yet he himself questioned orders several times when he felt strongly about an issue. In World War II, for example, while Ridgway was commanding the 82d Airborne Division, General Eisenhower ordered the division to drop on Rome in September, 1943. Ridgway thought the operation could result in disaster and went to Eisenhower's chief of staff to object to the mission: "I stated that in my opinion this mission, under these conditions, violated every principle we had developed in our training, and that my conscience compelled me to state my strong objections."[3] In so doing, Ridgway was aware that his objections would be made, as he put it later, "at the risk of my career." However, after a series of actions to confirm that the operation was as risky as Ridgway thought, Eisenhower ultimately canceled it.[4] In retirement, Ridgway took pride in his decision to question and oppose orders he thought unwise, and he reflected on that incident and his later opposition to a proposal for the 82d to force a crossing of the Volturno River during the Italian campaign: "To me such incidents most frequently found in war are those where the career of the leader is at stake, and where his actions or decisions well determine the saving or slaughter of many of his men. History is full of these cases. The lure of glory, the fear of being thought afraid, of losing personal power and prestige, the mistaken idea that blind obedience to orders have no alternative—all have been followed by tragic losses of lives with little or no gain."[5] In this context, he quoted Gen. George C. Marshall, whom he described as "one of the noblest men who has worn an American uniform since Washington," on questioning orders: "It is hard to get men to do this, for this is when you lay your career, perhaps your commission, on the line."[6]

It would appear that Freeman may have questioned orders at the risk of his career, certainly at the risk of losing command of his regiment. The speed with which General Almond ordered him relieved because of a minor wound, over the vigorous objections of the regimental surgeon and Freeman's strongly stated desire to stay in command at least through the end of the siege of Chipyong-ni, would seem to indicate that Almond was looking for a reason to relieve him as soon as possible.

It is axiomatic that in any military organization, questioning orders should always remain rare, but the corollary of that axiom is that military organizations should eliminate leaders whose orders inspire loyal subordinates to doubt their wisdom. At some level, probably at about battalion or regimental command, leaders have a responsibility to those whom they lead to question orders they think are inappropriate. The leader who believes he knows more about the military situation at the moment than the staff officer or commander who issued questionable orders has the responsibility to at least ask whether the current situation has been properly assessed. Likewise, the leader who assesses a mission as a forlorn hope in the absence of the life-or-death factors that made the defenders at Thermopylae hold out until the last man was killed are responsible for insuring to their own satisfaction that such a suicide mission is the only way to achieve success. Such missions have been and will continue to be necessary in war, but they should never become routine. As wags have expressed the dilemma, "If you do it right, you can only fall on your sword once."

Leadership

Both Freeman and Monclar were physically fit and required the same of their subordinates. This allowed them to set the example, as did the fifty-eight-year-old Monclar by climbing the daunting, ice-covered Hill 453 the day before the battle of Twin Tunnels—a challenging task for his youngest, fittest soldiers. It allowed both commanders the ability to walk and understand the terrain they expected their soldiers to fight on, and to appreciate the challenges and shortcomings of all their positions. This in turn enabled them to anticipate crises and be, as Wellington put it, "on the spot" when a crisis developed. The inspiration soldiers felt as they watched Freeman laboriously make his way around the perimeter with a walking stick the morning after he was wounded is immeasurable, because every soldier who saw him knew that Freeman was worried about their welfare.

Both commanders, and many of their subordinates, had a particular facility for planning in detail, assessing a changing situation, and continually assimilating large quantities of often-conflicting data. They combined this with their experience, intelligence, and moral courage to give them the flexibility to adapt to the circumstances they encountered. This adaptability allowed them to cut through the fog of war. Both officers had learned, through their experiences in both peace and war, to expect to have more information than was useful in making decisions; to have much intelligence that would prove to be false; to have the friction of war result in unexpected mistakes and accidents; and yet be able to call on the forces of character and courage to sustain themselves and their units to a successful outcome.

Freeman and Monclar required aggressiveness, audacity, and vigorous execution from their subordinates, and both they and their soldiers refused to accept defeat. They and their units continued with their missions in spite of casualties, their own wounds, lost equipment, and the shortage of supplies and ammunition.

The 23d RCT and the French Battalion each keyed on their leader and took on the leader's confidence and spirit. It is no exaggeration to say that Freeman and Monclar were the most decisive factor in building cohesion in their units. Although each was new to his unit shortly before it was committed to combat—Freeman just before embarkation, Monclar when the battalion was formed—each was key to the process of building that cohesion. By the time the 23d Infantry broke out of the Pusan Perimeter and by the time the French Battalion had participated in the battles around Wonju, their units had achieved a high degree of cohesion.

Both Freeman and Monclar had unquestioned integrity concerning his duties, coupled with a solid ethical foundation in matters dealing with combat, in the eyes of their soldiers. Both had a positive self-image and each refused to take counsel of his fears. Both enjoyed the respect of their subordinates and peers to a greater degree than that of their superiors, possibly a result of their unquestioned loyalty to the soldiers they led. Neither leader appeared to his soldiers to be intent on furthering his own career. Rather, they were perceived as trying to do the best they were capable of in leading the soldiers they commanded.

The leaders had prepared themselves for the challenge of combat without knowing where or when that challenge might come. Some officers had attended prestigious military colleges and military academies, including the U.S. Military Academy and the École Spéciale Militaire de Saint-Cyr, as well as specialized military courses and self-study programs. Other officers received their education in the military through experience, as was the case with the many "battlefields" present in the regiment—soldiers whose combat performance had earned them commissions in World War II or earlier in Korea. Enlisted soldiers were leaders as well, and the leadership of the sergeants and corporals at Twin Tunnels and Chipyong-ni contributed immeasurably to the victories.

The Individual and the Experience of Combat

Leaders can do nothing without followers, and every leader in the army of a democracy is himself a follower at some level. The soldiers of the 23d

Lieutenant General Ned Almond, X Corps commander, congratulates Lt. Col. Ralph Monclar, the French Battalion commander at the Twin Tunnels and Chipyong-ni, after awarding him the Silver Star. *Courtesy U.S. Army Military History Institute.*

RCT and the French Battalion were responsible for the victories as much as any of their leaders. They each knew in their own way that combat would test their skills and their reserves of character to the limit. Being human, most soldiers had at least some inner and unspoken doubts as to their ability to carry out their duties successfully, but each of them worked at evaluating and reinforcing his skill and character to build the resources necessary for survival. Most of this effort was unconscious, but no less real for being inadvertent. When soldiers talked to one another about their predicament, they were assessing their situation in light of others' perceptions. When they discussed their leaders and peers, they were evaluating whether they had the "right stuff" to endure the tests to come. At the same time, they boosted their own spirit and self-esteem by bragging about how good their unit was compared to the enemy's ineptitude.

The prospect was most challenging for soldiers who had not experienced combat. All had heard war stories from the veterans among them, many had read accounts of combat, and most had seen combat depicted in the movies and newsreels during the recent world war. But the common denominator among all the accounts was that each one was different and each inexplicable in its own way. For the veterans, although the prospect was more familiar, it was no less foreboding. Regardless of how much combat the veterans had seen, each incident was *sui generis*—the only example of its kind, unique in its own way. The veterans knew that they could never explain what combat was like to one who had not been there, and that however much they tried, any description would be a pale depiction of a life-changing experience.

Most soldiers faced the prospect of combat with worries about their own reservoirs of courage and whether or not they would stand up to the tests to come. Some took solace in deep religious convictions of divine protection. Others felt that matters of fate were out of their hands or influence, and that they had no choice but to do their best to survive in any situation. Many simply hoped that they would be up to anything that happened, that their courage would carry them through.

Courage is a slippery concept. Lord Moran, who wrote *The Anatomy of Courage* based on his experiences as a physician in World War I, compared it to a bank account that every soldier carried with him. Courageous soldiers began with more in their account, less brave soldiers with smaller accounts. Soldiers could build up their account in times between combat, through rest and reflection and the support of comrades. Battle, however, depleted every soldier's account, and every man's account could finally be depleted to insolvency. As he put it:

> Courage is will-power, whereof no man has an unlimited stock; and when in war it is used up, he is finished. A man's courage is his capital and he is always spending. The call on the bank may be only the daily drain of the front line or it may be a sudden draft which threatens to close the account. His will

is perhaps almost destroyed by intensive shelling, by heavy bombing, or by a bloody battle, or it may be used up by monotony, by exposure, by the loss of the support of stauncher spirits on whom he has come to depend, by physical exhaustion, by a wrong attitude to danger, to casualties, to war, to death itself.[7]

Others have disputed this analogy, and still others have tried to describe some of the many varieties of courage. What observers may see as courage can be merely fatalism that happens never to end badly, or it can be such confidence in one's abilities (or his weapons or his unit or other similar factors) that failure is not even an acknowledged possibility.[8] What can be said of courage from the accounts of the battles at the Twin Tunnels and Chipyong-ni is that soldiers often worried about their own courage and that of their comrades, and that they did everything within their power to assure themselves that they would not embarrass themselves when the test came. Many prayed; a few wrote detailed accounts of the action to their relatives or kept diaries; most took some reassurance in tendentiously checking and rechecking their equipment, cleaning and recleaning their weapons, and scrounging anything they thought they might need to survive. One of the strongest builders of individual courage was the confidence of soldiers in their own small group.

Analysts have recognized the cohesion of small groups of fighting men as a key factor in their success or failure throughout military history, but it remains an intangible factor, resistant to measurement by the analytical tools modern researchers use to quantify military effectiveness. Few commentators have exceeded in wisdom the ideas Monclar outlined in his chapter on cohesion in his "Catechisme de Combat." He discussed how living and working together helped soldiers learn to know one another like members of a family, and he observed that this forced coexistence built confidence in the unit and helped the men reinforce their own confidence. S. L. A. Marshall, from the experience of observing soldiers in numerous conflicts, described the phenomenon this way: "I hold it to be one of the simplest truths of war that the thing which enables an infantry soldier to keep going with his weapons is the near presence or the presumed presence of a comrade."[9] Few soldiers could survive without the assistance of the small group.

The Unit and the Cause

The memories of combat almost always touch on the unit the soldier served in. As far as he is concerned, his unit was either the best or one of the best units his nation sent to war. Those who have not experienced such an existence have a difficult time relating to the bonds that a soldier forms with his comrades in arms. His fellow soldiers often become more of a family than his relatives at home, and his existence is bonded with more closely to theirs than most people experience in civilian life. The soldiers of the 23d Regiment and the French Battalion became true "brothers in arms" through their life in the Korean War. The field soldier's existence revolves around his squad, platoon, or company, and to a lesser extent his battalion, regiment, and division. Many men may not remember which corps or army they were in, but no one forgets his small unit because the soldiers with whom he served became closer than most of his blood relatives. A man's deepest beliefs, secrets, and fears were revealed in the endless sessions of war stories and reminiscences of life before the war and aspirations of the life to follow. When combat threatened the unit, every soldier's very existence depended on the plans and actions of his officers and his fellow soldiers.

The pride of membership in the fraternity of soldiers often extends beyond the platoon and company, as it did in the 23d Regiment and the French Battalion. The confidence that veterans had in their unit encouraged acts that no soldier would perform of his own volition. The depth of the connections between wartime comrades is profound, and throughout history many observers have tried to describe its intensity. Shakespeare perhaps did it best when he penned the immortal words for Henry V before the battle of Agincourt on Saint Crispin's Day:

> If we are marked to die, we are enow
> To do our country loss; and if to live,
> The fewer men, the greater share of honor. . . .
> He which hath no stomach to this fight,
> Let him depart; his passport shall be made,
> And crowns for convoy put into his purse:
> We would not die in that man's company
> That fears his fellowship to die with us. . . .
> We few, we happy few, we band of brothers;
> For he to-day that sheds his blood with me
> Shall be my brother; be he ne'er so vile
> This day shall gentle his condition:
> And gentlemen in England, now abed
> Shall think themselves accursed they were not here,

And hold their manhoods cheap whiles any speaks
That fought with us upon Saint Crispin's day.[10]

Politicians have tried to use this profound sense of shared sacrifice and brotherhood to rally peoples to other causes than war—the "war on poverty" and the "war on drugs" to cite only two recent examples—but the element of danger seems to be necessary for the bonding to take place. Certainly those soldiers who fought on the Naktong, at Twin Tunnels, and at Chipyong-ni felt this bonding, and many have retained the sense of brotherhood with comrades for decades following the events that made them feel they were a band of brothers not unlike those Shakespeare described before Agincourt.

The real importance of small-unit cohesion in any conflict is that unless company-sized and smaller units undertake their missions with conviction and accomplish them successfully, larger units cannot be successful. The fifteen or so infantry companies in the 23d Regiment were the real key to its success. The support of such weapons as tanks, artillery, and aircraft were helpful—and at times essential—for success, but if the small units did not do their jobs with enthusiasm and efficiency, the supporting weapons were useless. Both Freeman and Monclar understood this and closely monitored all of their units for hints of problems, knowing that all the resources General Ridgway and his subordinate leaders could supply would be wasted if the infantry platoons and companies failed to carry out their assignments.

Unquestionably, the higher ideals for which the UN forces fought were profoundly important in the minds of the soldiers. If asked, many would likely have answered that they were fighting for those ideals: freedom for South Korea, the triumph of democracy over communist ideology, the "fight for our own freedom, for our own survival, in an honorable, independent national existence" that General Ridgway outlined in his letter to Eighth Army in January, 1951. Nonetheless, the Korean War was for many soldiers like wars described by earlier veterans: "one foxhole wide." Their survival was dependent on the survival of the small group of soldiers that made up their family, and they could not let them down. If a man abandoned his position, the Chinese might overrun the line and his comrades would perish. Thus, each man depended not only on his own actions, but also on the soldiers to his flanks. No one ever threw himself on a live grenade to save democracy, but countless soldiers have given their lives for their comrades.

The Synergy of the Leaders and the Led in the 23d RCT

The soldiers of the 23d Regiment and the French Battalion formed a cohesive, determined group. They trusted one another, they trusted their leaders, and they believed in their cause. The effect of this trust and cooperation toward the goal of defeating their enemies was to create a unit that was truly greater than any of its components.

Such units are rare in any army, although their creation is the goal of every high command. The 23d's leaders knew that if they gave an order, the men would do everything humanly possible to carry it out, even at the risk of annihilation. The regiment's soldiers, on the other hand, knew that their leaders would not give such orders without a compelling need for their efforts and sacrifices. This phenomenon caused both the leaders and the led to rise above their abilities to a level of performance that few units have equaled.

The components that come together to build such units are largely intangible. An army can have high standards for its members; it can supply them with the weapons, ammunition, and equipment to accomplish their missions; but the synergy that occurs to make a select unit truly elite is beyond the competence of any staff, however talented. It requires the coming together in a single organization of soldiers, sergeants, and officers each able to perform or to learn to perform the myriad tasks required in any assignment. It then takes time and good training or combat to weld the individuals into a group with ties as strong as in any family. Building individuals' confidence in not only their own abilities, but in those of their comrades as well as their leaders takes time and the successful surmounting of challenges and hardships. Shared danger and shared successes accumulate on one another to build attachments among the men and culminate in the belief that there is nothing the unit cannot accomplish. This feeling of solidarity usually extends only to the small group—squad, platoon, or company—but it can be built to encompass battalions, regiments, and even divisions.[11]

As with other soldiers in other wars, the actions of the men who served in the 23d RCT and its attached French Battalion remain alive in their memories a half-century after they occurred, as fresh as if they were last week. Hopefully their stories, told now to a new audience, may inform, educate, and inspire others in the profession of arms.

Notes

Introduction

1. Carl von Clausewitz, *On War,* trans. and ed. Michael Howard and Peter Paret (Princeton, N.J.: Princeton University Press, 1976), 119.

2. Tom Wolfe, *Mauve Gloves & Madmen, Clutter & Vine* (New York: Farrar, Straus, and Giroux, 1976), "The Truest Sport: Jousting with Sam and Charlie," 26–65.

3. With but a few atypical exceptions in American military history, men alone have engaged in combat. Although this exclusivity is changing and will almost surely continue to evolve, there were no women among the United Nations combatants at Twin Tunnels or Chipyong-ni, although the combatants found some female corpses among the Chinese casualties. For this reason, this book reflects the conditions when the historical events occurred and thus eschews such nongender-specific constructions as "humans" or "persons."

Chapter 1. The 23d Infantry Regiment and Col. Paul Freeman

1. Senior Officers Debriefing Project, "Interview of General Paul L. Freeman, Jr., by Lieutenant Colonel James N. Ellis" (hereafter Freeman Oral History), 1973–74, the Paul L. Freeman, Jr., Papers (hereafter Freeman Papers), Archives, U.S. Army Military History Institute, Carlisle Barracks, Pa. (hereafter MHI); Headquarters, 23d Infantry Regiment, Narrative Summary of Command and Unit Historical Report, (hereafter 23d Inf. Command Report) 9–31 July 1950. All of the various 23d Inf. Command Reports cited in this work are archived in the Freeman Papers.

2. J. Glenn Gray, *The Warriors: Reflections on Men in Battle* (New York: Harper and Row, 1959), 43, 45–46.

3. "Organic" units are those that are an integral part of the larger organization rather than "attached" or under "operational control" for a specific mission.

4. *Table of Organization and Equipment* (hereafter *TO&E*) *7–11N, Infantry Regiment* (Washington, D.C.: Department of the Army, 15 Nov. 1950); "Special Regulation SR 320–5-1," in *Dictionary of United States Army Terms* (Washington, D.C.: GPO, Aug., 1950), 52.

5. 23d Inf. Command Report, 9–31 July 1950.

6. Ibid.

7. Freeman Oral History. Active-duty soldiers and the sons of career military soldiers, among others, were eligible for presidential nominations. Because professional soldiers moved frequently, they usually had little or no contact with their congressional representatives, making this an important—and often the only feasible—category of academy nominations for their sons.

8. *Assembly,* Nov., 1990, 163.

9. Ibid.; Freeman Oral History.

10. *The Howitzer, 1929* (West Point, N.Y.: U.S. Military Academy, 1929), 135. "Beast Barracks" is the name given to stressful military training conducted by upperclassmen before cadets begin their

first academic year. Although "hazing" was against regulations, modified forms of what most reasonable individuals would consider to be hazing existed at West Point throughout the twentieth century.

11. Freeman Oral History; *Register of Graduates and Former Cadets* (West Point, N.Y.: Association of Graduates, 1990), 403, no. 8699; *Second Infantry Division* (Paducah, Ky.: Turner, 1989), 81.

12. *Assembly,* Nov., 1990, 164.

13. Ibid.; Ray S. Cline, *Washington Command Post: The Operations Division* (Washington, D.C.: Chief of Military History, 1951), 246–47.

14. *Assembly,* Nov., 1990, 164.

15. "Mission-type" orders are those which tell a subordinate commander what task is to be accomplished, rather than how to accomplish it, thus giving the subordinate maximum latitude and opportunity to use initiative and imagination.

16. Freeman Oral History.

17. *The Howitzer, 1940* (West Point, N.Y.: U.S. Military Academy, 1940), 190.

Chapter 2. Baptism by Fire on the Naktong River Line

1. Nena Vreeland and Rinn-Sup Shinn, *Area Handbook for North Korea* (Washington, D.C.: GPO, 1976), 39–46; Nina Vreeland et al., *Area Handbook for South Korea* (Washington, D.C.: GPO, 1975), 31–44.

2. For accounts of the origins of the Korean War using late-twentieth-century revelations from wartime archives, see Chen Jian, *China's Road to the Korean War* (New York: Columbia University Press, 1994); *Mao's China and the Cold War* (Chapel Hill: University of North Carolina Press, 2001); Xiaobing Li, Allan R. Millett, and Bin Yu, *Mao's Generals Remember Korea* (Lawrence: University Press of Kansas, 2001); Shu Guang Zhang, *Mao's Military Romanticism: China and the Korean War, 1950–1953* (Lawrence: University Press of Kansas, 1995); William Stueck, *The Korean War: An International History* (Princeton, N.J.: Princeton University Press, 1995); and the diverse papers of the Woodrow Wilson Center International Cold War History Project in Washington, D.C.

3. Merle Miller, *Plain Speaking: An Oral Biography of Harry S. Truman* (New York: Berkley, 1973), 273.

4. A readable account of the early phases of the war is in Clay Blair, *The Forgotten War: America in Korea, 1950–53* (New York: Times Books, 1987), chaps. 4–9. The Almond quote is on page 88.

5. Roy E. Appleman, *South to the Naktong, North to the Yalu,* U.S. Army in the Korean War (Washington, D.C.: Department of the Army, 1961), 7–18; Blair, *Forgotten War,* 55–56.

6. Freeman Oral History, 97f; 23d Inf. Command Report, 1–31 Aug. 1950.

7. Ibid. See also *TO&E 7–11N; TO&E 6–25N, Field Artillery Battalion, 105mm Howitzer, Truck–Drawn* (Washington, D.C.: Department of the Army, 15 Nov. 1950); *TO&E 44–27, Antiaircraft Artillery Automatic Weapons Battery, Mobile* (Washington, D.C.: Department of the Army, 4 Oct. 1948); *TO&E 5–17N, Engineer Combat Company, Divisional* (Washington, D.C.: Department of the Army, 4 Feb. 1948).

8. 23d Inf. Command Report, 1–31 Aug. 1950; Vincent J. Esposito, *The West Point Atlas of American Wars* (New York: Praeger, 1960), sec. 3, "The Korean War," Map 5. The term *main supply route* is self-explanatory. It is essential that a unit's MSR be kept open to facilitate resupply operations or withdrawal if necessary.

9. 23d Inf. Command Report, 1–31 Aug. 1950; Freeman Oral History.

10. "Banana clips," so named because of their curved shape, held thirty rounds as opposed to the regular magazines, which held only fifteen. "Double clips" were two magazines taped or welded together end-for-end, allowing the firer to quickly reverse them and thus maintain his volume of fire.

11. Quoted in Roger J. Spiller, ed. *Dictionary of American Military Biography* (Westport, Conn.: Greenwood Press, 1984), 2:796.

12. Cordite is a smokeless artillery and mortar propellant composed of nitrocellulose, nitroglycerin, and petrolatum. It burns with an unforgettable acrid chemical smell.

13. Freeman Oral History.

14. Ibid.

15. Clay Blair, *Forgotten War,* 240f; 23d Inf. Command Report, 1–30 Sept. 1950.

16. Blair, *Forgotten War,* 247; 23d Inf. Command Report, 1–30 Sept. 1950. A command post is the location from which the commander and his staff elements direct the battle. As a minimum, it ordinarily includes the commander, operations officer, communications personnel, and local security forces.

17. A blocking position is intended to keep enemy forces from moving through an area. The blocking force usually establishes physical roadblocks consisting of abandoned vehicles, felled trees, or whatever is at hand, and mans positions supported by direct and indirect fires on likely routes through the area.

18. 23d Inf. Command Reports, 1–31 Aug. and 1–30 Sept. 1950.

19. An obstacle is said to "cover" a position when it prevents another force from firing on it. Thus, a hill may cover a valley or a rice paddy dike may cover the ground near it. When something merely prevents observation, it is said to "conceal" it. Examples include foliage concealing a foxhole, and smoke concealing hostile movement. Some obstacles may provide cover from direct fire, but neither cover nor concealment from indirect fire. A camouflaged bunker might be said to offer both cover and concealment.

20. 23d Infantry Regiment S3 Journal (hereafter 23d Inf. S3 Journal), 1–30 Sept. 1950. All of the variously dated regimental journals are archived in Record Group (RG) 407, National Archives and Records Administration, Suitland, Md. (hereafter NARA); 23d Inf. Command Report, 1–30 Sept. 1950; Freeman Oral History.

21. 23d Inf. Command Report, 1–31 Aug. 1950.

22. Paul Freeman to Clay Blair, 26 Mar. 1986, quoted in Blair, *Forgotten War,* 249 (emphasis in original).

23. Blair, *Forgotten War,* 249f; Freeman Oral History; Roy E. Appleman, *Disaster in Korea: The Chinese Confront MacArthur* (College Station: Texas A&M University Press, 1989), 273. Meszar later said that the message recalling Freeman to the rear did not specify he was being relieved. It was ambiguous and unspecific as to why Freeman was being recalled. This meant that rather than reinstating a relieved regimental commander (thus overturning a previous order), Keiser could send a rested Freeman back to his command after Holden completed his fact-finding mission.

24. 23d Inf. Command Report, 1–30 Sept. 1950; Freeman Oral History.

25. Ibid.

26. 23d Inf. Command Report, 1–30 Sept. 1950.

27. Ibid.

28. Harold Martin, "The Two Terrible Nights of the 23rd," *Saturday Evening Post,* 19 May 1951, 23.

29. "Combat efficiency" is a commander's approximation of his unit's fighting strength. It is based on the remaining number of combat elements, ammunition and materiel supply, and such intangibles as morale and degree of fatigue. It is always subjective, and an experienced observer would likely evaluate an estimate as precise as 38 percent with some incredulity.

30. Ibid.

31. For a military unit to ford a river, the water must be shallow enough for vehicles to drive across without stalling. Serviceable entry and exit ramps, either existing or dug out by soldiers or engineer equipment, are needed to assure speedy ingress and egress, and the riverbed must be solid enough for vehicles to operate without getting bogged down. Sandbags can be used to "pave" the approaches as well as the riverbed in order to provide dependable trafficability.

32. 23d Inf. Command Report, 1–30 Sept. 1950; Freeman Oral History; Blair, *Forgotten War,* 302.

33. Freeman Oral History; Blair, *Forgotten War,* 301–303; Sherrard to Blair, quoted in ibid., 303.

34. 23d Inf. Command Report, 1–30 Sept. 1950; Freeman Oral History; Blair, *Forgotten War,* 303–304; Appleman, *South to the Naktong,* 580–81.

35. 23d Inf. Command Report, 1–30 Sept. and 1–31 Oct. 1950.

Chapter 3. Disaster in the North

1. Freeman Oral History. The intelligence report is mentioned in Clark C. Munroe, *The Second Infantry Division in Korea, 1950–51* (1952; reprint, Nashville: Battery Press, 1992), 51.

2. Unless otherwise noted, material on the Chinese People's Liberation Army (PLA) comes from the superb account in John A. English, *On Infantry* (New York: Praeger, 1981), 168–84. There is currently little reliable information from the Chinese side on their operations in the Korean War, particularly concerning diplomacy, war aims, motivation, strategy, and tactics. Any citations in paragraphs on the PLA are in addition to material in English's account. See also "The Chinese People's Army of Liberation in the Korean War," Minister of National Defense, Chief of Staff of the Armed Forces, 2d Division, 926 EMGFA/2/D/S/, Etat-Major de l'Armee de Terre, Service Historique, Vincennes, France (hereafter EMAT); "Infanterie Metropolitaine, Battalion Francais de l'ONU en Corée," box 271, EMAT.

3. "Chinese People's Army."

4. Speech by Captain Huchard, commander, 2d Company, French Battalion, n.d., text provided to author by Gerard Journet, copy in author's possession; "Chinese People's Army."

5. ATIS Enemy Documents, Issue 11, 74–82, captured by ROK 1st Division, 26 Nov. 1950, reproduced in Appleman, *South to the Naktong,* 720.

6. Ibid.

7. This and the following paragraphs on the effects of cold weather in Korea rely on Donald M. Thomas, "Korea, 1950–1951," unpublished typescript in author's possession; letters from Dr. Robert Hall, the 23d's regimental surgeon during the war; and the author's personal experience as a battalion commander in Korea in 1980–81.

8. Heat tablets, intended for heating canned rations, were combustible tablets a little larger than a cube of sugar that burned for about five minutes.

9. For a readable, detailed account of the Chinese intervention, see Blair, *Forgotten War,* pt. 7, "Drastic Miscalculations," and pt. 8, "Disaster and Retreat." For an account of MacArthur's psyche and "will to disbelieve," see the third volume of D. Clayton James's masterful study of MacArthur, *The Years of MacArthur: Triumph and Disaster, 1945–1964* (Boston: Houghton Mifflin, 1985), chaps. 15–18.

10. 23d Inf. Command Report, 1–30 Nov. 1950; Freeman Oral History; Blair, *Forgotten War,* 445; Thomas, "Korea, 1950–51," 3.

11. 23d Inf. Command Report, 1–30 Nov. 1950; Freeman Oral History; Blair, *Forgotten War,* 437.

12. 23d Inf. Command Report, 1–30 Nov. 1950; Freeman Oral History; Blair, *Forgotten War,* 445; Appleman, *Disaster in Korea,* 81, 195, 198.

13. 23d Inf. Command Report, 1–30 Nov. 1950; Freeman Oral History; Munroe, *Second Infantry Division,* 61; *America's Medal of Honor Recipients* (Golden Valley, Minn.: Highland Publishers, 1980), 222f.

14. 23d Inf. Command Report, 1–30 Nov. 1950; Freeman Oral History; Blair, *Forgotten War,* 446.

15. 23d Inf. Command Report, 1–30 Nov. 1950; Donald M. Thomas, "King Company," unpublished manuscript, Roy E. Appleman Collection, Archives, MHI (hereafter Appleman Collection), 6.

16. 23d Inf. Command Report, 1–30 Nov. 1950.

17. Munroe, *Second Infantry Division,* 61.

18. 23d Inf. Command Report, 1–30 Nov. 1950; Freeman Oral History; Munroe, *Second Infantry Division,* 61f; Blair, *Forgotten War,* 454.

19. 23d Inf. Command Report, 1–30 Nov. 1950.

20. Appleman, *Disaster in Korea,* 278–79.

21. 23d Inf. Command Report, 1–30 Nov. 1950; Munroe, *Second Infantry Division,* 62–66. The most detailed account of this action is in S. L. A. Marshall, *The River and the Gauntlet* (New York: Morrow, 1953), passim. It is, however, in error in places.

22. Robert F. Futrell, *The United States Air Force in Korea* (Washington, D.C.: Office of Air Force History, 1983), 254.

23. 23d Inf. Command Report, 1–30 Nov. 1950; Freeman Oral History.

24. 23d Inf. Command Report, 1–30 Nov. 1950; Freeman Oral History; Munroe, *Second Infantry Division,* 64–66; Blair, *Forgotten War,* 492f. Appleman offers the most complete account of Bradley's approval for the 23d to take the Anju road (*Disaster in Korea,* 309–11). Appleman is critical of Freeman for this movement, saying that it left the artillery and engineer units at the rear of the 2d Division column vulnerable to attack through the night of 30 November–1 December. Given the num-

ber of CCF troops that had already bypassed the 23d Infantry on their way south on 30 November, it is hard to believe the situation would have been much better had the 23d stayed in position. It most likely would have suffered far worse losses.

25. 23d Inf. Command Report, 1–30 Nov. 1950; Freeman Oral History; T. R. Fehrenbach, *This Kind of War* (New York: Macmillan, 1963), 344. Thermit is the trademark name for a mixture of aluminum powder and fine metallic oxides, usually iron, which burns at high temperatures and is used commercially for welding. Military units often carry Thermit grenades to destroy weapons and materiel. When placed in the breech of an artillery piece and ignited, the grenade welds the breechblock to the cannon tube rendering it worthless as a weapon.

26. 23d Inf. Command Report, 1–30 Nov. 1950; Freeman Oral History; Thomas, "Korea, 1950–1951," 13f.

27. Thomas, "Korea, 1950–1951," 13–14.

28. 23d Inf. Command Report, 1–31 Dec. 1950.

29. Captain Guthrie says some division staff officers accused Freeman of withdrawing without authority and that Freeman's promotion to brigadier general was delayed because of his actions (Blair, *Forgotten War,* 494).

30. Freeman, memorandum, 9 Dec. 1950, quoted in Appleman, *Disaster in Korea,* 316

31. Appleman, *Disaster in Korea,* 492 n 82; Marshall, *River and the Gauntlet,* 327–30, covers the withdrawal on the Anju road.

Chapter 4. The French Battalion and Lt. Col. Ralph Monclar

1. Appleman, *South to the Naktong,* 262; Doris M. Condit, *The Test of War, 1950–1953* (Washington, D.C.: Historical Office, Office of the Secretary of Defense, 1988), 48, 56–58.

2. "Le Battalion Francais de l'ONU en Corée, Decembre 1950–Novembre 1953," box 288, EMAT, 5.

3. "Le Battalion Francais," 5; Condit, *Test of War,* 56.

4. "Le Battalion Francais," 5–6; *The History of the United Nations Forces in the Korean War* (Seoul: Ministry of National Defense, 1974), 3:192.

5. Harold H. Martin, "Who Says the French Won't Fight," *Saturday Evening Post,* 5 May 1951, 19. The information for this and the following paragraphs on motivation is from personal experience and interviews with many veterans.

6. Ibid.

7. Serge Bererd was qualified to be a lieutenant but enlisted as a corporal. He served on the French general staff and performed the duties of a junior intelligence officer and liaison officer. In letters, interviews, and telephone conversations he amplified and clarified many details regarding the French Battalion.

8. "Le Battalion Francais," 5–6.

9. Ibid., 7; *History of the United Nations Forces,* 3:193.

10. "General Monclar," *The Indianhead* (newsletter of the Second Infantry Division Association), Nov., 1986, 1; reprinted from *Le Piton* (publication of the Association of Veterans of the French Battalion), June, 1986.

11. "General Monclar."

12. Pierre Collard, the source of these observations, acted as Monclar's aide-de-camp during part of his Korea tour.

13. Lt. Col. Ralph Monclar, "Catechisme de Combat," 7–14. This document is a typescript in the French military archives at the Château de Vincennes near Paris. It has never been published.

14. Ibid., 7.

15. Ibid., 7–9, 11.

16. Ibid., 9–10.

17. Ibid., 10–11.

18. Ibid., 12.

19. Monclar to Max LeJeune, secretary of defense, War Department, 16 Feb. 1951, box 296, EMAT.

20. Monclar to Max LeJeune, n.d., box 296, EMAT.

21. Monclar, "Catechisme de Combat," 13–14.

22. Paul Mousset, account of interview with Monclar in Paris, n.d., box 296, EMAT.

23. Martin, "Who Says the French Won't Fight," 19 (emphasis in original).

24. Information on the French Battalion derived through interviews with numerous veterans.

25. *History of the United Nations Forces,* 3:195; Phillip B. Davidson, *Vietnam at War: The History, 1946–1975* (Novato, Calif.: Presidio Press, 1988), 84–91.

26. *History of the United Nations Forces,* 3:195.

27. Ibid.

28. Ibid., 3:196; 23d Inf. Command Report, 1–31 Dec. 1950.

Chapter 5. Matthew Ridgway and a New War

1. Material on Ridgway's operations in Korea for this chapter is from Matthew B. Ridgway, *The Korean War* (Garden City, N.Y.: Doubleday, 1967), chap. 5; the quote is on page 83.

2. "Bug out" was a slang term coined by soldiers to describe the precipitate, out-of-control retreats that units often conducted when the Chinese attacked.

3. Harry S. Truman, *Memoirs,* vol. 2., *Years of Trial and Hope* (Garden City, N.Y.: Doubleday, 1956), 402.

4. Truman to MacArthur, 13 Jan. 1951, quoted in ibid., 456.

5. Ibid., 97 (emphasis in original).

6. "Rapport de General Monclar sur les Operations en Corée," chap. 2, "l'Exercice du Haut-Commandement vu du Groupement Tactique," Archives, École Militaire, Paris, 3.

7. Ridgway, *Korean War,* 264f.

8. Robert M. Hall, "Care of the Wounded of the U.S. Ground Forces during the Korean War," *Graybeards,* Jan., 1993, 10.

9. Ibid., 10–11.

10. Ibid. 11–12.

11. "Rapport de General Monclar," chap. 8, "Les Services," 2; ibid., chap. 3, "Movements," 4; "Note on How to Behave Around the Americans," n.d., box 287, EMAT.

12. 23d Inf. Command Report, 1–31 Dec. 1950. The command report amounts to an official record of the unit's activity. It reflects the views and opinions of the commander himself, whether actually written by him or not.

Chapter 6. Wonju and Patrols to Twin Tunnels

1. X Corps Periodic Intelligence Report (hereafter PERINTREP) no. 128, 1 Feb. 1951, and "Battle of the Tunnels Area." All X Corps documents cited in this work are archived in RG 407, NARA.

2. Quote and information on Almond's background is from David Childress, "Edward Mallory Almond," in Spiller, ed., *Dictionary of American Military Biography,* 1:25–27. For an appraisal of his generalship while leading the 92d Infantry Division in World War II, see Dale E. Wilson, "Recipe for Failure: Major General Edward M. Almond and Preparation of the U.S. 92d Infantry Division for Combat in World War II," *Journal of Military History* 56, no. 2 (July, 1992): 473–88. Almond's withdrawal of an award from the black officer is in Sherman W. Pratt, *Decisive Battles of the Korean War* (New York: Vantage Press, 1992), 155. Particularly valuable was a telephone interview with Maj. Gen. George C. Stewart (USA, Ret.), who, as assistant commander of the 2d Infantry Division in 1951, was in a position to observe Almond's generalship firsthand.

3. A quartering party is a detachment that deploys in advance of the main body when a unit moves. The quartering party is responsible for reconnoitering the route to the new location, organizing the position, designating areas for elements of the unit to occupy, and guiding the elements to their positions.

4. Appleman, *Ridgway Duels for Korea,* 99.

5. 23d Inf. Command Report, 1–31 Jan. 1951; Appleman, *Ridgway Duels for Korea,* 101.

6. *America's Medal of Honor Recipients,* 187.

7. Freeman Oral History; 23d Inf. Command Report, 1–31 Jan. 1951; 2d Infantry Division, Letter of Instructions, 6 Jan. 1951, RG 407, NARA.

8. Freeman Oral History; 23d Inf. Command Report, 1–31 Jan. 1951.

9. 23d Inf. Command Report, 1–31 Jan. 1951; 2d Infantry Division, Letter of Instructions, 090800I Jan. 1951, RG 407, NARA.

10. Appleman, *Ridgway Duels for Korea,* 118.

11. Freeman Oral History.

12. 23d Inf. Command Report, 1–31 Jan. 1951; 23d Inf. S3 Journal, 091630I—101630I Jan. 1951.

13. 23d Inf. Command Report, 1–31 Jan. 1951.

14. "Rapport de General Monclar," chap. 2, "l'Exercice du Haut-Commandement," 7, and chap. 6, "Le Combat Offensif," 4.

15. Monclar paraphrased this speech on 11 September 1951, when he made his farewell address to the French Battalion. "You have climbed too high to come back down. Prisoners of your past, you have condemned yourselves to the forced labors of glory. When you are engaged, remember that France is with you. And, as it is stated in the sacred book, 'God loves those who are as firm as an impenetrable wall'" (quoted in *Le Piton,* Sept., 1951).

16. "Rapport de General Monclar," chap. 2, "l'Exercice du Haut-Commandement," 10. Maj. Maurice Barthelemy, who related this story, was the battalion's third in command and was, in part, paraphrasing a speech Monclar gave in Brussels in 1953 describing the French Battalion's relationship with the 23d.

17. Ridgway, *Korean War,* chap. 5 passim; "Rapport sur le Guerre en Corée," box 287, EMAT, 63–64.

18. Almond Diary, 13 Jan. 1951, Appleman Collection; Maj. Gen. George C. Stewart (USA, Ret.), telephone interview by author, 18 Mar. 1993.

19. 2d Infantry Operational Directive, 240000I–242400I Jan. 1951, Annex.

20. Paul L. Freeman, "Wonju Thru Chipyong," n.d., Appleman Collection, 5–7.

21. Ibid., 7.

22. Ibid.; X Corps PERINTREP 232100I–242100I Jan. 1951.

23. Army Map Service Sheet 6726 III, AMS Series L751, Korea Scale 1:50,000, "Ip'o–Ri"; author's personal reconnaissance.

24. 2d Infantry Division Periodic Operation Report (hereafter PEROPREP) no. 503, 280001I–282400I Jan. 1951. All PEROPREPs cited in this work are archived RG 407, NARA.

25. 1st Battalion, 23d Infantry, Operation Report for 29–30 Jan. 1951, 17 Mar. 1951, "Battle of the Tunnels," Appleman Collection (hereafter "Battle of the Tunnels"); 23d Inf. Command Report, 1–31 Jan. 1951; Pratt, *Decisive Battles,* 148–49; Russell A. Gugeler, *Combat Actions in Korea,* (1954; reprint, Washington, D.C.: U.S. Army Center of Military History, 1987), 80–81.

26. 23d Inf. Command Report, 1–31 Jan. 1951; "Battle of the Tunnels"; Pratt, *Decisive Battles,* 149.

27. Ibid.; Freeman, "Wonju Thru Chipyong," 7.

28. Freeman, "Wonju Thru Chipyong," 8.

29. Ibid.; Gugeler, *Combat Actions in Korea,* 83–84. The origins of "Murphy's Laws" are shrouded in folklore, but the original Murphy's Law seems to have been, "If something can go wrong, it will." The law has grown into hundreds of elaborations stating how things can go awry in any endeavor.

30. Gugeler, *Combat Actions in Korea,* 85; 2d Battalion, 23d Inf. S3 Journal, 29 Jan. 1951; 2d Infantry Division PEROPREP no. 504, 290001I–292400I Jan. 1951.

31. Gugeler, *Combat Actions in Korea,* 86.

32. Ibid., 81–82, 86.

33. Gugeler, *Combat Actions in Korea,* 87–88. The term *beaten zone* refers to the area in which automatic weapons fire falls when fired on an area rather than directly at a target. It can comprise a large area in the case of large-bore (e.g., .50-cal. or 12.7-mm) machine guns.

34. Ibid., 87.

35. Ibid., 89. Tracers are bullets that leave a glowing trail so that the firer can see where his bullets are hitting. They are normally included in a 1:5 ratio in ammunition belts.

36. Freeman, "Wonju Thru Chipyong," 8–9; 2d Battalion, 23d Inf. S3 Journal, 29 Jan. 1951; Gugeler, *Combat Actions in Korea,* 90.

37. Gugeler, *Combat Actions in Korea,* 91; John Collins, "Tales from the Mosquito Squadron" *Atlantic Flyer* (copy provided by John Collins, n.d., n.p.). The quote is from John Collins, "Slow Ride to Hell," *Atlantic Flyer,* Aug., 1986, 9.

38. Gugeler, *Combat Actions in Korea,* 91; 2d Infantry Division PEROPREP no. 504.

39. Gugeler, *Combat Actions in Korea,* 92.

40. Ibid., 95–96; 2d Infantry Division PEROPREP no. 505, 300001I–302400I Jan. 1951.

41. Ibid., 96–97; "Battle of the Tunnels."

42. Freeman, "Wonju Thru Chipyong," 9.

Chapter 7. The Battle of Twin Tunnels

1. 23d Infantry S3 Journal, 30 Jan. 1951; "After Action Report Covering Operations of the 23d Regimental Combat Team During the Period 290630 Jan to 152400 Feb," 13 Mar. 1951, RG 407, NARA; 23d Inf. Command Report, 1–28 Feb. 1951; George C. Stewart, "Service in WWII and Korea," typescript furnished to author by Stewart, 7. An assembly area is an area where a unit gathers all units for a given operation to prepare to move out for an operation. Such tasks as food and ammunition distribution, refueling, and final briefings are usually carried out there.

2. Stewart, "Service in WWII and Korea," 7.

3. 23d Inf. Command Report, 1–28 Feb. 1951; Freeman, "Wonju Thru Chipyong."

4. "Rapport de General Monclar," chap. 6, "Le Combat Offensif," 1–3.

5. Information derived from a copy of Barthelemy's 1:50,000-scale map with positions of 31 Jan. 1951 still marked in pencil provided to author. See also "Rapport de General Monclar," chap. 4, "Preliminaries sur le Combat"; Freeman, "Wonju Thru Chipyong"; "Rapport sur la Guerre en Corée," 311; *TO&E 7–18N, Infantry Heavy Weapons Company* (Washington, D.C.: Department of the Army, 30 Dec. 1947).

6. "Rapport sur le Guerre en Corée," 66; "Rapport de General Monclar," chap. 7, "La Défense," 4.

7. "Rapport sur le Guerre en Corée," 64–65, 67.

8. Freeman Oral History; Gerard Journet, interview by author, Dec., 1992. I attempted to climb the hill in October, 1992, in pleasant fall weather. After a late morning start, it took me about four hours to make it two-thirds of the way up the hill before abandoning the climb at dusk.

9. Freeman, "Wonju Thru Chipyong."

10. "Rapport sur le Guerre en Corée," 52. See also Annex A, ibid., 309–310; 23d Inf. Command Report, 1–28 Feb. 1951; Appleman, *Ridgway Duels for Korea,* 210; map furnished by Barthelemy.

11. Freeman, "Wonju Thru Chipyong." "Firing in" defensive concentrations of all indirect-fire weapons (e.g., adjusting mortars and field artillery to hit positions so that data has been computed in advance) is standard practice when time and ammunition permit. The fires thus are available on short notice and are known to be accurate.

12. "Rapport sur le Guerre en Corée," 64–65.

13. Stewart, "Service in WWII and Korea," 7–8; Pratt, *Decisive Battles,* 151–52.

14. Pratt, *Decisive Battles,* 152, 154 (Freeman quote); Stewart, "Service in WWII and Korea," 8.

15. 23d Inf. S3 Journal, Forward Command Post, 1 Feb. 1951.

16. Stewart, "Service in WWII and Korea," 8–9.

17. Freeman, "Wonju Thru Chipyong."

18. 23d Inf. S3 Journal, Forward Command Post, 1 Feb. 1951; 23d Inf. Command Report, 1–28 Feb. 1951; "After Action Report . . . 23d Regimental Combat Team," 8.

19. "3e Company Journal de Marche," 1 Feb. 1951, box 288, EMAT.

20. "Rapport sur le Guerre en Corée," 69; "3e Company Journal de Marche"; Freeman Oral History; Freeman, "Wonju Thru Chipyong"; 23d Inf. Command Report, 1–28 Feb. 1951.

21. "Rapport sur le Guerre en Corée," 69.

22. François DeCastries, interview by author, Dec., 1992. This account differs from all accounts in the records and even from several accounts in the French archives. DeCastries assumes that the

archival accounts are wrong because he was too busy on the hilltop to report activities to his head-quarters. Additionally, he knew that there was nothing his headquarters could do to come to his aid. See also the report of Lt. Col. Oliver LeMire, "Aerial Support during the Battle of Chipyong-ni," box 404, EMAT, 9; and Freeman, "Wonju Thru Chipyong."

23. Freeman, "Wonju Thru Chipyong"; 23d Inf. S3 Journal, Rear Command Post, 1 Feb. 1951.

24. Freeman, "Wonju Thru Chipyong." A handwritten annotation on the copy in the Freeman Papers at MHI is the source for Captain LeMaitre dying in Freeman's arms. See also "Rapport sur le Guerre en Corée," 53.

25. "Rapport sur le Guerre en Corée," 312.

26. 23d Inf. S3 Journal, Forward Command Post, 1 Feb. 1951.

27. Freeman, "Wonju Thru Chipyong."

28. Ibid.; 23d Inf. S3 Journal, Forward Command Post, 1 Feb. 1951.

29. "3e Company Journal de Marche."

30. Freeman, "Wonju Thru Chipyong"; 23d Inf. S3 Journal, Forward Command Post, 1 Feb. 1951; "Rapport sur le Guerre en Corée," 54.

31. Freeman, "Wonju Thru Chipyong"; "3e Company Journal de Marche."

32. Stewart, "Service in WWII and Korea," 9.

33. Freeman, "Wonju Thru Chipyong."

34. *America's Medal of Honor Recipients*, 207.

35. Stewart, "Service in WWII and Korea," 9–10; Freeman, "Wonju Thru Chipyong."

36. Freeman, "Wonju Thru Chipyong."

37. Ibid.; Stewart, "Service in WWII and Korea," 10.

38. Freeman, "Wonju Thru Chipyong"; LeMire, "Aerial Support," 9.

39. Freeman, "Wonju Thru Chipyong"; "After Action Report . . . 23d Regimental Combat Team," 9.

40. Freeman, "Wonju Thru Chipyong."

41. Ibid.

42. Ibid.

43. Ibid.

44. Billy C. Mossman, *Ebb and Flow: November 1950–July 1951*, U.S. Army in the Korean War (Washington, D.C.: GPO, 1990), 249–51; mission statement in Freeman, "Wonju Thru Chipyong."

Chapter 8. Prelude to Chipyong-ni

1. 23d Inf. Command Report, 1–28 Feb. 1951.

2. Ibid., Freeman Oral History; Freeman, "Wonju Thru Chipyong."

3. Freeman Oral History; 23d Inf. S3 Journal, 3 Feb. 1951.

4. Freeman Oral History.

5. "Rapport de General Monclar," chap. 7, "La Défense," 7.

6. Ibid., 1–5, 7–8.

7. Ibid., 5–6.

8. Lt. Col. Ralph Monclar, "Compte-Rendu du Combat de Chipyong-ni (Coree) 13–14–15 Fevrier 1951," EMAT, 5.

9. 23d Inf. Command Report, 1–28 Feb. 1951.

10. Ibid.

11. Martin, "Who Says the French Won't Fight," 19.

12. Monclar, "Compte-Rendu du Combat," 5.

13. Freeman Oral History.

14. Historical Data Card (Form AGAZ 373) 23d Infantry Regimental Combat Team, Organizational History Branch, U.S. Army Center for Military History (hereafter CMH), Washington, D.C.

15. Walter Killilae and Clyde C. Hathaway, "*Accompli* at Chipyong," *Antiaircraft Journal*, July-Aug. 1951, 11.

16. *TO&E 5–17N*.

17. *TO&E 7–87, Ranger Infantry Company (Airborne)(Tentative)* (Washington, D.C.: Department of the Army, 17 Oct. 1950).

18. Freeman Oral History.

19. Ibid.; "Rapport de General Monclar," 1.

20. "Rapport de General Monclar," chap. 7, "La Défense," 7.

21. 23d Inf. S2 and S3 Journals, 4 Feb. 1951.

22. 23d Inf. S2 Journal, 4 Feb. 1951.

23. Lt. Col. James Edwards, "Siege of Chipyong-ni," typescript provided to author by the writer's son, 4–7; 23d Inf. S2 and S3 Journals, 7 Feb. 1951.

24. Ibid.

25. 23d Inf. S3 Journal, 7 Feb. 1951. In "Wonju Thru Chipyong," Freeman indicates that this was to be an "extended operation." However, the regiment's S3 journal includes a fragment of a warning order from division stating that the 9th Infantry should "be prepared to send its atk force." The operations officer notified the 3d Battalion to be prepared for the same mission, further specifying that "Should plan go into effect 3d Bn will return at 1600."

26. Freeman, "Wonju Thru Chipyong"; 23d Inf. S3 Journal, 8 Feb. 1951.

27. Ibid.; Edwards, "Siege of Chipyong-ni," 8.

28. 23d Inf. S3 Journal, 9 Feb. 1951; Pratt, *Decisive Battles,* 167–75. Pratt's version differs from the one in the S3 journal; he also refers to the hill as 503. The 1:50,000-scale tactical map shows it as 506, which is how the S3 journal refers to it.

29. 23d Inf. S2 and S3 Journals, 9 Feb. 1951; Edwards, "Siege of Chipyong-ni," 9–10. Edwards's account of the remainder of the 3d Battalion's patrol is garbled; he has them returning to Chipyong-ni on 9 February.

30. 23d Inf. S3 Journal, 9 Feb. 1951.

31. Ibid., 10 and 11 Feb. 1951.

32. Edwards, "Siege of Chipyong-ni," 9.

33. 23d Inf. S2 and S3 Journals, 9–12 Feb. 1951.

34. Ibid., 11–12 Feb. 1951; Edwards, "Siege of Chipyong-ni," 11–12. Edwards has the date wrong, placing the patrol on 10 February. He is also particularly disdainful of the Rangers as both a unit and a concept.

35. 23d Inf. S3 Journal, 12 Feb. 1951; Mossman, *Ebb and Flow,* 266–81.

Chapter 9. Isolated and Encircled at Chipyong-ni

1. Mossman, *Ebb and Flow,* 264, 284.

2. X Corps PERINTREP no. 137, 9–10 Feb. 1951, and no. 138, 10–11 Feb. 1951. The X Corps documents persistently identify PLA armies as "CCF Corps." Although roughly the same size as a U.S. corps, the organizations did not correspond in function. The PLA did not use a corps organization, moving directly from army to division without an intervening headquarters.

3. X Corps PERINTREP no. 139, 11–12 Feb. 1951.

4. 23d Inf. S2 and S3 Journals, 11 and 12 Feb. 1951; Appleman, *Ridgway Duels for Korea,* 256–57.

5. 23d Inf. S3 Journal, 13 Feb. 1951.

6. Ibid., 11 and 12 Feb. 1951; Appleman, *Ridgway Duels for Korea,* 256–57.

7. 23d Inf. S3 Journal, 12 Feb. 1951. Mossman, *Ebb and Flow,* and Blair, *Forgotten War,* say the aborted decision was made on 13 February. This is in error unless the regiment's S3 journal, a contemporary document, is wrong—an unlikely event. Almond visited the perimeter on 13 February, and a radio message at 1430 hours that afternoon reiterated that Ridgway ordered no change in position for twenty-four hours. Nevertheless, the order on 12 February seems to be the critical one.

8. 23d Inf. S2 and S3 Journals, 12 and 13 Feb. 1951; Freeman, "Wonju Thru Chipyong."

9. Edwards, "Siege of Chipyong-ni," 19.

10. Freeman, "Wonju Thru Chipyong"; Mossman, *Ebb and Flow,* 299; Appleman, *Ridgway Duels for Korea,* 288; Blair, *Forgotten War,* 697–98. The figure of fifty-four hundred troops at Chipyong-

ni is my best estimate based on veterans' reports of their unit strengths before the battle, including recent replacements.

11. 23d Inf. S3 Journal, 13 Feb. 1951.

12. Freeman, "Wonju Thru Chipyong."

13. Ibid.

14. Edwards, "Siege of Chipyong-ni," 22–23.

15. Ibid.

16. 23d Inf. S3 Journal, 13 and 14 Feb. 1951; "Compte Rendu Minute sur le Deroulement des Operations de Defense de Chipyong-ni" (hereafter "French Log, Chipyong-ni"). This is a minute-by-minute log of radio messages at Chipyong-ni furnished to the author by Barthelemy.

17. Freeman, "Wonju Thru Chipyong"; interview of King Company veterans and Meszar conducted by the Eighth Army command historian. Transcripts and tapes of this interview are available in the Office of the Command Historian, Headquarters, U.S. Forces Korea and Eighth Army, Unit no. 15237, APO AP 96205–0010. The shell that later wounded Freeman was *not* the same one that killed Shoemaker, as Freeman states in his oral history and Blair records in *Forgotten War*, 699.

18. Freeman, "Wonju Thru Chipyong."

19. Edwards, "Siege of Chipyong-ni," 9, 20; Gugeler, *Combat Actions in Korea,* 101–102. "Dead space" is any area to a unit's front that cannot be observed (and thus not fired on directly) from defensive positions. Defenders usually would mine such areas or target them with indirect fires to prevent attackers from approaching through them.

20. 23d Inf. S2 and S3 Journals, 13 Feb. 1951; Gugeler, *Combat Actions in Korea,* 105.

21. 23d Regiment S2 Journal, 14 Feb. 1951; Gugeler, *Combat Actions in Korea,* 105–106. Gugeler says the attack began at 2200 hours. However, this does not match the time in the S2 journal, which records the sound of tanks (probably amended later to the sound of digging) in front of George Company at 2217 hours—thirty minutes to an hour before the ground probe.

22. Edwards, "Siege of Chipyong-ni," 25.

23. Ibid., 20, 25–26.

24. 23d Inf. S3 Journal, 13 Feb. 1951.

25. 23d Inf. S2 and S3 Journal, 13 Feb. 1951; "French Log, Chipyong-ni"; Edwards, "Siege of Chipyong-ni," 26.

26. 23d Inf. S3 Journal, 14 Feb. 1951.

27. Ibid.

28. Freeman, "Wonju Thru Chipyong."

29. Clay Blair interview with Freeman, the Clay and Joan Blair Collection, Archives, MHI (hereafter Blair Collection). Freeman told Blair he was sitting on the ground in his tent and that the same round that injured him killed his intelligence officer. However, both Hall and Meszar state that the incident occurred as described in this account.

30. Freeman Oral History; Stewart, "Service in WWII & Korea," 18–19.

31. Ibid.

32. Freeman, "Wonju Thru Chipyong."

33. 23d Inf. S3 Journal, 14 Feb. 1951.

34. Ibid.

35. Freeman, "Wonju Thru Chipyong"; Freeman Oral History.

36. 23d Inf. S2 and S3 Journals, 14 Feb. 1951.

Chapter 10. Fighting and Surviving on the Second Day

1. 23d Inf. S3 Journal, 14 Feb. 1951.

2. Ibid.

3. Ibid.; Freeman, "Wonju Thru Chipyong"; "Rapport sur la Guerre en Corèe," 57.

4. Freeman, "Wonju Thru Chipyong"; Edwards, "Siege of Chipyong-ni," 34; 23d Inf. S2 and S3 Journals, 14 and 15 Feb. 1951.

5. 23d Inf. S3 Journal, 14 Feb. 1951; "Rapport sur la Guerre en Corèe," 57; LeMire, "Aerial Support," 9.

6. 23d Inf. S2 and S3 Journals, 14 and 15 Feb. 1951; "Rapport de General Monclar," 5; Edwards, "Siege of Chipyong-ni," 34–35.

7. The account of fighting in George Company relies primarily on Gugeler, *Combat Actions in Korea*, chap. 8, 100–125. Although the chapter is entitled "Chipyong-ni," it is almost exclusively devoted to the action in George Company's sector. Gugeler interviewed many of the participants during the war.

8. Capt. Edward G. Williamson, 4th Historical Detachment, "SUBJECT: Set of Interviews: Company G, 23d Infantry Regiment," 28 Nov. 1951, copy at CMH. This document is the cover letter describing notes of Captain Williams's interviews with Lt. Paul J. McGee.

9. Edwards, "Siege of Chipyong-ni," 39.

10. 23d Inf. S2 and S3 Journals, 15 Feb. 1951.

11. Edwards, "Siege of Chipyong-ni," 39.

12. "French Log, Chipyong-ni."

13. 23d Inf. S2 and S3 Journals, 15 Feb. 1951; Edwards, "Siege of Chipyong-ni," 41; Huchard speech, 9.

14. Curtis, "Chipyoung-Yi," Korean War Survey, 23d Infantry Manuscripts, Curtis, Robert, MHI, 1.

15. Ibid., 2.

16. Edwards, "Siege of Chipyong-ni," 39; Curtis, "Chipyoung–Yi," 1, 2.

17. Curtis, "Chipyoung-Yi," 2–3.

18. Ibid., 3.

19. *TO&E 7–87;* Freeman, "Wonju Thru Chipyong"; Edwards, "Siege of Chipyong-ni," passim.

20. Curtis, "Chipyoung-Yi," 4.

21. Ibid., 4–5; Gugeler, *Combat Actions in Korea*, 118–19.

22. Curtis, "Chipyoung-Yi," 5; Gugeler, *Combat Actions in Korea*, 119–20.

23. Curtis, "Chipyoung-Yi," 6; Gugeler, *Combat Actions in Korea*, 121.

24. Curtis, "Chipyoung-Yi," 8.

25. Ibid.

26. Ibid.

27. 23d Inf. S3 Journal, 15 Feb. 1951; Munroe, *Second Infantry Division*, 107.

28. Curtis, "Chipyoung-Yi," 9–10. There are several eyewitness accounts of what happened in the area behind George Company in the early morning hours. Gugeler presents a version in which Captain Ramsburg and two sergeants are the last out of the area, and does not mention the artillerymen staying on their guns until morning. I find this version more convincing after examining all accounts.

29. Curtis, "Chipyoung-Yi," 10–11. Williamson and Junot also mention direct fire by artillery. See Williamson, 4th Historical Detachment, "SUBJECT: Set of Interviews." Information on artillery position in ibid., interview with Elledge.

30. Williamson, 4th Historical Detachment, "SUBJECT: Set of Interviews," Inclosure 1, Narrative Report, 16.

31. Ibid., 16–17; Junot interview in Williamson, 4th Historical Detachment, "SUBJECT: Set of Interviews." Perhaps no single action at Chipyong-ni is as hard to sort out as the events on George Company hill during the daylight hours of 15 February. This appears to be because of the participants' desire to avoid blame or take credit for actions there. Pratt claims he reached the crest on the north side and held it all day. He says his company's actions were the "only reason that the [relieving armored] force reached us by dark" and that had Baker not taken the hill, "the whole course of the war would have taken an entirely and disastrously different turn." He blames his company's failure to take the southern slopes of George Company hill on the poor fighting positions the George Company soldiers constructed there (Pratt, *Decisive Battles of the Korean War,* 190–209). No other account confirms all these details, and several contradict them. Just as tendentious in his own way, Edwards,

blames Pratt personally for the failure to retake the hill more expeditiously ("Siege of Chipyong-ni," 48–50). Edwards is positive in his description of the positions. For example: "all units improved their positions whenever they were not engaged in combat or on patrols. The 2d Battalion Commanding Officer insisted that all foxholes and weapons emplacements be of the standing type with overhead cover. He personally checked the siting of each automatic weapon. This extra labor saved many lives in the savage fighting that followed" ("Siege of Chipyong-ni," 1–2.) The points about "standing type with overhead cover" are refuted by participants' accounts; for the checking of all positions, see, e.g., the reminiscences of one of Edwards's company commanders, Capt. Bickford "Buz" Sawyer of Easy Company: "I find it quite amazing that no one from battalion or regimental headquarters came down to check my defensive positions at Chipyong. I know that I went to the battalion headquarters every day, but no one ever came to see me. What were these people doing for the week prior to the battle?" (Sawyer to author, 9 Feb. 1993.) Certainly it is possible for a battalion or regimental commander to visit a unit such as company without the company commander knowing, but the level of detail that Edwards claims makes that seem unlikely. With regard to the fighting positions on the George Company hill, a walk through the foxholes in 1992—which included excavating several with a trained archaeologist and a metal detector—showed that they could not have been more than three to four feet deep, even allowing for erosion and filling over a forty-year period. That said, they were not appreciably different than positions anywhere else on the perimeter, as Pratt alleges they were. Finally, Col. Marcel Crombez credits his tank-infantry task force with achieving the crucial victory. It would appear that the truth lies somewhere among these extreme positions.

32. 23d Inf. S3 Journal, 15 Feb. 1951; Lt. Richard Kotite, General Headquarters, Far East Command, Military Intelligence Section, General Staff, to Maj. Roy Appleman, 3 Dec. 1951, Appleman Collection. This letter is in response to Appleman's request for Kotite's account. It is ambiguous and clearly suspect in some respects, but has some useful details. See also Edwards, "Siege of Chipyong-ni," 48–49. Although useful in some respects, as elsewhere, this differs from more reliable reminiscences as well as contemporary documents. Edwards, for example says the first air strikes came in at 1415 hours, while Kotite's letter and the 23d Inf. S3 Journal for 15 Feb. 1951 both say the first air strikes came in before 1039, location not specified. Another air strike specifically in support of Baker's attack on George Hill was logged in at 1136 hours.

33. Donald O. Miller to Roy Appleman, 11 Sept. 1951, Roy E. Appleman Collection (hereafter Appleman Collection), MHI.

34. John Collins, "'Mosquito Spirit' Leads 'Operation Punch' Through Dark Days," *Atlantic Flyer*, Mar., 1988, A6. In the article, Collins says the date was 14 February, but a photocopy of his flight log provided to the author shows the date as "15 Feb 51."

35. 23d Inf. S3 Journal, 15 Feb. 1951.

36. Ibid.

37. Futrell states that "six H-5s [evacuation helicopters] delivered blankets, blood plasma, and medical supplies [to Chipyong-ni] and took out the most serious casualties, each helicopter making three trips on the afternoon of 15 February 1951" (*United States Air Force in Korea,* 578). He asserts that four more sorties were made the following day, evacuating a total of fifty-two casualties over two days. The author could find no evidence of these actions, and the regimental surgeon is convinced that his notes, which indicate only twenty casualties were evacuated on 15 February, all by army aircraft, are correct. A photo at the Eighth Army historian's office in Seoul appears to be of Major General Ruffner (two stars are clearly visible as blurred dots; the face is not recognizable) in a USAF H-5 helicopter; all other helicopter photographs seen by the author are of army helicopters.

Chapter 11. Task Force Crombez Runs the Gauntlet

1. Casualty figures from Gugeler, *Combat Actions in Korea,* 133.

2. *The Howitzer, 1935* (West Point, N.Y.: U.S. Military Academy, 1935), 214. "Guardhouse lawyer" is soldier slang for a man who often argues, quotes, and discusses military law, regulations, and soldiers' rights.

3. *The Register of Graduates and Former Cadets, 1802–1990,* number 10366.

4. Norman F. J. Allen to Victor Fox, 19 Nov. 1979. Copies of all Allen–Fox correspondence cited in this work were provided to the author by Fox.

5. *The Howitzer, 1925* (West Point, N.Y.: U.S. Military Academy, 1925), 99.

6. Blair, *Forgotten War,* 212.

7. An oversize eagle, grenade, and cavalry scarf are all visible in photographs of Crombez taken during the war.

8. Joe W. Finley, "Information on Korean War Experiences," typescript provided to author.

9. Allen to Fox, n.d., 1979; Clay and Joan Blair interviews with 5th Cavalry veterans, Blair Collection.

10. Ibid.; Appleman, *South to the Naktong,* 420–21.

11. Allen to Fox, 4 Feb. 1985.

12. Allen comments to Fox, 28 Apr. 1985, telephone transcript, 9.

13. 5th Cavalry Regiment, Command Report, Feb. 1951, RG 407, NARA; Martin Blumenson, interviews with Task Force Crombez veterans (hereafter Blumenson interviews), Appleman Collection; Gugeler, *Combat Actions in Korea,* 126.

14. Blumenson interviews.

15. Ibid.; Allen comments to Fox, narrative dated May, 1984, 16; Blair, *Forgotten War,* 548.

16. 23d Inf. S3 Journal, 14 and 15 Feb. 1951.

17. Victor Fox to Don Knox, Sept., 1985, copy provided to author by Fox, 43.

18. 1st Cavalry Division Command Report, 15 Feb. 1951, RG 407, NARA; Gugeler, *Combat Actions in Korea,* 126, 128.

19. 1st Cavalry Division Command Report.

20. Ibid.; Gugeler, *Combat Actions in Korea,* 128; Blumenson interviews.

21. Blumenson interviews; Blair, *Forgotten War,* 706; 23d Inf. S3 Journal, 15 Feb. 1951.

22. Blumenson interviews; 1st Cavalry Division Command Report.

23. Blumenson interviews; Allen comments to Fox; Blair, *Forgotten War,* 706–707.

24. Gugeler, *Combat Actions in Korea,* 128–29.

25. Allen comments to Fox; Gugeler, *Combat Actions in Korea,* 129.

26. Blumenson interviews.

27. Ibid.; Allen comments to Fox.

28. Blumenson interviews; Gugeler, *Combat Actions in Korea,* 130

29. Fox to Knox.

30. Blumenson interviews.

31. Ibid.; Gugeler, *Combat Actions in Korea,* 131–32.

32. Edwards, "Siege of Chipyong-ni," 49–51.

33. Ibid., 51–52.

34. Monclar, "Catechisme de Combat," 7.

35. Edwards, "Siege of Chipyong-ni," 52–53.

36. Mossman, *Ebb and Flow,* 300. Ridgway's characterization of Crombez's decision was in an interview with Appleman, 2 Nov. 1951, Appleman Collection.

37. 5th Cavalry Regiment Command Report, Feb., 1951.

38. Captain Robert Hall, the regimental surgeon, was present at the time and remembers the incident. He recalls a lieutenant who had been wounded and lost his entire platoon echoing the same sentiments.

39. Blair, *Forgotten War,* 709.

40. Ibid.

41. 1st Cavalry Division Command Report.

42. Ibid.; 5th Cavalry Command Report; Blair, *Forgotten War,* 708.

43. Rutherford Poats, "5th Cav GIs Asking CMH For Treacy, 3d Bn CO," n.d., unnamed newspaper clipping provided to author by Preston G. Richard.

44. Norman Allen to James Cardinal, 27 Apr. 1984, copy provided to author by Allen.

45. Blair, *Forgotten War,* 708.

46. Fox to Knox. Allen says the account of Ridgway's actions came from Hodes's aide-de-camp (Allen to Fox, 11 Sept. 1982).

47. Headquarters, I U.S. Corps, Armor Combat Lesson Bulletin no. 7, 7 Mar. 1951, "Observation on Task Force [Blank], 15 Feb 51," Appleman Collection.

48. For other criticisms, see Gugeler, *Combat Actions in Korea,* chap. 9, esp. 134–35.

Chapter 12. Aftermath and Reflections

1. "After Action Report . . . 23d Regimental Combat Team," 6; 23d Inf. Command Report, 1–28 Feb. 1951.

2. Blair, *Forgotten War,* 719.

3. Matthew Bunker Ridgway, memorandum "Development of Operation Giant," 9 Sept. 1943, quoted in Clay Blair, *Ridgway's Paratroopers* (Garden City, N.Y.: Doubleday, 1985), 136.

4. This story is told in detail in ibid., 135–43.

5. Matthew B. Ridgway, "Leadership," *Military Review* 46, no. 10 (Oct., 1966): 40–49, reprinted in Robert L. Taylor and William E. Rosenbach, eds., *Military Leadership: In Pursuit of Excellence* (Boulder, Colo.: Westview Press, 1996), 111f.

6. Ibid., 112.

7. Lord Moran, *The Anatomy of Courage* (1945; reprint, Garden City Park, N.Y.: Avery, 1987), passim. The quotation is on xvi.

8. For a lively discussion of this subject, see William Ian Miller, *The Mystery of Courage* (Cambridge, Mass.: Harvard University Press, 2000).

9. S. L. A. Marshall quoted in William Darryl Henderson, *Cohesion: The Human Element in Combat* (Washington: National Defense University Press, 1985), 5.

10. William Shakespeare, *Henry V* (1599), act 4, sc. 3.

11. The phenomenon of building highly capable units is similar to the popular 1980s theory called "transformational leadership" or "theories of excellence." To avoid jargon and to keep this discussion a historical analysis of a single regiment, I have omitted the theoretical underpinnings of this concept. Readers interested in an introduction to transformational leadership should see Kevin S. Donohue and Leonard Hong, "Understanding and Applying Transformational Leadership," *Military Review* 74, no. 8 (Aug., 1994): 24–41, reprinted in Taylor and Rosenbach, eds. *Military Leadership,* 42–52.

Suggestions for Further Reading

Literature on the Korean War has been undergoing its latest revision since about 1990, when the breakup of the Soviet Union began opening archival materials to researchers. Since any exhaustive recommendations for reading on the war are likely to be outdated with the publication of materials relying on the new archival releases, I have chosen to list several basic works dealing with aspects of the war that should give an outline of the subject but not be completely outdated by new revelations. It is a list of personal favorites and is not exhaustive.

The serious student of the war will want to consult Lester H. Brune's *The Korean War: Handbook of the Literature and Research* (Westport, Conn.: Greenwood Press, 1996) as well as Harry G. Summers Jr.'s *Korean War Almanac* (New York: Facts On File, 1990), bearing in mind that the accelerating pace of revelations on the war will outdate both. William Stueck, in *The Korean War: An International History* (Princeton, N.J.: Princeton University Press, 1995), masterfully synthesizes myriad aspects of a war that the author argues forestalled World War III. The Woodrow Wilson Center's Cold War International History Project is an invaluable source of information on and tentative interpretations of the war. The Wilson Center, located in Washington, D.C., publishes interim findings as they become available and sponsors a variety of meetings for the discussion of Cold War issues.

For a general outline of the war, James L. Stokesbury's *A Short History of the Korean War* (New York: William Morrow, 1988) is concise and useful. Matthew B. Ridgway wrote *The Korean War: How We Met the Challenge; How All-Out Asian War Was Averted; Why MacArthur Was Dismissed; Why Today's War Objectives Must Be Limited* (Garden City, N.Y.: Doubleday, 1967) as the American role in Vietnam was accelerating. In it he warned of how America's experiences in Korea provided insights into the phenomenon of limited war. It has stood the test of time better than some accounts by participants and supplements his shorter coverage in the six chapters of *Soldier: The Memoirs of Matthew B. Ridgway* (New York: Harper and Brothers, 1956) that deal with the war. Other general histories of the war abound; those most useful for the novice include Max Hastings's *The Korean War* (New York: Simon and Schuster, 1987, for a British perspective, and Clay Blair's *The Forgotten War: America in Korea 1950–53* (New York:Times Books, 1987), with its wealth of anecdotes. Both share a failing of many accounts of the war by emphasizing the first year of combat, when maneuver was predominant, giving inadequate coverage of the last two years, when stalemate and frustration were the norm. T. R. Fehrenbach's *This Kind of War: A Study in Unpreparedness* (New York: MacMillan, 1963) is a vivid and readable account with considerable editorializing on America's shortcomings in waging war.

Doris M. Condit's *The Test of War, 1950–1953* (Washington, D.C.: Office of the Secretary of Defense, 1988), the second volume in the History of the Office of the Secretary of Defense, gives insight into the policy makers and their view of the war. Volumes 4 and 5 of the History of the Joint Chiefs of Staff—Walter S. Poole's *The Joint Chiefs of Staff and National Policy, 1950–1952* and Robert J. Watson's *The Joint Chiefs of Staff and National Policy, 1953–1954* (both Washington, D.C.: Office of Joint History, Office of the Chairman of the Joint Chiefs of Staff, 1998)—provide perspectives from the highest levels of the U.S. military. Roy E. Appleman, who had access to oral and official accounts of the Korean War as one of the U.S. Army's official historians, places Chipyong-ni in context in his masterful *Ridgway Duels for Korea* (College Station, Tex.: Texas A&M University Press, 1990). The military services' official histories are useful at recounting the deliberations and operations of the armed forces, although none avoids intermittent touches of parochialism.

Little literature is available on Chinese forces, and details are often difficult to pin down. Coverage is most complete at the strategic level, where Chen Jian's *China's road to the Korean War: The Making of the Sino-American Confrontation* (New York: Columbia University Press, 1994) and *Mao's China and the Cold War* (Chapel Hill: University of North Carolina Press, 2001) give insights into the emerging interpretations. Shu Guang Zhang's *Mao's Military Romanticism: China and the Korean War, 1950–1953* (Lawrence: University Press of Kansas, 1995) outlines a philosophical interpretation of Chinese strategy, which Xiaobing Li, Allan R. Millett, and Bin Yu *Mao's Generals Remember Korea* (Lawrence: University Press of

Kansas, 2001) supplements in detail. Sergei N. Goncharov, John W. Lewis, and Xue Litai handle the international aspects of Communist strategy superbly in *Uncertain Partners: Stalin, Mao, and the Korean War* (Stanford, Calif.: Stanford University Press, 1993). Several Chinese political and military leaders published memoirs. Students should, however, use them with an awareness of China's political climate at the time they were published.

On basic elements of Chinese operations and tactics, the single chapter coverage in John A. English's *On Infantry* (New York: Praeger, 1981) is basic, concise, and accurate. Alexander L. George, *The Chinese Communist Army in Action: The Korean War and Its Aftermath* (New York: Columbia University Press, 1967); Samuel B. Griffith II, *The Chinese People's Liberation Army* (New York: McGraw-Hill, 1967) ; and John Gittings, *The Role of the Chinese Army* (New York: Oxford University Press, 1967), are all useful, but no comprehensive study of the tactical details of Chinese operations in the Korean War is yet in general publication. Charles R. Schrader covers the neglected topic of supply operations exhaustively in *Communist Logistics in the Korean War* (Westport, Conn.: Greenwood Press, 1995).

On the topic of men and conflict and the physical and psychological ramifications of war more broadly defined, every military historian has personal favorites. Mine is J. Glenn Gray's *The Warriors: Reflections of Men in Battle* (New York: Harper and Row, 1967), in which a philosopher, drafted in 1941, examines his experiences retrospectively. The multivolume series on *The Ineffective Soldier* published by the Columbia University Press, based on the U.S. Army's experiences in World War II, highlights the difficulties the army faced, many of which persisted into the Korean War. William Ian Miller effectively dissects *The Mystery of Courage* (Cambridge, Mass.: Harvard University Press, 2000), and gives a more nuanced view than that of Lord Moran in *The Anatomy of Courage* (London: Constable 1945), which remains useful even though debunked by many leadership scholars.

Index

ISBN 1-58544-232-1

90000